# Irish Poetry after Joyce

*DILLON JOHNSTON*

University of Notre Dame Press
Notre Dame, Indiana

The Dolmen Press
Mountrath, Ireland

Copyright © 1985 by
University of Notre Dame Press
Notre Dame, Indiana

Published in Ireland by
The Dolmen Press Limited
Mountrath, Portlaoise

Manufactured in the United States of America

**Library of Congress Cataloging in Publication Data**

Johnston, Dillon.
　Irish poetry after Joyce.

　Bibliography; p.
　Includes index.
　1. English poetry—Irish authors—History and
criticism.　2. English poetry—20th century—History
and criticism.　3. Ireland in literature.　4. Joyce,
James, 1882–1941—Influence.　5. Yeats, W. B. (William
Butler), 1865–1939—Influence.　I. Title.
PR8491.J63　1985　　　821'.914'099415　　　84-40819
ISBN 0-268-01158-3 University of Notre Dame Press
ISBN 0-85105-437-4 The Dolmen Press Limited

*For Kathleen & Devin*

# Contents

# *Preface*

This book developed from sympathetic readings of individual poems to the discovery of eight to ten remarkable Irish poets, then to some general assumptions about Irish poetry and its audience, based on these poems by these poets. Poetry, then, meaning a specific body of poems by certain poets, is the paramount word in the title.

"Irish poetry" means what most of the English-reading world recognizes: poetry written in English, from or pertaining mostly to Ireland. More specifically, my subject is poetry written recently by poets whose national identity is Irish and who write chiefly in English. I realize this excludes a half-dozen interesting poets who write in Irish and who, strictly speaking, may more validly claim to write Irish poetry. Yet, no other term serves my subject. Because the term Anglo-Irish has been used by critics such as Thomas MacDonagh and Daniel Corkery to depreciate the Ascendancy class, it remains too colored and limited for use here. "Irish poetry in English" is both clumsy and imprecise because it fails to distinguish dialectical differences between the language spoken and written in southern Britain and that employed by over 99 percent of the Irish.

"After Joyce" fences off as a field of study four decades of poetry that have a starting boundary—within the nearly boundless history of poetry written by the Irish—of 1941, the year of James Joyce's death.

"After Joyce," rather than the usual "after Yeats," may seem only perverse. Within these forty years, Yeats, probably the outstanding modern poet in English, has influenced Irish poetry more than any other writer. In fact, his influence hindered and even thwarted the development of his immediate successors: F. R. Higgins, Padraic Fallon, Donagh MacDonagh, W. R. Rodgers, John Hewitt, Austin Clarke, Patrick Kavanagh, Denis Devlin, Brian Coffey, and Louis MacNeice. The best of these threw off or absorbed Yeats's troubling presence, and thereby liberated recent poets from all but the salutary aspects of Yeats's influence.

In adapting his voice to his dramatic concept of "the mask," Yeats created an authoritative tone which seemed inappropriate to those complexities of the nuclear age that concern recent poets and to the diverse audience of colleagues, neighbors, countrymen, English, Americans, and other readers of English whom they address. For an interplay of dramatic voices, more appropriate to their subject and audience, these poets looked to Joyce, as well as to American poets, for a more helpful example of how to replace the poet's singular lyric or odic voice either with a more variable speaker or with dramatic speakers who maintain a strategic relation to the audience. The greater need to account for Joyce's influence is acknowledged by specifying his name in the title.

A definition of this title hardly constitutes a justification of the topic, which is nothing if not insular. The pleasures of observing a literature in transition or reading together poets who derive from the same related traditions will reward the reader who shares this study with me. That Irish poets deserve our attention more than English or American poets I cannot establish. I can claim, however, that the late-nineteenth-century chromosomal or environmental miracle that produced our century's most accomplished poet, novelist, and, perhaps, playwright writing in English within a detached corner of Europe no bigger than Maine, Jordan, or Panama has stirred again in Ireland's favor and produced five or six poets who deserve an international audience. Rather than insisting on, or celebrating, the fact of this poetic renaissance, this book attempts to study the background and poetry of this remarkable gathering of poets.

In pursuit of this, the opening chapter, mostly history, observes the poets' various situations at the time of Joyce's death, considers the legacy for these poets of Yeats and then Joyce, and surveys events that affected their poetry from 1941 to the present. The final section of chapter 1, theory derived from the poetry, characterizes recent Irish poetry in terms of tone, the strategic relation of speaker to an audience within the poem. By resorting to dramatic speakers or various versions of the self, the poet attempts to share with his audience his present and his past or, in other words, to recreate with his audience a version of his tradition. In the four successive chapters, each of four immediate successors to Yeats is paired with a living poet to suggest, generally, four living versions of the Irish poetic tradition. Within these four chapters, various critical methods are used to ease the reader's access to the eight poets studied, and neither the concept of tone nor the characterizing version of the tradition is applied so uniformly that it takes precedence over the effort to illuminate the poetry. Finally, chapter 6 discusses some practical aspects of tone and audience and introduces certain contemporary poets not included within the four pairings.

I am gratefully beholden to all of the living poets featured in this book, and their families, for their generous cooperation; to Anthony Bradley, Terence Brown, Peter Fallon, and David Dalton who read and advised me on all of this book, and to Lee Potter, Michael Roman, Jim Hans, Liam Miller, Bert Hedin, Bill Moss, Dick Johnston, Patrick O'Neill, and Mark Waelder, who read and commented on individual chapters — all of whom I would hold responsible for remaining errors if they and I did not know better; to scholars Stephen Amidon and Robert Matteson, to the staff of Wake Forest's library, to the American Committee for Irish Studies, to my Stoots Mountain neighbors, and, especially, my colleagues in the English Department, who have been kind and supportive; to Wake Forest University for a Reynolds Leave, and to her Yeats scholar and provost Edwin Wilson for his wise encouragement and for his vision in the founding of Wake Forest University Press; to the National Endowment for the Humanities for the godsend Research Fellowship and a Summer Seminar with John Hollander; to James Langford and Richard Allen who have been gentle and humane in their publishing of this book, and to Iris Tillman Hill for helpful publishing advice; and especially to Guinn Batten, who has advised and supported me at all stages of this book.

May I also thank the following for permission to include copyright material in this book:
The Dolmen Press Ltd. and Liam Miller and Mrs. Nora Clarke for selections from Austin Clarke's *Collected Poems* (© 1973); The Dolmen Press for selections from Padraic Colum's *The Poet's Circuits* (© 1981); The Dolmen Press, Brian Coffey, and Stephen Devlin for selections from *The Heavenly Foreigner* (© 1967) and Maria di Gropello for selec-

tions from Devlin's *Collected Poems* (© 1964); The Dolmen Press for selections from Padraic Fallon's *Poems* (© 1974); The Dolmen Press and Thomas Kinsella for selections from *Poems 1956–1973* (© 1980) and *Peppercanister Poems 1972–1978* (© 1979); The Dolmen Press and John Montague for selections from *The Rough Field* (© 1972, 1978, 1984), *A Slow Dance* (© 1975), *The Great Cloak* (© 1978), *The Dead Kingdom* (© 1984).

Farrar, Straus & Giroux, Inc., Faber & Faber, Inc., and Seamus Heaney for selections from *Field Work* (© 1976, 1979), *Poems 1965–1975* (© 1966, 1969, 1972, 1975, 1980), *Preoccupations: Selected Prose 1968–1978* (© 1980), *Station Island* (© 1985).

Faber & Faber, Inc. for selections from *The Collected Poems of Louis MacNeice* (© 1966); Faber & Faber, Inc. and Paul Muldoon for selections from *Why Brownlee Left* (© 1980) and *Quoof* (© 1983); Faber & Faber, Inc. and Richard Murphy for selections from *High Island* (© 1974) and *The Price of Stone* (© 1985).

Gallery Press, Peter Fallon, and Eiléan Ní Chuilleanáin for selections from *Site of Ambush* (© 1975) and *The Rose Geranium* (© 1981).

Peter Kavanagh Hand Press and Peter Kavanagh for selections from *The Complete Poems of Patrick Kavanagh* (© 1972).

Katherine B. Kavanagh for selections from the selected poetry and prose of Patrick Kavanagh.

Macmillan Publishing Co., Inc., Michael and Anne Yeats, and Macmillan London Limited for selected material from *Autobiography* by W. B. Yeats (© 1916, 1936 by Macmillan Publishing Co., Inc., renewed 1944, 1964 by Bertha Georgie Yeats); *Essays and Introductions* by W. B. Yeats (© Mrs. W. B. Yeats, 1961); for these selections from *The Poems of W. B. Yeats,* edited by Richard J. Finneran: "Adam's Curse," "The Ballad of Moll Magee," "The Fascination of What's Difficult" (© 1912 by Macmillan Publishing Co., Inc., renewed 1940 by Bertha Georgie Yeats), "The Second Coming" (© 1924 by Macmillan Publishing Co., Inc., renewed 1952 by Bertha Georgie Yeats), "The Tower" (© 1928 by Macmillan Publishing Co., Inc., renewed 1956 by Georgie Yeats), "Vacillation" and "I Am of Ireland" (© 1933 by Macmillan Publishing Co., Inc., renewed 1961 by Bertha Georgie Yeats), "Under Ben Bulben" and "High Talk" (© 1940 by Georgie Yeats, renewed 1968 by Bertha Georgie Yeats, Michael Butler Yeats and Anne Yeats).

Oxford University Press and Derek Mahon for selections from *Poems 1962–1978* (© 1979) and *The Hunt by Night*; Oxford University Press and Medbh McGuckian for selections from *The Flower Master* (© 1982) and *Venus in the Rain* (© 1984).

Wake Forest University Press for permission to quote from works by Ciarán Carson, Austin Clarke, Thomas Kinsella, Michael Longley, Derek Mahon, John Montague, Paul Muldoon, Richard Murphy, and Eiléan Ní Chuilleanáin.

# Abbreviations

| | |
|---|---|
| *CCP* | Austin Clarke, *Collected Poems* |
| *CBC* | Austin Clarke, *Twice Round the Black Church* |
| *DCP* | Denis Devlin, *Collected Poems* |
| *DHF* | Denis Devlin, *The Heavenly Foreigner* |
| *HFW* | Seamus Heaney, *Field Work* |
| *HP* | Seamus Heaney, *Poems 1965–1975* |
| *HSI* | Seamus Heaney, *Station Island* |
| *JP* | James Joyce, *A Portrait of the Artist as a Young Man* |
| *KCP* | Patrick Kavanagh, *The Complete Poems* |
| *KPC* | Thomas Kinsella, *Peppercanister Poems 1972–1978* |
| *KP* | Thomas Kinsella, *Poems 1956–1973* |
| *MCP* | Louis MacNeice, *Collected Poems* |
| *MHN* | Derek Mahon, *The Hunt by Night* |
| *MP* | Derek Mahon, *Poems 1962–1978* |
| *MCL* | John Montague, *A Chosen Light* |
| *MDK* | John Montague, *The Dead Kingdom* |
| *MGC* | John Montague, *The Great Cloak* |
| *MPL* | John Montague, *Poisoned Lands* |
| *MRF* | John Montague, *The Rough Field* |
| *MSD* | John Montague, *A Slow Dance* |
| *MT* | John Montague, *Tides* |
| *MWBL* | Paul Muldoon, *Why Brownlee Left* |
| *MHI* | Richard Murphy, *High Island* |
| *YP* | W. B. Yeats, *The Poems* |

## CHAPTER ONE

# The Irish Poet & his Society, 1941–1985

## 1. The Situation of Irish Poets in 1941

Because writers are both guardians and composers of their literary tradition, the actual situation of Ireland's creative writers in the 1940s can help us understand recent Irish literature. In the opening years of World War II, many of the talented Irish literary figures, including Joyce, Beckett, O'Casey, and MacNeice, had abandoned the relative security of their neutral nation for more vulnerable homes in Britain or Europe. Yet, in contrast to this apparent rejection of Ireland, their literary creations, letters, and conversations reveal, if not a preoccupation with their homeland, frequent patches of nostalgia for native light or landscape or for old friends or Irish faces. These writers remained exiles rather than emigrants or expatriates according to the following distinction: "An expatriate is someone who sloughs off his country like an old skin; an exile on the other hand, however far he may go, has his country always on his mind."[1]

If we dismiss this overly restrictive adverb "always," then Joyce qualifies, even in his closing years, as an Irish exile. According to his friend Louis Gillet, a member of the French Academy, "Nothing interested him more than the news from his fatherland."[2] Gillet continued in this obituary note of 1941:

> He never stopped corresponding with a lot of faithful friends and former college comrades who constituted his secret party, as if he were a pretender in exile keeping in touch with his agents in his old country.[3]

Joyce's *Letters* reveal that, in his closing years, he maintained a correspondence with only C. P. Curran, Alf Bergan, and Michael Healey among his friends in Ireland although he also exchanged letters with Yeats, O'Faolain, and Maurice Craig. Yet, if we turn to his fiction, on which he expended most of his adult hours, we concede again how much he lived within his re-created city of Dublin.

On the other hand, he flew by the nets of his nation as vigorously in 1940 as he did in 1904. The record of his last months in Saint-Gerard-le-Puy reveals how unwaveringly Joyce had rejected any official affiliation with Ireland. Having published *Finnegans Wake* earlier in the year, Joyce left Paris with Nora in December of 1939 for this hamlet in Allier near Vichy, because his grandson Stephen was enrolled in Maria Jolas's school there. Excepting a two-month sojourn in Vichy, this was Joyce's first rural residence, which he retained for a year, receiving war bulletins and irregular news of the mental collapse of his daughter and daughter-in-law, grumbling about the reception of his masterwork, and pacing the short-circuit of St. Gerard, pockets weighed with stone arsenals for the village dogs with whom he kept no truce.[4] Joyce's adopted village became a temporary refuge for Samuel Beckett, who had taken one of the last trains from Gare de Lyon, for Lucie and Paul Leon, and for Joyce's son George who, during the next six months, had to dodge prevailing drafts by both the German and Vichy governments. The safety of George and his daughter Lucia, whom he sought to transfer from Pornichet to a Swiss asylum, became the preoccupations of Joyce as he delved in several bureaucracies for both permissions to leave France and visas for residence in Switzerland. After receiving the visa in late November, the Joyces had to renew British passports and secure the *permis de sortie* before the expiration of the visa on December 15th.

In Joyce's penumbral nightmare of flight and restraint, his treasured family in jeopardy and an undiagnosed ulcer searing his duodenum, he was offered one last, supreme opportunity to relent toward his homeland. The Irish Minister in Vichy, through the mediation of George, offered Irish passports which would have certified the Joyces as neutrals and given them the simplest egress from France. Joyce rejected the offer, as George told Ellmann in an interview, because "he should not accept in wartime something he did not desire in peacetime."[5] Ellmann details the last heroic odyssey of this restless man from Vichy to Geneva to Lausanne to Zurich and finally to the narrow bed in Fluntern Cemetery overlooking Zurich where only Nora's muted Galway accent and a green wreath with interwoven lyre reminded his European mourners of Joyce's native birthplace.

The ambivalence of other exiles in 1941 was less extreme than Joyce's. Beckett, for example, was not loath to receive neutrality papers from the Irish legation in Paris. He joined the French underground in October 1940, after the Nazis had seized for the crime of Jewishness his and Joyce's friend Paul Leon. Within his resistance reseau, termed "Gloria," he was known as *Irlandais,* or merely Sam. When news of Joyce's death reached him in Paris, he joined with friends at Lucie Leon's apartment on February 2nd to commemorate Joyce's birthday and hear a recorded paean to Anna Livia in the master's own voice.[6]

Among the nonresident writers, Denis Devlin was as international as Joyce or Beckett. While living in France, Italy, Turkey, and the United States, he remained linked to Ireland by his position in the Irish foreign office. In 1941 as first secretary in the legation to Washington, he was composing *Lough Derg,* a complex poem, richly ambivalent about the Jansenist strain in Irish Catholicism, and mingling in literary circles that eventually would include Allen Tate, Robert Penn Warren, and Katherine Anne Porter. In his official capacity, this cosmopolitan intellectual became an effective, even eloquent, defender of the neutrality policy of his leader and friend, Eamon de Valera.[7]

Neutrality and censorship were political policies that contributed most to the intellectual miasmus of Ireland in 1941. Neutrality increased the strain of Louis MacNeice's ambivalence toward his native island. In late 1940, he returned from the United States to England, having been, with Austin Clarke, one of the two losing candidates for the Chair of English at Trinity College, Dublin. He settled permanently in London where this Heraclitean poet served as a fire watcher in the House Guard. In several months, he assumed a position in the BBC and, like Sean O'Casey, remained in England nearly until his death. In a poem in a 1943 journal, MacNeice appealed to "the neutral island" to "look into your heart." "You will find such ducats of dream and great doubloons of ceremony / As nobody to-day will mint":

> But then look eastward from your heart, there bulks
> A continent, close, dark, as archetypal sin,
> While to the west off your own shores the mackerel
> Are fat—on the flesh of your kin.
>
> (*MCP,* 208)[8]

Because neutrality was merely symptomatic of Ireland's "intense introspection,"[9] an absorbing preoccupation with questions of nationhood, MacNeice's countrymen were unlikely to divert their gaze from Ireland's own heart to view the horrors off her coast, as MacNeice probably realized. Augustine Martin's characterization of Irish society at this time helps explain why this self-absorption tended to isolate the Irish writer, even the Catholic writer, within his own society:

> a society which was stunned and unsettled by a revolution and a civil war, which was predominantly Catholic, middle-class and conservative; which wished to exclude from its ethos those elements that were associated with the Protestant ruling class of the pre-revolutionary period. One of these elements happened to be literature. . . .[10]

Looking back from 1953, the editor and writer Sean O'Faolain was less sympathetic than Martin in characterizing "Ireland After Yeats":

> Change-over from a stratified society—ranging from aristocrat to outcast —to a one-class . . . farming population, rarely induces a fertile awareness either among its people or its writers. Even before the Revolution Irish writers—Joyce, Shaw, Wilde, dozens besides—felt this, in so far as our awareness was then all going down the drain of politics and nationalism, and left Ireland for the more interesting life of the island next door.[11]

In 1941, not all of Ireland's writers had fled eastward or to America, however. Yeats's poetic successors, for example, Austin Clarke and Patrick Kavanagh, had abandoned their own exiles in London and returned to Dublin in 1937 and 1939 respectively. Kavanagh would later regret his return, saying if he had remained in London in 1938, he would have conquered that town eventually.[12] Yet in the year of Joyce's death, he was hopeful for a Dublin career as journalist and poet. In that year, he was germinating ideas for his major work, *The Great Hunger* (1942), writing pieces for the *Irish Times* and *Irish Press,* and drinking in the court of the *Times*'s editor, R. M. Smylie, at the Palace Bar in Fleet Street. Writers gathered at the Palace, as at the Pearl, where they would be on tap for the odd assignment from the *Irish Times* which was Dublin's steadiest employer of poets and prose writers. After visiting Dublin in 1941, Cyril Connolly described the atmosphere of the Palace Bar:

It is as warm and friendly as an alligator tank. Its inhabitants, from a long process of mutual mastication, have a leathery look, and are as witty, hospitable, and kindly a group as can be found anywhere.[13]

In perhaps Dublin's most spacious snug, the Palace's large rectangular room, closed off from the bar by a wall of frosted glass, Connolly would have encountered, on a normal working day, Kavanagh himself and, across the room from him, Austin Clarke whose Palace associates would have been F. R. Higgins, who died in that year, Padraic Fallon, and Seamus O'Sullivan.[14] Other fluid coteries included Brian O'Nolan, Donagh MacDonagh, Lynn Doyle, and Maurice Walsh, and a dozen other literary luminaries in Dublin.

Yet, in 1941, light from these luminaries was hidden under the bushel of Irish neutrality. First of all, the writers suffered the same stasis and isolation that enveloped all Irish citizens. There may have been a dynamics of neutrality with diplomatic and terrorist circles: the pressure from other nations to abandon neutrality heightened as Catholic Poland was invaded by the Nazis and then subsided as Italy joined the Axis powers; de Valera frequently voiced the Republic's intolerance of a draft being instituted in the North of Ireland; IRA operatives collaborated with Nazi spies; and Dublin was a whispering gallery for agents of many nations.[15] For the average citizen, however, the war, referred to as "The Emergency," intruded only on rare occasions such as the blitz of Belfast in mid-April and early May of 1941 and the accidental bombing on the North Strand of Dublin. The Belfast bombings killed nearly a thousand citizens and drew assistance from fifty-eight fire departments from Dublin and its environs.[16] While bombers flying from Toomesbridge and the Erne base became as familiar as jackdaws and corncrakes to the infant ears of Seamus Heaney and the attentive eyes of John Montague in the Northern provinces of Derry and Tyrone, the Southern skies were off-limits to military flights.[17] Routinely, however, for most of the war, the average citizen must have felt at two removes from the war. Papers remained so even-handed that they misrepresented the Nazi's ruthless and brutal invasions of their European neighbors. The Irish suffered no severe shortages of staples such as meat, eggs, milk, or Guinness stout, and the scarcity of petrol required only the retrieval from a short rustication of bicycle or horse, neither of which had passed into desuetude in Irish society. The reappearance of a "staggering array of wheeled carriages"[18] must have added substance to the observer's impression that while embattled Europe was suffering the malign application of modern technology, Ireland had backed off several decades from the technological age.

Irish neutrality placed additional burdens on the resident writer. Cyril Connolly speculated that the allied nations' impatience with Ireland's neutrality had curtailed foreign interest in Irish writers in 1941.[19] Unsupplemented by foreign readers, the half-million population of Dublin, or even the three million in the Free State, could not provide enough royalties even to keep the Palace guard in drink.

With access to British publishers impeded, the Irish writer could turn to no responsible Irish publisher at home. The average Irishman's indifference to the publishing vacuum, which must have added insult to the injured pockets, is evident in the narrow chauvinism of this notice in the *Irish Times* on March 15, 1941, of the First Irish Book Fair:

> Dublin is always in the foreground with new ideas as far as culture is concerned, and this later venture will do much to further a reputation which already is firmly established.[20]

We can only imagine how the remainder of the announcement would have fretted the patience of the Irish writer, say Brian O'Nolan, who had no real publisher and whose two novels — *At Swim-Two-Birds* (1939) and *An Beal Bocht* (1941) — had disappeared at birth as surely as if they had been launched in the bullrushes or given to a wet-nurse wolf:

> The stall holders included such booksellers and publishers as the Talbot Press, Browne and Nolan's, the Sign of the Three Candles, Eason's, Government Publications, the Irish Photo-Engraving Company, James Duffy, the Nassau Library, Fred Hanna, Hodges and Figgis, and Combridge's.[21]

For a serious publisher of literature, writers would have to wait for the founding of the Dolmen Press in 1951.

Finally, during neutrality, the writers' sense of being out of touch with the world's crisis was probably more harmful than the loss of the heroic or nightmarish subjects that an observing writer would have absorbed. Commenting on the poems that had appeared on the literary page of the *Irish Times* up to 1944, R. M. Smyllie observed: "Those poets who have been writing in Ireland have been almost wholly un-affected by the impact of the world struggle."[22] However, Sean O'Faolain's characterization, in "Ireland After Yeats," of writers during the forties may explain the complexities of the writers' "unaffectedness":

> Whatever the cause, Irish writers, still tuning-in, as writers always do, to the intellectual stations of the world do so now almost like men in an occu-pied country listening to forbidden voices. The writer who has the feel of the world rises from his grapevine excited by the sense of the world and turns to his page to write as he feels. But with what? With whom? What characters will act and speak for him, in his poem, play, or novel?[23]

An additional question confronted the writer, one that would help define poetry in the last four decades: to whom would the writer ad-dress himself? The responses of vigilance committees, playgoers, and reviewers to literary works during the first decade of the Irish Free State suggest that most Irish readers would approach poetic truth only if it was consistent with the political and moral assumptions the read-ers shared. Official censorship, therefore, represented a popular reaction to centuries of British suppression and second-class citizenship within the Empire and an expression of the Irishman's need to emerge as ra-cially, nationally, and religiously purer than the antagonists.

Passage of the Censorship of Publications Act (1928) led to the ap-pointment of a Censorship Board in 1930, the suppression of 1200 books and 140 periodicals before 1940, and the maintenance of what Robert Graves would later call "the fiercest literary censorship this side of the Iron Curtain. . . ."[24] Although all Irishmen were stunted by censor-ship, the writers were also persecuted by these laws. Not only could years of a writer's work be suppressed by nonreaders on arbitrary grounds, but a spirit of censoriousness intruded between the artist and his muse like a duenna or maiden Irish aunt. The effect on the writer, recorded often in his own words, is summarized in Peter Costello's only some-what hyperbolic statement:

> Irish laws and Irish attitudes effectively made the writer an outlaw in his own society: one did not have to leave the country to become an exile, there was also an internal state of exile. A writer's work was ever open to the irreversible decision of the law, which might prevent him speaking to his own people. . . .[25]

Furthermore, just as neutrality distanced the writer from the political and military activities of Europe, so also censorship muted the intellectual controversies from the continent. When we witness Austin Clarke railing against "modernism" and the "anti-traditional school," we can recognize that writers suffered nearly as much from the suppression of European "modernist" books and journals as from the banning of Irish books, against which Clarke, for one, took his stand.[26]

The most effective resistance movement against excessive censorship was waged by the founders and editors of *The Bell.* Beginning a decade after the closing of the *Irish Statesman* in 1930 and a decade before the founding of *Envoy, The Bell*'s first full year of publication offers another reason for considering 1941 a landmark year. Peadar O'Donnell and Sean O'Faolain founded the journal, O'Faolain serving as editor until the spring of 1946 when he passed on editorial duties to his co-founder.

*The Bell* gave voice to Cork's hedge-school of writers, O'Faolain and Frank O'Connor, whose tutor had been Corkery, and revealed the emergence of several important poets in Ulster. While also praising Roy McFadden and W. R. Rodgers, who published a book in 1941, *The Bell* particularly supported the poetry of John Hewitt who would not publish a book until 1948.[27] During O'Faolain's tenure, the offices of *The Bell* became not a mere literary enclave but a command center with outposts in Cork, Belfast, and wherever a single reader clandestinely received his special order of *The Bell,* from under the counter, and was encouraged to contribute his own story or poem.[28]

*The Bell*'s skirmishes against censorship flared into controversy, which resulted in public hearings and, eventually, reform of the Censorship Board in 1945. This partial victory against censorship can be seen as one front in a broader war O'Faolain would wage against provincialism. Augustine Martin has written that *The Bell* subverted Ireland's disabling myths: the Gaelic language myth and the myth of the noble peasant.[29] Certainly, O'Faolain intended to deconstruct myths that balked imaginative progress, as he indicated in his inaugural editorial:

> That was why we chose the name of 'The Bell'. . . . We could not have used *any* of the old symbolic words. They are as dead as Brian Boru, Granuaile, the Shan Van Vocht. . . . These belonged to the time when we growled in defeat and dreamed of the future. The future has

arrived and, with its arrival, killed them. All our symbols have to be created afresh. . . .[30]

However, as unswerving as O'Faolain was in his own antipathy to narrowness, dead abstractions, and poetic interference with creativity, he nevertheless opened his journal to divergent views so that *The Bell* reflected healthy ambivalences and even self-contradictions, especially concerning nationalism and internationalism. Perhaps O'Faolain was predicting this contradiction in this same opening essay when he wrote, "The Bell will ring with a note this way and a note that way. The wind will move it and a faint sigh will come from the top of the tower."

Readers must have often felt, during O'Faolain's reign, that his poetry editors, especially, were directing their notes in directions contrary to those of other editors and writers in *The Bell.* In addition to encouraging contributions from the North, editors and other writers frequently reminded readers that an international community existed beyond the shores of neutral Ireland. For example, in an article entitled "When Peace Breaks Out in Dublin," Roy Greacen wrote: "Undoubtedly the presence of so many foreign troops on our streets is having the affect of drawing on the imagination of local people and of blowing a wholesome spirit through a closed in and soured atmosphere."[31] In the next issue, O'Faolain complained: "We have become . . . alienated from Europe to such an extent that we sometimes seem less to belong to it than barely to adhere to it. . . ."[32]

Yet the poetry within O'Faolain's own journal might have been composed before the wireless or the bomber was invented, so completely did it ignore everything but nature and farm life. On rare occasions, poems by Valentin Iremonger or Roy McFadden introduced a different theme such as death or religion, but the bias toward budding trees or sheep was quickly reclaimed. In the July issue (1943), Roy McFadden complained of this predominance of "pastoral poems," but the poetry editor Geoffrey Taylor defended his selections as the best of the poetry submitted to him.[33] The testimony of R. M. Smylie, quoted above, would suggest that poetry in the *Irish Times* was as remote from modern life as that of *The Bell.*

These submitting poets might have appeared to be heeding Yeats's parting advice to "sing the peasantry," advice which poets featured in this study came to deride. These poets and editors alike were probably more influenced by the conservative dicta of the first poetry editor of *The Bell,* Frank O'Connor, who was himself influenced by both Yeats and Daniel Corkery. Before closing his nine-month tenure at *The Bell,* O'Connor advised his general reader: "Education is a preparation for life, and the only suitable preparation for Irish life is Irish literature" —recommending especially the poetry of Yeats, Colum, Higgins, and Kavanagh. To the poets he counseled:

> Don't write verse unless you have to, and don't write it under the influence of any English or American poet, no matter how good he may be. Poetry is the most national of the arts, and its colouring must be distinctive.[34]

One wonders how different might have been the contours of recent Irish poetry if younger poets such as Kinsella, Montague, and Heaney had followed O'Connor's prescription and thereby avoided the influence of such foreign poets as Hardy, Williams, Auden, Duncan, Frost, and Hughes. In fact, every poet included in this study, even Clarke, reacts more or less against O'Connor's form of literary nationalism as each recognizes that statements such as this Belfry advice are based on the illusory assumptions that there is a recognizably monolithic literature and one Irish audience. With hindsight of nine years, Patrick Kavanagh provided this rebuttal of O'Connor's sort of restrictiveness:

> As far as I am concerned, Auden and Dylan Thomas, Moravia, Sartre, Pound are all Irish poets. They have all said the thing which delighted me, a man born in Ireland, so they must have a great deal of Irish in them.[35]

Only in a rough way do O'Connor and Kavanagh's statements define the two sides of the central literary controversy of the 1940s. On the one side, an aftergrowth of Irish nationalism would impose one cultural tradition and one racial identity—Gaelic, Catholic, rural—that might exclude or judge as irrelevant many Irish writers. Emigration and public opinion had, in fact, reduced the number of resident writers not cast in the nationalist mode, as Frank O'Connor observed in 1941: "Since Yeats's death, Irish literature has passed almost entirely into the hands of writers of Catholic Irish stock. . . ."[36] Characteristically,

O'Faolain's view of this same phenomenon, though partisan, was more penetrating. In *The Irish* (1949), describing the demands on the Irish writer by the emancipated Catholic reader, O'Faolain said,

> A simple illustration is his attitude to the Anglo-Irish tradition. He thinks he has conquered it whereas in fact it has absorbed him. . . . Nor can he develop a blood test for pure Eireanns, not with such un-Celtic national heroes as Tone, Parnell and De Valera. Unable to make up his mind to accept the warp and woof of history, he keeps on nagging at the Irish. . . . And all this is so because he wants to take over the town-life the Anglo-Irish bequeathed to him and does not know how to handle it.[37]

The major poets of the last four decades, however, have not capitulated in their poetry to nationalist prescriptions, regardless of the poets' own degree of attraction to Irish political causes. In recognizing the necessity to recreate their own distinctive version of the tradition, they have embodied their ambivalences in their art, as we shall see, as well as in their lives. The reactions and attractions we have observed in the attitudes toward Ireland in the forties, of both exiles and resident writers, become an identifying characteristic of Irish poetry after Joyce. It was Joyce, after all, who most clearly demonstrated how "to take over" as a literary subject "the town-life the Anglo-Irish bequeathed to him."

For this study comparisons of Yeats and Joyce are relevant only in relation to their legacies for the younger writers. Although recent poets have developed strands of their tradition independently of these two literary giants, such as the Irish language, traditional music, sectarian violence, and disruptive commerce, Yeats and Joyce remain a major part of the tradition that their followers must revise and recreate. As we assess these legacies, we must recognize their relativity because each poet is an independent reader and because critical interpretations and even the texts of these writers have varied from generation to generation of their followers. If we recognize the importance of the new corrected text of *Ulysses* and the newly revised *Collected Poems* and of critical studies that will incorporate understandings of *Finnegans Wake* and of Yeats's occult preoccupations, then we can extend Auden's assumption that the legacies of great writers such as Yeats and Joyce "are modified in the guts of the living."

In his person Yeats seems to have had no direct influence, or at least no positive personal influence, on the best of his immediate successors. After he retired from the Irish Senate in 1928, Yeats lived a more secluded life, restricting his public activity in his last decade to founding the Irish Literary Academy and directing the Abbey Theatre. When he moved to Rathfarnam in 1933, he tightened his circle of regular visitors to Oliver Gogarty, Frank O'Connor, F. R. Higgins, Captain McManus, and a few others, seeing additional acquaintances rarely and by appointment. Out of Yeats's earshot, city gossip depicted him as stuffy, eccentric, and slightly comic. Those young writers who were not deterred from visiting Yeats by these mock-heroic pub-tales were often turned away by the poet himself.[38]

Austin Clarke suffered a more serious rebuff. Having been among the precious few who attended all of Yeats's later plays, he recalls that he "enjoyed the poet's curtain-lecture, almost as if it were a special benefit performance for myself."[39] However, neither this devoted attendance nor a pilgrimage to Coole Park spared Clarke from Yeats's rebuff. First in a 1936 interview at the Saville Club in London, Clarke followed a line of questioning for a projected biography of Yeats that led into the personal life of Yeats, to his privileged moment with Maud Gonne, and quickly to a stillborn interview, and an aborted biography. That same year, Yeats's *Oxford Book of Modern Verse,* which implicitly set itself against the modernist "Ezra, Eliot, Auden School"[40] that Clarke opposed, could find no room among the ephemeral lyrics of Coppard, Gibson, Flecker, Cornford, Grenfell, Mathers, or Church for a single poem by Austin Clarke, though it reprinted seventeen by Yeats's friend Gogarty (whom he called "one of the great lyric poets of our era")[41] and seven by his neurotic devotee, Margot Ruddock.

To those writers such as Gogarty and Higgins of whom he approved, Yeats could be magnanimous; a number of writers shared Francis Stuart's gratitude for Yeats's "generosity toward younger writers, which he showed by never failing to praise those of us with whom he felt some kinship, however slight."[42] Yet, Yeats's worst fears about his own family—". . . what if my descendants lose the flower/Through natural declension of the soul,"—seem more appropriate presentiments for his poetic kinship. If we except his fraternal support of John Synge, we might agree with the judgment of Frank O'Connor, a self-professed protege, that Yeats "had fathered more bad art and literature than any great writer of his time."[43]

## 2. Yeats's Legacy: An Antithetical Art

In 1941, Irish writers mourning the passing of Yeats and Joyce may well have wondered if their literary lot had improved in the fifty tumultuous years that brought independence to part of Ireland and the brilliant Irish literature to the world. *After* looked depressingly like *Before.* Mary Colum describes the intellectual situation, shaped by the views of Thomas Davis and the young Ireland movement, that Yeats inherited:

> The country Yeats faced had had its intellectual life twisted awry with political and defensive preoccupations and its artistic life made anemic through the writers' making themselves mere auxiliaries of political leaders.[44]

Fifty years later, the reigning patriots would ignore or even isolate those writers they could not dragoon into political image-making, a reclothing of national images in moral terms in an effort to preserve an illusion of an Ireland free of the impurities of English social and religious life. Richard Loftus characterizes the poets' heritage after Yeats: "Nationalism . . . became a narrow creed reflecting the values of a middle-class society, and its spokesmen . . . demanded that the poet respect the forms of conventional morality and taste. . . ."[45] From within the island came the despairing notes of novelists and poets such as Frank O'Connor writing in 1942: "Ireland has used her new freedom to tie herself up into a sort of moral Chinese puzzle from which it seems impossible that she should ever extricate herself."[46]

Yeats's reaction in the thirties to the stultifying middle-class morality must have seemed increasingly reactionary, and at times anachronistic and unrealistic. Had the younger poets actually gathered for a reading of Yeats's last testament, their glances would have caromed and their hands stifled the snicker:

> Sing the peasantry, and then
> Hard-riding country gentlemen
> The holiness of monks, and after
> Porter-drinkers' randy laughter

Sing the lords and ladies gay
That were beaten into the clay
Through seven heroic centuries.
                    ("Under Ben Bulben," *YP,* 327)[47]

John Montague pronounces the writers' verdict on these lines when he characterizes them as "a catalogue of subjects that could only be legitimately treated in parody."[48] Yet, in their reaction to an institutional Yeats, his successors could only emulate the absolute integrity which spurred Yeats himself to oppose any institution that threatened to conscript his art or enroll his free voice in a chorus. They absorbed Yeats's Blakean injunction to create a system or be enslaved by another man's. Even if they eschewed Yeats's systematic mythologizing, they practiced nonetheless his total independence in reporting their own personal and communal experience and thereby avoided ratifying, in Heaney's words, "the sectarian categories which had us where we were."[49]

Earlier in his career, Yeats had learned that an independently conceived poetry could make something happen. His belief in the isolated hero, his interest in indigenous literature, and his setting of the Cuchulain myth contributed to the outline of the nation's emerging self-image, a contribution examined at length by historians and critics such as F. S. L. Lyons and William Irwin Thompson.[50] Yeats's play "Cathleen Ni Houlihan" and early poems may well have sent "Out / Certain men the English shot" ("Man and the Echo," *YP,* 345). The leader of the 1916 Easter insurgents Patrick Pearse was reported to have said, "In days to come, people will say that this was the age of Yeats."[51]

Yeats worked actively for the nationalist cause for a dozen years or so from his creation of the *Countess Cathleen* in 1891. He was instrumental in creating central images around which the nation could cohere. As Seamus Heaney has stated,

> When . . . he sought a badge of identity for his own culture, something that would mark it off from the rest of the English-speaking world, he found this distinctive and sympathetic thing in the magical world view of the country people. It was a conscious counter-culture act against the rationalism and materialism of late Victorian England.[52]

Inevitably, his artistry became too complex merely to re-etch nationalist icons such as the noble cottager, the chaste and self-willed woman,

and the nationalist martyr starkly enough to distinguish an Irish stereotype from an English. By 1907, the figure of the peasant was so en-
sconced as the national touchstone that he could no longer be safely
cast in a comic situation, as John Synge attempted to do in *The Playboy
of the Western World.* Stirred by nationalistic attacks on Synge's play,
members of Sinn Fein and other patriots rioted through four first-week
performances of this masterpiece. In defending the riots against the
*Playboy,* the *Freeman's Journal* argued that "no traducer of the Irish people ever presented a more sordid, squalid, and repulsive picture of Irish
life and character"[53] than did Synge's play. When Yeats complained that
strong leadership and principle had been replaced by organized opinion
and strategy—"Instead of a Parnell, a Stephens or a Butt, we must obey
the demands of a commonplace and ignorant people . . ."[54]—he already
knew that his heroic, aesthetic, and elitist ideals of the nineties had
been subordinated to nationalists' ends. F. S. L. Lyons depicts the actual
Irish priorities Yeats was encountering in 1907: "Every cultural initia-
tive, every artistic experiment, every work of literature, was liable to
be judged by a single criterion—whether it helped or hindered the breaking of the English connection."[55]

Spokesmen for the nationalist views, who may have once been swayed
by Yeats's inspiration, declared a shift in the currents between aestheticism and nationalism. "Art evolves from the nation, not the nation from
art,"[56] asserted an anti-*Playboy* editorial in *Sinn Fein,* not as a premise
to be examined but as a prescription for the Irish hierarchy of values.

The fruitless debate concerning whether or not the *Playboy*'s characterization of the peasant was realistic forced Synge to defend the work
as an "extravaganza,"[57] and further seasoned Yeats's distaste for realism.
It is not remarkable, then, that Yeats defined his art mythopoeically
or that his new mythical figures—such as the betrayed Parnell-like martyr, the antinomian hero isolated in his own creative potency, and the
aristocratic coterie of 'hound voices'—supported the artist's independence from the demands of Young Ireland politics reclothed as the Sinn
Fein ethos.

During the Playboy riots of 1907, the positions of artists and nationalists were established in crude outline by Yeats and by Arthur Griffith,
who would become the first leader of the Irish Free State in 1922. Consequently, the "Irish Literary Renaissance" became an antithesis to Sinn

Fein nationalism and to the more violent Fenians. Its major works, most
of which appeared after the *Playboy* curtain rose, are politically attuned,
implicitly directed at national issues, and frequently created around pro-
tagonists who are not nationalist models but Yeatsian masks or anti-
dotes for the prevailing nationalist types. Although friends have dis-
claimed political motives for Synge and Joyce, one need consider only
such satiric butts as the Saint in *The Well of the Saints,* the Citizen in
*Ulysses,* or the schoolmaster Jones, Shaun, or the Ondt in *Finnegans Wake*
to recognize that these writers' political hackles are up. Of course none
of the masterpieces of modern Irish literature, such as *The Playboy of
the Western World, Hail and Farewell, Ulysses,* and *The Plough and The
Stars,* holds up a simple mirror to political reality or offers a mechanical
opposite. Yeats himself recognized that antithetical art transmutes as
it reflects and that even realistic art may be called a "mirror-resembling
dream."

In addition to offering his Irish contemporaries the most complex
model of antithetical art, Yeats also affected the practical conditions from
which the Renaissance developed. George Moore argues that Lady Gregory "never would have written a play if she had not met Yeats, nor
would Synge . . . and perhaps . . . if I had not met Yeats . . . I should
not have written *The Lake* or *The Untilled Field,* or the book I am now
writing."[58] Perhaps, this assertion is more certifiable than Moore's conclusion that "all the Irish movement rose out of Yeats and returns to
Yeats," but Yeats created the conditions for a literary estate in Ireland
that counterbalanced the excesses of the revolutionary political estate.

Yet, the historical views of the Sinn Fein adherents who spoke for
the nationalist movement after the turn of the century and those of
Yeats were equally remote from any realistic representation of Irish history. Seamus Deane finds the nineteenth-century aesthetic tradition, from
which Yeats developed, antipathetic to historical realism:

> The aesthetic heritage with which we still struggle clearly harbors the
> desire to obliterate or render nugatory the problems of class, economics,
> bureaucratic systems and the like, concentrating instead upon the es-
> sences of self, nationhood, community and Zeitgeist.[59]

Avoiding direct criticism of Yeats's mythmaking, Deane complains
about the recent literalization by his contemporaries of Yeats's myths,

especially the intellectual claims for Protestant Ireland. Deane worries that "a tradition which continues to interpret its culture in such exclusive terms is in danger of petrifaction." This echoes Yeats's own assertion, made seventy years earlier, that contemporary nationalists had made of Davis's ideas fixed dogma:

> The more ambitious . . . tried to see the world as Davis saw it. No philosophical speculation, no economic question of the day, disturbed an orthodoxy which, unlike that of religion, had no philosophical history. . . ."[60]

Although many of Yeats's own ideas about a nationalism rooted in history were derived from Davis's essays,[61] Davis too often wrote without an imaginative grasp of history, and his concepts dried into condescending shibboleths and arrested concepts:

> Happy boys! who may grow up with such ballads in your memories. Happy men! who will find your hearts not only dutiful, but joyous, in serving and sacrificing for the country you thus learned in childhood to love.[62]

In sharp contrast to Davis's static journalistic history, Yeats developed a "philosophical history" derived from continental and English writers such as Shelley, Carlyle, and Nietzsche, who opposed the Enlightenment's mechanistic concepts of history as they came to be formulated by Taine, the Positivists, and sociological demographers. Victorian science's absolutist claims to truth raised questions about the sources of historical truth, made epistemologists and historiographers of historians, and finally collapsed the causal bridge between past and present. Robert Langbaum describes the reaction of writers such as Eliot and Joyce who followed, according to Eliot, the "method already adumbrated by Mr. Yeats":

> Eliot and Joyce show with uncompromising completeness that the past of official tradition is dead, and in this sense they carry nineteenth-century naturalism to its logical conclusion. But they also dig below the ruins of official tradition to uncover in myth and underground tradition, an inescapable because inherently psychological pattern into which to fit the chaotic present.[63]

Thomas Whitaker has argued convincingly that Yeats's own approach was dualistic: he assumed a panoramic view of historical patterns or he dramatized characters from his own actual experience.[64] Whitaker allows Yeats to answer the critics of romanticist history:

> History as vision is limited by one's own mental breadth and depth; history as dramatic experience is limited by the extent to which one has, in one's own lifetime, gone over the whole ground. But to seek history in any other way is to compile anatomies of last year's leaves and not to see or create a living forest.[65]

Yet, Yeats's visionary and dramatic historical representations can be applied to actual situations only obliquely because Yeats strips his characters of contexts, much as he sets characters on a bare stage. "All knowledge is biography,"[66] wrote the aging Yeats, for whom the cultural and linguistic disjunctions of the great famine seemed aside from the point of history. If the poet could restore to his people the heroic spirit and fierce integrity of earlier heroes, as he imagines them, he believed he could reunify his culture. In *Trembling of The Veil* Yeats wrote,

> Nations, races, and individual men are unified by an image, or bundle of related images, symbolical or evocative of the state of mind, which is . . . the most difficult to that man, race, or nation; because only the greatest obstacle that can be contemplated without despair rouses the will to full intensity.[67]

Yeats believed that he had discovered and transmitted the nation's masks through his own writing, as he claimed in 1922:

> As I look backward upon my own writing, . . . it seems I have found something hard and cold, some articulation of the Image, which is the opposite of all that I am in daily life, and all that my country is.[68]

Although these poetic articulations may be inhuman images — the gray rock, a "cold and rook-delighting" sky, or "a laughing string / Wheron mad fingers play / Amid a place of stone" — they may also be types, such as the Connemara fisherman, or mythical figures, such as Cuchulain, or historical personages, such as Swift. In a more fully developed exposition, we might also explore the mask-like functions of the odd contrary types that people Yeats's poetry. Because he liked to flip hard-shelled opinions on their back and watch them kick, he seems to have inverted or troped some of the most sacred, and therefore stalest, representations of Ireland. Crazy Jane, for example, slut and seer, is both a version of the Hag of Beare and a debased form of Cathleen Ni Houlihan just as Ribh represents the first order of the Irish clergy. These characters are hardly models for action in themselves but means of purging clichés and counterbalancing lopsides of the emerging Irish character.[69]

Swift and Berkeley serve less plausibly as masks for Ireland because they are derived from history, yet Yeats draws them far enough from history to stress their passion and personality over their historical situation. Consequently, he offers them as images to his nation:

> These two images . . . Swift and Berkeley, concern all those who feel a responsibility for the thought of modern Ireland that can take away their sleep.[70]

Yeats opposes them implicitly to the values associated with the sons of Young Ireland, based on Utilitarianism, industrialization, and urbanization.[71] To counter them Yeats offered not the values of Georgian Ireland but of "the solitaries" within that society: a "sense for what is permanent, as distinct from what is useful"; the belief "that abstract ideas are mere words"; a "disbelief in Newton's system and every sort of machine"; "delight in the particulars of common life"; and the "conviction that all States not grown slowly like a forest tree are tyrannies." Yeats emphasized these values in the writings of Berkeley, Swift, Goldsmith, and Burke who "found in England the opposite that stung their own thought into expression and made it lucid."[72] Ironically, the Free State replaced England in the antinomies of the early thirties, as Yeats viewed them.

Yeats's extolling of these Anglo-Irish thinkers seems more reactionary than racial or sectarian. Although Yeats occasionally referred to the Anglo-Irish "race," he as frequently maintained the reference he assumed in the nineties to "my own people, the people of a Celtic habit of thought."[73] He argued that the Anglo-Irish were so interbred that racial distinctions were meaningless:

> The newest arrivals soon inter-married with an older stock, and that
> older stock had inter-married again and again with Gaelic Ireland. . . .
> Ireland, divided in religion and politics, is as much one race as any mod-
> ern country.[74]

As a non-Christian Yeats seems as sympathetic, and unsympathetic,
toward Catholicism as toward his family's religion, the Church of Ireland. His preference for the views of Swift and Berkeley over those of
O'Connell and Davis, the latter of whom was also Protestant, does not
seem motivated by religious considerations. Yeats redirected his anger
from nationalism to Catholicism, as in the Senate speech of 1925 against
divorce, only when religious consensus replaced a political consensus
as the major threat to his freedom, as an Irishman and an artist. Yeats's
diagnosis in that Senate speech seems unhysterical:

> For the last hundred years Irish Nationalism has had to fight against
> England, and that fight has helped Fanaticism. . . . The basis of Irish
> nationalism has now shifted, and much that once helped us is now
> injurious. . . .[75]

A misunderstanding of Yeats's antithetical art more serious than
these exaggerated assumptions about racialism or sectarianism has been
promoted almost into popular acceptance by Conor Cruise O'Brien.
Cruise O'Brien has argued that Yeats's political statements would lead
to fascism if they were extended only somewhat along the linear scale
on which we locate political positions.[76] Although almost certainly
Yeats's plays, and perhaps even his poetry, influenced the course of Irish
history, no repressive political system could be justified on the basis of
his art. Yeats cannot suppress contrary views, those of young Ireland,
for example, because he is engaged in an imaginative dialectic in which
his ideals, such as Parnellite integrity, Swiftian indignation, and Burkean
traditionalism implicate, and therefore depend on, their opposing Sinn
Fein values. In a 1934 preface, Yeats argued that Parnell symbolized his
era's antithetical relation to O'Connell and his milieu: "He was the symbol that made apparent, or made possible, . . . that epoch's contrary:
contrary, not negation, not refutuation: . . . contraries are positive."[77]
To extend Yeats's political ideas on a linear political scale ignores his
assumption that they are conjoined to their antithesis. Rather than fly-

ing off into extremes, Yeats's ideas become centripetal, in tension with their polarities and moving about a center.

They also represent history as cyclical. In this 1934 preface Yeats recalled the lament of Aogán Ó Rathaille, Swift's Gaelic contemporary and superior poet, for his overthrown Jacobite patron and especially their predecessors: "My fathers served their fathers before Christ was crucified."[78] Just as the Irish leadership passed from Jacobite to Georgian to O'Connell to Parnell, so will it return to Catholic heroes, Yeats foretold.[79]

We might pause here to suggest how Yeats's antithetical art served as a legacy for younger poets. While clearly finding the democratic and pluralistic content of Joyce's art more appropriate for Irish society than the aristocratic and elitist content of Yeats's, poets of the last forty years have found Yeats's actual role in society a more helpful model than Joyce's. Whereas Joyce represents an extreme example of the independent artist who rejects his society in order to create its conscience, Yeats demonstrated that a poet could testify to his personal experience—psychological, intellectual, perceptual—while actively playing a public role. By opposing prevailing collective views in his poetry (as, for example, his randy characters are antithetical to popular images of purity), Yeats shielded his poetry from those common assumptions and acceptable phrasings that convey no human's actual experience. Consequently, in their disappointment with a reactionary social climate, his successors, most specifically Clarke and Kavanagh, could slip into an adversarial role prepared for them by Yeats.

More recently poets have played Yeats's double role of active citizen and priestly poet. Kinsella, Montague, and Heaney, for example, lecture, translate, review, and administer to enhance the place of art in Ireland, and to feed their families. In their poetry they may oppose popular assumptions or, in any case, scrupulously avoid widely-held beliefs. For example, in a poetry of recovery, they comment indirectly on the widespread irredentist aspirations of their countrymen. Rather than writing directly on the recovery of their homeland from colonial rule, Kinsella more often has developed the theme of re-invasion, based on *The Book of Invasions* but correlative to his interest in Jungian recoveries from the unconscious; Heaney constructed and then abandoned a tentative myth concerning exploration of bogland and the elevation into the pres-

ent of a multi-layered past; Montague defines the limitation of language
or of any vehicle by which we attempt to return to our homeland. The
more personal and profound treatments of recovery call into question,
as they can revise, popular myths. Heaney found in Yeats this lesson
that "art can outface history, the imagination can disdain happenings
once it has incubated and mastered the secret behind happenings."[80]

Saving for the end of this section a final comment on Yeats's antithetical art as poetic heritage, I will summarize other important, but less
significant, Yeatsian legacies to Irish poetry, beginning with the means
by which Yeats spoke of public events in a personal poetic voice.

Samuel Hynes has praised Yeats for his "willed assimilation of political experience, the public emotion, into personal life. Yeats was the
first poet to do this, to accept contemporary history as a subject, and
to respond to it as a poet".[81]

Although Yeats brought contemporary events into the presence of
imaginary concepts more frequently and systematically than other poets,
poets from Horace to Milton to Shelley have written topical poems.
Stephen Spender characterizes Yeats's adaptation to public historical
topics in terms of the poet's "voice," "his power of making a kind of
public historic statement of a general kind which yet strikes us as having a great particularity."[82]

This poetic voice is never merely spatialized words, nor is it a song —
ballad or lyric — a dance or chant, but rhythmical and elevated speech,
or, as Yeats phrased it, "written speech." The tone and diction of this
"written speech" are consistent enough for us to characterize the speaker
of most of the poems as a version of the poet, but usually of the poet
speaking in a particular place and time. Even in the most public, vatic,
or visionary poems, such as "The Second Coming" or "Nineteen Hundred and Nineteen," which begin by overturning the speaker's iamb
with the oracular trochee or dactyl, the personal speaker appears for
long enough to be identified and located.

Certain recurrent words and phrases and rhetorical habits, however,
both generalize and particularize this written speech. Adjectives — *old*,[83]
*ancient, bitter, gay,* and *proud*; phrases that combine abstractions — "old
wrong," "fabulous, formless, darkness"; or vague key-words — "things
fall apart," "everything that man esteems" — could be a vocabulary from
almost any decade after *Paradise Lost.* Even the celebrated tough diction

—"rail and sweat," "slouches," "marrow bones," "cold grey stones"—
which entered Yeats's poetry in the twentieth century—could have been
used by Swift. These words, however, have an emotional base, as if they
are drawn from the inside out to find their application in the world.
Furthermore, Yeats has recombined these and similar words so frequently that only a slightly extended concordance would identify this
post-Victorian author. Words that could be of many ages serve as the
signature of one poet speaking in a particular context.

We are also familiar with certain rhetorical patterns in Yeats's verse,
which are reminiscent of older, more elevated forms of address but
which become recognizably Yeatsian through recurrence. Among the
devices Yeats employs, perhaps *chiasmus,* as in "Make all Platonic tolerance vain / And vain all Doric discipline" (specifically, antimetabole),
or more general forms of parallel structure become signatures, but the
most familiar rhetorical device is the ubiquitous parathesis, Yeats's habitual interposing of additional modifiers or of afterthoughts between
his subjects and their actions. For examples of Yeats's parenthetical patterns we need only scan his prose where repeatedly a simple question
or statement is qualified into complexity by some interposed phrase.
Among the abundant examples of parenthesis in his poetry, we might
consider the complex blending of a general statement with particular
qualifiers in four lines of "The Tower":

> Did all old men and women, rich and poor,
> Who trod upon these rocks or passed this door,
> Whether in public or in secret rage
> As I do now against old age?

(YP, 197)

Of the historical, legendary, and fictional characters that people his
imaginative Kiltartan district, he asks this basic ten-word question: "Did
all old men and women rage against old age?" The question, though
not historical, is general and timeless. Between subject and verb, however, he places parenthetical qualifiers to add a further generalization—
"rich and poor"—that rhymes with a particularization—"Who trod upon
these rocks or passed this door." He wants to know about the aged
of all classes and all epochs (the archaic trod demonstrates his accommodation to their indefinite pasts) but only if they shared this particular

place. The next parenthetical phrase seems paradoxical: if the preceding generations raged in secret, who would know? In this personal colloquy, this knowledge can arise only from his own imagination, where Hanrahan, Raftery, and Mrs. French reside. The final parenthetical phrase, which brings us to the moment of the poet's anguish, renders immediate and personal a question that was asked about the broadest general audience, "all old men and women." Finally, although the parenthesis heightens as it elaborates on the question, it also interiorizes the question and makes it immediate by revealing the mind musing and qualifying. Because parenthesis is habitual with Yeats, the four lines convey the general question through the private thoughts of one individual whom we recognize. Although the proportion of the private and public, the particular self and the general human condition, vary from poem to poem, Yeats's "written speech" remained an effective instrument for reflecting the outside world within the poet's "mirror-resembling dream."

Yeats's "written speech" has been a mixed blessing to his poetic successors. Imbued with Yeats's sense of the beauty and loftiness of language, they cannot set their places with his silver phrasings without seeming antique. Derek Mahon has confessed that only a lobotomy could remove from his mind the Yeatsian line,[84] which he, like MacNeice, exorcises by placing elaborate diction within ironic sentences. Other poets follow Kavanagh's escape from Yeats through plain diction and flat colloquial sentences.

It may have been easier for succeeding poets to eschew or transform the Yeatsian style than to avoid literary headlines that proclaimed Yeats's international stature. Although many references in Yeats's poems were addressed to an Irish audience, he was overheard in England and America, if not on the continent, by readers amazed that a tiny nation could house great writers. The effect of Yeats's international reputation on his immediate successors was expressed by Austin Clarke in 1949:

> So far as the younger generation of poets are concerned, here in Ireland, Yeats was rather like an enormous oak-tree which, of course, kept us in the shade, and did exclude a great number of rays of, say, the friendly sun. . . .[85]

If Clarke was present in the Abbey audience in 1940 to hear T. S. Eliot deliver the first annual Yeats lecture, as he probably was, the English critic ignored his presence, as a poet in that audience or even in Ireland. "Certainly, for the younger poets of England and America, I am sure that their admiration for Yeats's poetry has been wholly good,"[86] declared Eliot, apparently incapable of conceiving of an Irish poetry after Yeats. Yet, if acclaim for Yeats deafened critics and readers to the voices of other Irish poets, it also troubled the Irish poets with questions of how far to pitch their voices beyond the immediate Irish audience. The crucial questions of audience, which are part of Yeats's legacy, are addressed in the last section of this chapter.

A more sustaining gift for the major talents, if not for the minor poets, was Yeats's professional attitude toward poetry. First, he dispelled certain nationalist and utilitarian assumptions about poetry which are evident in John Mitchel's praise of Thomas Davis:

> From a calm, deliberate conviction that among other agencies for arousing national spirit, fresh, manly, vigorous national songs and ballads must by no means be neglected, he conscientiously set to work to manufacture the article wanted.[87]

Yeats would admit that the creative process requires the equivalent, at least, of hand labor, as he does in these familiar lines from "Adam's Curse:"

> Better go down upon your marrow-bones
> And scrub a kitchen pavement, or break stones
> Like a pauper, in all kinds of weather;
> For to articulate sweet sounds together
> Is to work harder than all these. . . .
>
> (*YP*, 80)

The test of a poem's utility, however, Yeats set at a level unapproachable by Davis. Yeats's adaptation of Wilde's saying that "all the most valuable things are useless"[88] does not deny to poetry secondary functions, such as "arousing national spirit," but it would bring the poem to an ultimate test beyond the measure of utility:

> Begin the preparation for your death
> And from the fortieth winter by that thought
> Test every work of intellect and faith,
> And everything that your own hands have wrought
> And call those works extravagance of breadth

That are not suited for such men as come
Proud, open-eyed and laughing to the tomb.
                    ("Vacillation," *YP,* 250)

No art for art's sake, this elevated sense of the poetic mission derives from English anti-utilitarian writers of the nineteenth century such as Shelley, Blake, Pater, Hopkins, and Rossetti. The extent to which Yeats has absorbed and extended Victorian aestheticism is evident in the magnificent late poem "Lapis Lazuli" where the work of art establishes tragic types and offers the script for living this tragic life, where art rebuilds after destruction, involves the audience in the creative act, solaces, and offers an overview of tragic life that allows humans to accept and affirm life in a spirit of "tragic gaiety" (*YP,* 294–95). By reestablishing such hieratic functions for the poet, Yeats may have made it easier for his successors, particularly those who grew up in Ulster, to resist demands to respond poetically to the Troubles.

Yeats also established that the priesthood of poetry is a life's espousal. Beyond negative examples such as Wordsworth's long loveless post-honeymoon with the muse, Yeats offers the healthiest example of an extended and fruitful career maintained by energetic renewals, only some of which, such as those following the *Playboy* controversy and the 1916 Rising, were forced on him by the vicissitudes of Irish politics. Seamus Heaney, echoing T. S. Eliot's Abbey lecture, finds in Yeats's example support for his own poetic mid-life crisis:

He is, indeed, the ideal example for a poet approaching middle age. . . .
He bothers you with the suggestion that if you have managed to do
one kind of poem in your own way, you should cast off that way and
face into another area of your experience until you have learned a new
voice to say that area properly.[89]

Surely, Yeats's example must have burned brightly for Austin Clarke who, at age fifty-nine after a seventeen-year preoccupation with drama, returned to strike off from his soul's smithy nearly a dozen volumes of poetry before his death at age seventy-eight.

In retrospect, the dramatic shifts in Yeats's poetry seem inevitable rather than capricious. This effect of a designed career results in part from the shape Yeats gave to each volume of his poetry and finally to the relation of volumes within the vast design of *The Poems.* His practice of shaping books out of individual poems has challenged most of his successors to envision designs structured of, but more commodious than, individual lyrics.

Not all of Yeats's legacies were created and handed down in defiance of orthodox views within Ireland. We might argue that Yeats passed even Daniel Corkery's exclusive test of the Irish writer: that he be preoccupied with Catholicism, nationalism, or the land.[90] Whereas one might find argument in asserting that Yeats's apparent rejection of religion and nationalism was actually a delving beneath Victorian and Jansenist overlays on the roots of Irish nationalism and belief, Yeats's lifelong interest in the land—the countryman, the ancient agrarian traditions, and the landscape—is more evident. Frank O'Connor has claimed that Yeats "had lived so long with the folk mind, the nonreasoning, instinctive mind, that he had an infallible sense of what belonged to it."[91] Yeats imbued his early stories and poems and his plays based on the Ulster cycle with details from folk life, but he rarely describes a landscape. We know that Yeats could perceive acutely, as in this vagrant's view of the unwelcoming lanes, which anticipates Christy Mahon's poetry of the road:

> The window and the doors were shut,
> One star shone faint and green,
> The little straws were turnin' round
> Across the bare boreen.
> ("The Ballad of Moll Magee," *YP*, 23–24)

Yet, excepting perhaps in a few poems about Thoor Ballylee and Coole Park, such details rarely compose a coherent realistic picture of Irish landscape. Yeats's image of Ireland is composed otherwise, as Thomas Flanagan contends: "Indeed, in certain of his poems, this image of Ireland is totally autonomous, a Platonic form of which the actual island is but a smudged and imperfect copy." Flanagan determines that this Platonic Ireland is "wrought from inchoate and fragmentary materials and yet is more pure than a candle's flame. . . ."[92]

Yeats seems to have composed his island from fragments of the real world which he infuses with emotions, as Yeats himself suggested in his description of the nation's mask, which I quoted earlier, as "an image, or bundle of related images, symbolic or evocative. . . ."[93] Although he abandoned the "overcharged colour" inherited from Rossetti and Burne-Jones, he derived a concept of a "spiritualized landscape" from the Pre-Raphaelites who were once his father's standard.[94]

Ironically, a generation of Yeats's readers, perhaps those born east of Crumlin or west of the Skelligs, can observe in the West of Ireland a Yeatsian landscape composed of cold gray stone, cold light, and tumbling clouds and imbued with a "cold emotion." Like all great artists, Yeats has altered the way we view the world we live in, as he has altered the Irish tradition we share with him. As I will argue later, the strong artist recreates with his audience a version of that tradition, which is the most vital means by which the tradition can live.

It may seem seditious that the poet can insinuate into our views an image of Ireland antithetical to any orthodox sense of Irish realities. Yeats confesses,

> It is perhaps because nature made me a gregarious man, going hither and thither looking for conversation, and ready to deny for fear or favour his dearest conviction, that I love proud and lonely things.[95]

The proud and lonely thing, of course, is implicit in the gregarious, as for Yeats all things imply, in the imagination, their opposite. Yet, far from being a mechanical polar opposition, an imaginary antithesis is a vividly conceived contrary to orthodox opinions or routine habits of thought or action. Although it may transform reality, antithetical art can not retreat from or reject the world we inhabit, Yeats suggests in his ironic escape poem, "Sailing to Byzantium." Having imagined an antithesis to the Romanticist poet's dream of becoming a "selfsame song," Yeats's speaker would become a mechanical golden bird. The immigrant to Byzantium escapes to "an artifice of eternity," which is the mirrored form of what we call an eternity of art. "Once out of nature" and exiled from "whatever is begotten, born, and dies," the poet-bird can sing only of the mirror-image of that natural world, "of what is past, or passing, or to come" (*YP*, 194).

### 3. Joyce's Legacy: History and the Speaker's Voice

When James Joyce had "sailed the seas and come" to Trieste, Zurich, and Paris, he could only turn back like Yeats's escaping poet to take as his subject the life-and-death processes of his homeland. Joyce's desire to remain detached from the social, national, and religious problems of Ireland was more compelling than Yeats's, who only migrated or mounted his tower when he wished to escape Irish politics. At the beginning of his career, Joyce underscored this difference by attacking Yeats's "treacherous instinct of adaptability" which Yeats demonstrated to Joyce by collaborating in the Irish National Theatre: "If the artist courts the favor of the multitude he can not escape the contagion of its fetishism and deliberate self-deception. . . ."[96] Consequently, Joyce applauded, from the distance of Rome, the *Playboy* controversy which seemed to confirm this prediction of 1901.

In his attack on Yeats and especially in his self-exile we witness a puritanical severity of faith in his art and its ability to affect his society, the sort of intransigent faith that made, in other ages, heresiarchs and martyrs such as St. Stephen and Bruno of Nola or, in his own epoch, "priests of eternal imagination" such as Ibsen, Pater, and Flaubert, all heroes of Joyce. Although Joyce declared *Dubliners* a "moral history" in which he took "the first step towards the spiritual liberation of my country,"[97] "for Joyce, the freeing of the individual was the main issue, indeed the only one,"[98] according to a critic who has also recently demonstrated that Joyce habitually associated the enemies of individual freedom with his Irish nemeses, English imperialism and Roman Catholicism.

However, Joyce separated himself from any possibility of interfering in Irish politics by the Irish Sea and the English Channel. A practical consequence of this celebrated exile was to make Paris, especially, a literary Van Diemen's Land where Irish writers such as Beckett, Denis Devlin, Brian Coffey, Thomas MacGreevy, and John Montague lived part, if not most, of their lives. Furthermore, Joyce's aligning of the Irish writer with the great European literary tradition set a standard for eclectic reading and polyglot writing that was not lost on these exiles or on poets of the next generation such as Derek Mahon and Seamus Deane.

Whereas *Finnegans Wake* employs a complex amalgamated language built around a core of Irish-English, *A Portrait* remains a primer of the Irish writer's relation to English. Although the entire book demonstrates Stephen's development of linguistic skills and attitudes, the opening of chapter 5 serves as a crucial text to Joyce's successors. Having risen too late for his English lecture, Stephen meditates on the works of Hauptmann, Newman, Cavalcanti, Ibsen, and Jonson, as he follows his own course to the university. He arrives in time to engage the Dean of Studies in a conversation in which fire and water alternate as images of truth. After Stephen allows that "thinking must be bound by its own laws," the image of fire is contained within a discussion of lamps.[99] Stephen then informs the Dean that the funnel by which one fills a lamp is called a *tundish*. According to the *OED*, which cites *Measure for Measure* as a source Stephen would have appreciated, a tun-dish, a bowl with a funnel, actually is used to fill a tun or some other large container. If this funnel is attached to the Dean's lamp, as it seems to be, Stephen has reversed the direction of the fuel's flow much as he has changed the direction by which an understanding of English is usually disseminated: "It is called a tundish in Lower Drumcondra, said Stephen laughing, where they speak the best English" (*JP*, 188). This passage serves as a pre-text for Seamus Heaney in the conclusion of *Station Island:*

> there is a moment in Stephen's diary
> for April the thirteenth, a revelation
>
> set among my stars—that one entry
> has been a sort of password in my ears,
>
> the collect of a new epiphany
> the Feast of the Holy Tundish. . . .[100]

In the diary entry Heaney refers to, from *A Portrait's* conclusion, Stephen recollects the discussion of *Tundish,* damns the Dean for his ignorance, and asks, "What did he come here for to teach us our own language or to learn it from us?" (*JP*, 251).

It is the self-consciousness of Stephen and his compatriots toward English that leads to mastery. In the original encounter with the Dean, Stephen muses:

How different are the words *home, Christ, ale, master,* on his lips and on mine! I cannot speak or write these words without unrest of spirit. His language, so familiar and so foreign, will always be for me an acquired speech. I have not made or accepted its words. My voice holds them at bay. My soul frets in the shadow of his language. (*JP*, 189)

The self-consciousness extends to Latin, learned through church and school, and then to other languages (*JP,* 90).

Acknowledging his own tentative hold on language, the artist grows to recognize his obligation to forge a language that will transmit his inner state to an audience:

> How could he hit their conscience or how cast his shadow over the imaginations of their daughters. . . . And under the deepened dusk he felt the thoughts and desires of the race to which he belonged flitting like bats. . . . (*JP,* 238)

Although the uncreated conscience of his race may have been Joyce's central concern, his sense of potential audience widened eventually to include all Europeans falsely preoccupied with World War II rather than *Finnegans Wake.*[101] Joyce's great integrity and independence never freed him from an anxiety about the size and commitment of his readership.[102] He must have known that his innovative narrative methods were especially daunting to those most familiar with his subject matter.

The subject of Joyce's art, however, remained parochial, specifically his Dublin parish of street corners, small shops, pubs, and idiosyncratic citizens. His autobiographical Stephen Hero, in "evangelising" his mother, might have been addressing the incipient author of "Sailing to Byzantium":

> Art is not an escape from life. It's just the very opposite. . . . An artist is not a fellow who dangles a mechanical heaven before the public. The priest does that. The artist affirms out of the fulness of his own life. . . .[103]

The "fulness of life" that Joyce brought to the pages included that commercial class Yeats condemned as "paudeens" and the bustle of "pavements grey" the poet would escape. Furthermore, by attending to the meekest and poorest urban characters, Joyce broadened the Irish writer's longstanding respect for the rural poor to an all-embracing literary democracy.

By turning away from the country and countryman, Joyce opened up the city as a legitimate Irish landscape. In assaying Joyce's choice of settings, some critics have separated out as a secondary motive a reaction to Yeats, "a half uncomprehending detestation of Yeats's involvement with peasant and primitive Ireland."[104] Joyce assigns his strongest statement on the Irish peasantry to Stephen, in *A Portrait,* who reacts anxiously to his classmate's tale of meeting an Irish-speaking country-man in Connacht:

> I fear him. I fear his redrimmed horny eyes. It is with him I must strug-gle all through this night till day come, till he or I lie dead, gripping him by the sinewy throat till . . . Till what? Till he yield to me? No. I mean him no harm. (*JP,* 252)

Bernard Benstock emphasizes Stephen's recognition of a "personifica-tion of hopeless ignorance that persists as an eternal threat to the world he lives in"[105] whereas clear allusions to Jacob's all-night stalemated grapple with God's champion (Genesis 32), which critics have not overlooked,[106] suggest that Stephen, within a fortnight of his departure for Paris, will continue to wrestle with the firbolgian shadow-side of the Irish char-acter even though it may wear an urban guise (*JP,* 249–50).

If Joyce was to touch, as Stephen wished, "the thoughts and desires of the race to which he belonged," he must take as his subject the clamor and clamber of Dublin. "For myself, I always write about Dublin, be-cause if I can get to the heart of Dublin I can get to the heart of all the cities of the world," Joyce confessed to Arthur Power at the publica-tion of *Ulysses.* The world's great writers "were national first, and it was the intensity of their own nationalism which made them inter-national in the end. . . . "[107] In this advice, Joyce anticipates Patrick Kavanagh's distinction between the parochial writer—who wrote with assurance about the particular life he knew—and the provincial writer —who would sell local color on the mass markets. Kavanagh recog-nized in Joyce not only a fellow parishioner but, with George Moore, one of the "two great Irish parishioners."[108]

With that recognition by the true peasant-poet, Joyce nullified the privileged position of the peasant in Irish literature. Just as Irish poetry matured beyond the pastoral verse of AE, Colum, and Higgins, the ca-reer of Austin Clarke progressed beyond the influence of early Yeats to that of the author of *A Portrait.* Poems such as Clarke's "Ancient Lights," "Inscription for a Headstone," and "Emancipation," Kavanagh's "If Ever You Go to Dublin Town" and his canal-bank sonnets, and Kin-sella's "Baggot Street Deserta" had established before 1960 a new urban poetic landscape that owed its foundation to Joyce, whom Kinsella confesses was "definitely his [early] hero,"[109] although Auden, Eliot, and MacNeice were also influences on the Irish urban poetry.

Secondly, Joyce's faithful descriptions of mundane nonpoetic aspects of the city encourage Irish poets, urban and rural, to create from the actual details of their own lives. To a great extent, this influence has been transmitted by Patrick Kavanagh, whom Seamus Deane calls "the man who has most deeply influenced contemporary Irish poetry."[110] Ironically, Kavanagh's misreading of Joyce's writing as a sort of documentation confirmed the poet in his views: "*Ulysses* . . . is almost entirely a transcription of life. Joyce added nothing—except possibly Stephen. . . ."[111]

In fact, the apparent naturalism of *Dubliners* has dissolved into a dizzying multiplicity of styles by the midpoint of Bloom's Odyssey. Hugh Kenner argues that the dissolution of naturalism in Joyce's own work was determined by the premises of the nineteenth-century novel: "Reality, Joyce learned early, does not answer to the 'point of view', the monocular vision, the single ascertainable tone. A tone, a voice, is somebody's, a person's, and people are confined to being themselves, are Evelines, are Croftons, are Stephens."[112] To the extent that the novelists shared assumptions with nineteenth-century historicists—that past eras were distinctive from the present and recoverable by recreating the distinctive *race, moment,* and *milieu* of each era—they came to realize that historical validity depended on an authority of judgment and imagination that no person could legitimately claim. Consequently, Joyce leads the shift from a single point of view to a more dramatic form of narration in which the reader arrives at judgments formerly proclaimed by the narrator. As no insignificant byproduct of this narrative shift, Joyce suggests to the Irish poets a way of freeing their vision from historical determinism which has had a killing hold on the Irish consciousness.

Perhaps the most successful evasion of the monocular point of view occurs in the climactic "Ithaca" chapter of *Ulysses,* where a catechism of questions and answers compounds information on expansive scientific fields—such as the universe—and on the most personal proclivities and opinions of Bloom. Walton Litz describes the effect of this narrative method:

It is as if we were viewing Bloom and Stephen from a great height, against a vast backdrop of general human action and knowledge, while at the same time standing next to them and observing every local detail. It is this parallax achieved by the macrocosmic-microcosmic point-of-view which gives the episode, like Hardy's *Dynasts,* the grandeur and sweep that Joyce certainly intended.[113]

This term *parallax* is introduced into *Ulysses* by Bloom before the Ballast Office clock, the site in *Stephen Hero* of Stephen's controversial explanation of *epiphany,* a term appropriate to a monocular point of view.[114] Parallax is a method of locating a celestial body by measuring the apparent shift in the position of the body when sighted from two points of view, or from the same observation point at two different times. Critics have observed that these methods of determining "geocentric" parallax have their analogues in the multiple points of view in *Ulysses* and that the term can be applied to the way the reader must "locate" Stephen and, especially, Bloom from a number of partial or even inaccurate sightings. *Parallax* implies not the incompleteness of any one character, as Ellmann has suggested,[115] but the incompleteness of any one viewpoint within the novel, as well as being a strategy for involving the reader in the search for meaning.

Of course, our application of the term *Joycean* to even, or especially, the most disparate points of view in his novel suggests that the author has not refined himself out of existence. As the reader of *Ulysses* collates and interpolates from the various points of view, he also distills the Joycean undertone from the various speakers. This undertone becomes a Joycean tone only in the totality of the novel.

The aftereffects of Joyce's example on Irish poets' control of tone are considered more closely in the final section of this chapter. Here, we need say only that writers who followed Joyce could hardly assume a monocular point of view or a univocal tone unreflectively, whether in poetry or fiction. For example, the multiple points of view and voices in John Montague's *Rough Field* and *Great Cloak,* which are that poet's way of displacing judgment to the reader, must be derived, at least in part, from *Ulysses,* as are the subtle shifts of voice in Kinsella's later poetry. However, even when direct influence cannot be established, we may assume the Irish poets' particular skeptical and sophisticated adaptation of tone evolves in part from Joyce's discarding of the objective viewpoint in *A Portrait, Ulysses,* and *Finnegans Wake.*

In the quotation above, Litz applies Joyce's term *parallax* not merely to various narrative perspectives but specifically to the alternation between panoramic and approximate perspectives on Stephen and Bloom. Litz argues: "On the literal level, bounded by the twenty hours of the novel's action, Stephen and Bloom are mock-heroic figures; but on the figurative level they take on heroic and creative possibilities."[116]

To readers who would complain about the lack of resolution in *Ulysses*—Stephen's unwillingness to recognize Bloom as a spiritual father who can teach him "what the heart is and what it feels" (*JP*, 252); Bloom's failure to attach Stephen to his domestic triangle—Litz suggests that the union of Stephen and Bloom occurs symbolically to the reader who has been invested with Joyce's split-focus, when the two heroes urinate in the garden under a shooting star that intersects Orpheus's Lyre and Leo.[117]

These astronomical references and Bloom's knowledge of the stars derive from *The Story of the Heavens,*[118] a book in Bloom's library by Sir Robert Ball, the Royal Astronomer of Ireland. Later, in "Ithaca" Joyce transforms Ball's complex term *parallax* into an elaborate concept by fusing with it certain reflections on time that are only secondary and accidental in Ball's study. Bloom muses on

> the parallax or parallactic drift of socalled fixed stars, in reality ever-moving from immeasurably remote futures in comparison with which the years, threescore and ten, of allotted human life formed a parenthesis of infinitesimal brevity.[119]

Bloom has paraphrased the "group-parallax" method which Ball explains in chapter 16 of his book. To parallax's two senses of spatial relativity—an object will appear different to two simultaneous viewers or to one viewer at two times of day—Joyce adds two pages later a complex idea of temporal relativity of observation: the radiance of an object being observed in the present may be an emanation from the past:

> an infinity, renderable equally finite by the suppositious probable apposition of one or more bodies equally of the same and of different magnitudes: a mobility of illusory forms immobilised in space, remobilised

in air: a past possibly had ceased to exist as a present before its future spectators had entered actual present existence.[120]

As an ancient form may have a visible reality in the present, so metaphorically or even ontologically Bloom may emanate Odyssean qualities.

In writing to Frank Budgen about "Ithaca" Joyce said that through the process of catechistic method, "Bloom and Stephen thereby become heavenly bodies, wanderers like the stars at which they gaze."[121] "Ithaca" answers Stephen's morning question — "Am I walking into eternity along Sandymount strand" — by casting Stephen and Bloom against the infinite spaces and thus freeing them, at least in the reader's mind, from causal history, from a total restriction to June sixteenth's problems of paternity, adultery, guilt, and residence that confine them in their Dublin perambulations.

This infinite space that contains all time becomes, as well as these characters' field of travel, a metaphor for the human mind as Vico taught Joyce to understand it:

> To Vico history was the actualization in time of possibilities that could be deduced by study of the individual mind; it moved in patterns discoverable in that mind. Croce rephrased Vico in the sentence, "Man creates the human world, creates it by transforming himself into the facts of society: by thinking it, he recreates his own creation."[122]

As a spatial representation of time, Joyce's use of the heavens accords with modern physics and with ancient Irish traditions. In the countless *Immra* — Irish voyage sagas — the hero frequently travels into a past time or a transcendent state. Bloom's "Utopian" heaven has its analogues in Yeats's adaptation of *Tir na nOg,* O'Brien's otherworldly police precinct, Clarke's "next to nothing," a coterminous world hidden from ours by an invisible curtain — the *faed fiad* — and even to Kinsella's seeds and larvae and Heaney's archaeological stria. All of these are spatial representations of multiple layers of time, and, perhaps more significantly, almost individualistic recreations of traditional Irish modes of understanding reality.

The absence of any sense of protracted history in *Ulysses* Hugh Kenner attributes to "Joyce's own lack of any feel for the past." Kenner can credit Joyce with only "one deliberate time-journey in *Ulysses,*"[123] a description of the Elizabethan Globe theatre at midsummer. Although we might protest that *Ulysses* offers other time-journeys, such as the fourteenth-century whale slaughter (p. 45), and that the evasion of a predetermined historical development is part of Stephen's, and Joyce's, intention, nevertheless we can agree with Kenner that Joyce's fiction approaches Saussure's definition of the "synchronic: all that exists exists only now, and the past is really only as I imagine it."[124] This idea offers liberation to Joyce's successors as it does to Stephen who had complained that "history is a nightmare from which I am trying to awake."[125] By implication, the mortmain of nationalist history could be slackened, and the poet could clarify his own Irish experience according to the light of his own imagination as it illuminated certain intractable facts of his and his nation's existence. To the extent that each writer wins an audience to his revision, to that extent he has reshaped his nation's tradition.

For the writer to maintain his independent vision and recreate an audience that will be nourished by this vision, he may need to endure isolation and calumny from that audience. Through autobiographical novels and his personal example, Joyce suggested that this martyrdom was the writer's professional responsibility. Before Joyce's intellectual legacies could be inherited, his immediate successors among the poets had need of this example of his personal integrity which made Joyce the "cultural hero"[126] of this generation. It would be the generation of Kinsella that would inherit Joyce's complex revision of point of view, tone, and narrative sequence and restructure their poetry and their relation to an audience in light of this inheritance.

As the second generation after Joyce has ascended, the influence of both Joyce and Yeats has altered. In 1965, Stephen Spender observed: "The Yeats who exercised an influence on young poets in the twenties and thirties seems very different from the Yeats who may be influencing work of some writer in London or New York today."[127] Spender's observation seems accurate not only because critics have clarified many obscurities in Yeats's *A Vision* and Joyce's *Finnegans Wake* but also because the world to which the writers would apply their legacies has altered so drastically. The world of the recent generation of Irish poets, if it was encompassed by the imaginations of Yeats and Joyce, is larger and more complex than would have been envisioned in the amber light of the Palace Bar in 1941.

### 4. *Irish Poetry in the Last Forty Years*

In most cases of assumed literary influence, some gap remains between evidence and proof. One can not prove that the ideas, attitudes, and artistic virtues of Yeats and Joyce caused certain effects in recent Irish poetry, although in the works discussed throughout this book, Yeatsian and Joycean cognates nearly announce their paternity. Neither can we delineate precise stages by which poets absorbed Yeats's examples and began imbibing Joyce's bracing influence. The major benefits and impediments in Yeats's legacy were probably available in 1941: he moved Irish literature from the backwater to the center of the literary map; he defined the poet's priestly function and declared poetry's independence from social or political dominance; he inspired his successors with a majestic cadence. Yet, in this uneasy interregnum between successively brutal wars, who has the authority to assume this elevated tone — "Mere anarchy is loosed upon the world, / The blood-dimmed tide is loosed, and everywhere / The ceremony of innocence is drowned" ("The Second Coming," *YP*, 187) — without navigating the eye of the apocalypse or broadcasting from the celestial command center?

Joyce, and American poets such as Pound and Eliot who acknowledged Joyce's example, would lead Yeats's successors beyond this problem of the narrator's authority. In 1941, Joyce's reputation for independence was established, but readers were only beginning to digest those ideas on history, point of view, and dramatic voice that, I have argued, affect recent poetry. In the decade following the death of Joyce, readings in his work may have encouraged the irony in MacNeice, the rhetorical evasions of Devlin, and the role-playing of Kavanagh by which these writers eased the burden of authority in their poetry. Whereas in "Nationality and Literature" Yeats had postulated an inevitable development of national literatures from epic to dramatic to lyric,[128] Stephen, we know, informed Lynch that art progresses from the lyrical to the epical to the dramatic form in which the audience must proceed without the authoritative intermediacy of the artist.[129] The recent tendency toward dramatic poetry — the use of dramatic speakers or of various versions of the poet-narrator, addresses to the audience, and shifting distances between speaker and audience — suggests that Stephen Daedalus's sense of literary evolution applies to Irish poetry more accurately than Yeats's.

In this section, we must turn from such broad speculation to the actual events that affected these poets' progress from wartime isolation and postwar stagnation to a new flourishing of Irish poetry. The situation of Irish poetry characterized in section one of this chapter — isolation from the outside world caused by censorship and neutrality, and alienation within Ireland enforced by the absence of publishers and the government's hostility toward artists — actually persisted until the fifties. When the wartime's economic hypertrophy abated in the late 1940s, the lack of real productivity and the thorough dependence on England became apparent once again. An Irish government that displayed symbols of its cultural independence — its advocacy of Gaelic as a replacement for English, its espousal of an agrarian rather than an urban society, its continuing recitation of claims on the six northern counties — could nevertheless not free itself from English mercantilism. Furthermore, the inadequate attempts to develop industries, more strenuous before the war than immediately after, took precedence over social reform so that, as F. S. L. Lyons has pointed out, the new Ireland maintained "a regime wedded to the economic ideas of Griffith rather than to those of Connolly."[130] Politicians' hypocritical lip-service to revolutionary policies was as disappointing to writers and other idealists as the limited vision of the economic policies.

Emigration soon became the most alarming symptom of postwar stagnancy, and the most apparent, in the continued export of workers from Dun Laoghaire to jobs in England. Furthermore, a steady shift of population from the Gaeltacht and the west of Ireland generally — the spiritual heart of Ireland — toward Dublin further threatened the continuity of the Irish language and of rural traditions important to Ireland's national identity. Having been apprised by *The Bell* early in the decade that "all our symbols have to be created afresh,"[131] the Irish audience was nevertheless distracted from literature by economic exigencies. As Terence Brown has written, "For many, literature, art, intellectual endeavor or architectural innovation would have seemed luxurious irrelevancies set against daily struggle for survival in years of economic despair."[132]

In Ireland's depressed postwar economy, Joyce probably had few readers. Of the major writers, perhaps only Yeats's public and prophetic voices resonated above penury's drone. Yet those poets who imitated the master's voice soon sounded hollow and false. In one sense, F. R. Higgins fails to enter the story of Irish poetry after Joyce because he died in 1941. On the other hand, he failed to reach the level of accomplishment of the poets included in this story because he sang the peasantry, with a rhetoric too close to Yeats's, while lacking Yeats's discipline to learn his trade.

Padraic Fallon has a more serious claim to be numbered among the Irish poets after Yeats and Joyce. However, as a fully employed customs official and father of six sons, Fallon devoted too little of his time to poetry. Consequently, he lacks the output and intensity of his four contemporaries studied in this book.

Poems published separately in journals were gathered into a book only in 1974, the year of Fallon's death. Occasionally, in poems such as "The Head," we encounter a poetic imagination virile enough to free him from Yeats's influence.[133] For the most part, however, *Poems* reveals the extent of Fallon's entanglement with Yeats, from whom he tried to extricate himself in one whole section of the book. Frequently, as in "Johnstown Castle," what should be counterstatement results in burlesque:

> An ornamental water
> Should be backed with mercury that the sculptured swan
> May be ideal swan forever.
> Here one shiver shows the mud
> And I am glad because a swan
> Can turn up his end and shatter mood
> And shatter mirror,
> Till the woods massed in an architecture shake
> Because a real swan mucks up a lake.[134]

Like Fallon, who lived in Wexford, all of Yeats's poetic successors worked independently of any strong Irish literary center. MacNeice and Devlin returned to Ireland only sporadically, although for a period MacNeice was poetry editor for *The Bell.* Living in their nation's capital in the forties, Clarke and Kavanagh worked without significant support or encouragement beyond that offered by *The Bell* and by *The Dublin Magazine,* which published, with a year's interruption between 1923 and 1950, poetry, short stories, scholarly articles, and reviews of such an elevated tone that they often seemed detached from the actual society of Ireland. During this decade, Clarke wrote plays and founded a theatre for poetic drama, but like Kavanagh he relied on reviewing and hack journalism for his sustenance.

Perhaps Sean O'Faolain and Brian O'Nolan provided the meager core of Ireland's literary world. O'Faolain continued to edit *The Bell* until 1946 when he yielded the editorship to his co-founder Peader O'Donnell. Although two journals appeared in Belfast in the forties—*Lagan* (1943–47) and *Rann* (1948–53)—northern writers such as John Hewitt, W. R. Rodgers, Roy McFadden, Sam Hanna Bell, Maurice Craig, and Robert Greacen published regularly in the Dublin journal, which offered added encouragement with a special Ulster issue (July 1942). *The Bell* published many young poets, such as Donagh MacDonagh, Pearse Hutchinson, Valentin Iremonger, Ewart Milne, and Anthony Cronin, who, if nurtured in a different milieu, might have flourished as poets. At his retirement from *The Bell,* O'Faolain characterized this climate of the forties: "We were born into this thorny time when our task has been less that of cultivating our garden than of clearing away the brambles."[135]

Brian O'Nolan could not claim even this purgative, scourging role, but, as Myles na gCopaleen, his "Cruiskeen Lawn" column for the *Irish Times* goaded the stiff-backed Irishman and reminded other writers that wit and imagination were the traditional Irish escapes from repression.

Before *The Bell* fell silent in 1954, other journals appeared for intense, fugitive careers, each intending to offer some center where writers and readers could meet. Yet, *The Bell*'s persistent complaint—for example, from Peader O'Donnell (April 1946 and November 1950) and Valentin Iremonger (April 1947)—concerned the "want of a centralizing force among Irish poets."[136] That no poetic center could hold in postwar Ireland became manifest with the demise of John Ryan's *Envoy* (d. July 1951), David Marcus's *Poetry Ireland* and *Kavanagh's Weekly* (d. 1952), and *The Bell* (d. December 1954) within several years. (The last issue of *The Bell* contained no poetry!) As if to confirm the Bodkin Report, a state paper that concluded in 1949: "No other country in

Western Europe cared less, or gave less, for the cultivation of the Arts,"[137] these three years witnessed also Kavanagh's public humiliation in his court case against a newspaper that libeled him, the closing of Clarke's poetic-dramatic productions, and the destruction by fire of the Abbey Theatre.

Yet, the post-Yeatsian poetic movement arose from these ashes. In the publication of Sigerson Clifford's ballads, "an extremely amateur piece of book production"[138] offered by Liam Miller to inaugurate his Dolmen Press, one might have ignored the first peep of the poetic phoenix. Within eight years, however, Dolmen had published first books by Thomas Kinsella, Richard Murphy, and John Montague, leaders of the ascending generation of Irish poets. Miller helped Austin Clarke emerge from his poetic silence of seventeen years by setting the private Bridge Press edition of his 1955 volume *Ancient Lights,* and he thereby earned Clarke's confidence and the right to publish later volumes. In the quality of his printing and design and the excellence of his early eclectic choices, Miller set a high standard for subsequent publishers of Irish poetry such as Gallery Press, started by Peter Fallon in 1970, and Blackstaff Press, founded in Belfast in 1971. When this era can be judged, Robin Skelton's encomium for Miller may not be extravagant: "If, as some critics have maintained, another Irish artistic renaissance is beginning, it will be the Dolmen Press that must eventually be thanked."[139]

The formation of a national arts council in 1951, the founding by Mary O'Malley of the Lyric Theatre in Belfast (followed in 1957 by the first issue of its magazine *Threshold*), the reemergence of Austin Clarke as an active poet, and the "spiritual rebirth" of Patrick Kavanagh in 1955 further strengthened the resurgence of poetry in Ireland. That these signs preceded the recovery of the economy, which began in the late fifties, probably indicates a complementary rather than dependent relation between financial and artistic health in Ireland. The impetus for this economic recovery is often attributed to a government paper, written by T. K. Whitaker in 1957 and entitled *Economic Development,* and the economic policies based on this paper and guided by Sean Lemass, who became the Taoiseach in 1959. By setting clear objectives for industrial development and by encouraging foreign investment in Ireland, the Irish enjoyed an improved standard of living until the recent international recession created unemployment and painful inflation.

This relative prosperity affected poetry directly and indirectly, as it altered the Irish society. Increased industrialization accelerated the population drift from west to east. Whereas in the burgeoning population of 1841 (8.5 million for the island) only 15 percent lived in towns,[140] by 1971 over half of the nation lived in urban areas.[141] To the extent that "proudly independent scattered farms and the weakness of long-established village communities" have molded the Irish personality,[142] then demographic shifts have created an identity crisis which only fiction writers such as John McGahern, and poets such as Clarke and Kinsella, have documented.

Furthermore, this prosperity confirmed the ascending power of pragmatists and developers over idealists and poets. Politicians' routine, hypocritical references to republican ideals, to the virtue of Gaelic language, and to the preservation of folkways became so far beside the actual objectives of the state that many writers felt summoned once again to recover and defend some version of the Irish tradition. Whether in defense of the Viking settlement at Wood Quay in Dublin or in some real effort to recover Gaelic literature, the writers of the sixties and seventies were often aligned against the powers that controlled the economy.

If the writers were coming to see a need, as great as that in the late nineteenth century, to free the cultural tradition from colonial manipulation (this time by entrepreneurs with an eye toward tourism and the EEC), they also enjoyed direct benefits from the improved economy in the form of tax relief for artists' income, higher salaries in universities, arts council bursaries, and income supplements from Aosdana, which was established in 1981. With arts council assistance, poetry readings developed as an intellectual entertainment, beginning perhaps with a reading in Dublin's Black Church, organized by Liam Miller in 1957, and reaching wide acceptance in the Dublin Arts Festival whose first readings in 1970 were held in the fashionable showrooms of the Brown Thomas department store.[143] The readership for poetry evolved sufficiently to offer marginal success, if not prosperity, to several publishers of poetry beyond Dolmen, such as Gallery Press, Goldsmith Press, New Writers Press, Blackstaff, and Raven Arts. The literary and social criticism that had issued from *The Bell* found re-expression in new journals, notably the well-balanced *Irish University Review* and the more probing *Crane Bag,* which is developing into one of the foremost quarterlies in the British Isles. *The Honest Ulsterman* and *Cyphers,* with the revived *Poetry Ireland,* have become the important periodicals for poetry in Ireland.

In the ideal history of Irish poetry in the last four decades, events such as the reemergence of the Troubles with the Protestant attacks on civil-rights marchers in Burntollet in 1969 and the Republic's entry into the EEC in 1972 probably should weigh lightly beside the poets' moments of new insight, mostly hidden from record, and the publication dates of these developed insights, recorded on the verso of the title pages of volumes such as Kavanagh's *Come Dance with Kitty Stobling* (1960), Clarke's *Flight to Africa* (1963) and *Mnemosyne Lay in Dust* (1966), Kinsella's *Notes from the Land of the Dead,* Montague's *Rough Field,* and Heaney's *Wintering Out* (all three in 1972).

Within this annotated chronology, we can mention only the outstanding titles and the recognition these poets received within the Irish community—Kinsella won the Devlin Award in 1967—within the American Irish communities—Montague won the Irish-American Cultural Institute Award in 1976—and within the American literary realm— Heaney won the esteemed and lucrative Bennett Award in 1982. In fact, the extraordinary international reputation of Seamus Heaney figures as an important element in any history of this period because it indicates a partial recognition by a wider English-reading public that Ireland could produce significant poets after Yeats. Often called Ireland's finest poet after Yeats, unquestionably Heaney is the most widely read and acclaimed Irish poet since the master's poetry first appeared in the curricula of American and English universities some fifteen years after his death. The first-month sale within the British Isles of six thousand copies of *North* (1975)[144] clarioned the arrival of Heaney as a popular poet and rendered likely the eventual recognition of Kinsella, Montague, Heaney, Mahon, Murphy, Longley, and Muldoon, as well as of younger poets, as the sort of remarkable gathering of talent usually described as a poetic renascence (or renaissance).

Any history of this era in Irish poetry must also recognize the publication of Kinsella's translation of the Irish epic, *The Táin* (1969) and of *An Duanaire* (1981), poems from the Irish between 1600–1900 chosen by Sean O'Tuama, of *The Faber Book of Irish Verse* (1974), edited by Montague, and of Heaney's translation of *Buile Suibne* (1984), as well as of Kinsella's *Oxford Book of Irish Verse* (forthcoming). As an indication of the poets' labors to recover traditional literature, these publications direct us to a major characteristic concern of recent Irish poets.

Realizing that a progressive Irish government will allow repositories of the past to be destroyed—bogs scraped to bare rock and Viking settlements to foundation stone for a new Corporation building—recent poets can assume both Yeats's antithetical posture and his antiquarian motives in reaching back for some accommodation with the Irish past. Because recent historians are dredging up this past in disparate pieces and because the poets differ from each other in their geographical, religious, or social backgrounds, the traditions they offer their audiences can only represent discrete strands of a hypothetically unified tradition, perhaps buried irrecoverably in prehistory and the Irish unconscious.

Although the poets may individualize their traditions, they all show an interest in most of the following traditional fields: a historical era or historiographical theory developed by recent historical work; Gaelic language and literature; traditional music; religion; geography; and the ancient provincial divisions, especially as manifested politically in the British partition of Ireland. Elaboration of some of these concerns appears in the last section of this chapter.

With more historical accuracy than Yeats had, all of his successors but Mahon and MacNeice reflect in their poetry a preoccupation with past eras. However, the recent publications of a number of very competent historians, probing in their research and revisionary in their conclusions, give credence to F. S. L. Lyons's claim that Ireland is enjoying "an Irish historiographical revolution."[145] Works such as the Royal Irish Academy history of Ireland proposed by T. W. Moody and numerous individual studies move beyond a preoccupation with biography and politics to a new concern for social and economic history.[146] Estyn Evans and Henry Glassie have observed the influence of geography and folk customs on the formation of an Irish personality.[147] In some cases, contemporary historians have so narrowed the chasm between documented and undocumented history that the poetic imagination can leap to a sympathetic understanding of obscure eras. Clarke's poems and fiction about the early monastic church, Murphy and Montague's long poems exploring the colonial past, and individual poems by Kinsella and Heaney attempt to speak for previously silent social types and epochs.

Through understanding and translating Gaelic poetry, the poets also attempt to let these areas speak for themselves. As the population of native Gaelic speakers declines below one percent toward extinction,[148] the life of the Gaelic language depends on that four percent of the population, living mostly in Dublin and Cork, who have learned to speak Gaelic "very well," and the additional eighteen percent who speak it "fairly well," as a second language, according to one recent survey.[149] After an unsuccessful forty-year campaign by a zealous government to enforce the recovery of Irish, the responsibility for the intensive care of the language has shifted back to the scholars and the writers. With this shift, so too has revived some of the amateur's enthusiasm for Gaelic that was evident in the early Gaelic League but desiccated by bureaucratic enforcement. For the writer, Gaelic opens a privileged view of the past which he could share with his reader. This enthusiasm for Irish is demonstrated in a recent festschrift — *The Pleasures of Gaelic Poetry* — in which all the essayists, "with one or two exceptions . . . learned Irish as a second language."[150] Among these essayists, perhaps, Thomas Kinsella best expresses the new spirit of the Gaelic recovery:

> It is a relief to sense the effective and enlarging sympathy between some whose natural language *is* Irish, and whose business is Gaelic literature, and some who are merely very interested, like myself. It is not so long since a total commitment was asked as the price of fellowship, a commitment that involved abjuring the English element in the Irish inheritance . . . as falsifying as the related narrowness that sees nothing beyond Anglo-Irish. . . . There is a sense that it is up to us to overcome the old dividing idiocies and employ our energies directly, as best we can, on the actual material of the vital inheritance that unites and divides us.[151]

Many of the poets writing in English are reliable readers of modern Irish poets such as Mairtin Ó Direain, Sean Ó Ríordáin (d. 1977), Maire Mhac an tSaoi, and younger poets associated with the journal *Innti*. I am incapable of saying what influences these poetries may have exchanged, but occasionally translations from modern Irish by poets in English seem to blend successfully the translator's unique voice with the poet's. Consider Paul Muldoon's "The Mirror," an adaptation of Michael Davitt's poem in Irish, from which I quote the final encounter with the dead father:

There was nothing for it
but to set about finishing the job,
papering over the cracks,
painting the high window,
stripping the door, like the door of a crypt.
When I took hold of the mirror
I had a fright. I imagined him breathing through it.
I heard him say in a reassuring whisper:
*I'll give you a hand, here.*

And we lifted the mirror back in position
above the fireplace,
my father holding it steady
while I drove home
the two nails.[152]

We can also imagine a hand from a past tradition steadying Muldoon in this remarkably fresh revision of his recurrent theme of mirroring realities.

An enthusiasm for traditional Irish music seems as pervasive among the poets as their interest in Gaelic, if not as influential on their writing. The recovery of the songs and lyrics of a sophisticated tradition began early in the century with the collections of Captain Francis O'Neill of the Chicago Police Department and other folklorists. Ireland's reawakened music reached the public's attention through the work of the Irish composer Sean O'Riada in the sixties. O'Riada formed Ceoltóirí Cualann, a band of traditional musicians, and reset music for ensemble that conventionally had been played solo or in duet. As O'Riada himself withdrew into the Gaeltacht to integrate music, language, and song within one community, his band, transformed into the Chieftains, and several other groups such as the Bothy Band and Clannad, reached the broader community usually reserved for popular music.

One is tempted to seek parallels between the poetic counterpoint of rhythm and dramatic voice and the drone and melodic line of traditional music, but such parallels remain analogies in the ear of the auditor. More verifiably, traditional music offers the Irish poet an encouraging example of a wide audience responding enthusiastically to a traditional art. Furthermore, in an age of egocentric poetry, the self-abasing attitude of the Irish musician toward his music could serve as a chastening reminder of the relation of tradition and the individual talent. As a tragic example of self-abasement before the tradition carried to the point of self-neglect, Sean O'Riada, who died in 1971, became the subject of extended poetic sequences by Kinsella and Montague and an elegy by Heaney.[153]

Orthodox religion is not a preoccupation of recent Irish poets. It is less to the point that few Irish poets are among the 87 percent of the Republic who regularly attend church services[154] than that orthodox views are anathema to any poetry unless reformed into the poet's unique expression. In observing their culture independently, poets have often arrived at a poetic representation of the following point made by E. Estyn Evans:

> I became convinced that a significant factor in what is sometimes called the essential unity of Ireland has been the retention, persisting in many areas into modern times, of certain attitudes toward the world and the otherworld, of traditional customs, beliefs and seasonal festivals which had often assumed the guise of Christian poetry, but which had their origins in the Elder Faiths of pre-Christian times.[155]

In Yeats's Ribh poems and in Clarke's novels and early poetry, these poets recognized the persistence in early Christian culture of pre-Christian practices and beliefs. In *North,* Heaney assigned to Nerthus, a Celtic earth-goddess, a cult of blood sacrifice. Montague and Devlin recognize some feminine principle working in Irish history, and in *One* Kinsella insinuates masculine and feminine principles of unity and multiplicity. By eschewing religious orthodoxy, these poets delve into a more radical tradition.

Although poets must recognize the distinctiveness of various groups within Irish society, they cannot adopt the sociological overview that would assign these differences merely to geographical diversity. Usually, the poet only represents his own individuality against a nurturing or alienating society. However, the geographical historian Estyn Evans attributes cultural diversity not only to the boglands and drumlins that have separated groups within Ireland for millenia but also to Ireland's insularity and to the accessible harbors that have attracted other cultures to intrude.[156] Traditionally, writers have recognized a division between the western half of Ireland and the eastern region of the Pale.

Conversely, a series of drumlins surrounded by patches of bog, north of the ancient earthworks called the Black Pig's Dyke, restricted travel between Ulster and the rest of Ireland and created the distinctiveness of the north of Ireland, recorded in the *Táin* and in much of Ireland's literature.

Ulster's separation by geological barriers is complicated by its proximity to Scotland. The first Irishmen were probably Mesolithic adventurers who crossed from Scotland.[157] In turn, the Ulster subkingdom Dal Riata established an important colony in Scotland, and Columba developed a Christian colony on Iona. Warriors from the Hebrides, the gallowglasses, fought for Irish kings of Ulster in the thirteenth century, and the Scots Bruces ruled parts of Ireland in the fourteenth century.[158] Neither Ulster's ancient interchange with Scotland, which was only somewhat more active than the traffic between Leinster and England and between Munster and France, nor the geographical partition of Ulster, which obstructs traffic only a little more than the midland bogs divide Connacht in the west from Leinster, constitute a valid basis for political partition unless one insists on subpartitioning the island to preserve various relatively monolithic cultures.

Recently, historians have argued that traditionally Ireland is culturally pluralistic and politically clannish or regional rather than nationalistic.[159] As a political arrangement, a confederation of provinces would seem more consistent with this definition of the traditional Irish community than either a republic or a partitioned island. Such issues have been forced on the poets' attention by the extended colonial rule and terrorists' reaction in Northern Ireland. Although poets have devoted major poems to the Northern crisis, most notably Montague's the *Rough Field*, Heaney's *North*, Kinsella's "A Butcher's Dozen," and Paul Muldoon's *Quoof*, usually they address the Troubles only indirectly in what Heaney calls "semaphores of hurt." Nevertheless, all would admit that the issue registers at some level as a compelling theme which challenges them to weigh the value of political poetry and to examine the distinction between private and tribal emotion.

If the partition of Ireland violates the traditional Irish community, then so does the political and journalistic partition of the Irish poetic community, which is based on the argument that the poetic revival is restricted to poets from the North of Ireland. Serious critics make no

claims for the superiority, or even existence, of a Northern Irish school.
Neither Terence Brown's critical survey, *Northern Voices: Poets from Ulster* (1975), nor Frank Ormsby's anthology, *Poets from the North of Ireland* (1979), argues that Ulster poetry constitutes a distinctive tradition.
Brown begins his study with this foreword: "The poets studied in this
volume . . . contribute not to a separate Ulster poetic tradition but to
an Anglo-Irish and/or British poetry. . . ."[160] Recently the editors of
*The Penguin Book of Contemporary British Poetry* named Heaney as the
most important British poet "of the last fifteen years, and the one we
very deliberately put first in our volume. . . . "[161] About Heaney and
the five other Ulster poets represented in this volume, the editors asserted: "So impressive is recent Northern Irish poetry. . . . that it is not
surprising to find discussion of English poetry so often having to take
place in its shadows."[162] On his own behalf, Heaney retorted in a recent
Field Day broadside that he was not British.[163] Nevertheless, American and British reviewers have argued for the superiority of a school
of Northern Irish poetry[164] which has a founding father, a date of origin, a central hero, and an impressive list of titles attributed to it.

In fact, in the early sixties, poets in Belfast were greatly encouraged
by Philip Hobsbaum, a British poet and critic and former member of
"The Group" in London, who was teaching at Queens University on
a temporary appointment. In 1963, he and his wife invited certain young
writers to gather at his house on Fitzwilliam Street and to bring copies
of poems and stories to be read and discussed critically. Hobsbaum maintained these Monday-night meetings until 1966 when he left Belfast
for Glasgow. Seamus Heaney picked up the leadership, but poetic energies were soon dissipated in the civil rights fervor of the late sixties
and the resumption of the Troubles. Among the group's members, chroni-
clers number Heaney, Michael Longley, James Simmons, Derek Mahon,
critics Michael Allen and Edna Longley, and, later, Paul Muldoon and
Frank Ormsby.[165]

Poems from the Group found their way first into Harry Chambers'
journal, *The Phoenix,* and, before the Group disbanded, into the newly
founded *Honest Ulsterman,* which Simmons began in 1968 and eventually passed on to Michael Foley, and which has been edited recently
by Frank Ormsby. Their work also appeared in pamphlets published

by the Queen's University Festival and the Arts Council and soon after in a steady series of books offered by the most esteemed London publishers or by Belfast's Blackstaff Press, which was founded by Jim and Diane Gracey in 1971.

Curiously enough, Belfast, a field salted with political hatred, has become a fertile ground for writers. Those who make no claim for the Group's aesthetics still value the friendships begun there in a spirit of helpful criticism. The friendship of Catholic poets—beneficiaries of the Education Act of 1947 which provided fairer access to the universities— and Protestant poets serves also as a political model for a new integrated society. If Hobsbaum and then Simmons have fostered this poetic community through the Group and the *Honest Ulsterman,* Michael Longley's avuncular patronage and encouragement from his position as assistant director of the Arts Council have extended this spirit. Even today, this cooperative spirit is generally evident in regular but unscheduled meetings in Belfast pubs of such writers as Longley, Muldoon, Ormsby, Ciarán Carson, and John Morrow, but it was symbolically manifest in a city-hall ceremony in the spring of 1983 when the senior Belfast poet, John Hewitt, who returned from a fifteen-year exile in Coventry in 1972, was given "the Freedom of the City." "I thought I already had it," was Hewitt's reassuring reply.[166]

Although this cooperative spirit in Belfast probably has encouraged young poets, the major poetic achievements from the North of Ireland, those attended to in this book, cannot easily be attributed to the influence of a poetic school. The major volume concerning the troubled North, Montague's *Rough Field,* was written by a poet who never visited the Group and who has lived more of his years on the south side of the border than on the north. As it has been later revealed, Derek Mahon, who has taken up residence in London, attended only one session of the Group, as a guest. Seamus Deane, a contemporary of Heaney's, an accomplished poet, and perhaps Ireland's most acute critic of poetry, seems not to have attended any meetings. Michael Longley asserts that he "didn't alter one semi-colon" as a result of Group discussion.[167]

On the other hand, Heaney has acknowledged the mutual help of the Belfast poets during their apprenticeship:

> When I was in Belfast, we almost did committee work on each other's
> poems; they were circulated in manuscript and sat upon, and before you
> had a book your poems had graduated and the canon was settled.[168]

It may be that without Hobsbaum's Monday evenings, *Death of a Naturalist* (1966) would not have appeared so early or so impressively as it did. Yet, who can believe that Heaney would have remained a mute, inglorious Milton without the Group's supporting criticism? In the same interview in which he acknowledged the Group's assistance, Heaney recalled his need to escape their sessions and establish his own independence.[169]

In fact, the threat to poetic independence is the one cause that might evoke a uniform response, and even a solidarity, among the Ulster poets. The closer these poets live to "the explosion's heart," in Muldoon's phrase, the less do they speak out their private political views. It is conceivable, although not probable, that they will be drawn into the political discussion generated by Field Day, an organization established in 1980 by the playwright Brian Friel and the actor Stephen Rea. Initially founded as a production company to manage an Irish tour of Friel's play *Translations,* it soon produced a series of touring plays, extensive playbill notes, and a series of six pamphlet-essays. Published in 1983 by Tom Paulin, Seamus Deane, and Heaney (the verse epistle to the Penguin editors) and in 1984 by Deane, Richard Kearney, and Declan Kiberd —these essays attempt to expose the myths with which inhumanity is rationalized in the North.[170] Although most of these pamphlets develop cogent intellectual arguments, they have not yet tinctured a line of poetry in Ireland, where even Heaney, who is a director of Field Day and who dedicated his most recent book to Brian Friel, juggles his ambivalences. It is unlikely that, even now, Deane would deny each poet's right to interpret his tradition independently, without constraint from the blinkering terms by which politicians and journalists characterize the Troubles. A decade ago, he could even articulate the poets' resistance to a propagandistic or politicized role:

> Commitment is too early a demand. It would merely lead to the kind
> of poetry politicians would quote when they needed it. As far as poetry
> is concerned, nothing in the world is intransitive; . . . But the poet must
> define the connexion in terms of his art in order to save it from the
> kinds of claim a public world as ominous as ours would make upon him.[171]

If this assumption draws common assent from poets such as Mahon, Muldoon, Longley, Carson, Simmons, Ormsby, McGuckian, and Heaney, who live or have recently lived in Northern Ireland, then it also enhances their diversity and casts them in the Irish poet's traditional antithetical role inherited from Yeats and Joyce.

Of course in a revolutionary society, such as Ulster, or even a society rapidly evolving such as Ireland, the poet must win his readers to his revision of society and his renewal of their shared traditions. In such a volatile society as Ireland has become, in which the tradition can nevertheless still draw reader and writer together, the poet's relation to his audience becomes a central concern which actually enters into poetry itself. In the final section of this chapter, I will argue that this poetic relationship of the speaker and auditor within the poem is an identifying characteristic of Irish poetry.

### 5. Tone in Recent Irish Poetry

Perhaps the most distinctive characteristic of Irish poetry resides in the dynamic relation between the poet and his tradition. This relation is stronger and more insistent than in American poetry and more unsettled than in British poetry. The poet's relation to a tradition, which is a shared body of essential cultural assumptions, is most immediately a relation to its adherents, in this case those who read or hear Irish poetry and who support and are nourished by it. In Ireland's relatively homogenous but rapidly changing culture, however, the poetic tradition is not easily separated from the larger cultural tradition which is in transition. Most simply stated, the Irish poet shares with his audience an extensive Irish history and two literatures: an ancient literature in Irish, much of which is lost to the air in which it was recited, and an Anglo-Irish graft, two-and-one-half centuries old, on literature in English. The bilingualism and mixed Gaelic and English heritage of most of these writers heightens their interest in other languages, cultures, and reading audiences. Consequently the Irish poet addresses not only an immediate audience, an insular orchestra, but also the more remote lower and upper tiers of British and American readers. He displays an ambivalence toward his tradition and his audiences in his speaker's attitude toward the poetic object and toward the audience addressed in the poem, or in what we call *tone*.

Of the living Irish poets, Kinsella most often has wondered aloud about audience and tradition and has experimented most frequently with poetic tone. Consequently, I will extract a single poem from Kinsella's artfully constructed sequence, which begins with "Phoenix Park" and continues through his latest publications to illustrate the dynamics of tone in Irish poetry. The lyric's subordination to the longer sequence and its relation to particular poems around it actually becomes a characteristic of tone. "Minstrel" appears toward the middle of the Pepper-canister chapbook *One* to extend the volume's theme of regeneration, reconquest, and the recreation of one out of many.[172] Placed between "38 Phoenix Street" and "My Father's Hands," the poem contributes to a progression of ideas about the child's growth: his individuation, his own creativity, and his relation to his multiple pasts and to the chance conditions out of which he was born and grows:

> He trailed a zither from
> melancholy pale fingers, sighing.
> A mist of tears lay still upon the land.
>
> The fire burned down in the grate.
> A light burned on the bare ceiling.
> A dry teacup stained the oil cloth
> where I wrote, bent like a feeding thing
> over my own source.
>
> A spoonful of white ash fell
> with a soundless puff, undetected.
> A shadow, or the chill of night,
> advanced out of the corner.
> I stopped, my hand lifted
> an inch from the page.
>
> Outside, the heavens listened,
> a starless diaphragm
> stopped miles overhead
> to hear the remotest whisper
> of returning matter, missing
> an enormous black beat.
>
> The earth stretched out in answer.
> Little directionless instincts

uncoiled from the wet mud-cracks,
crept in wisps of purpose, and vanished
leaving momentary traces
of claw marks, breasts,
ribs, feathering prints,
eyes shutting and opening
all over the surface.
A distant point of light
Winked at the edge of nothing.

A knock on the window
and everything in fantasy fright
flurried and disappeared.
My father looked in from the dark,
my face black-mirrored beside his.

The reader's difficulties with this poem arise from the poet's paradoxical precepts: on the one hand, the poetic object is thoroughly external in that the poem renders even cerebral events public and objective, and, on the other hand, the object remains thoroughly internal in that even documented history becomes a poetic event only through the poet's imaginative conception. Reinforced with the Jungian belief that the world we explore within ourselves contains a version of the history and substance of the world without, Kinsella reduces the distinction between external and internal realities, which may account for the dwindling of his readership. As Christopher Clausen writes,

> The boundary between the inner and outer is often not very clear or important in poetry, which is one major reason that the typical modern mind finds poetry so unsettling. For the 'modern' view of the world derived from popularization of science is based on a rigid separation of the two, and sees the inner as being of dependent and secondary importance.[173]

To the "post-modern" reader, however, acquainted with cellular biology, particle physics, or depth psychology, Kinsella's poetry can have a special appeal.

As the title implies, "Minstrel" opens with the borrowed tradition of the court poet, three lines derived from some archaic European model but also from the deliberate archaisms of W. H. Auden. The stanza's final, and the poem's only, iambic pentameter line distributes the stress on the Victorian pun *still* and renders the verb more passive. The pathetic fallacy anticipates the act of creation later in the poem in which the projection of emotion on nature is strategic.

As the poem shifts into the second stanza, we may be reminded that *minstrel* is derived from a word for "a household servant" or worker.

> The fire burned down in the grate.
> A light burned on the bare ceiling.
> A dry teacup stained the oil cloth
> where I wrote, bent like a feeding thing
> over my own source.
>
> (*st. 2*)

The shift in mode, pronoun, and age and attitude of the reflective speaker alerts us to observe that the first stanza is a youthful creation, rather like Kinsella's first poems written in 1948–9. Characteristic of his dynamics of tone, the shift in tone and mode between stanzas one and two requires the reader to participate in, as he comprehends, the poet's strategy and to identify the speakers *dramatically* as he would in a Joyce short story, such as "An Encounter" and "Araby."

In the second stanza of "Minstrel," the correspondences between the grate and the ceiling, between the object's stain and the poet's signs, and between the poet's frame and the writing surface, establish two contraposed surfaces as a controlling image. The predatory poet feeding on his own memory and imagination recalls the earlier "Baggot Street Deserta" and the opening poems of *Notes from the Land of the Dead*.

Kinsella's poetic persona and the autobiographical subject are distinguished: the memory of the younger poet cradling his emerging poem is contained by the overarching presence of the mature poet:

> A spoonful of white ash fell
> with a soundless puff, undetected.
> A shadow, or the chill of night,
> advanced out of the corner.
> I stopped, my hand lifted
> an inch from the page.
>
> (*st. 3*)

Although the mature poet and his audience hear, detect, and measure what the ephebe only sensed, the form in which night advances remains unspecified so that engulfed, in a sense, in the same darkness as these two poets, we depend for guidance on the speaker's voice and the images offered us, which are mostly nonvisual. When full stops or caesuras direct us, we halt or pause to keep pace with the narrating poet in the dark.

As in Joyce's "Ithaca" episode of *Ulysses,* the third stanza expands our scope toward the heaventree:

> Outside, the heavens listened,
> a starless diaphragm
> stopped miles overhead
> to hear the remotest whisper
> of returning matter, missing
> an enormous black beat.
>
> (*st. 4*)

The rhymes with feminine endings *listened* and *whisper* cradling the quatrain suggest the echoing surfaces of the animate universe, but it is the third rhyming word *missing* that indicates how we have shifted from study to starless diaphragm. Only the reflective poet, and his audience, hears what the attentive heavens missed: the systole of poetic creation. The reader of Kinsella's sequence, which begins with "Phoenix Park," will also recognize in the stanza's final line the flight of an owl or other predatory bird initiating on behalf of the muse Hecate or Persephone the predatory act of creation. (The line's three stresses can enforce the pumping of an owl's wings or of the human heart.) As these myths project internal psychological processes, so the reflective poet projects organic processes such as the rhythm of the heart in motile or organic images, reminding us that the remotest cosmic whispers that we can detect must be contained within the ultimate diaphragm of the human imagination. In this Coleridgean sense, the missing beat becomes also a murmur of the universal heart contained within the creating imagination.

By extending the images of the predatory hunt and of the corresponding surfaces, the fifth stanza suggests the completion of the quaint poem begun in stanza one or, more likely, the first awakening and nourishing of the full poetic imagination:

> The earth stretched out in answer.
> Little directionless instincts
> uncoiled from the wet mud-cracks,
> crept in wisps of purpose, and vanished
> leaving momentary traces
> of claw marks, breasts,
> ribs, feathering prints,
> eyes shutting and opening
> all over the surface.
> A distant point of light
> Winked at the edge of nothing.
>
> (*st. 5*)

Again, the enclosing horizontal surfaces echo, mirror, or correspond with each other. The heavens-awaited "whisper" emerges as "wisps of purpose." Earth answers the wings' beat by offering inchoate instincts and memories to what, in the context of the "feeding poet," we recognize as the predatory imagination. In the murkiness of this stanza, we find our way by sibilant sounds and tactile images.

In witnessing the dark creative beginnings in the poet's life, we also glimpse the creative beginnings of Ireland, mythologized in the twelfth-century compilation called *Lebor Gabála Érenn: The Book of the Taking of Ireland* (*The Book of Invasions*).[174] In "Minstrel" the allusion is made in the fifth stanza by a return to phrases and images employed in three poems that precede "Minstrel" in this volume *One* and which employ voices of two mythic poets, Amergin and Tuan. *The Book of Invasions*, which records six successive conquests of the island, emblemizes, for Kinsella, the need to evolve by conquest, loss, recovery, and repossession. So stated, the myth of successive invasions becomes for sea-bound Ireland what the myth of endless frontiers was for nineteenth-century America. Within Kinsella's poetry, the repossession of homeland becomes a paradigm for the progression of art, the renewal of love, the growth of family, and, as the embryonic imagery of "Minstrel" implies, the evolution of the species.

The creative moment of stanza five sparks only some light, "a distant point," but enough to extend the imagination to "the edge of nothing" from which the youthful poet is recalled by a summons at the window:

> A knock on the window
> and everything in fantasy fright
> flurried and disappeared.
> My father looked in from the dark,
> my face black-mirrored beside his.
>
> (*st. 6*)

The creative act ends in a doubling, similar to the boy's self-definition in the preceding poem, "38 Phoenix Street," when he is twinned by a neighbor's child held up above the garden wall to meet his own startled face in mirror-reflection of himself. The scene also recalls a hallucinatory moment in Joyce's "Circe," when Stephen, standing beside the kinder and worldly-wiser Bloom, sees their complementary images compose Shakespeare's face in the mirror's reflection. In "Minstrel," the poet finds his own face reflected beside his father's actual face. In the mirror of the poem, however, the father's face, emerging unexpectedly from the dark, seems spectral, representing the succession the poet has now assumed by completing his creative act.

"Minstrel" suggests the kinds of difficulties the reader must encounter and resolve to understand Kinsella's poetry, as well as much recent Irish poetry. Through interrelated poems and ipso-relative allusions, Kinsella's poetry encompasses personal and family history, artistic and biological processes, and portions of Irish myth. In his distinctive way, Kinsella's dramatized poets become conduits for tradition. To comprehend the various levels of Kinsella's poetry, we often must parry, or yield to, the speaker's dramatic affronts or blandishments, follow his voice into the dark, learn to interpret the levels of the dramatic voice, apprehend meaning from the dramatic experience of the poems rather than from what the poem "says," and experience poems as units in an expanding sequence.

Kinsella replaces the transmissive speaker with a dramatic relationship because he recognizes that an understanding of the human situation depends on phenomenological experiences, Protean language, and shared premises, all of which are uncertain bases for truth. As he remarked in an interview in 1975,

> Poetry is a two-way process: the reader completes an act of communication initiated by the poet. For that action to be completed—for such

a thing to be shared — certain common foundations must be shared. There have been times, fortunate times, when many things were shared, so that complex utterances were possible without questioning one's means, as in Dante's time. This is not one of those times. What we share is a general sense of unease and distress, betrayal and disappointment. There are very few bases on which we can share an understanding of great, enormous nouns like love, faith, and so on. Acts of communication involving objects of that kind have now to be managed very carefully. . . . I don't feel I can rely in my poetry on anyone else's understanding what I'm saying in large, unquestioned terms; I have to particularize, to prop my statements up, specialize them, and give the context with the object.[175]

In representing the poem as a "two-way process," Kinsella implicitly recognizes a triangular relationship among the poet, the reading audience, and the poetic object, representative of the "many things . . . shared," which I have called *tradition*. The readers, who have an independent relation to the tradition, renew that relationship through the poet. Within this cultural relationship exists the more concentrated triangular relationship of the poem — as the actual reader encounters it — comprised of the speaker, the poetic object, and the implied or implicit reader. At various points in literary history, this triangular poetic relationship has been distorted or ignored. For instance, in interpreting symbolist poetry as it arose in France and England and was developed by modernist poets, critics concentrated on the poetic object, ignoring the relationships by which we perceive that object. Poets themselves shifted the focus, as symbolist poets abandoned naturalistic premises, by which the setting correlated with the speaker's attitudes, to fixate within this setting certain objects which returned increased significance for their additional emphasis. The New Critics soon asserted that the poem was as autonomous as the poetic object was assumed to be, and they represented the poet's relations to his audience as merely strategies for attaining objectivity. As Charles Altieri has pointed out, "Modernism tended to ignore questions of audience because it treated poems as the construction of objectified perception available to all who would put in the necessary interpretive labor."[176]

According to Altieri's characterization the modernist reader might have represented with a straight line, rather than a triangle, his relation to the poetic object or event on which the poetic speaker served merely as an objective commentator. Likewise, today's reader might also misrepresent the poetic relationship linearly, but with the poetic speaker standing directly between the reader and the poetic object. Of course, unless the poet gibbers, the public nature of language always gives the reader access to the poetic object—more or less access, depending on the degree to which the reader shares the language and premises of the poet, as Kinsella has pointed out. Whereas Kinsella regrets the lack of "common foundations," he might also have pointed out that the current degradation of language, and therefore of perception, has created an orthodoxy of obtuseness and of misusage which the poet must counteract to be understood. For example, in a celebrated poem Elizabeth Bishop draws the reader from his tame Bullwinklish misconception toward the "dim smell" that is represented by the word *moose,* as Murphy, Montague, and Heaney must redepict, seal, swan, or badger, as "not at all what he's painted," in Heaney's phrase. On almost any subject, the Irish poet must assume an antithetical position, as he tries to dislodge the reader from petrified attitudes and fixed responses to their shared language.

Therefore, the contemporary Irish poet attempts, as Kinsella says, to "give the context with the object" in order to create a poetic experience rather than to evoke shared values or appeal to a specious common experience. Consequently, he will often emphasize that the poetic object demands on the apprehension of a poetic speaker, the conveyance of his language, and the receptiveness of some auditor or reader. Conceiving of the poem as the dramatization of a set of interdependent relationships rather than as a well-wrought container of symbolic meaning, the poet must address readers who, as a consequence, often misunderstand him. For example, one critic, applying Modernist criteria to recent Kinsella poetry, regrets the absence of a comfortable decorum toward the reader, who is "placed . . . where surfaces are illusory" and where he is treated "as an element in the poem's strategy."[177] Such a static view of the poem may arise from Formalist assumptions about a fixed relationship between the reader and the poetic speaker, who becomes a transparent medium through which we view the object.[178]

To fill our role as humans reading, however, we will characteristically seek meaning in words which we attribute to a speaker. From our first encounter with words we associate them not merely with a speaker but with a speaker in a particular context (not merely, "This is Daddy speaking," but "Daddy's just in a bad mood!"). As Stanley Plumly argues,

> The poet's voice, his way of presiding over his material, whether the intention is to inspire or illuminate, whether the terms are those of a persona or one of a trinity of personal pronouns, is inevitable. The question is never one of the fact of a voice but of the effective control or disclosure of that voice.[179]

"Effective control or disclosure of . . . voice" becomes one of the strategies by which the poet draws the reader into the triangular poetic relationship and communicates, as he influences a reader's response to, a poetic experience. The difference between the limited sense of tone —the poet's static attitude toward object and audience—and this expanded sense—the various strategies by which the poet dramatizes poetic relationships—becomes a question of the poet's deliberateness or emphasis. Consequently, within literary history this emphasis may be transitional, a temporary means of reeducating the reader, reducing his aloofness, and educing from him certain responses which become part of the "meaning" of this poetic experience. To dramatize the poetic relationships, the poet draws our attention to the speaker, who no longer merely transmits information. The poet may create several speakers, a quirky persona, or a mysterious anonym. Like the prototypical Ancient Mariner, the speaker may be intrusive, insistent, and even offensive, as he plucks our sleeve and solicits our complicity. He may address an auditor directly, enlist him with his pronouns, or otherwise "intend toward" the reader, so that implicitly there is another presence on the dramatic scene.

The poet of tone will adjust rhythm, line length, stanzaic formation, or his speaker's diction to accommodate the experience dramatized in each poem. If the poet does not vary these poetic aspects, he may achieve a recognizable poetic voice, which I will call *timbre,* but he will fail to develop *tone.* The poet can remind us that our access to any poetic object depends on this speaker-auditor relationship by reducing visual imagery, darkening the setting, and frequently introducing tactile, auditory, and nonvisual imagery. Finally, the meaning of the poem resides within the dramatic experience, which depends on the reader's response but only to the same degree that earlier poems depended on his objective interpretive skills. The poetic experience is created by the poet and remains largely under his direction.

Although *tone* is comprised of poetic strategies, which are given precedence over the continuity of a speaking voice from poem to poem (*timbre*), these strategies may help us, ultimately, to characterize the poet. When approaching living poets, *tone* assists us more than *temperament*, David Kalstone's term for "the voice and writing self" of the poet, because it describes the dynamic unfolding of attitude rather than the static final characterization.[180] As our key to understanding contemporary poets through their poetry, tone assumes the central position held by formal control in an earlier period. Until the advent of free verse, the poem introduced itself to us before our reading, creating in its length and form definite expectations and guiding us within lines to stress certain words. Meaning tended to unwind, fulfilling or playing off against generic expectations.[181] Now a more colloquial sort, the poem may withhold meaning or shift it drastically at its conclusion, as the speaker reveals or alters tone. Line length, which is a unit of concentration, may reveal stages of the speaker's attitude, which we must recognize continuously. As the context widens, our understanding of the poet's tone deepens, from line to poem to section to book to series of books. Just as we ultimately observe Joyce behind all the characters and voices in *Ulysses* and *Finnegans Wake,* so do the various dramatized attitudes and the dramatic strategies come to compose a recognizable tone, the poet's overarching disposition toward his reader and toward their shared traditions, which are created or renewed through the poetic experiences.

Identifying a poet by tone would reform our standard characterization of the poetic spirit we recover from a poet's corpus. The overstrained term *vision* has served through several decades and countless book-titles to characterize first the transcendental experience and scope of the Romanticists, then the immanentist experience and scope of post-Romanticist poetry, and finally any idiosyncratic attitude and angle of vision the post-modern poet adopted toward his or her domestic experience. In other words, much of the current sense of "vision" could be re-fenced within the domain of "tone." In thus extending *tone,* we will eventually augment our critical vocabulary. Among words associated with sound and touch, we have no word suggesting the transcendence of *visionary,* unless we resort to an erotic vocabulary. In describing the recovery of meaning in a poem, *apprehend, transform, assess,* and *prehension* might replace terms such as *perceive, review, focus,* and *insight.* Eventually we might even find *touch* and *tone* associated in the *Princeton Encyclopedia of Poetry and Poetics* where the entry on *tone* now begins: "Traditionally, 'tone' has denoted an intangible quality. . . ."[182]

Georges Poulet, through his approach of "intersubjectivity," would recover from the literary text, usually a novel, an organizing consciousness. I quote him because his procedure is analogous to the act of recognition by which we discover a poet's tone:

> It is not a question of going from the work to the psychology of the author, but of going back, within the sphere of the work, from the objective elements systematically arranged, to a certain power of organization, inherent in the work itself, as if the latter showed itself to be an intentional consciousness determining its arrangements and solving its problems.[183]

Whereas for Poulet this organizing consciousness finally absorbs the literary text, "tone" remains only an aspect of the poem and one characteristic of poetic intention. However, study of the strategies by which we are involved with a poetic speaker leads us toward the poet, if not quite to the poet. For a final qualification of the concept of *tone,* before applying it to individual poets, we might turn to a passage from Kinsella, with whom we began this section. The passage reminds us that this most personal aspect of a poem, like the poem itself, is interventional, a deliberate artifice that mediates between the human and the natural world, and remains therefore not merely human. Kinsella describes this process of reading:

> eyes bridging the gap, closing a circuit.
>
> Except that it is not a closed circuit,
> more a mingling of lives, worlds simmering
> in the entranced interval: all that you are
> and have come to be
> — or as much as can be brought to bear —
> 'putting on' the fixed outcome of another's
> encounter with what what he was
> and had come to be

impelled him to stop in flux, living,
and hold that encounter out from
the streaming away of lifeblood, timeblood,
a nexus a nexus
wriggling with life not of our kind.

(KPC, 92)

No single characteristic of tone is peculiar to Irish poetry, nor will the cumulative components of tone either apply evenly to each Irish poet or exclude all American or English poems. However, when recent verse is surveyed, tone emerges as a characteristic that distinguishes contemporary Irish poetry from that of England or America. First, with noticeable frequency the Irish poet directly addresses some auditor or audience — a *you,* a circumscribed or intimate *we,* an unnamed lover or friend, or a specified correspondent or dedicatee. These direct addresses will no longer take the form of the blanket imperatives or the "Come let us" Yeats employed, although the master-poet as often addressed as described the aristocracy of art from which he would build his unity of culture. The recent poets are more deliberate and varied in their address. The most specific audience emerges in the poetry of Derek Mahon who dedicates or addresses, to one individual or another, about a fourth of his poems. Seamus Heaney, who has dramatized his speaker and audience only in recent volumes, composes mortuary poems and postcards to the dead or addresses a tribal *we* in *Field Work* so that audience takes on a new presence. In Muldoon's bleak volume *Quoof* the *you* addressed often remains mysterious or even sinister, as in "Beaver" where Death may be the guest invited to "Let yourself in by the leaf-yellow door. / Go right up the stairs."[184] In "Cherish the Ladies," the *you* would divert the poet from a gentle elegy for his father to the theme of loveless breeding that poet and reader share in other poems. Montague's speaker, who frequently addresses an intimate audience of wife, lover, forebear, or child, becomes himself the audience addressed in several poems in *The Great Cloak* so that our affiliation with the autobiographical subject is redirected and our sympathy, thus, reinforced.

In recent Irish poetry we observe, even as we are involved in, the relation between the speaker, who may be an implied author, and a fictive audience, an explicit *you* or *we* or an implied reader. The relation between the implied reader and our practical selves is as mysterious as, and analogous to, the relation of the poetic voice to the practical poet, but as readers we become complicit in the poetic fiction. For example, to the extent that we accede to the eloquent voice in Derek Mahon's volume *Snow Party,* who says,

> Extraordinary people
> We were in our time,
> How we lived in our time
>
> As if blindfold
> Or not wholly serious,
> Inventing names for things
>
> To propitiate silence.
>
> (*MP,* 61)[185]

we audition to that extent for Mahon's roles of ironic survivor, sophisticated revenant, or futile onomast. In Mahon's poem "Leaves" the language of Beckett's Vladimir addresses us as if we were his fellow attendant Estragon:

> Somewhere there is an afterlife
> Of dead leaves,
> A stadium filled with an infinite
> Rustling and sighing.
>
> Somewhere in the heaven
> Of lost futures
> The lives we might have led
> Have found their own fulfilment.
>
> (*MP,* 59)

To resolve the problematics of tone, we may first have to revise Coleridge's description of the reader's "willing suspension of disbelief" to admit instances when poetic invitations draw in the reader and make him complicit with the poet's fiction. We may also have to readjust the phrase "aesthetic distance" to whatever lack of distance may exist between the reader and the experiential process in which he is also involved, or to the understanding of that engagement upon rereadings.

Central to any full study of the Irish poet's involvement of the reader in the poetic experience would be Kinsella's carefully structured series of poems, especially his volume *Technical Supplement* which opens with nine pathological poems. In verse supplemented by the anatomies and terrifying illustrations in Diderot's *Encyclopedie,* the direct address and imperatives are most insistent, and yet these are Kinsella's most affronting poems, those in which we are the least willing to be complicit.

The volume opens by introducing the obtuse anatomist Blessed William Skullbullet who then instructs the poet:

> You will note firstly that there is no containing skin
> as we understand it, but 'contained' muscles
> — separate entities, interwound and overlaid,
> firm, as if made of fish meat or some
> stretched blend of fibre and fat.
>
> *(KPC, 77)*

Just as obliquely, the poet speaks on behalf of a self-dramatizing child in the act of dismembering her dolls: "Is it all right to do this?" A speaker, presumably Skullbullet, begins another poem: "How to put it . . . without offence / —even though it is an offence, / monstrous, in itself. // A living thing swallowing another. // *Lizards:*" (*KPC,* 83). The cold anatomist is genteel enough to turn our head, and with that movement we become witnesses.

The *you* the speaker addresses in the poems is also the poet. From his first book of poetry, *Poems* (1956), Kinsella has insinuated a parallel between a psychological analysis of self and any poet's publicizing of his private life. In the sixteenth poem of *Technical Supplement* Kinsella writes, "It is a question of / getting separated from one's habits / and stumbling onto another way. The beginning / must be inward. Turn inward. Divide." (*KPC,* 89). This growth by division, basic to the amoebic procreation represented elsewhere in Kinsella's poetry, is presented here as a disconcerting fun-house schizophrenia: "Where is everybody? / Look / in the mirror, at that face. / It began to separate, the head opening / Like a rubbery fan. . . ." The division is sacrificial and painful: "That day when I woke / a great private blade / was planted in me from bowels to brain. . . . From that day forth I knew / what it was to taste reality / and not to; to suffer tedium or pain / and not to; . . ." (*KPC,* 94–96). The poet's awareness of his own psychic division is prerequisite to his self-integration, the healing process Jung called the quest for individuation. This quest parallels and contributes to Kinsella's probings of the most basic impulses to live. Insofar as the reader resists the encyclopedic evidence that this life-force in man is worm-blind and ephemeral, then he may enforce experientially the book's theme that this force is precious as it is vulnerable. In this regard, Kinsella's reader bears out Wolfgang Iser's contention that meaning in modern literature "is no longer an object to be defined, but is an effect to be experienced."[186]

Frequently in recent Irish poetry our objectivity and our independence of the speaker's guidance yield as the setting darkens and vision becomes impaired. Whereas we have experienced a suppression of visual imagery in other recent poetry, that of Theodore Roethke and Ted Hughes for example, the dethroning of vision began with the Romantics. As John Hollander has observed, because the Romantics associated vision with reason, they often represented eyesight "giving way to the ear at a particular kind of heightened moment,"[187] on Mount Snowden or beneath the nightingale, for examples. Phenomenologists have emphasized that vision distances and that focus diminishes the object. Extending the Romanticists' assumption about the limitation of vision, most recent Irish poets promote touch in the hierarchy of senses. In the work of Richard Murphy, Montague, Heaney, and Kinsella, we feel angle, curve, and texture. In Seamus Heaney's poetry particularly, images of sound and touch make natural objects impinge on the boundaries of the self. For example, when the housewife in "The Shore Woman" lay "in an open rocking boat / Feeling each dunt and slither through the timber" (*HP,* 145),[188] onomatopoeic nouns convey to us the threatening bump and brush of huge porpoises that molest her through the garment of the boat.

The unreasonable contiguity to nature produced by touch and the rational distancing of vision become overt themes in several recent Irish poems. Seamus Heaney, revising the *fili*'s prescription to "compose in darkness," to "trust the feel of what nubbed treasure / your hands have known" ("North"), creates in the poem "The Bog Queen" subtle associations between darkness, touch, and the unconscious mind. Although the "point of view" is that of Ireland's own bog-corpse, a Viking exhumed in County Mayo, we do not see through her eyes so much as

feel through her pores—"My body was braille"—while rationally secured distinctions between self and soil deliquesce. Helen Vendler, in
the *New Yorker*, has pronounced Heaney's poems on the Ulster dead
"wholly devoid, for moral purposes, of resurrective power."[189] Although
she offers this comment over her shoulder, she could have been referring
to "The Bog Queen," which represents a mock-resurrection. Our experience of the physical dissolution of the bog-queen as she is brought
to light is enforced by the soft network of vowels, aspirates, sibilants,
and apocopated rhymes which melt into a swill of *s*s and *h*s in the middle of the poem:

> My sash was a black glacier
> wrinkling, dyed weaves
> and phoenician stitchwork
> retted on my breasts'
>
> soft moraines.
> I knew winter cold
> like the nuzzle of fjords
> at my thighs—
>
> the soaked fledge, the heavy
> swaddle of hides.
> My skull hibernated
> in the wet nest of my hair.

Ironically, only in her "resurrection," when the speaker has been dismembered and shoveled from her grave, are we permitted a purely visual image:

> and I rose from the dark,
> hacked bone, skull-ware,
> frayed stitches, tufts,
> small gleams on the bank.
>
> (*HP*, 188–89)

As Heaney's remarkable diction enmeshes us aurally and palpably in the
experience of recovery, the poem declares our necessary failure to bring
to light and to envision the actual poetic object, that mysterious otherness interred in the human unconscious.

Like Heaney, Derek Mahon employs nonvisual imagery to involve
the reader in unconscious processes that approach the border between
animate and inanimate life, as in "A Disused Shed in Co. Wexford."
Rather than yield point of view to the inanimate subject, which in this
poem is a colony of mushrooms, the speaker approaches them anthropo-
pathetically, remaining on the human side of the border:

> They have been waiting for us in a foetor
> Of vegetable sweat since civil war days,
> Since the gravel-crunching, interminable departure
> Of the expropriated mycologist.
> He never came back, and light since then
> Is a keyhold rusting gently after rain.
> Spiders have spun, flies dusted to mildew
> And once a day, perhaps, they have heard something—
> A trickle of masonry, a shout from the blue
> Or a lorry changing gear at the end of the lane.
>
> (*MP,* 79–80)

Almost in spite of the narrator, the experience of mushroom-endurance
sifts to us through the ironic *expropriated,* the inhuman's synonym for
*arrested* or *detained,* and through the delicate tactile and auditory images
of these last four lines and others throughout the poem. The point is
that, like Heaney, Mahon manipulates the point of view and reduces
visual images to involve us in an experience of unconscious or inanimate
life that may be otherwise inexpressible.

Although the tone may guide the reader into the experience of the
poem, it may also be used to withhold the poet's attitude, deflect it
to a dramatic speaker, or refract it among several speakers. In *The Great
Cloak,* for example, Montague assigns to various speakers the awkward
and clichéd statements inherent in love poetry. For the book's subject
of failed love and remarriage, painfully private and increasingly universal, no new language exists. Rather than attempting to be more coy
or radiant than countless other love poets, Montague confronts the problem directly by declaring the cliché and then by attempting in his short,
clean lines to renew this worn language of love. The initial cliché he
often places in the mouth of another speaker: the wife, the lover, or
one of several French or Gaelic poets whose translations are included

in the text. For example, the volume opens with a passage in French
from Stendhal of twenty-eight words which is followed by the poet's
version of the same idea, rendered in eleven words. Later, a translation
of André Frénaud's general statement about love-making is followed by
the poet's version of the same poem set in a contemporary urban setting. Frénaud's conclusion—

> Blithe, surprised,
> we refind our bodies.
> So far, there is only someone else.
>                               ("The Hunt")

—is improved in the mirror-image of Montague's poem, which ends:

> Before, disentangling,
> through rain's soft swish,
> the muted horns of taxis,
> whirl of police or fire engine,
> habitual sounds of loneliness
> resume the mind again.
>           ("Do Not Disturb," *MGC,* 10–11)[190]

Within this dramatic context, Montague is not afraid to introduce references to butterflies or the moon in this language of love, turning and
dusting the images until they reflect light. He even appropriates from
Bord Failte a tower, rather like Yeats's, but it is introduced through
the speech of the abandoned wife: "But I have lost both faith and hope,
and live on sufferance, an old tower crumbling by the water's edge"
("She Daydreams By the Blue Pool," *MGC,* 29). Later, Montague justi-
fies these lines by converting the tower to a lighthouse set across channel from the poet:

> Upstairs my wife & daughter sleep.
> Our two lives have separated now
> But I would send my voice to yours
> Cutting through the shrouding mist
> Like some friendly signal in distress.
>                      ("The Point," *MGC,* 61)

In discussing *The Great Cloak,* we may more appropriately speak simply of shifting speakers rather than of shifting tones, because the tones

seem necessary extensions of the dramatic situations of the speakers. In "She Daydreams . . . ," for example, the rejected wife bemoans her pain and isolation. Her tone is sincere, and we may prefer to accept her as a credible character in a long dramatic sequence rather than as an aspect of tone. However, when we consider the poem in the entire sequence, irony enters and the poet's strategy toward the reader becomes apparent. The "implied author" has her introduce in prose the image of the tower that he will render poetic in "The Point." To speak of a secondary ironic tone in "She Daydreams . . . " becomes appropriate after all. The form of the poems—prose poem and lyric in five-tetrameter-line stanzas—directs us to the tone which in turn directs us to the sequence's ultimate meaning: that while the book contains various voices and three stories, it also is bound to contain only one voice and one story. The wife's plea in the beautiful poem "Herbert Street Revisited"—"don't betray our truth"—contains a double irony. The entire book is an attempt to betray that truth, yet the betrayal is incomplete: language and negative capability can recover only so much of the wife's and lover's stories.

In his first three volumes, Heaney unfalteringly maintained a rich lyric and nondramatic poetry. In two poems of *Wintering Out,* however, he yields his point of view to a fisherman's wife ("Shore Woman") and a Bye-child ("Good-Night"), but he maintains a recognizable timbre—an identifying quality of voice constituted in Heaney's case by a consistent diction, nearly unvarying line lengths (and even stanza forms), and a comforting, clearly positioned speaker. At times in *Wintering Out, North,* often in *Field Work,* and throughout "Station Island," however, he assumes the point of view of his subjects, brings a past self into relation to a present self, or dramatizes the discrete traditions out of which he composes, so that the reader now must experience and interpret that which the earlier poetry would have asserted. Consequently, "tone" offers a helpful approach to Heaney, as well as to other Irish poets, because it reminds us that the poet deliberately employs his speaker to withhold or disclose meaning and attitude, to lead the reader into the poem's experience, and to mediate that experience only to the degree that consciousness, memory, and language necessarily intrude into, as they shape, poetic recreations.

Although tone is cast by the writer, the term signifies a relationship, and therefore raises questions about the poet and his community or, in Stanley Fish's terms, about "intention and understanding":

> . . . each of which necessarily stipulates (includes, defines, specifies) the other. To construct the profile of the informed or at-home reader is at the same time to characterize the author's intention and vice versa, because to do either is to specify the contemporary conditions of utterance, to identify, by becoming a member of, a community made up of those who share interpretive strategies.[191]

We can postpone the broad questions concerning the contemporary Irish poet and his community until the final chapter of this book. The particular unstable, transitional relation within this community renders the Irish poet self-conscious about "interpretive strategies" and deliberate in approaching his audience through the poem. Eschewing orthodox interpretations of the Irish tradition yet embued with a sense of community, the poet must win his audience to a common ground. This understanding of a poet's work in relation to its tradition, by Irish readers and others who care to delve, becomes another, experiential version of the Irish tradition.

To illustrate variations on the Irish tradition that are refracted through poetry, each of the following four chapters pairs a poet in the generation after Yeats with a contemporary poet to suggest four recreations of the Irish poetic tradition.

## CHAPTER TWO

# Clarke & Kinsella

The Dublin childhoods of Austin Clarke and Thomas Kinsella were set in similar overteeming conditions although they were separated by miles, decades, and social class (Clarke's father was highly placed in the Dublin Corporation whereas Kinsella's father was a worker in the cooperage and a shop steward in the Guinness Corporation). Neither Clarke's middle-class home nor the unusual intraurban village which cloistered Kinsella could immure them from the inhumane overcrowded conditions of Dublin. Having lost eight of twelve children, Clarke's family contributed to Dublin's grim distinction of having one of the highest child-mortality rates in Europe. Conditions had not improved between Clarke's birth in 1896 and Kinsella's in 1928, when, among other unspeakable statistics, 24,849 persons were recorded living within 2,761 families of nine persons each in warrens of only two rooms.[1] Raised as Catholics in this urban setting, Clarke and Kinsella share sensibilities closer to Joyce's than to Yeats's. They developed a wounded sense of the disparity between the real and the ideal world and a keen, almost pathological awareness of offending aspects of the sensible world. As a student in Joyce's old school Belvedere College, Clarke found that *A Portrait of the Artist* "had long since become confused with my own memories or had completed them. . . ."[2] Although, as Clarke recognized,[3] O'Sullivan and Stephens had already established the city as an Irish poetic setting, Clarke and Kinsella were the first to depict, in the manner of Joyce, both details of the cityscape and particular urban characters: Dick King, Little Agnes, Martha Blake, or Miss Marnell, rather than "the people and beasts who have never a friend," about whom Stephens wrote. As children Clarke and Kinsella took their keen eyesight to the countryside as avid cyclists, but their poetry usually renders a mobile sweep rather than the countryman's stationary view of hedgerows, fields, and bogs we get in Kavanagh's and Heaney's poetry. As city dwellers their heritage seemed even more tenuous than it did to their rural contemporaries immersed in the Gaelic world. Separated from the last great Irish Catholic poets by their urban and modern settings and by their loss of the mother tongue, they developed a special attachment for Irish and for poets such as Carolan, O Bruadair, and O Rathaille. Consequently, Clarke and Kinsella often adopt the role of intermediate copyist or redactor for the lost dark ages of Irish poetry. Dispossessed of much of their Irish inheritance, they make an uneasy accommodation to the modern age. Frequently satiric in their view of Church and State, they withhold elegance and often clarity from their readers. Clarke especially congeals his language to guard rather than reveal aspects of his personal life, whereas, like Joyce, Kinsella disperses the burden of revelation among various, often unidentified, speakers. In the discussion that follows, we need not twang the tonal chord to remind the reader that the crucial questions of Clarke's and Kinsella's deliberate use of their poetic speakers can now be seen as questions of *tone*.

Because many of Clarke's obscure poetic passages gather in autobiographical poems, we feel a need to know more about his life. We know that as a boy he was less a scholar than an enthusiast—for violin, scientific experiments, and Gaelic language and myth, at various stages. Because of a vivid imagination, the young Clarke especially suffered fear of the other-world and from sexual guilt inculcated by the Victorian and Jansenist Church and its chilly monitor, Clarke's mother. Having absorbed this admonishment, he later suffered a mental breakdown, an inoperative betrothal, and a lifelong preoccupation with sexuality, with which he came to terms in his poetry. After achieving first-class honors in English at University College Dublin, he was appointed assistant lecturer to replace a mentor, Thomas MacDonagh, who had been executed for his role in leading the Easter Rising. His first book of poetry, the lyrical epic of *The Vengeance of Fionn*, published in 1917, was greeted by one of Ireland's leading scholars as a work of "mature splendour . . . power walking in radiant beauty."[4]

A reaction to such overpraise may account for Yeats's unprofessional and inhumane omission of Clarke from the *Oxford Book of Modern Verse* in 1935. Yeats may have been offended by Clarke's indiscreet questioning when the younger poet was preparing a biography of him, later abandoned, or Yeats may have mistaken Clarke for an imitator. In 1935 Clarke's and Yeats's poetic directions were contrary: as Yeats attempted to reach a wider audience through ballads, Clarke was developing more arcane diction and more obscure allusions that would distance him from his audience. His remoteness from his audience I will return to at the conclusion of my discussion.

In 1922 Clarke moved to London to work as an editor and reviewer. After four major volumes and a fifteen-year exile, he returned to Dublin in 1937 to publish a *Collected Poems* and, then, *Night and Morning* (1938), his last volume of poetry until 1955. During this seventeen-year poetic silence Clarke founded the Verse-Speaking Society and the Lyric Theatre Company, reviewed regularly for Radio Eireann and local journals, and produced eight of his own plays. In 1955 he resumed his poetic career with a series of "poems and satires," three knotty volumes that are relieved somewhat by "Forget-me-not" (1962) and the increasingly autobiographical and narrative poems into which he eases in the half-dozen volumes that close out his rejuvenated poetic career. *Flight to Africa* (1963), winner of the Denis Devlin Award, and a poetic account of his breakdown, *Mnemosyne Lay in Dust* (1966), were particularly heralded by readers and critics.[5]

A poetic career so disjunct and changing has been as difficult to characterize as the legendary elephant fondled by the blind keepers. Critics have been reduced to declaring that the essential Clarke is the portion they can handle: usually the lyricist of *Pilgrimage* and *Night and Morning,* the satirical Clarke, or the author of the confessional *Mnemosyne Lay in Dust.* For example, the eminent British critic Donald Davie, in a 1974 essay on Padraic Fallon, Edwin Muir, and Clarke, focuses on the satires and poems of the late fifties and early sixties to characterize Clarke as a non-mythopoeic poet "who trusts the local and contingent through thick and thin." He contrasts Clarke's mode with that in Muir's "The Horses":

> As in nearly every poem that Muir wrote, the action takes place in a visionary or fabulous time that clocks and calendars do not measure.
>
> In other words Muir is a mythopoeic poet. And I recall him so as to present the bleakest possible contrast with Austin Clarke, who is further from mythopoeia than any poet one might think of.[6]

Even if we apply Davie's own definitions, Clarke can be recognized as essentially a mythopoeic, rather than a historical, poet. In contradicting Davie, we can follow his lead by beginning our discussion with Clarke's first autobiography, *Twice Round the Black Church*, which is "still the best introduction to his poetry," according to Davie.[7]

Critics have referred to *Black Church* only as a personal history, perhaps because the subtitle, "Early Memories of Childhood and Youth," encourages this treatment. However, a book that mentions Shakespeare in its first sentence and *Paradise Lost* in its last, that contains over a dozen ruined gardens or apple trees, that is pervaded by water imagery, and that interweaves scenes from maturity and childhood into a meaningful pattern must be interpreted rather than merely cited. Clarke's autobiography fulfills Michael Leiris's concept of this genre: "Everything leads back, whatever one does, to a specific constellation of things which one tends to reproduce, under various forms, an unlimited number of times."[8]

*Twice Round the Black Church* (published in 1962, Clarke's 66th year) seems to be structured on a series of opposites, such as the Mother and the Grandfather, city and country, governance of the Catechism and the freedom of Nature, the present and the past. These sometimes appear as moral alternatives because they were so presented to Clarke by his puritanical mother and her Victorian Church. As we come to see, they actually represent the familiar parochial world contrasted with the unfamiliar world beyond the narrow parish of the child's mind. This latter realm, which raised fear or desire in the child, was clothed in Christian myths by the child and, by the maturing hero, in the eclectic myths spawned by his artistic imagination.

Of these myths, suggestions of Eden are most recurrent. It is an autobiographical, as well as Romanticist, convention to depict certain stages of childhood as Edenic, as in the autobiographies of Wordsworth, Ruskin, Gosse, and Yeats. In *Black Church*, however, even for the child Eden is a beckoning mirage that recedes into the past or some other unattainable realm. Numerous suggestions that urbanization had ruined Paradise are reinforced by the principal paradigm in the autobiography, what Clarke calls his "governing myth," a story encountered in childhood that "dominates us even though we have lost all memory of it" (*CBC*, 124). According to Clarke's myth, rediscovered when he was thirty-

three, a small boy and girl, longing to escape their suburban neighborhood, follow a magic ball which leads them to the deserted seashore:

> Theirs was all the delight which Adam and Eve had never known. Un-
> fortunately, despite inward warning of what would happen if they did
> not behave themselves, the little splashers had a tiff one day and imme-
> diately the shore grass was hidden by a mile-long promenade. The next
> time they sulked with one another, a pier with a bandstand was there.
> To make a short story even shorter, with every quarrel, terraces and hotels
> spread along the sea front, empty, silent, reproachful. (*CBC,* 124)

Clarks asserts that this "little story has encompassed me because it is
still coming true. The old house in which we live at Templeogue Bridge
in the deepening shade of trees has been rapidly surrounded by a new
suburb" (*CBC,* 125). Yet, the autobiographical hero never enjoys an un-
spoiled Eden. As the children are only resituated in the urban home
from which they sought escape, so the suburbanite Clarke is drawn back
from "the deepening shade of trees" to the sooty bosom of his childhood setting.

It was in the trees' sheltered darkness that the autobiographical hero
discovered, in one case, a hanged doll, a reflection of his own guilt,
and, in two other cases, bizarre images of Satan beside a Tree of Life.
The autobiographer comments on one of these encounters: "As we explore our own small past imaginatively, we find the fears and joys of
childhood have taken on new meanings for us. All has become legend—
and symbols are waiting for us" (*CBC,* 18).

In fact, Clarke's mythopoeic projecting seems almost compulsive both
in the child and, in its more eclectic form, in the adult. Nevertheless,
he does attribute to nature an animus which has opposed him throughout his life. On his first visit to the country, the child found himself,
Clarke writes, "without guidance, in a region that seemed to me beyond the catechism" (*CBC,* 57). About one country misadventure in
which a culpable girl accused him of frightening "a broody hen . . .
off its clutch" (*CBC,* 58), Clarke comments: "The country itself was
even more deceptive than that small Eve whom I met in the garden.
Those fairy tales which Eileen read out to me sometimes or told me
when we were walking past the sweetshops in Capel Street all seemed
to be true. Nothing was quite what it seemed . . ." (*CBC,* 57–58). This
charge of nature's animus recurs.

Chapters 9 and 10 of the autobiography's 14 leap ahead to describe his life in London during his twenties and early thirties, as some of the earlier chapters advanced to comment on the adult Clarke. At least in part, Clarke's intention is to obscure our sense of chronological progression and to establish points of comparison between the mature writer and the earlier self-version that is the hero of the narrative.

In his encounters with nature, Clarke frequently was reacting against the mysterious or deceptive aspects of the reproductive cycle. Confronted with teeming nature, the child willingly retreated to the security of urban ordinance. For example, in another twilight encounter, while the child was awaiting the train to the city, a huge bull, "black and horned against the last light of the west," struck in him an elemental dread which the autobiographer traces to the oral accounts he heard in the Liberties of Dublin, of the *Tain Bo Cuailgne.* He rushed for refuge to the train, and "in its noise and smut we were swept back to the city and the catechism" (*CBC,* 61).

Here, dramatized but not explained, is Clarke's personalized version of the Romanticist dilemma: he is separated by time and temperament from the past and from nature, for which he constantly yearns, and which he conceives of in terms of parochial folklore and mythology. The autobiography concludes with a radiant statement in which the Mt. Argus tree, under which he had seen a satanic figure, and the tree of Paradise merge. The hero claims conversion, under Milton's influence, to a form of Arianism which might incorporate other mythologies. Several pages from the conclusion, speaking of Milton's fallen angels, Clarke says, "Their secondary names brought me glimpses of other mythologies. . . . The next world had become a mental refuge. So much did I feel the power of Milton's imaginative vision . . ." (*CBC,* 172).

This mythopoeic poet can relieve his dilemma only through the transforming power of imaginative vision. At one point he describes the child's midnight epiphany of a gleaming flood, rather like Wordsworth's experience on Mt. Snowden, recorded in *The Prelude.* Commenting on this recurrent vision, he says, "I was much pleased, as water is a symbol of vision. The Gaelic poets were accustomed to think out their poems beside stream or loch . . ." (*CBC,* 69). This vision is a key to an earlier scene in which the child discovered, within a rain puddle near his grimy coal-shed, a reflected world of inverted housetops and deep blue heavens:

"It seemed to me," he says, "that this was the celestial city of which all spoke" (*CBC,* 22). The reflecting water transformed even the terrifying Black Church of the title. According to an ancient Dublin legend, if one dares to circle this Protestant church three times, he will meet the devil himself on the third lap.[9] Twice around the Black Church indicates the limits imposed on Clarke and his peers by parochial mythology and the fear of Protestantism inculcated in many Catholic children. Yet, the frightening world is transformed within that water's other "hemisphere in which all is different. There the Black Church, which I feared so much when I looked at it, was radiant, lovely and enskied" (*CBC,* 23).

The reflecting pool initiated the conception that matured under Milton's influence. As Clarke says, "Children can enact in their little way the primary myths, find for themselves the ancient ritual of fear" (*CBC,* 2). These powerful myths, which seem inherent and necessary to him, can be transformed and shaped by "imaginative vision," the liberating power to which he is attracted in Milton.

If the reflecting pool and the Gaelic symbolism of water were the exclusive characterizing aspect of *Black Church,* we would seem to be describing an author of romance or escape literature. Though this is an element in Clarke's writing, we need to reconsider the other paradigmatic passage, that of the "governing myth," in its full context. The autobiographer of sixty-six recalls a younger self at age thirty-three who, while working for *Argosy Magazine* in Ludgate Circus, came across a picture of two children bounding through that very same London square. This picture recalled to him the tale, which he had read sometime in childhood. The tale itself was written before his birth and was, of course, imaginary. Within the tale the children escape to an idyllic life by the sea: to this point . . . romance with opportunities for lyricism. Then, from their own fallen natures springs the urban blight: a condition for pathos, or satire. If we keep in mind that the romance-satire is contained within a frame of memory, the older Clarke reflecting through various self-versions on a past that is legendary or imaginary yet highly personal, then, I think, we can recognize Clarke's most characteristic mode, even as it manifests itself so differently in the three stages of his poetic career.

Clarke himself characterizes this mode clearly in the preface to his

first published poem, *The Vengeance of Fionn*, a retelling of the elope-
tale of Diarmuid and Grainne:

> The poem begins in the middle age of Diarmuid and Grainne, and changes
> rapidly, visionally, to their youth and love,—so that the reader has an
> awareness of the past—ideal in itself, yet further idealized by memory—
> in the present.[10]

This poem contains rhyme in varying and irregular patterns and a diction and syntax closer to Tennyson's or Morris's than Clarke's later highly
wrought style, but as in the later poetry, the style reminds us that we
have suspended disbelief. The disparity between historical reality and
imaginative fiction is enforced when the narrator occasionally dips into
a mock-epic tone.

The conclusion of *The Vengeance of Fionn* adds yet another reflecting
surface to the poem. As earlier in the narration the two lovers had sighed
over their own lost possibilities for love—"But O that we / Had seen and
loved like Lovers long ago; / Self-found, each in the other's mystery"
(*CCP,* 33)—so now two adolescent lovers comment on the widowed
Grainne, who is "wrinkled and ugly," and swear they will "never, never,
grow old." The poem concludes with the boy's ejaculation: "O shiny
Dew / O little wild Bird of the air / Youth only is wisdom and it is
love" (*CCP,* 40). We assent, as we smile, not to the lover's assertion
but to the psychological truth that the fantasy of idealized love survives
even the conflict with a disillusioning reality. Because the conclusion
echoes the language of the mythic heroes, Diarmuid and Grainne's earlier exchange of vows, we are reminded that even this final idle longing
for love is a literary expression, a recollection that is enforced in the
reader's mind by the rhyme, poetic diction, and mock-heroic tone.

Clarke's first poem introduces more than a poetic mode combining
memory and imagination to place events outside of history into an idealized past. It also suggests his dominant theme: the alternation between
an ideal, evoked by imagination and memory and associated with literature, and historical reality, which is here only suggested by mock-
heroic tone and strategies of nonchronological plot (in Clarke's second
stage, I will argue, historical reality is described and the ideal is implied). Stated another way, Clarke illuminates not the Fall but man's
preoccupation with the Fall, his persistent projection through imagina-

tion and memory of an ideal state, and the heroic pathos of maintaining this ideal alternative reality. The stories of elopement to an erotic state without ordinance, the shifts into surreal states of dreaming and drunkenness, the representation of Eden and of the *faed fiad,* which is the veil between coexistent worlds, the aisling poems, and a pervasive literariness that obviates verisimilitude are all manifestations of Clarke's theme in the poetry and three novels.

Within the first phase of Clarke's poetic career, which closes in 1938, the poet shifts his topic from the heroic Irish myths to the early medieval church community in Ireland, and then, ostensibly, to modern conflicts between faith and reason. One critic has described Clarke's historical subject, which Clarke called the "Celtic-Romanesque Church," as a "historical objective correlative for a more personal and anguished dialogue." [11] We know from *Black Church* that the culdee's and hermit's struggles against the flesh parallel Clarke's experience, but in a more subtle manner Clarke introduces his own, or at least a modern, perspective into poems ostensibly recited by a medieval narrator. For example, the pilgrim to the holy sites in "Pilgrimage" (1929) is undeniably a medieval Christian. At his second station the devotee says:

> O Clonmacnoise was crossed
> With light: those cloistered scholars
> Whose knowledge of the gospel
> Is cast as metal in pure voices,
> Were all rejoicing daily,
> And cunning hands with cold and jewels
> Brought chalices to flame.
>
> (*CCP,* 153)

Voices once, in the present tense of the poem, as clear as bells can now be evoked only by their metalwork which maintains their pitch. Similarly, the craftsman's flame will reside in the radiant jewel-work after his kiln is snuffed. The sources of the images, bell and jewel, deliquesce into a past activity, an idea that Clarke will develop into a technique, where things such as candles or angels become actions: "candeling" or "angeling." The effect in "Pilgrimage" is to suggest that a modern narrator is recovering an imaginary medieval itinerary through the stimulus of ancient artifacts.

In this 1929 volume, Clarke borrows the antiquarian approaches of writers of the Celtic Twilight, but, just as Montague, Murphy, Kinsella, and Heaney will later do, he stakes out and explores his own distinctive, "neglected and almost forgotten" era.[12] Along with this interest in the early Gaelic monasticism, he had developed some knowledge of Gaelic literature which led to his most celebrated recovery, certain assonant effects adapted from Irish poetry.

It is difficult to determine to what extent these innovative adaptations from Irish were based on a command of the language or a considerable understanding of Irish poetry. Although nonacademic contemporaries deferred to him on matters of poetry in Irish, in the company of Gaelic scholars Clarke became shy and defensive about his Irish.[13] In his discussions of the literature, he usually cites translators or scholars such as Standish Hayes O'Grady, Douglas Hyde, George Sigerson, Herbert Trench, and Thomas MacDonagh, rather than Gaelic poets, although he must have worked closely with the dual-language versions of older sagas offered by the Irish Texts Society.[14]

Whatever his command of Irish, Clarke seems quite clear about the kind of Irish-poetic effects he would import into English:

> Assonance, more elaborate in Gaelic than in Spanish poetry, takes the clapper from the bell of rhyme. In simple patterns, the tonic word at the end of the line is supported by a vowel-rhyme in the middle of the next line. Unfortunately the internal patterns of assonance and consonance in Gaelic stanzas are so intricate that they can only be suggested in another language. . . . By cross-rhymes or vowel-rhyming, separately, one or more of the syllables of longer words, on or off accent, . . . lovely and neglected words are advanced to the tonic place and divide their echoes. (*CCP,* 547)

Robert Welch has argued that such adaptations from Irish poetry constitute "perhaps the main achievement of Austin Clarke's many-faceted career."[15] In an informative essay, Welch demonstrates these reconstructions which he believes freed Clarke from dependence on English prosody and on Yeats's model. However, to the extent that Gaelic-like internal intricacy congealed the flow of Clarke's lines or led him into obscure diction, Clarke's borrowings also seem restrictive and, as Montague has said, "at least a partial failure."[16]

At times Clarke remembers his admonishment that Irish prosody can
only be suggested in English, and he employs his greater cross-references
of vowels for his own ends, which are often unconventional. For example, consider his description of the Connaught estate of an English
landlord, probably during the era of the Penal Laws, in "The Planter's
Daughter." In this poem from *Pilgrimage,* he anticipates by four decades Seamus Heaney's distinction between Gaelic and English: "river
tongues . . . flood, with voweling embrace, / Demesnes staked out in
consonants" (*HP,* 111). As the Irish narrator approaches the subject of
the poem, his words indeed "divide their echoes," as in <u>sea</u> / <u>beauty</u> /
<u>music</u> / <u>few:</u>

> When night stirred at sea
> And the fire brought a crowd in,
> They say that her beauty
> Was music in mouth
> And few in the candlelight
> Thought her too proud,
> For the house of the planter
> Is known by the trees.

Within the two vocalic stanzas, Clarke seems to assign to the background elements, such as the native onlookers, the sea, and the trees,
front sounds of *i* and *e,* and to the admired subject back vowels such
as *o* and *u:*

> Men that had seen her
> Drank deep and were silent,
> The women were speaking
> Wherever she went —
> As a bell that is rung
> Or a wonder told shyly,
> And O she was the Sunday
> In every week.
>
> (*CCP,* 173)

The exclamatory *O,* her bell-note, becomes also her signature as the
countrymen are entitled to the weekdays and, implicitly, to the trees
sheltering her house, which were once everyone's. According to this

reading, Clarke's vowels establish a thematic counterpoint, which is not a conventional use of vowels within Irish poetry.

From his small production of poetry in the thirties, Clarke gathered a beautiful pamphlet of poems which he called *Night and Morning* (1938) to suggest the alternation of cowering faith and reason. "The Straying Student," the most anthologized of all Clarke's poems, is situated in the middle of this sequence to maintain a "historical objective correlative" for the poet. The speaker, a student forced to study on the continent during the era of the penal laws, is seduced from his studies by an aisling, a vision of a beautiful woman, who represents not Ireland but the Renaissance ideal of beauty and wisdom. The conclusion could be Clarke's plaint as well as the scholar's:

> And yet I tremble lest she may deceive me
> And leave me in this land, where every woman's son
> Must carry his own coffin and believe,
> In dread, all that the clergy teach the young.
>
> (*CCP*, 189)

Conversely, the voice of "Repentance," which can be recognized as Clarke's, can also be that of the "straying student." Although the poem draws on Clarke's tour of the West during the Irish Civil War, the point of view in the poem is of one traveling east, as from Aran:

> I crossed the narrows of earthward light,
> The rain, noon-set along the mountain,
> And I forgot the scale of thought,
> Man's lamentation, Judgment hour
> That hides the sun in the waters.
>
> (*CCP*, 186)

At the conclusion of "Repentance," the speaker wonders if, at the moment of judgment, he will be able to free himself from pernicious thought. As does the imagination, religion offers an alternative to a ravening nature and to historical reality, but one based on anxiety rather than desire.

W. J. Roscelli has written of Clarke's preoccupation with man's search for an alternative reality. He praises Clarke for his "sympathetic understanding of the human condition—the ceaseless quest for Eden which inevitably leads us to the cloister or the bed, which makes ideas into

abstractions and turns our lust to ashes. . . . [17] After *Night and Morning*
Clarke dismisses the religious alternative and dwells discontentedly in
this world, in his satirical poetry of the fifties and sixties, before his
poetic subject becomes bedridden in the erotic final stage of his career.

In a subtle manner Eden remains present in these earthbound poems
of 1955 through 1966, which are Donald Davie's total concern. Each
outrage or limitation against which Clarke protests in these poems is
a thorn in the crown persecuting poetry and the expansive imagination
(images of spikes and thorns recur frequently). The adversary of the
imagination is no longer the anxious conscience but the institutions
and practices of the actual world:

> So think, man, as Augustine
> Did, dread the ink-bespattered ex-monk,
> And keep your name. No, let me abandon
> Night's jakes. Self-persecuted of late
> Among the hatreds of rent Europe,
> Poetry burns at a different stake.
>
> ("Ancient Lights," *CCP,* 200)

Critics hover over the title poem of the 1955 volume, "Ancient Lights,"
because portions of the poem offer attractive images from Clarke's youth
and because the poem seems to declare its own importance. The poet
recalls the dual worlds of his youth: the daytime world of man which
he and his sisters explored like little Alexanders, and the nighttime haunted
by religious injunctions and fears of the next world, which pervade the
dark confessional and sanctuary as well. After recalling his first confession, in which the questions by Christ's priest advertise the rites of Onan,
of which the boy was innocent, he recalls leaving the church on another
occasion, suffering from the priest-induced self-consciousness:

> Once as I crept from the church-steps,
> Beside myself, the air opened
> On purpose. Nature read in a flutter
> An evening lesson above my head.
> Atwirl beyond the leadings, corbels,
> A cage-bird came among sparrows
> (The moral inescapable)
> Plucked, roof-mired, all in mad bits. O
> The pizzicato of its wires!

Goodness of air can be proverbial:
That day, by the kerb at Rutland Square,
A bronze bird fabled out of trees,
Mailing the spearheads of the railings,
Sparrow at nails, I hailed the skies
To save the tiny dropper, found
Appetite gone. A child of clay
Had blustered it away. Pity
Could raise some littleness from dust.

The keepers agree that this limb of the elephant is important, but they are hard pressed to know how it works. Augustine Martin believes the boy becomes "piercingly aware of nature's beneficence,"[18] which seems dead wrong. Craig Tapping asserts that Clarke "sees himself as the cage-bird, weakened and victimised by rigid thinking, orthodoxy and dogma," which seems reasonable. However, to then conclude that "freedom is to think and liberate oneself from such a cage-like superstructure of belief"[19] is to ignore nature's lesson in the savage rending of the bird by the wild sparrows. The most intrepid, and most penetrating, interpreter of "Ancient Lights" is Adrian Frazier. He suggests that Clarke's identification with the cage-bird's fate, "because he is a poet and because he has been shut up from Nature by his religious education," also has its parallel in the story of Orpheus who is dismembered by wild Nature. However, then Frazier subordinates the poet's ambivalence concerning nature and order to the theme of a virile nature oppressing the civilized but impotent singer, a "tiny-dropper." According to Frazier,

> "Ancient Lights" contains references to the initial point in the history of Clarke's psychic conflict: guilt over masturbation; the medial point: impotence from guilt. . . . This drama took fifty years to run its course. The ultimately liberating conversion . . . did not really take place until the poem itself was written. "Ancient Lights" is the conversion it recounts.[20]

Thoughtfully, Frazier has opened Clarke's poetry to the type of psychological criticism Clarke seems to invite in his autobiographies. In *Penny in the Clouds* Clarke attributes his mental breakdown to sexual guilt and "overindulgence in continence"[21] in his bundling with Lia Cummings. When Frazier attributes a seventeen-year silence, which he claims is broken by only one poem, to Clarke's ignorance of or inhibitions concern-

ing the origins of his sexual guilt, he overstates his case, as he does
in seeing this one poem as the drama of its own purgation, which releases "stores of aggression" to energize his satires. Finally, Frazier regrets Clarke's obscurity, presumably even that of "Ancient Lights," much
of which he has dispelled, and praises those poems in which Clarke
writes clearly and "completely free of chains." As his "best example"
of this superior type, he offers "The Blackbird of Derrycairn," published in *Ancient Lights.*

Frazier seems unaware that "The Blackbird . . . " actually appeared
during Clarke's seventeen-year silence. It was published in 1943 and recited in 1942 as lines in Clarke's play, *As the Crow Flies,* a work that
can remove some shadows from "Ancient Lights." In this play, sheltered
from a tempest in a cave above the Shannon River, three seventh-century
monks overhear a grim conversation among demons, who are actually
celebrated animals from pre-Christian Irish myths. As prelude to the
conversation, Father Virgilius comforts Brother Aengus concerning their
mission for the Abbot: "Perhaps he sent you here / To learn the mercy
of the elements."[22] As the play unfolds, these lines develop the same
irony as the lines in "Ancient Lights" concerning nature's vespers. "Nature read in a flutter / An evening lesson" undercuts its gentler meaning with an echo of "Nature red in tooth and claw," which becomes
the ultimate "moral inescapable." The immediate moral, that the moral
life cannot be escaped from, is dramatized by the sparrows' mugging
of the strayed cage-bird.

The next stanza retains the density of a black-hole that blocks a clear
vision of "Ancient Lights." The only proverb I know concerning sparrows appears in Luke XII and Matthew X, but the proverbial victims,
whose fall God observes, have become the inhumane aggressors. Furthermore, nature's naked aggression is associated with the Church's oppression: her railings become armed spearheads, the sparrows crucifiers.
About the identity of the "bronze bird" I have false leads, especially
when I track remote literary possibilities such as Yeats's golden bird,
Peter's cock, or Sweeney's songs of nature, and one anticlimactic hunch
that *bronze* merely describes the color of a bird, "moderately yellowish
to olive brown," who is named *sparrow* in the fifth line's appositive.
Perhaps he "fabled out of trees" to the extent that "knowledge is found
among the branches," as the Blackbird of Derrycairn declares. In any

case, as in the passages from *Twice Round the Black Church* discussed earlier, the boy confronts his dilemma between a restrictive oppressive Church and a free aggressive nature, here in a seemingly overwhelming alliance. Implicitly, as a rite in this dark passage, savage birds initiate the boy into the rapaciousness of nature, which is the explicit theme of *As the Crow Flies*:

> every creature
> We know is eaten by disease
> Or violent blow! We are unseasoned,
> unsensed, unearthed, riddle-diddled
> By what is hidden from the reason.
> How can the forethought of defilement
> Be reconciled with any faith
> That teaches mortals to be mild?[23]

The poet of "Ancient Lights" does not flinch from this forethought: "So think, man, as Augustine / Did . . . / And keep your name," though he would like to abandon "night's jakes," roomed with fears. These fears are absolved and his dilemma relieved in the solution of an "awful downpour" which purges sexual guilt and fear of nature's sparrow-like rapacity:

> Waste-water mocked
> The ballcocks: down-pipes sparrowing,
>
> .  .  .  .  .  .  .  .  .  .  .  .  .  .
>
> I heard
> From shore to shore, the iron gratings
> Take half our heavens with a roar.
>
> (*CCP,* 200–01)

In the final section the poet can absolve himself in part because he has reacted against his dilemma in the middle stanzas. Although Frazier has argued that these two stanzas reflect "impotence from guilt"[24] and that cage-bird and boy suffer a loss of appetite, the boy acts, shouting at the sparrows, who had been demonstrating appetite, and therefore chasing them away.

> I hailed the skies
> To save the tiny dropper, found
> Appetite gone. A child of clay

> Had blustered it away. Pity
> Could raise some littleness from dust.

Although the boy's outcry is bluster, which succeeds in recovering only "some littleness," it is a defiant and creative act, in imitation of God's raising man from the dust, which precedes Clarke's absolution. If the poem releases "stores of aggression" into the satires of this period, as Frazier asserts, it also sets their tone of a self-absolving but ineffective defiance.

The tone of the satires is not savage indignation but a petulance and frustration that are suggested by the offhandedness of such complaints as "The Dead Sea Scrolls," "Christmas Eve," "Medical Missionary of Mary," "Intercessors," or "The Choice," or in such impenetrable poems as "The Hippophagi." As Martin Dodsworth observed, "The poet's protest is half defeated by its understanding of the order of events which give rise to it."[25] Perhaps we can come no closer than analogy to an explanation of the tone of diverted attention I sense in the satires of the fifties and sixties.

Clarke's portrayal of *coitus interruptus,* farcically in "Phallomeda" and *Tiresias,* or more developed in his first prose romance, *The Bright Temptation* (Dublin: Dolmen, 1932, 1965), may provide us with a metaphor for his state of mind in the second phase of his career. In the romance, the innocent "straying student," Aidan, interrupts the mounting excitement of his first congress with Ethna, his "bright temptation," to gather firewood for their bower. He becomes lost and then kidnapped by a gregarious Firbolgian giant, the Prumpalaun, who, deaf to Aidan's plaints, carries him farther and farther from his tryst. One senses that the Prumpalauns of Church and State, which Clarke assails in the satires, are forces beyond correction and aside from his center of interest, the lost bright moment from which we are carried by the world at birth but which we retain in our literature and our imaginations.

Some of the poems in this second stage are merely querulous and bitchy, and others so enmesh with the topical that they attain the mouldy obscurity of last decade's page-two journalism. However, in spite of a certain number of opaque topical poems in the six volumes of Clarke's second phase, I cannot agree with Davie's assessment that "Austin Clarke is an extreme case of the poet who trusts the local and contingent

through thick and thin, who refuses to rise above the congested hetero-
geneity of the world as we experience it . . . of *this* time in *this* place."[26]

Rise Clarke does, and through active intercourse between the sounds
of words and phrases, he suggests the dominance of poetic fancy or even
erotic fantasy over the "local and contingent." Denis Donoghue argues
that Clarke's "high jinks in language are related to standard speech as
freedom to constraint: sexual freedom, mostly. Homonyms give their
speaker a double life, not one life amplified but two separate lives, prosaic and poetic, conventional and exotic, the daily life and the life of
fantasy."[27] Donoghue illustrates his observation with a passage from
"More Extracts from a Diary of Dreams":

> Why should the aged be unhappy,
> Mope in the dark, when the unhappenable
> Is theirs and they can glide between the shades
> Of meaning in a dream, talk to the shades,
> Unchaperoned, watch every jog of nature
> That proves the midnight merriment innate—
>
> (*CCP,* 394)

It simply amplifies Donoghue's point to indicate that often in the second line the homonym hems in its partner:

> All dress, remark that lunch is late, or
> Tidy the pair in perambulator.

This rhyming of homophones, *rime riche,* like the more frequent internal rhyme and assonance, suggests a mating that originates in the imagination rather than in nature.

Clarke's unusual verbs contribute indirectly to his theme. Often constructed from nouns or adjectives, these verbs can hypostatize Eden by
suggesting a displacement from some advantageous state or an attempt
to regain it. Martha Blake was "angeling the road," a clerk "halo'ed
the candles," a stag was "uncragging," bombers "unwombed the frightened cities," and "that mighty unhousing / A mile away, rooks elm-
ing in a flock." Clarke's unusual diction also serves to elevate sexuality
above the level of the Liberties' graffiti through words with Chaucerian
lineages—"swiving," "pintel," "sporran," "Smugging" or botanical
associations—"Thalamus," "Caprifigging," "introrsely."

One might point out that this elevated diction is derived from nature and that the elaborate interlacings of sound in Clarke's verse, insofar as they inscribe the aural equivalent of the zoomorphic swirls in ancient Irish art, are substitutions for nature's patterns. The haunting "Forget-me-Not" (1962) begins by discussing the relation of sound and meter to the jog-trot of horses: "For what is song itself but substitution?" Yet, whatever its origins, song offers in contrast to the discordant and sullied world an imaginary structure of sounds and idealized images. In this most historical, nostalgic poem, the neglect and slaughter of horses are shamed by contrast not so much with man's historical relationship to horses as with the idealized horses of literature: Pegasus, the Trojan Horse, Rosinante, the Gray of Macha, the Sagittary carved on the royal arch of Cormac's chapel. Davie consents that whereas the sacrilege of hippophagy is condemned in this poem, a certain "sacredness is affirmed."[28] We need to go further and assert that even in this most historical of Clarke's poems, Clarke suggests that idealized structures and images persist in man's mind so that he can not remain insistently of "this time in this place." Speaking of a tradition he emulated, Clarke said:

> Gaelic poetry is based on one of the seven deadly sins, that of pride. The aristocratic world in which these poets lived was fairer than reality. The human form, as in Greece, was celebrated under an ideal aspect.[29]

This ideal extends even to the horses he defends in this untypically historical poem.

So, I would argue that the enduring theme of Clarke's poetry, the lost Eden hidden in man's memory and created by his imagination, even lurks behind the satires of the second stage. This theme is confirmed, if not created, by the third stage of Clarke's poetic career which is announced by a poem granting general absolution, "Sermon on Swift" (1967), after being prepared for by the restorative *Mnemosyne Lay in Dust* (1966).

My discussion of *Mnemosyne,* which many critics consider Clarke's masterwork, will extend only to some comments on the popularity and the place in the canon of this detailed fictionalization of Clarke's breakdown and recovery within St. Patrick's asylum, to which he was committed in 1919. First, the poem, in all of its eighteen sections, greets the reader as refreshingly comprehensible. Most obscure passages can be clarified by reference to other works by Clarke, such as "Fragaria" (*CCP*, 323), "Old Fashioned Pilgrimage" (*CCP*, 357–58), and the autobiography *Penny in the Clouds*. The reader remains thankful to Clarke for his uncharacteristic efforts to meet him halfway. Secondly, among the number of reviewers who extol the work as confessional poetry equal to Plath's or Lowell's, one senses some admire the work especially because it is un-Clarkean, or even un-Irish, and that others know too little of Lowell's verse from which they believe they are borrowing splendor.

Clarke's work may be as vivid and well constructed as *Life Studies,* Lowell's major confessional work, but it does not contribute incrementally to the larger significance of Clarke's work as *Life Studies* does to Lowell's concern for private and public history. *Mnemosyne* comments on sexual frustration and pathological self-consciousness and implies that the arrest of urges toward the future, sex, and hunger, also blocks access to the past, leaving him in a timeless state of endurance: "The bearded face was drawn / With sufferings he had forgotten. // Sunlight was time . . ."(*CCP*, 332). Intimations of release and future happiness are gathered from overheard whispers concerning "the Gate, the Garden, and the Fountain," which are associated with Eden and his childhood conceptions of the Garden, but which actually represent the immediate future that will greet him outside the hospital walls as he recovers (see sections II, IX, X, XIII). In *Mnemosyne,* because the Edenic promise that brackets our lives is represented as arising from the universal and last remnants of the functioning mind, the Garden is introduced naturalistically, independent of literary language and allusions. Consequently, the work remains anomalous, a masterful confession that clears the stage for Clarke's next phase but which may simply join a list of other masterful poems by Clarke when this poet is better understood.

No curtain drop or seventeen-year scene-change interrupts Clarke's second phase. His poetry unknots, becomes more prosaic, and absorbs itself in the theme of sexuality, but gradually so that *A Sermon on Swift and Other Poems* (1968) serves as well as the transitional volumes—*Old Fashioned Pilgrimage* and *Echo at Coole* (1968)—to introduce Clarke's final phase. As a prologue to this phase, the opening poem concludes not with an account of personal absolution, as in "Ancient Lights," but of the heresy attributed to John Scotus Erigena and to Jonathan Swift: "Eternal Absolution" for the human race. After the full disclosure of *Mnemosyne,* Clarke can refer easily in the "Sermon . . ." to his own sojourn in St. Patrick's Hospital, the "mansion of forgetfulness," which Swift willed to Ireland. He also promises to take as his text "privy matters" of which Swift also wrote.

Clarke fulfilled this promise to the discomfort of certain critics who have dismissed the late works, including the accomplished "The Healing of Mis" and *Tiresias* as the sexual fantasies of a superannuated adolescent, what one otherwise discerning critic mistook as Clarke's "perennial smut."[30] Such dismissals ignore the deliberate literariness of these anacreontics which renders as the basic subject the real estate of the Edenic bower in the literary imagination. In the major poems of the last phase, "The Healing of Mis" and *Tiresias,* this subject is treated lightly but self-consciously, so that the poet or bard's relation to sexual fantasy is represented.

In "The Healing of Mis," the physician is a poet, or at least a harper, who employs music and sex to sate, sedate, and restore the dream-frenzied princess, Mis. The story is rendered succinctly but lucidly in a six-stress line that permits very rapid shift of speakers:

> "Are you a man?" she asked. "I am." "What's that you are holding?"
> "A harp." "I remember the triangle." "Pluck it."
>
> (*CCP,* 511)

The poem is organized in stanzas of seven long lines of twelve syllables or more and a foreshortened line that provides dramatic or lyrical closures that are frequently surprising: "The bushiness above her knees" or "Of a lonely sorrow time could not cure." This stanza allows Clarke enough slackness for shifts of speakers and tone while still permitting lyricism, as evident in the eighth stanza which introduces the poet's healing instruments:

> Holding his harp, the consolation of his bosom,
>     He played a suantree with grace-notes that enspelled
> Traditional tunes and, smiling quietly at his ruse,
>     Waited. Soon his sense knew that loneliness
> Stood by, a bareness modestly draped in tangle-black hair,

With timeless hands, listening to the special
Melling that drew and soothed her mind as she stared
In surmise at his rising flesh.

*(CCP,* 511)

The poet and Mis confect a bower of fennel bloom, wildering wood-
bine, and braided daisies, and in this place with song and sex Mis is
healed and restored by the poet to the respectful court "that had laughed
him one night from the feast," a victory for erotic poetry, for Clarke's
surrogate, and for Clarke as well, who receives "Blessing, / Victory,
to him who relates this story!" *(CCP,* 516).

Writing in 1966 Denis Donoghue praised Clarke for achieving "a
singing line which moves with the vigor of his own best prose,"[31]
praise which seems particularly applicable to "The Healing of Mis."
As with most of the successful poems from the second and third phases,
these verses are most effective if we yield to the enjambment and read
the stanzas as discourse from which we are drawn toward poetry by
a spirit of traditional Irish verse, the assonance and near-rhyme that
haunt the poem.

*Tiresias* (1971) features another surrogate for Clarke, the aged seer
who is petitioned by Jove and Juno to recount the seven-year period
when he had been changed into a woman after touching two sacred
coupling snakes. The gods want him to settle their wager over which
sex derives more pleasure from coition. Doubting his gift of foresight
and "second sight," which is granted to ancient Irish poets as well,
Tiresias relies on memory and the unusual transsexual experience to describe in detail the woman's experience of love. For such experience the
modern poet could consult Kinsey or Masters and Johnson rather than
the sacred snakes, but Clarke's negative capability is sanctioned within
the poem by Jove, who to win his wager—that woman's pleasure is
greater—may have induced in Tiresias preorgasmic pleasures. Clarke's
imaginary transsexualism finds precedence in literary history where writers such as Rabelais, Chaucer, Browning, George Eliot, and Joyce have
attempted to bridge the sexual divide.

*Tiresias* suggests complex connections between the seer's interior vision across the ages, his sensual response to external vision, and his
transsexual experience. Before encountering Jove and Juno, the seer is
nearly blinded by the "preternatural bloom" of mountain flowers *(CCP,*

517). The moment foreshadows his accidental intrusion on Pallas Athene
in her bath for which offense he is punished by blindness, as he is compensated with forevision. Before he is stricken blind, he mistakes Athene
for Pyrrha, his transsexual self from another period of his life: "O why
had Pyrrha not recognised me? / With open arms, I came out. / . . .
Body / Wanted its other self" (*CCP*, 532). The narrative suggests that
the transsexual's memory, the seer's foresight, and the poet's vision cross
barriers in human experience and complete the self. The story also suggests that for Clarke's surrogate, at least, all such gifts are fading into
the past, as the poem concludes with the seer's wife calling him home:

> "Come in, dear
> Friend, for the purple-robed hours pass by. Luna has led her
> Star-flocks home — and your cup of hot milk waits on the table."
> (*CCP*, 540)

In his last year Clarke wrote a version of the Irish legend "The Wooing of Becfola" which was published posthumously in his *Collected Poems.*
In less than one hundred lines, this poem tropes several situations familiar to readers of Clarke's romances. It appears that, as in *The Sun
Dances At Easter,* a woman trysts so vividly in dreams that this otherworldly experience becomes an alternative reality affecting her situation
in this world. Becfola's lover shares his bower with her but sends her
back to her husband faithful and aroused:

> And now you are like a honey bush.
> All May and murmur as if you had hid in
> A raid of kisses. Why is it, I wonder?
> (*CCP*, 543)

By suppressing the fact, evident in the legend, that Becfola is actually an immigrant from the Otherworld,[32] Clarke allows dream- and
psychological-analysis to serve as means of interpretation in place of legend and credulity. Whereas innocent sexuality, or whatever the Eden
that resides in man's mind, cannot be attained on this side of the invisible curtain that separates us from the Otherworld, the idea of this
alternative reality is nevertheless ineradicable. Occasionally, ideal images from this world impinge on and affect the events of our "reality."
Clarke shares Wallace Stevens' understanding:

There may be always a time of innocence.
There is never a place. Or if there is not time,
If it is not a thing of time, nor of place,

Existing in the idea of it, alone,
In the sense against calamity, it is not
Less real. . . .
                    (from "The Auroras of Autumn")

Clarke's poetry is often autobiographical because the human imagination associates eroticism and possibilities lost in a past, a fact Milton recognized when he located the bower at the center of his Paradise lost. Yet, whereas Milton's myth has an extratextual reality for his seventeenth-century audience, Clarke insinuates that his ideal depends on its literary expression. As he conveys this idea through complex diction, literary allusions, deliberate rhyme that bridles discursive poems, chiming vowels, and mythical topics, much of which he adapted from Gaelic literature, this poetic priest often seems as remote from his audience as he does from the ideal that haunts him. Insofar as Gaelic literature, and the Irish language itself, produced the elopement myths and the aislings that embody Clarke's erotic ideals, they become associated with the irrecoverability of the ideal itself, as the abandonment of the language exposes the apostasy of the laity. Consequently, the difficulty of Clarke's poetry may be seen as his test of the reader's fidelity to vehicles and ideals that Clarke himself knew could no longer be "a thing of time, nor of place."

*&*

Thomas Kinsella would never accept the dark habit of the Irish tradition's priest which Austin Clarke routinely wore.[33] In fact Kinsella has denied the continuity of an Irish tradition. Nevertheless, as Clarke in his generation, Kinsella has done more than his poetic contemporaries to revitalize that tradition, through his translations of the *Tain* and of Irish poetry in *An Duanaire* and through the incorporation of Irish materials in his own verse. Both poets have paid the price in obscurity and in their shrinking readership's perplexity, caused, in part, by gaelicized diction and prosody in Clarke's verse and by shadowy allusions

to Irish legend in Kinsella's. Excepting perhaps only Maurice Harmon and
M. L. Rosenthal, critics who supported Kinsella's early poetry, with its
clear antecedents in the Romantics, Yeats, and Auden, have tended to
neglect his recent verse, from *Nightwalker and Other Poems* to the present.[34]

To suggest the demands Kinsella places on his critics, consider the
reaction of Calvin Bedient to "Survivor," which appears in the middle
section of the sequential *Notes from the Land of the Dead* (1973). An eloquent explicator of the early poetry, Bedient has come to cite the following lines as an example of Kinsella's "guilt and weariness freezing
his animal faith":[35]

> There is nothing here for sustenance.
>   Unbroken sleep were best.
> Hair. Claws. Grey.
>   Naked. Wretch. Wither.

However, we can no longer attribute these emotions to the poet or accept Bedient's characterization of the last six words as "Kinsella's latest
summa," once we acknowledge the dramatic post-diluvian setting ("this
cave escaped the Deluge") and identify the speaker as Fintan, a survivor
of the first invasion of Ireland and her ur-poet. His escape from fifty
life-sapping women and his hibernation through the Flood in a womb-
like cave are recounted in the *Lebor Gabála Érenn*, or *The Book of Invasions*, where Fintan says,

> I had a year under the Flood
> in strong Tul Tuinde;
> I found nothing for my sustenance,
> an unbroken sleep were best.[36]

It is pertinent to ask whether an American critic writing in 1973
can be expected to recognize "Survivor" as a loose rendition of an episode in the ancient myth of the settlement of Ireland, which has been
translated by A. Stewart Macalister and published between 1938 and
1941 by the Irish Texts Society. Even if we extend Bedient a reprieve,
we cannot exonerate critics in the 1980s who ignore this and other sources
which are available in most libraries, which Kinsella has mentioned in
interviews, and which have been less or more explained by the only
book on Kinsella's poetry and a long dissertation on his work.[37] The

latter work by Carolyn Rosenberg offers copious detailed information concerning the poet's life and his literary references. Even in 1973, before such glosses were available, *The Book of Invasions* was probably better known to Kinsella's audience than the sources of *The Wanderings of Oisin* and "The Madness of King Goll" were to Yeats's readers when those works appeared in 1889.

Yet, Yeats reduces his readers' ignorance with his titles, which appeared with these poems in 1889, and his notes which were published in 1895. Conversely, Kinsella offers in "Nuchal," "Survivor," "Finistere," "The Oldest Place," and "His Father's Hands" only those clues to his source that appear in the setting or in the snatches of direct translation. Whereas Yeats's rhyme, diction, and Pre-Raphaelite coloring depict the world of Goll and Oisin as antique, literary, and remote from our own, Kinsella's spare diction and dramatic presentation draw us too close to his subject to be comfortable or objective spectators. As in a dream, we experience the speaker's plight before we recognize it. In fact, much of Kinsella's recent poetic recovery of personal and public history can be clarified by the dream-analysis of Carl Jung and by the process Jung calls "individuation." As Jung defines it, individuation requires both the recognition within the self of the arbitrariness of the public persona and a healthy communication between the conscious mind and the personal and collective unconscious.[38]

For this purpose *The Book of Invasions* serves as a metaphor for the collective unconscious; specifically, it represents the Irish nation's collective memory of successive invasions and of the necessity for repossession, as this memory manifests itself in dreamlike images within one individual's consciousness. The sixth wave of invaders, the Celtic Milesians, have driven their predecessors into the underworld, just as Ireland's prehistory has been interred in the racial memory. The poet's descent into himself represented in *Notes from the Land of the Dead* and subsequent poems finds its analogue in a return to the invaders' landing site in Munster, known in Irish legend as "the land of the dead," and a burrowing into the various strata of Irish prehistory. The following excerpt from a long passage in *The Book of Invasions* suggests two other parallels to his own poetry that Kinsella develops:

> The island of Ireland is situated in the west; as the Paradise of Adam
> is situated on the southern coast of the east, so Ireland is in the northern

portion, toward the west. These lands are as similar by nature, as they
are similar by their positions on the earth: for as Paradise hath no nox-
ious beast, so the learned testify that Ireland hath no serpent, lion, toad,
injurious rat. . . . Moreover the country is called Eriu for the heroes.
[Let him who readeth perspire!][39]

First, the curious equation of mirror-opposites supports Kinsella's assumption, and Jung's, that contraries are interdependent. Secondly, the
concluding "Sudet qui legit" is added by a Latin scribe, a redactor of
one of the eleven separate sources from which Macalister's translation
is constructed. Kinsella frequently plays the role of the redactor as he
reviews the past necessarily in terms of the present and splices into legendary material personal asides.[40] For example, consider this interruption of Fintan's soliloquy in Kinsella's "Survivor":

> From Paradise . . .
> In the southern coast of the East . . . In terror
> —we were all thieves. In search of a land without sin
> that might go unpunished, and so prowling
> the known world—the northern portion, toward the West
> (thinking, places answering each other on earth
> might answer in nature).
>                                     (*KP*, 156–57)[41]

The interjection of the parenthetical comment from section 1 of *The
Book of Invasions* into Fintan's monologue, drawn from section 3, can
be attributed to Kinsella's narrator-as-redactor. The redactor makes a
subtler appearance in *One* when Amergin, the narrator and first poet
of the Celtic "race," describes in "Finistere" the invasion of Munster
by his people. As the poet Amergin approaches the shore, he comments,
"I had felt all this before . . . ," suggesting the continuity of the poetic
view through the various invasions' succeeding poets but also insinuating the view of the redactor who has gathered this history of repossession. As Amergin steps on shore, evading the she-hiss of waves, the
first prayer-poem is raised: "'Our Father . . . ', someone said / and there
was a little laughter" (*KPC*, 59). The full ironic inappropriateness of
the Christian paternoster in this maternal, pagan setting could have occurred only to the post-Christian redactor, set in further ironic contrast
to the Romanesque scribe of the original text. Then, Amergin composes from "the old words once more" (*KPC*, 59) Kinsella's version of

the legendary first poem of Ireland. As his poem reaches its inspired peroration, he interrupts himself:

> When men met on the hill
> dumb as stones in the dark
>     (the craft knocked behind me)
> who is the jack of all light?
>
> (*KPC*, 60)

Whereas we attribute the narrative aside concerning the landing-boat to Amergin, the punning comment on inspiration outdistancing poetic skill probably should be ascribed to the redactor. By importing into dramatic poems the various narrative levels of the ancient text, Kinsella intensifies those particular challenges to the reader described as *tone* in chapter 1.

In addition to employing the invasions of Ireland as the collective racial content of his own dreams and memories, he uses the six successive re-takings, numbered 0–5, to structure the stages of his repossession of a personal past. In *Notes,* for which the egg-shaped *0* becomes a thematic glyph, the poet clarifies memories of his earliest childhood among ancient and threatening women, just as Fintan recalls his survival from Cessair and forty-nine other women in the pre-diluvial invasion which was narrated but not counted in *The Book of Invasions*. In *One* and *The Messenger,* Kinsella recalls his masculine succession — grandfather, father, and the emergence of the self. As the title implies, the unfinished *Two* will divide the unit and treat the relation of brothers, perhaps in a Shem-Shaun duality.[42] Kinsella offers the best summary of his own psychological delving and his use of *The Book of Invasions*:

> The things that happened to me happened in Irish contexts. . . . And it is in rooting back into my own identity and finding Irish fathers and grandfathers, Irish history, that my model of the emergence of the psyche would necessarily take Irish forms. Hence it is naturally significant that I would go back and attempt to identify with the legendary first Irish poet Amergin, and speak in his voice, and feel that what I am attempting to do has something to do with primal creation.[43]

The reader's access to Kinsella's poetry was remarkably unobstructed until the publication of *Nightwalker and Other Poems* in 1968. Whereas an archaic formalism often sequestered the poet from his audience, it gave them secure poetic objects to contemplate:

> Some, who have comely daughters, watch
> A spray of God's wit light the gloom,
> A tree of nerves vividly breaking.
> All that drifts into the tomb
> Is a body still or a body speaking.
> ("The Fifth Season" from *Another September*)[44]

Otherwise, the reader was untroubled by tone which remained consistent. If an overreliance on Auden and Yeats, as in the opening and closing, respectively, of the stanza above, forecast another derivative poet, this poet seemed well-grounded in his craft. Beyond these two modern masters, Kinsella echoed Keats (frequently in the 1956 and 1958 volumes), Shelley (as in "Downstream" and "Mirror in February"), and Clarke ("Baggot Street Deserta," "Dick King," "Downstream").[45] His themes were predictably a young man's themes: love, old age, off-season, and, most frequently, the role of the poet. Kinsella's permanent themes, such as evolution and order, also emerge in the early volumes. From the second volume to the present Kinsella has often formed his insights around peripatetic structures, as in the imaginary foray of "Baggot Street Deserta" (in the manner of Clarke's poetry), "Downstream," and "A Country Walk" ("I turned," "Into the final turn," "They turned . . ."). For such spatializing of mundane consciousness Kinsella probably owes something to Eliot and Joyce as well.

Among other important sources for Kinsella's poetry, perhaps the most pervasive and least specific are incidents from his own life.[46] Although his biography rarely is crucial to understanding a poem, some familiarity with his life can confirm a reader's interpretation. The poet's childhood neighborhood becomes the setting for a few early poems, such as "Dick King," and for most poems in *Notes* and *One*. This setting can be reached by proceeding east and west from Ireland's Bastille, Kilmainham jail in west Dublin, along the pastoral Inchichore Road and Kilmainham Lane, bound on the one hand by the gully of the Camac River and on the other by Memorial Park and the Royal Hospital. This enclave provided Kinsella a stable community, some of the quiet and roving spots of the country, but with a gray urban overcast.

The child attended a model national primary school and an O'Connell secondary school where the Irish language and heritage were emphasized. From his interests in science, languages, literature, and geography, he chose science as his course of study for one term at University College Dublin before joining the Civil Service. At night he completed university study in public administration, and at lunch and during other breaks from the Land Office he mixed with a group of day-students with literary interests. At this time he began writing poetry seriously.

In 1951, he met his future publisher Liam Miller and wife Eleanor Walsh, probably the most important influences on his development as a poet. Miller not only eventually published Kinsella's poetry but also instructed him in printing and book-design, organized his first poetry readings, and shared his literary enthusiasms. Kinsella began courting Eleanor Walsh while she was a tuberculosis patient in St. Mary's Hospital in Phoenix Park, visits recollected in his major love poem, "Phoenix Park." From 1960 Eleanor Kinsella revealed the more alarming symptoms of myasthenia gravis which abated under proper medication in 1967. She serves as the model in several poems for the woman whose courage and intuitive insight complement and ease the poet's compulsion for structural order.

Organizational skills advanced Kinsella to a high administrative level in the Ministry of Finance where he assisted T. K. Whitaker, an architect of Ireland's economic recovery in the late 1950s. With Whitaker's help he secured leave in 1963 to consult scholars at Harvard concerning his translation of the *Tain*. During this semester he read at the Poetry Center in New York, encountered a number of American poets, and altered his views of a culture he had once depreciated. Within two years he had left the Irish civil service to fill what was nearly a sinecure at Southern Illinois University which afforded him time for his translation and Eleanor more advanced medical supervision. Three years later he accepted a position at Temple University in Philadelphia, and by developing an Irish Studies program for Temple students in Dublin, he managed to divide his academic year between Philadelphia and his new residence on Percy Place facing Dublin's Grand Canal.

Both migratory directions have influenced the development of Kinsella's poetry. When he first visited America, his formal verse had won him the esteem of Irish critics and readers. Of a handful of serious poets writing in 1962, which included Clarke and Kavanagh, Frank O'Connor remarked that "Kinsella may well be the leader as I suspect he is the artistic conscience."[47] For the publication of *Wormwood* in 1966 he was awarded the Denis Devlin Award for the best volume of Irish poetry over a three-year period. Yet at this time Kinsella was developing the looser forms which eventually would scatter his readership and baffle his staunchest critics, one of whom began a review of Kinsella's masterwork in this manner: "'Notes from the Land of the Dead'—mere 'notes.' Ireland's best living poet has brooded himself to pieces."[48]

The looser forms that Kinsella develops from *Nightwalker* forward express his own phenomenology of perception. As he said in a recent interview,

> I believe the significant work begins in eliciting order from actuality. We're surrounded and penetrated by squalor, disorder and the insignificant, and I believe the artistic impulse has a great deal to do with our trying to make sense out of that.[49]

To accommodate the ordering mind to the reality of the world, Kinsella developed *ad hoc* forms, a practice confirmed by, rather than modeled on, the work of American poets such as Williams, Pound, Roethke, and Lowell. On first moving to America in 1965, Kinsella declared that the "growth point of contemporary poetry" had shifted to America:[50]

> It is out of ourselves and our wills that the chaos came, and out of ourselves that some order will have to be constructed. It is at this point that I have the sense of growth in modern American poetry, the idea of a common front of individual activity, the meristematic area of the poetic organism.[51]

Kinsella asserts that coming to understand in an American context the poetic voice of William Carlos Williams became "the single most helpful thing" in liberating the Irishman from the "entrapment" of traditional forms.[52] Kinsella admires Williams' "creative relaxation in the face of complex reality."[53] Lowell taught him not to tighten the unit of each poem but to leave the doors open to a poetic sequence that develops a progressive experience shared with the audience.[54] Pound affected Kinsella's point of view within the poems by employing a poetic speaker who was intermediate to levels of consciousness and epochs of history, and Roethke demonstrated that the autobiographical subject could be explored independently of the confessional mode.

If emigration led Kinsella to more flexible forms, repatriation confirmed him in his subjects and themes. His own retaking of Ireland, with his recovery of childhood memories, finds its parallel in *The Book of Invasions,* as we have seen. Furthermore, with the help of scholars interested in Gaelic, such as Proinsias MacCana, Liam de Paor, and Sean O Tuama, Kinsella has sharpened his skills as a translator and drawn his English-speaking culture into contact with the Gaelic matrix, what Kinsella has called parts of "our imaginative bedrock."[55]

Before examining individual poems, we must consider one other change in Kinsella's poetry which appeared in the *Nightwalker* volume. Within poems and in an interview, Kinsella has applied the term "allegory" to his shift from observation to speculation or commentary on that observation. For example recently he said,

> The obsession with fact, with specific individual data, wouldn't seem to me to make much sense unless it had some allegorical drive behind it. Experience by itself, however significant, won't do.[56]

Although poems such as "Death in Ilium" and "Soft Toy" express reasonable skepticism about human objectivity, Kinsella nevertheless wants to distinguish between observation and the ordering of observation through abstraction and generalization. In the early poetry, Kinsella occasionally used anachronistic personifications from Christian allegory to make an ironic point. By *Nightwalker* the word allegory had lost its moral associations. As he uses the term in one poem, "Ballydavid Pier," it seems to indicate merely the coexistence of different levels of thought, in this case particular observation and scientific generalization. The generalizations in this poem seem related to those of Pierre Teilhard de Chardin who sees in the ageless evolutionary process some promise of a higher moral order. Without fully subscribing to Teilhard's evolutionary teleology, Kinsella considers the phenomenon of the individual in relation to the vast evolutionary processes, and wonders at both.

Of the process of each life, he says,

> Being born, growing up, learning, maturing, procreating, decaying, extinguishing: it's an astonishing process. We take cover from it by being busy. . . . On the other hand, certain things force awareness on us and

we sense our predicament for exactly what it is. The deaths of beloved people. . . . Once you understand that life is portioned out, your concentration on it, if you're lucky, increases and you don't waste it. . . .[57]

Kinsella's poems, then, become acts of attention to life in process. Just as the process of growing and dying elicits Kinsella's wonder, so too do both the individual's futile but relentless efforts to impose order on life and the collective record of these intellectual attempts we call our "civilization."[58]

Both life's process and intellectual processes become the explicit subjects of "Ballydavid Pier," the poem in *Nightwalker* that introduced readers to the radical shifts in Kinsella's form, tone, and type of "allegorical" speculation. The poem is set in a fishing village on the tip of the Dingle peninsula, on the west coast of Ireland, at noon, the boundary between morning and afternoon. From an intermediate position on a pier, an observer watches the tide advance on the shore where he sees "a film of scum / . . . / cloudy with (I remember) / Life . . ." (*KP,* 80–81). The parenthetical comment, a recollection that the earth's first life formed in such a sea broth, calls attention to what the "redactor" is adding to the empirical description. He then looks into the shallows beneath him before glancing toward deeper water where he observes "a bag of flesh, / Foetus of goat or sheep." The poem dramatizes the observer's thoughts as he attempts to rationalize this intermediate life, which has experienced neither birth nor death. The poem progresses through five stanzas of a variable number of three- or four-beat lines. In the second stanza, the speaker claims, "Allegory forms of itself," as the harbor divides into three stages: the advancing life-bearing scum, the clarity following its wake, and waste that cannot share in this advance. The poem could be a dramatization of the evolutionary concepts of Teilhard who contemplates the "pattern defined by the following properties: constantly increasing unification, centration, and spiritualization—the whole system rising unmistakably toward a critical point of final convergence," as he soon reminds us that "the tide of consciousness of which we form a part is not produced simply by some impulse that originates in ourselves."[59]

The speaker then addresses the foetus in the third stanza:

> Small monster of true flesh
> Brought forth somewhere

In bloody confusion and error
And flung into bitterness,
Blood washed white:
Does that structure satisfy?

Of course the question, concerning whether or not allegorical structures can justify wasted lives, is also asked of the reader. The fourth and fifth stanzas conclude the poem:

The ghost tissue hangs unresisting
In allegorical waters,
Lost in self-search
—A swollen blind brow
Humbly crumpled over
Budding limbs, unshaken
By the spasms of birth or death.

The Angelus. Faint bell-notes
From some church in the distance
Tremble over the water.
It is nothing. The vacant harbour
Is filling; it will empty.
The misbirth touches the surface
And glistens like quicksilver.

Apparently describing the foetus, the fourth stanza actually represents the idea of the foetus in the "allegorical waters" of the observer's mind. It is this unborn idea, rather than the bag of flesh whose features are submerged, that is "lost in self-search" and which remains embryonic. The thought of this creature defines itself only ironically, as a modern biological counterpoint to the Angelus, a summons of believers to contemplate the mystery of the Incarnation. In such a place this summons, "faint bell notes," is "nothing." Cycles of life and death continue. In the final line the surfacing misbirth assumes like quicksilver a visual vitality that belies its inertness. As the short-*e* recurrences parallel the visual glistening, the ordering poetic mind gives momentary life to an accidental residue of life's processes.

In a study of the psychic opposites as represented in alchemy, Jung associates quicksilver with Mercurius and with Nous, "wisdom . . . that lies hidden and bound in matter. . . ."[60] "Those mortals who wished to attain consciousness could renew themselves in this baptismal bath.

. . . Its maternal aspect as the matrix and 'muse of all things' makes it an unsurpassable analogy of the unconscious."[61] Should we read in the poem's final word a reference to alchemy or to a Jungian interpretation of alchemy, then this final image of the misbirth takes on a particularly bitter irony.

With eight to ten equally effective short poems and three remarkable long poems, *Nightwalker and Other Poems,* with *Notes from the Land of the Dead,* is one of the least conventional volumes ever published in Ireland, and therefore one of the most difficult to characterize. For example, in the title poem, "Nightwalker," the narrator rambles through a coastal suburb of Dublin which is transformed by a sinister moonlight. The moon, suggestive of the predatory muse of earlier poems, threatens to invade the earth's atmosphere or draw the speaker from it. Glimpses of scenes or echoes of lines from *Paradise Lost, Sorrows of Werther,* Yeats's poetry, Synge's plays, and the works of other writers brush across the baroque narration as in a literate dream, like Earwicker's in *Finnegans Wake.*

Joyce becomes, in fact, an overseer in the poem, whom the nightwalker invokes within or behind or beyond or above a setting that could be Joyce's: "Watcher in the tower, be with me now / . . . / Turn your milky spectacles on the sea . . ." (*KP,* 108). Joyce may also be present as an influence in those metaphors Kinsella employs in "Nightwalker" and later poetry that provide rapid transport between modes of perceiving our private world — sexual, anatomical, psychological — and modes of perceiving or structuring shared experiences — history, myth, the commercial urban conventions. For example, in "Nightwalker" the speaker reminds us with phrases such as "musing thus" that these metaphorical hinges are merely opening different levels of his own thoughts: we track him easily as he observes televiewers, then imagines them to be, first, spirits in a Necropolis and, next, larvae in a waxen hive. In one passage (*KP,* 105), the nightwalker, observing the Gemini, remembers the German twins who consulted him that morning about investing in Irish land. He recalls their faces, "livid with little splashes of blazing fat." The next statement, "The oven door closes," forms an inevitable but complex poem-in-itself which evokes fables about acquisition and burning such as the Nibelungenlied, Hansel and Gretel, and the rationalization of the Jewish holocaust. The transitions of "Nightwalker" are suppressed in the later poems where these various levels of response are presented dramatically, often in disjoined sections of the poem. The reader must move into the narrative center, draw relations, and allow himself to be reminded of significance as it has evolved elsewhere in the series.

Whether or not Joyce influenced Kinsella's hinged images, his character Stephen provides a foil for the nightwalker who eavesdrops on the seamew's song. As Maurice Harmon points out, the seamew sings a portion of Amergin's song, a version of which appears in Kinsella's "Finistere," which we have discussed.[62] The scene echoes the close of *A Portrait* where gulls cry to their brother-in-flight Dedalus: "Come. And the voices say with them: We are your kinsmen. And the air is thick with their company, as they call to me, their kinsman, making ready to go . . ." (*JP*, 252). Conversely, to the seamews' invitation the nightwalker replies:

> A dying language echoes
> Across a century's silence.
> It is time
> Lost soul, I turned for home.
>
> (*KP*, 111)

Like Joyce himself, Kinsella aspires to understand and thereby repossess home, family, and his own childhood.

His homing instinct finds expression in "Phoenix Park," a love poem for which three other lines from "Nightwalker" are also prologue: "I believe now that love is half persistence, / A medium in which, from change to change, / Understanding may be gathered" (*KP*, 112). In lieu of the love song for which the woman asks, "Phoenix Park" offers "one positive dream," a crystalized understanding, ultimately expressed in poetry, of the lovers' past ordeals. He remembers his lover's confinement to a tuberculosis sanitorium in Dublin's Phoenix Park, where like Prince Charming or Sigfried he dared to approach her through enclosing glass and her consuming fever.

As "preparation" for the "positive dream," he recalls himself and his daughter as infants stooping like Persephone to eat some deadly fruit and to enter into a relationship with death. In our great hunger for life, the poem asserts, we eat our way toward death through a series of ordeals. Although the meaning and understanding of these ordeals, when shared within the medium of love, may crystalize into "laws of order" crowded "with light," the couple must recognize that the initial impulse to life, the principle of hunger, is finally not valuable in itself but a terrifying phantasm "who'll come painfully in old lewd nakedness" (*KP*, 121). By association, the fiery fever that consumed the patient creates an ordeal that she must overcome in her hunger for life. As an ambiguous sign of life's hunger, fire itself is interpreted by darkness. His hunger for order leads the speaker to a spatialized vision of the cycles of the Phoenix's self-conflagration:

> The orders of stars fixed in abstract darkness,
> Darknesses of worlds sheltering in their light;
> World darkness harbouring orders of cities,
> Whose light at midnight harbours human darkness;
> The human dark pierced by solitary fires . . .
>
> (*KP*, 125)

The solitary human fires may "gutter and fail" returning us to the initial darkness of the abstract, earthly, and human nights.

In the final stanza, the human tongue, which is associated with the serpent and man's knowledge of death, begins to feed on the darkness in order to form and articulate life:

> A snake out of the void moves in my mouth, sucks
> At triple darkness. A few ancient faces
> Detach and begin to circle. Deeper still,
> Delicate distinct tissue begins to form,
>
> (*KP*, 126)

This coda, which also becomes the opening four lines of the prologue to the three acts of *Notes from the Land of the Dead,* gains resonance from a symbol on the title page of this later volume. A broken zero represents both an egg and the uroboros, a snake ingesting its own tail. As uroboros, the *0* signifies nous, the potential, male wisdom inherent in the world[63] and, implicitly, in the boy who is the subject of this volume. The fifth line in this prologue-poem — "hesitate, cease to exist, glitter again" — suggests the volume's three stumbling stages, as recalled by the poet, of the child's development — threatened preconsciousness, torpid emergence, and the child's first continuous self-awareness.

The prologue-poem itself prepares us for the poet's descent in the semi- and preconscious world of his dreams and earliest memories. In the manner of Goethe's Faust or the Irish poetic caste, the *filid,* the poet enacts a ritual and reclines in the dark before descending into his subject. Like an egg losing its protective shell, he falls into his unconscious self where he encounters ancient women, the Irish cailleach, like MacBeth's witches guarding a cauldron. This vat, presumably, contains the pottage of his earliest childhood experiences. These women also represent, as Rosenberg argues, the *anima* which, as Jung defined it, is "an imprint or 'archetype' of all the ancestral experiences of the female" which every man carries within him.[64] Although threatening when repressed,[65] the *anima,* when integrated into consciousness, can give "relationship and relatedness" to man.[66] In the first stage of *Notes,* the old woman is a terrifying protectress of his childhood memories. With the aid of a key —wand, pen, penis, knife—he fends off the cailleach and recovers the cauldron from which he draws the subjects of his sequence.

*Notes from the Land of the Dead,* and indeed the series that unfolds from "Nightwalker" on, is an analogue to Jung's process of individuation: Jung commented that "one understands nothing psychological unless one has experienced it oneself";[67] Kinsella presents these memories dramatically, involving the reader in the experience. Furthermore, whereas "the secret of psychic development can never be betrayed, simply because the development is a question of individual capacity,"[68] it can be presented metaphorically. For this purpose, Kinsella reminds us, through allusions, that his loss of the protective shell of his persona and his descent into the self enact an ancient paradox and one story retold in most cultures. According to the paradox, expressed by Christ and other seers, we must die to be born again. Buddha's parable of the egg reminds us that the actual birth occurs not at the appearance of the egg but at its breaking. The shaman risks re-entering a cavern and descending into the underworld in order to lead his soul back to light,[69] as Orpheus descended for Eurydice or as Demeter, disguised as an old woman, and Hecate, her lunar character, await Kore's (Persephone's) release from the underworld.[70] The motif of the hero's descent into hell to recover soul, wisdom, or crucial information, called the *nekyia,*[71] recurs in Christ's descent into hell, Odysseus's visit to his mother among the shades, Dante's tour of hell and purgatory, and Faust's *walpurgisnacht,* as well as in countless other legends. Although Kinsella challenges his readers to ransack their learning, his recovery of personal memories and Irish legend against a background of the world's mythologies finally seems practically exoteric.

Kinsella's ability to enfold his reader in psychologized experiences which resonate with mythical allusions and references accumulated within the series constitutes his prime achievement. As a substitution for the reader's own experience of the series, I will refer to one incident in the celebrated poem "Hen Woman" which follows the prologue-poem. The poem recovers a simple event: the poet recalls the child watching a neighbor rush from her cottage, seize a hen about to lay an egg, fumble the emerging egg, and then comment resignedly when the egg breaks, "It's all the one. / There's plenty more where that came from!" (*KP*, 137) The reader observes immediately the parallels between this hen-woman and the *cailleachs* in the surrounding poems. The egg and cave motives amplify meaning in the hen-yard:

> The cottage door opened
> a black hole
> in a whitewashed wall so bright
> the eyes narrowed.
>
> > (*KP*, 134)

as does the volume's signature, a zero-glyph, and the Phoenix idea of light being created from darkness:

> The black zero of the orifice
> closed to a point
> and the white zero of the egg hung free,
> > (*KP*, 135)

The slow-motion fall of the egg re-enacts, or is re-enacted by, the poet's descent into himself in the prologue:

> it floated outward, moon-white,
> leaving no trace in the air,
> and began its drop to the shore.

The reflections of the complex psychic descent in the simple domestic fumble yields one of the poem's pleasurable complexities. The extensive commentary on the simple act establishes the primary relation not between the woman and hen but between the mature poet and a scene that has incubated in his memory for many years.

Rosenberg seems to have identified most of the allusions in the poem, explaining, for example, that the brief epilogue — "Hen to pan! / It was a simple world." (*KP*, 137) — is derived from a gnostic motto which appeared with the symbol of the tail-swallowing snake to suggest the ultimate unity of life's processes. She also discusses the following brief interlude in the drama:

> There was a tiny movement at my feet
> tiny and mechanical; I looked down.
> A beetle like a bronze leaf
> was inching across the cement,
> clasping with small tarsi
> a ball of dung bigger than its body.
> The serrated brow pressed the ground humbly,
> lifted in a short stare, bowed again;
> the dung-ball advanced minutely,
> losing a few fragments,
> specks of staleness and freshness.
>
> (*KP*, 135)

In Egyptian mythology, the god of the rising sun, Khepri, appeared as a scarab-beetle perambulating its eggs in a dung-ball.[72] Symbolizing for the Egyptian "the renewal of life and the idea of eternal existence,"[73] the beetle also functions in "Hen Woman" as a comic analogue to the poet. As the self-preoccupied poet has recovered the cauldron of memories, so this insect struggles with the waste-enclosed larvae, its future concealed within its past, in a compound of Sisyphus's task and Ajax's Augean labors. The reader's ability to appreciate the self-mockery, which in this case enriches rather than deflates the allusive significance of the beetle, becomes another challenge of tone.

Reminded of the significance of certain mythological figures, such as Hecate, Selene, Orpheus, and Persephone and their attendant symbols — moon, owl, pomegranate — and armed with some knowledge of *The Book of Invasions,* the reader can begin to enjoy the resonant interrelation of poems in the three sections of *Notes.* For a condensed example of this serial interplay, we can begin with "Endymion," from the second section, which like the following poem "Survivor," places its title-

character in a cave. Although the hen-sphincter and womb-cave spawn
life in earlier poems, in section two the cave only harbors the potential
life of the moon's lover and of Fintan. As the goddess of the waxing
moon, Selene, bends toward Endymion, the cave's light kindles "from
the interplay of our two beings," but when she "straightened up," the
moon passes into its waning phase, governed by the more predatory
Hecate in her owl-form:[74]

> and the ruddy walls with their fleshy thickenings
> —great raw wings, curled—a huge owlet-stare—
> as a single drop echoed in the depths.
>
> (*KP,* 154)

The cave, from which the human has not awakened, nurtures the life-
cycles of the moon-goddess, muse, and anima, but the only sign of human life is the seminal drop, which, we learn from "Crossroads," is
also the owl's predatory drop on its prey. This negative contact between
anima/muse and the cave-dweller precedes his awakening and ascent
which begins in section three of *Notes.*

The difficult opening poem of this section, "All Is Emptiness, /And
I Must Spin," sets its subject in a modern version of Fintan's and Endymion's enclosures: an H-Block shack, Gulag cell, or the St. Stephen's
psychiatric ward of which Austin Clarke wrote. Although promise is
truncated in the closing lines—

> Fantastic millions of
> fragile
> in every

—in this aposiopesis hope resides in the words omitted: *droplets* and
*drop,* which from prior poems we know signifiy seed and the dispersed
psyche.

In the final poem, after the turn toward home in the attractive "Liffey Hill," the boy enters his own bed where the adult voices from an
adjoining room intersperse with his encroaching dream. As in the *Nightwalker* poem "Before Sleep" and the prologue-poem from *Notes,* he de-
scends "to a drowned pit," a "nothingness / inhabited by a vague animal light / from the walls and floor" (*KP,* 172). Life begins to form
in this dream-pit as crystals formed in the ordeal-cup of "Phoenix Park"

and foetuses appeared in the caves of section two. Here, the images have a remarkable anatomical quality as if the sleeping boy with "ear pounding— / peering eye apples, unseeing" were observing details of his own slumbering body:

> and (faintly lit from within)
> clusters of soft arms gathering down
> tiny open eyes, finger-tips, pursed
> mouths from the gloom, minute
> drifting corruscations of light, glistening
> little gnat-crescents of hair!
>
> (*KP,* 172)

Perhaps in response to the adults' wakeful homilies—". . . would you agree, then we won't / find truths, or any certainties . . ."—the poet records the boy's unconscious discovery:

> we cannot know them, . . .
> daylit, we are the monsters of our night,
> and somewhere the monsters of our night are . . .
> here . . . in daylight that our nightnothing
> feeds in and feeds, wandering
> out of the cavern . . .
>
> (*KP,* 173)

The enfolding of his conscious and unconscious lives suggests the alternation of light and dark in the Phoenix-vision of "Phoenix Park." Because "the unconscious processes stand in compensatory relation to the conscious mind," as Jung said, an understanding of this dream-wisdom will allow the poet to divest himself "of the suggestive power of primordial images"[75] which educes the speaker's "blood vision" in "Ely Place" and, perhaps, "Sacrifice." The volume concludes when the speaker emerges "out of the cavern" and "ungulfs a Good Night, smiling," a positive step in his repossession of the past.

Much of Kinsella's poetry since *Nightwalker* stands aside from this repossession of self and homeland and comments indirectly on the sequence: by examining the craft of poetry, considering parallel situations of other artist-thinkers, such as Jung or Mahler, or, as in *Technical Supplement,* by exorcising "the blood vision" that rises from the concentrated foreknowledge of evil Jung calls "the shadow" or from the suppressed anima. The sequence develops over a decade from "Nightwalker" in 1968 through "Phoenix Park" to *Notes, One,* the second half of *Technical Supplement* to *The Messenger* in 1978.[76] Because the poems of *The Messenger* in themselves form an evident sequence, they confirm in miniature Kinsella's larger, evolving intentions. Consequently, examinations of poems in *One,* such as "38 Phoenix Street" and "His Father's Hands," and in *Technical Supplement,* volumes that have entered into our discussion, must be postponed for a more spacious study of Kinsella's verse.

In *The Messenger,* Kinsella's most recent *Peppercanister* chapbook, the poet seeks in his father's life compensation for the sour last years and the nightmare image of his corpse. Kinsella's intention is rather like Roethke's in "The Lost Son" sequence ("I've seen my father's face before / Deep in the belly of a thing to be,") as characterized by Charles Molesworth: Roethke makes "the father something realizable instead of given, a future to be grown toward rather than a past to be fled."[77]

As in *One, The Messenger* begins with an awakening. Dreams have brought him "Something to discourage goodness":

> A dead egg glimmers—a pearl in muck
> glimpsed only as the muck settles.
> The belly settles and crawls tighter.
>
> (*KPC,* 119)

He also recalls the grating comment of a well-wisher at his father's funeral:

> "His father before him . . . Ah, the barge captain . . .
> A valued connection. He will be well remembered . . .
> He lived in his two sons."
>
> (*KPC,* 122)

To rebut this suggestion that the father was merely an intermediate between grandfather and grandchildren, the poet reverses life's process where "hour follows hour" and regresses stage by stage to the father's childhood.

First, he recalls the father's final years when the father had absorbed into his psyche unfulfilled aspirations of his youth. These form a hard cyst of disappointment which the poet retrieves as he would a pearl from its bed.

The poem regresses through courageous moments in his father's political career to the evening of the poet's conception beside a Wicklow river with a dragonfly as witness, then to a scene in the grandfather's cobbler shop: "Son and father, upright, right arms raised. / Stretching a thread. Trying to strike right." Finally, the poem arrives at the climax, an account of his father's first day of employment, as a messenger boy. If the book were arranged chronologically, the description of the boy's bright eyes and keen aspirations might form the opening chapter in the sort of nineteenth-century *bildungsroman* by Butler, or even Flaubert, that can lead only to disappointment, decay, and death. However, this narrative recedes to its heroic climax:

> Deeper. The room where they all lived
> behind the shop. It is dark here too—shut off
> by the narrow yard. But it doesn't matter:
>
> it is bustling with pleasure.
> A new messenger boy
> stands there in uniform, with shining belt!
>
> He is all excitement: arms akimbo,
> a thumb crooked by the telegram pouch,
> shoes polished, and a way to make in the world.
>
> His eyes are bright,
> his schoolmaster's tags fresh in mind.
> He has a few of the Gentlemen's Sixpenny Library
>
> under the bed—*A Midsummer Night's Dream,*
> *Sartor Resartus, The Divine Comedy,* with a notebook,
> Moore's *Melodies,* a trifle shaken. . . . Shelley, unbound . . .
>
> he unprops the great Post Office bicycle
> from the sewing machine and wheels it through the passage
> by odours of apron and cabbage-water and whitewashed damp
>
> through the shop and into the street.
> It faces uphill. The urchin mounts. I see
> a flash of pedals! And a clean pair of heels!
>
> (*KPC,* 133)

By running the film of the life in reverse, the poet frees his father's youthful figure from historical causality, making of him a type of fresh beginnings and human aspirations. The tactful humor of "a way to make in the world," of the list of the child's reading, and of the final line, suggest in a reversal of roles, the poet's fatherly love for this boy. We see the boy as less the intermediate between generations than the typal go-between, the messenger Mercury whose picture faces the poem. We might be reminded that Mercury, or Hermes, invented the lyre which he never played but passed on to Apollo.[78]

On the final page of *The Messenger,* when the poem cycles back to the funeral, the father's death has also been transformed to a sort of beginning:

> He rolled on rubber tyres
> out of the chapel door. The oak box
> paused gleaming in the May morning air
>
> and turned, sensing its direction.
> Our scattered tribe began gathering itself
> and trudged off onto a gravel path after if.
>
> By their own lightness
> four girls and three boys separated themselves
> in a ragged band out from our dull custom
>
> and moved up close after it, in front,
> all shapes and sizes,
> grandchildren, colourful and silent.
>
> (*KPC,* 134)

As does the larger series, in miniature *The Messenger* answers Kinsella's own appeal, fifteen years ago, for "an exploration into the interior to find what may guide us in the future."[79] Such Jungian introspection entails a regressive method, beginning with the present and stepping both backward and inward. *The Messenger*'s transitions support this: "It is outside . . . ," "Inside . . . ," "Deeper . . ." mark three stages of regression. If it is out of ourselves that history came, then also we contain within ourselves the pattern of the past.

To represent this relation of self to world, Kinsella employs hinged images that suddenly open the partition between the present and past, as I have shown, and between the subject and the object, such as the dragonfly that witnesses the parents' coition at the moment of the poet's conception. As the seed enters the womb, "a gossamer ghost" floats overhead, his "body, a glass worm, is pulsing."[80] Like the egg-seed, this dragonfly contains at this moment the code of its past existences, as larva, cocoon, and imago. The poem's advance through the stages of the poet's recovery—from nightmare of the body's putrescence and vulnerability to the resplendent image of fresh beginnings—has its analogue in the dragonfly's rise from slime into "insect-shimmering" beauty:

> Trailing a sunless instinct,
> a saw-jawed multiple past,
> an edible (almost liquid)
> vulnerability,
> and winged!—weightless and wondrous!—
> up from the bloodied slime
> through the arms of a black rainbow
> scooping down in beauty
> he has come, he has arisen
> out of the pool of night!
>
> (*KPC*, 129)

Such intricate matching of part to whole—here, the microscopic image to the macroscopic process of the volume—extends to the relation of the volume to the sequence, although the complexity and inclusiveness of the sequence requires our faith on this point. The pleasure in reading Kinsella arises from the resonance among parts of his work, between a part and the whole process of repossession, and among parts of Kinsella's and related works. In attention to sequence, he seems, on occasion, to lose coherence, becoming too fragmentary, as in the conclusion of "Survivor" which Calvin Bedient criticized. However, when we recognize the dramatic nature of his poetry and learn to identify which poetic self is speaking—the anima-muse, the redactor, the order-seeking poet—or which character, then even fragmentary patches often seem appropriate. Furthermore, one can argue that Kinsella has drawn the fragmentary and inchoate into art, reminding the critic that such aspects of real discourse as muttered words, broken syntax, and fragmentary sentences have their legitimatizing classical tags: parataxis, anacoluthon, and aposiopesis, if you will. Although Kinsella has written as lyrically as any Irish poet in poems such as "The Shoals Returning," he can relinquish graceful phrasing to manifest the truth of the turbulent world and its shadow psyche.

Perhaps the best summary assessment of this major poet is Heaney's, who seems graciously to offer Kinsella the bays:

> Kinsella is by now I suppose his own firm and major man. He is the poet who affirms an Irish modernity, particularly in his treatment of psychic material which is utterly Irish Catholic. In this sense he is somewhat akin to the Joyce of *The Dubliners* who found a form for that unspoken world. Kinsella has found a language which is both at ease with exemplars like Joyce and Eliot, and also capable of speaking very much out of his own world and intellect. . . .[81]

## CHAPTER THREE

# Kavanagh & Heaney

Patrick Kavanagh (1904–67) has influenced recent poetry in Ireland more than any Irish writer after Yeats and Joyce, and, with Beckett and Flann O'Brien, he remains the writer immediately after Joyce who can still steam up a literary discussion. Even dispassionate critics of his verse, should such exist, could find themselves arguing about different bodies of poetry, so uneven are his *Complete Poems* and so erratically selected his *Collected Poems.*[1] While culling our own thin, essential selection from the *Complete Poems,* we recognize that even the appearance of a slender, judiciously selected volume, which we have long needed, would never muffle the extra-textual wrangling concerning both the poet's life—his peasant origins in County Monaghan, his outcast status in Dublin, his strident journalism, his attitude toward women, his libel suit, his public drunkenness, his untimely death—and his value as a liberating model relative to Austin Clarke's, or his successors'.

So pure, frail, and simple is Kavanagh's gift that it can easily slip out of focus for critics, as it did for Kavanagh himself during the decade following 1942. We apply the term *lyric* to Kavanagh's poetry only synesthetically, as a metaphor for his especially lucid vision. He can incarnate the beauty of common people and things so freshly that he evokes ideas of creation and of creators, poetic and providential. Coleridge's characterization of the poetic act—"as if all had then sprang forth at the first creative fiat"[2]—exactly describes the effect of certain Kavanagh lyrics. Critics who offer praise, such as "The 'business of love' is Kavanagh's fundamental concern,"[3] recognize that his poems depict not merely images but a relationship which weds the creative, mirroring mind with the beloved object.

As in most marriages, Kavanagh's poetic relationship includes a familial support, a third party comprised of the audience which he at-

tends carefully. In an excerpt from "Wisdom," written while Kavanagh
was recovering from the removal of a cancerous lung in 1955, he characterizes, rather than exhibits, the ingredients of his poetry:

> Isn't it extraordinary to have discovered
> That a man who has read, thought, suffered
> More than many and has met
> Thousands of interesting people yet
> Can only offer to the hungry mass
> Unkempt water and the immortality of grass.
>
> (*KCP,* 279)

For several productive years after this operation, Kavanagh would return to his lyric gift rather than develop a narrative, drama, or myth
that validates what he has "read, thought, suffered." Having "no system, no plan / Yeatsian invention" (*KCP,* 330) and lacking "an ancient
saga for . . . instrument" (*KCP,* 335), Kavanagh could dispense with
elaborate strategies of tone, complex historical relations, or the complexities of self.

His best poetry will "name" the forms of nature, "unkempt water
and the immortality of grass." Elsewhere he declares, "I simply choose
to name / Something not hitherto involved with time" (*KCP,* 299) and
"Sufficient to name these things / That knew the immortal part in me"
(*KCP,* 255) and "Naming these things is the love act and its pledge"
(*KCP,* 280). In rhymes such as "discovered / suffered," he will imitate
the fluid "unkemptness" of nature or represent the tension between the
forms of poetic perception — sonnets, stanzas, rhymes — and the unbound
emergency of nature.

Less explicitly than in "Wisdom," Kavanagh's poems will address an
audience, "the hungry mass." Echoing this phrase, Kavanagh once wrote
of the poet, "It is the pressure of a people's need for a voice which is
his power."[4] In the final issue of *Kavanagh's Weekly,* the short-lived journal Patrick founded with his brother Peter to instruct his readership,
Kavanagh said, "An audience makes a writer as much as a writer makes
an audience."[5]

In this characterization of Kavanagh's poetry through six lines of
"Wisdom," we digress only a little away to wonder if *mass,* rather than
*masses,* is selected to relate the readership to poetic ritual and to a com-

munity celebrating the incarnation of spirit. Yet, the misplaced *only* warns us of the slackness of this poem and suggests that *mass* was selected merely to rhyme with *grass* (*grasses* would have subdivided the genus). Unlike Heaney, Kavanagh often ignores secondary meanings of words, evoking them only when he cares to tune the language of the entire poem. In such poems, associations hidden in Kavanagh's religious and communal sense of language emerge, almost intuitively. His comment on Auden indicates his own hit-or-miss approach to composition: "There is something of the prospector's luck about a great poet's success."[6]

The final ingredient of a Kavanagh poem is "a man who . . . offers" images of water and grass. Within the poetry Kavanagh represents himself generically as poet and seer rather than merely autobiographically. With the exception of a few sections of the esteemed narrative poem *The Great Hunger* and a few other poems, we receive from Kavanagh's poetry an impression of the mirroring poetic mind or the poet's statement about his relation to the image. At times we recognize that the poet is too remote from the object, or too enmeshed with it, so that focus on the poetic relationship is blurred. Kavanagh defined poetry as "a point of view," and, suggesting the Romanticist metaphor of the poet as source of light, he wrote: "To look on is enough / In the business of love. . . . To have a point of view which is a man poised with a torch."[7]

Kavanagh's poetic successes occur when he is able to focus his point of view—more specifically, when he balances the distances between speaker, object, and audience represented within the poem. We turn, then, to questions of *tone,* in this case not elaborate dramatic strategies but the adjustments Kavanagh made over three stages of his life to focus the poetic relationship.

Kavanagh's career fulfills the Romanticist dialectic by progressing from thesis (innocence or primal sympathy) through antithesis (experience, human suffering) to a synthesis (radical innocence, the philosophic mind). Kavanagh's own description of this dialectic may be adapted from Blake, whom he often echoes: "There are two kinds of simplicity, the simplicity of going away and the simplicity of return."[8] Kavanagh embodied this "simplicity of going away" in his major work before 1943: *Ploughman and Other Poems* (1936), his fictionalized autobiography *The*

*Green Fool* (1938), *The Great Hunger* (1942), and two other long poems written before the end of 1942, most of which work reflects his ambivalence toward his simple gift. Kavanagh suffered through a second stage, a decade of reviews and criticism, sour satirical poems, one novel *Tarry Flynn* (1948),[9] and a few lyrics of quality. Finally, facing the failure of his satirical journal, libel, and weakening health, Kavanagh began a reformation of his poetic powers around 1952 that became evident in 1955.

Kavanagh's uncertain control of point of view and his social alienation, obvious in his criticism of the forties and early fifties, actually appear during his poetic apprenticeship in Inniskeen, Monaghan, some fifty miles northwest of Dublin on the border of the Six Counties. On farms too cribbed for agricultural planning, the principal crops were potatoes, turnips, cabbage, and grass. These rocky drumlins were an unlikely cradle for poetry according to *The Green Fool*:

> There was no love for beauty. We were barbarians just emerged from the Penal days. The hunger had killed our poetry. . . .[10]

In such a setting, the peculiar sort who took language away from the easy rounds of hedge gossip to the privacy of desk or bed was looked on with suspicion: "In the country places of Ireland writing is held up in certain awe: a writer was a dangerous man from whom they instinctively recoiled."[11] Such suspicion has its justification: the wonderful Brueghel-like peopled landscapes in *The Green Fool* were not developed by overapplying the hoe or ploughing straight furrows, and a man so attentive to his neighbors' idioms and intonations probably has not provided his fair share of the local news. Both *The Green Fool* and *Tarry Flynn* recount the hero's growing sense of estrangement from his people.

The word *poet* recurs from the earliest of the poetry, and a certain literariness suggests that Kavanagh took as much time reading dead or distant poets as hearing his neighbors. Years later he confessed, "When a country body begins to progress into a world of print he does not write out of his rural innocence—he writes out of Palgrave's *Golden Treasury*."[12] Kavanagh's attic room in Inniskeen must have also housed poetry by Herrick ("Not yet half-drest / O tardy bride!"), Blake ("For you are driving your horses through . . ."),[13] and, in spite of his own disclaimers, Yeats. Presumably accepting the testimony of *The Green Fool*, Alan Warner asserts that Kavanagh had not read Yeats in 1929.[14]

Yet, in that year, this Monaghan apprentice-cobbler wrote the following imperative: "Speak no more / A thread-worn story," and soon echoed Yeats in other poems.[15]

Yet, even in the early derivative poetry we often encounter the Kavanagh signature: precise observation and rhythm and diction adjusted to the broken music of his parish. If we compare an earlier portrayer of the "peasantry," Padraic Colum, we can assess this new note. Colum describes the native poet and the poem's gestation:

> And I could hear,
> The door being open, certain birds that flew
> Between the clouds and bog, and I could hear
> The cattle moving in the byre, the horses
> Stirring in their short sleeps, and while I sat,
> My mind took to itself a murmuring,
> And there were words that it was fitted to,
> Words that turned in furrows or in verses,
> And took shape, and went with certainty
> Among surprises, and became a poem.[16]

These lines accommodate themselves to the mind's "murmuring" rather than to the sounds of night, excepting perhaps the lovely descriptions of the horses, "stirring in their short sleeps." Everything is generic—cattle, horses, bog, poet—befitting a writer who knows the etymology of *verses* but cannot specify what bird flies at night.

To depict the Gaelic poet parturient with the word, Kavanagh recalls the actual poet of the South Ulster school, Art McCooey, whom he locates in the townland of Shancoduff.[17] Although earlier in his poem Colum names various tasks, none appears with such memorable pungency as McCooey's carting of dung: "The steam rising from the load is still / Warm enough to thaw my frosty fingers."[18] Although he overloads the final stanza with adverbs, they enforce the mystery of the poetic occupation in contrast with the detailed account of the dung trade. The lines adjust to the rhythm of the work:

> Wash out the cart with a bucket of water and a wangel
> Of wheaten straw. Jupiter looks down.
> Unlearnedly and unreasonably poetry is shaped
> Awkwardly but alive in the unmeasured womb.
>
> (*KCP*, 77–8)

By observing detail and adjusting rhythm to the harshness of work, rather than to an ideal, Kavanagh's poem seems set in a fallen world whereas Colum's poet, like his other characters, is sanctified by his peasant state.

Kavanagh rarely contrives a persona such as McCooey. Presenting himself as the poet, he achieves in his best poems a balance between detachment and specificity, love and indifference, which characterizes this stage which he called "the simplicity of going away." Perhaps his most satisfying poems of this first stage are "Shancoduff" (1934) and "Inniskeen Road: July Evening" (1935), both of which portray the poet's ambivalence about his poetic situation.

"Shancoduff" opens with a reminder that *dubh* (black) often suffixes the names of northern-facing mountains[19] (Shanco*bane,* white Shanco, slopes southward behind Shancoduff):

> My black hills have never seen the sun rising,
> Eternally they look north towards Armagh.
> Lot's wife would not be salt if she had been
> Incurious as my black hills . . .
>
> > (*KCP,* 13)

These lines explicitly identify the poet with the dark hill and implicitly relate Sodom with Dublin or perhaps London. Shancoduff and its poet-owner seem parochial rather than provincial according to the often quoted distinction Kavanagh developed in 1952:

> Parochialism and provincialism are opposites. The provincial has no mind of his own; he does not trust what his eyes see until he has heard what the metropolis—toward which his eyes are turned—has to say on the subject. . . .
>
> The parochial mentality on the other hand is never in any doubt about the social and artistic validity of his parish. All great civilizations are based on parochialism. . . .[20]

Loved deeply, the hills reveal their wealth to the imagination and become the type of even the greatest mountains. Yet in the final stanza of "Shancoduff" the urban standard intrudes through the disparaging opinions of drovers, unrooted roving merchants who serve the British market.[21] To the drovers' question of ownership the poet responds with an ambiguous question: "'Who owns them hungry hills / . . . ? / A poet? Then by heavens he must be poor' / I hear and is my heart not badly shaken?"

The much-explicated "Inniskeen Road: July Evening" develops a similar ambiguity toward the poet's isolation. The road at two hours—the half-seven thoroughfare for neighbors going to a dance and the silent boreen left to the poet—represents the actual world and the poet's imagination:

> Half-past eight and there is not a spot
> Upon a mile of road, no shadow thrown
> That might turn out a man or woman, not
> A footfall tapping secrecies of stone.
>
> (*KCP,* 18)

As Seamus Heaney has written, "The power of the negated phrases . . . establishes a ghostly populous atmosphere."[22] Deprived of actual dancers, the poet prepares his imaginative compensation for the dance: "footfall tapping secrecies of stone." Among that "ghostly populous" he is "king / Of banks and stones and every blooming thing." *Blooming* strikes the Kavanagh note of ambiguity poised on a colloquialism. The word belittles the objects of the poetic landscape ("bloody") just as they are issuing from the "unmeasured womb" ("blooming").

Toward the end of his first phase, Kavanagh concentrated on narration. In 1938 he published *The Green Fool,* an autobiographical account of the poetic consciousness emerging among the small fields of Monaghan. Although gentler in tone than his other iconoclastic narratives, *The Green Fool* begins Kavanagh's thorough dismantling of the nationalist myth of the pure Irish peasant. If this fictionalized autobiography shakes the pedestal, *The Great Hunger* (1942) demolishes the monumental image of the peasant. This long narrative poem recounts several stages in gravity's conquest of the small farmer Patrick Maguire and of his dreams, based on the stock salutation and toast, "of health and wealth and love . . ." (*KCP,* 87).

Blocked by his mother and the Church from natural functioning, Maguire slides from dreams of love to sexual fantasies that weigh on his will. Interpreting from the poem's opening line—"Clay is the word and clay is the flesh—", John Jordan has reminded us that the Word forever being made flesh is the prototype of the act of love, as well as the central truth of Christianity. On this basis, he reads "The Great Hunger" as "the analysis of an extended blasphemy against Creation."[23]

Specifically, Maguire refuses incarnate grace, God's spirit transubstantiated into flesh:

>                               But he dreamt of the
>     Absolute envased bouquet—
> All or nothing. And it was nothing. For God is not all
> In one place, complete
> Till Hope comes in and takes it on his shoulder—
> O Christ, that is what you have done for us:
> In a crumb of bread the whole mystery is.
>
> He read the symbol too sharply and turned
> From the five simple doors of sense
> To the door whose combination lock has puzzled
> Philosopher and priest and common dunce.
>
> Men build their heavens as they build their circles
> Of friends. God is in the bits and pieces of Everyday—
> A kiss here and a laugh again, and sometimes tears, . . .
>
>                                  (*KCP,* 88)

Critics concur in their judgment that *The Great Hunger* is a flawed masterpiece although they characterize the flaw differently. Terence Brown and an editorialist of the *Honest Ulsterman,* "Jude the Obscure," align the poem with the realistic novel, a genre that Brown sees clogged for Irish writers by the inadequacy of Irish life.[24] Jude assigns the flaw to Kavanagh's static narration: "The focus has been so narrowed to catch the detail that it cannot catch the movement in time."[25]

Not a consistent myopia, however, but an unsteadiness of focus flaws the poem. As the poem opens, the speaker stands closer to his companion Imagination than to Maguire: "If we watch them an hour . . . ," ". . . why do we stand here shivering?" "Come with me, Imagination, into this iron house. . . ." From this perspective, he can observe the minutest details of Maguire's life against a larger cultural background: "October playing a symphony on a slack wire paling:" "He stands in the doorway of his house / A ragged sculpture of the wind." The narrator's analysis, above, of Maguire's graceless state reveals a sophisticated religious understanding and a thoughtful sympathy for this humble man. In other words, in all of these passages I have cited, Kavanagh has balanced his speaker effectively between the poetic object and his audience. This point of view carries the narration so successfully that certain intrusive, sarcastic asides blur the focus:

> The poor peasant talking to himself in a stable door —
> An ignorant peasant deep in dung.
> What can the passers-by think otherwise?
>
> (*KCP*, 91)

This seems both too defensive of Maguire and too conscious of a viewpoint irrelevant to the poem. The long digression on peasantry in section XIII which begins, "The world looks on / And talks of the peasant," seems provincial in Kavanagh's terms of having one's eyes turned toward the metropolis.

Among the long narratives of this first stage, which ends in 1942, "Jude the Obscure" would include "Why Sorrow," a fragment which is usually dated in the mid-forties and from which poem "Father Mat" was excerpted. He argues persuasively that the work must have been finished by 1942 when a more sophisticated treatment of penitents on Lough Derg was completed by Kavanagh.[26]

In 1942, Kavanagh traveled to the ancient island retreat of Lough Derg in Donegal to write a feature for *The Standard,* intended later to be part of a best-seller on Irish pilgrimages. Kavanagh recorded journalistic impressions of this pilgrimage along with novelistic insights into the lives of three pilgrims in a long poem "Lough Derg," apparently completed in 1942 but never published by the poet. Although the poem has received extravagant praise,[27] again apparent confusion of points of view — specifically, disconcerting shifts in tone — have led many critics to ignore the poem or often to consider it as an unpolished draft. Alan Warner approves of a conversational comment by Brendan Kennelly that in "Lough Derg," Kavanagh "doesn't know whether he's on his knees or on his feet."[28] However, Kavanagh's narrator does not pop up and down like a Mass-goer. Rather he progresses from sarcasm to sympathy much as does his central character, a literate farmer. If we can understand the shift in point of view as a controlled progression, then the work seems more finished and significant.

At the opening of the poem the speaker condescends toward the other pilgrims:

> They come to Lough Derg to fast and pray and beg
> With all the bitterness of nonentities, and the envy
> Of the inarticulate when dealing with the artist.
> Their hands push closed the doors that God holds open;
>
> (*KCP,* 104)

At this stage of the poem, he recognizes supplicants only by their social roles, glossing over the individual tragedies:

> Solicitors praying for cushy jobs
> To be County Registrar or Coroner,
> Shopkeepers threatened with sharper rivals
> Than any hook-nosed foreigner.
> Mothers whose daughters are Final Medicals,
> Too heavy-hipped for thinking,
> Wives whose husbands have angina pectoris,
> Wives whose husbands have taken to drinking.
>
> (*KCP,* 105)

Only slowly does the pilgrim mass dissolve into individuals. On the third page, the speaker recognizes "the Castleblaney grocer," "a young woman," "an old monk," and "a fat lawyer."

Soon the journalistic view yields totally to offer insight into three lives:

> On Lough Derg, too, the silver strands
> Of the individual sometimes show
> Through the fabric of prison anonymity.
> One man's private trouble transcending the divinity
> Of the prayer-locked multitude.
>
> (*KCP,* 108)

The favored characters are an ex-monk from Dublin, a skeptical and literate farmer who "talked heresy lightly," and a beautiful girl shielding her secret of an illegitimate child whom she killed at birth.

At this point the narrator offers asides that would have been conventional for medieval scribes translating sacred texts: "The truth must go on as it occurred . . . O God of Truth / Keep him who tells this story straight, / Let no cheap insincerity shape his mouth." He begins to close his account of these three lives with an astounding statement about his point of view:

> The ex-monk, farmer and the girl
> Melted in the crowd
> Where only God, the poet
> Followed with interest till he found
> Their secret, and constructed from
> The chaos of its fire
> A reasonable document.
>
> (*KCP*, 115)

Only an anacoluthon or an omitted comma guards him from claiming God's insight and responsibility. More explicitly, the poet shares God's taste in literature: "Christ Lord / Hears in the voices of the meanly poor / Homeric utterances, poetry sweeping through."

Assuming God's privilege, the poet hears the penitential prayers, four of which are formed in sonnets which should be admired even by critics who dismiss "Lough Derg." Kavanagh never again assumed this exalted point of view that allowed him to sympathize so dispassionately with his countryman, as with this one unemployed laborer:

> O Sacred Heart of Jesus I ask of you
> A job so I can settle down and marry;
> I want to live a decent life. And through
> The flames of St. Patrick's Purgatory
> I go offering every stone-bruise, all my hunger;
> In the back-room of my penance I am weaving
> An inside-shirt for charity. How longer
> Must a fifty-shilling a week job be day-dreaming?
> The dole and empty minds and empty pockets
> Cup Finals seen from the branches of a tree,
> Old films that break the eye-balls in their sockets,
> A toss-pit. This is life for such as me.
> And I know a girl and I know a room to be let
> And a job in a builder's yard to be given yet.
>
> (*KCP*, 120)

We can appreciate how much more lightly this floats toward heaven than Yeats's "A Prayer for My Daughter." To give us a moment's insight into a humble religion and a peasant soul, Kavanagh dispenses with any metaphysical, religious, or historical complexities.

As history and religion have grown more burdensome in Ireland,

Kavanagh's successors have found in his first and third phases numerous poetic models for avoiding nationalistic rhetoric and the worn symbolism of Yeats and other writers of the Irish Renaissance. When praising Kavanagh's example, however, admirers are as likely to cite the journalistic invective or poetic diatribes of his second phase as the fine earlier and later poetry.

Kavanagh's distaste for the literary establishment of Dublin, which became evident soon after he settled there in 1939, grew steadily until the end of his life. Undoubtedly, in his satirical writings Kavanagh exposed some talentless writers, certain unfounded nationalist assumptions, and the tasteless residue of Yeats's aestheticism. Given his belief in the poet's elevated role, Kavanagh might well seethe at comments such as Valentin Iremonger's sweeping Wildean assertion that "poetry has little to do with Truth, Sincerity, or what-have-you," printed in *The Bell* in 1944.[29] This same reviewer claimed that poetry in *The Bell* was as good as that during any era of Irish literature.[30] To such provincialism, Kavanagh responded with increasing frequency and vehemence, dismissing most current poetry, the Irish Literary Renaissance, and all forms of "Irishness." In 1947 while dispatching F. R. Higgins as a "gallivanting" poser who "never became adult and sincere," he discovered "the absurdity and the lie called 'the Irish Literary movement',," according to his own recollection.[31] He would later call the movement "a thoroughgoing English-bred lie."[32] Kavanagh's criticism often sinks into vituperation or exposes the author's prejudices and ignorance. On Radio Eireann in 1952 he could claim "that in a thousand years Ireland has not produced a major poet or indeed a good minor poet."[33]

John Nemo has demonstrated that throughout Kavanagh's criticism "the one intention that remains constant . . . is the desire to establish an intelligent audience by preaching creative ideals."[34] Yet, Kavanagh's invective suggests he was also kicking against the pricks, merely reacting against those Dublin patrons and editors unwilling to employ him steadily. Soon after he moved to Dublin from Monaghan, he began writing occasional pieces for the *Irish Times,* from which he drifted to the *Irish Press,* and then the *Standard* in 1946. In that year he published *A Soul for Sale.*[35] Some of the best poems in this volume, such as "Advent," "Art McCooey," "A Christmas Childhood," and "Father Mat," were written during his first phase before the publication of his previous volume in 1942. In 1948 he published his autobiographical novel *Tarry Flynn*. Although this work is marred by Kavanagh's ambivalence concerning his own departure from his home, as reflected particularly in the curious climax of the novel, it represents his major achievement of this middle phase of his career. In 1949 he was hired to write a regular "Diary" for *Envoy* by the Editor, John Ryan, who later said of Kavanagh: "Ten awful years of writing film reviews and leaders for a religious newspaper had, it seemed, emptied the last of his poetic reserves."[36] In 1952 with his brother's funds, he launched *Kavanagh's Weekly*, a medium for his own editorial views, which foundered within three months.

Throughout this insecure career of journalistic drudgery, Kavanagh directed much of his resentment against the institutional Yeats. He made the distinction between Yeats and his reputation most clearly in an *Envoy* "Diary" of 1950:

> The mentality which was Yeats's enemy is everywhere in power, and that mentality thrives by praising Yeats. The adulation of Yeats and Joyce has become a menace to the living, for when a dead poet is praised, something is praised that isn't the real thing at all. Death changes the whole position, so that to be on the side of truth one would need to damn dead poets.[37]

Yet, as Robert Garratt has argued, Kavanagh was often inclined himself to use Yeats as a stiff to beat living poets.[38] Through grudging praise, Kavanagh reveals a profound admiration for Yeats's "gay youthfulness and his authority."[39] Much of Kavanagh's sense of the poet's role is derived from what he observed of Yeats's life. Kavanagh's illusion that there existed a "sort of arch-poet position which only one man could occupy" sprang from Yeats's predominance, as Anthony Cronin has observed.[40] Yeats's defense of writing plays for the drawing room rather than for the Abbey Theatre provided a convenient model for Kavanagh's frequent rationalizations that he sought only a small elect as audience.[41] He would not have drafted this elect, however, from Dublin's bars or Bohemian catacombs, the source of his most vocal disciples. According to John Ryan's unflattering summary, Kavanagh dreamed of achieving "the private esteem of poetic greats; the quiet background murmur of mandarin approval and the nodding fellowship with the beautiful people,

from whom just enough money rubbed off to make life tolerable. . . ."[42]
That this lucrative rubbing-off would occur with beautiful women was
Kavanagh's persistent, unfulfilled fantasy.[43] His frequent advertisements
for this patron-paramour suggest that Yeats's associations with wealthy
women influenced Kavanagh's expectations concerning the poet's benefits: "Yes, Yeats, it was damn easy for you protected / By the middle
classes and the Big Houses / . . . / . . . sheltered by the dim Victorian
Muses," (*KCP,* 349) he complained.

If his view of the poet's role was influenced by Yeats's life, Kavanagh's best poetry owes little directly to the master. I cannot agree with
Garratt's half-truth that Kavanagh is "a revisionist" and that, therefore,
"Yeats makes Kavanagh's poetry possible."[44] It does seem, however, that
during this middle decade Kavanagh spent pages looking over his shoulder
at Yeats and lacking the courage of the parochial writer, who "is never
in any doubt about the social and artistic validity of his parish."[45] As
a consequence of this, the parish disappears from the page and leaves
only a page, a place for the poet and reader to meet with no agenda:

> The problem that confronts me here
> Is to be eloquent yet sincere;
> Let myself rip and not go phoney
> In an inflated testimony.
>> ("Auditors In," *KCP,* 242)

Replacing the poetic object, *here* leaves the poet and reader in the situation
of Coleridge's mariner and wedding-guest with no tale and no compulsive confession: the poet can only poke the guest's shoulder self-consciously
and play variations on "how's it going, buddy." In this 1951 poem, lacking confessional compulsion or tale, Kavanagh can only address himself—
as *him, you,* and *I*—or evoke the freedom from tradition he has given
his reader, as in this parody of the conclusion to Joyce's *Portrait*:

> Mother Earth is putting my brand new clothes in order
> Praying, she says, that I no more ignore her
> Yellow buttons she found in fields at bargain prices.

"Auditors In" is actually a transitional turn away from satire, which he will
soon recognize as "unfruitful prayer" (*KCP,* 275), toward "the parish."

He reached this third stage, the "simplicity of return," in 1955 with a series of sonnets written during convalescence from his lung operation. In his "Self Portrait" he declares, "As a poet, I was born in or about nineteen-fifty-five, the place of my birth being the banks of the Grand Canal."[46] In this third stage, he reaches the parish not by map but by turning his eyes back to some familiar territory and observing closely natural detail and his own loving response. As he later remarked of his life's three stages, "We begin by being simple and then for years plough through complexities and affectation to come back to where we begin."[47]

However, as in the dialectic of a Romanticist, the third stage represents a synthesis of the first two stages. Into the "simplicity of return," a few poems in the third phase continue to spring from a reaction to Yeats and other writers. For example, the title poem in *Come Dance with Kitty Stobling and Other Poems* (1960) defies understanding unless we read it as a reinterpretation of Yeats.[48] Originally entitled "High Journey," this enigmatic sonnet revises many elements of Yeats's "High Talk." As the self-regarding Yeats mounts elaborate metaphor to elevate his verse— "All metaphor . . . stilts and all. A barnacle goose / Far up in the stretches of night" (*YP*, 343) — so the Yeats-attending Kavanagh once assumed the same elevation in order to describe beauty: "my rhyme / Cavorting on mile high stilts . . . (*CP*, 291). The message he offers his groundlings may also echo a refrain in a late Yeats poem: "I am of Ireland . . . // Come . . . / . . . dance with me in Ireland" (*YP*, 267). Rather than inviting his readers to more Irishness, Kavanagh would match them with "Kitty Stobling" which sounds demotic and actual. The final couplet suggests that with this great stalking ended, he gratefully returns to "madness . . . nearly," perhaps the condition of "not caring" which he adopted in this third phase.

The fruits of this period Kavanagh harvested in this 1960 volume. His first British publication in thirteen years, this book also contained some of his most successful poems from the second phase: "Kerr's Ass," "On Looking into E. V. Rieu's Homer," "Epic," and "Auditors In." Among the two-dozen successful poems of the last phase, most are sonnets. Of this form Kavanagh said in his 1956 lectures at University College, Dublin:

I am very fond of the sonnet form, and not merely because it has been
the most popular vehicle for the expression of love but because of its
strict rules, which like other rules Shakespeare broke so wonderfully,
forces [*sic*] the mind to moral activity but is itself not forced.[49]

In these sonnets Kavanagh recovers the naturalness of his first phase,
not merely with images from nature but with his approximation within
strict forms of spontaneous expression and uninhibited, unpretentious
thought. His objective, he said in his "Self Portrait," was "to play a
true note on a dead slack string."[50]

This play between the formal and extemporaneous expression becomes a theme of his most successful sonnet, "Canal Bank Walk," which
celebrates the poet's new parish. The Grand and Royal Canals enclose
Dublin from the south and north. Kavanagh's haunt—the Grand Canal
between Baggott Street and Leeson Street—is nature restricted to a
fifty-yard ribbon of grass, stone, and water shared by strollers, ducks,
and detritus. The sonnet reflects the contained but natural quality of
this setting:

> Leafy-with-love banks and the green waters of the canal
> Pouring redemption for me, that I do
> The will of God, wallow in the habitual, the banal,
> Grow with nature again as before I grew.
> The bright stick trapped, the breeze adding a third
> Party to the couple kissing on an old seat,
> And a bird gathering materials for the nest for the Word
> Eloquently new and abandoned to its delirious beat.
> O unworn world enrapture me, encapture me in a web
> Of fabulous grass and eternal voices by a beech,
> Feed the gaping need of my senses, give me ad lib
> To pray unselfconsciously with overflowing speech
> For this soul needs to be honoured with a new dress woven
> From green and blue things and arguments that cannot be proven.
>
> (*KCP*, 294–5)

In addition to freedom and restraint, the poem balances other apparent
contraries such as beauty and banality, external and imagined beauty,
inherent and divine spirit. The poem opens at the moment of creation,
the banks flourishing as they are touched by the sympathetic imagina-

tion. The canal waters reward and encourage his poetry, redeeming him *because* he does, and *in order that* he do, God's will. The breeze offers the same paradoxical imagination, actually visiting the kissing couple but in imaginative language becoming a "Party," more festive than a presence.

The commonest natural creature must stand in for the Holy Ghost as it builds a nest for the Word, with which it rhymes. Within the poem this divine spirit will become "abandoned to its delirious beat," spirit free in the poet's territory, in the poetic tempo, and in the rhythm of the bird's wing. The seventh and eighth lines both prepare for and welcome the arrival of the Word, but the poet then substitutes the freshly-perceived *world* for the *Word* in his invocation, a prayer that his soul find a new containment in a web or newly woven garment, that his senses gain food, and that his pen find "ad lib." This journalistic phrase for extemporaneous speech is derived from the musical instruction *ad libitum,* "to perform with freedom" or according "to desire," within a prescribed musical score. The slant-rhyme with *web* restores the central paradox of freedom within containment; so does the final "not . . . proven" as he seems to slip it extemporaneously and intuitively into uneasy harness with *woven.* In this final down-beat rhyme Kavanagh parallels the trailing off of the Irish *sean-nos* singer who rapidly slides out of his moving lyric. Both artists depend on the audience's sense of the form against which the poet or singer plays. Kavanagh appeals to an audience that appreciates the difference between this ad hoc quality and a moment's monument.

Encumbered with his system and embroidered mythologies, Yeats never walked so naked as Kavanagh does in this sonnet. A poem such as "Canal Bank Walk" is worth thousands of Kavanagh's prosaic summons to forget Irishness and to celebrate one's place and moment in appropriate poetic forms. Some poems from his first and third phases established for younger writers a detour around Yeats's highly constructed poetry, much as William Carlos Williams' spare colloquial poetry freed American poets from the elaborate academic quality of T. S. Eliot's poetry. We can regret that Kavanagh created too few poems of this quality, so that poets whom he helped to liberate from Yeats, such as Seamus Heaney and John Montague, have already eclipsed his real but stunted accomplishment.

Unfortunately, Kavanagh's career entered a fourth phase in which he could invoke no muse or build no nest for the Word. In a 1964 interview in *Hibernia* when asked about his rebirth in 1955, he responded, "I am beginning to disbelieve in it."[51] Well he might have agonized over the iron stool of forced creations, analyses of his own dead-end, or self-parodies.[52] Whether spirits came in when the spirit left, or vice versa, Kavanagh's grim public example may make him the last important Irish poet to die of alcoholism. If he demonstrated the great value of poetic insight, he also showed how quickly this frail gift can expire.

*&*

Seamus Heaney has already proven himself a more careful steward of a more copious talent than Kavanagh's. Like Kavanagh's verse, Heaney's poetry immediately attracts the reader: the images are vivid and precise; the speaking voice is reassuring; the lines seem, as Heaney said of Kavanagh, "lyrically opportunistic,"[53] incorporating radiant moments of ordinary rural life. For example, consider this description of Heaney's aunt from the first dedicatory poem of *North*:

> Now she dusts the board
> with a goose's wing,
> now sits, broad-lapped, with whitened nails
>
> and measling shins:
> here is a space
> again, the scone rising
> to the tick of two clocks.
>
> (*HP*, 161–62)

This depiction of time as gestation, which has already reappeared in major anthologies, probably has pleased more readers than Kavanagh's finest lyrics, which are seriously underread. Gauged by the number of major journals that have featured Heaney and the extraordinary sales of his recent volumes,[54] his success approaches that of novelists and the most celebrated American poets such as Ashbery and Warren.[55] Kavanagh's fantasies about fame and fortune, which he mocked in his own verse, could hardly have flared so high as to reach Heaney's actual success.

Nevertheless, an ingredient of Heaney's appeal, as revealed in this

"Mossbawn" poem, is the observant eye, patient ear, and celebratory tone that he found in the poetry of Kavanagh. Kavanagh had already demonstrated that the subject they would share—vignettes from routines on the small farms of Ulster—carried an extraordinary nostalgic appeal. Although Heaney's birthplace on the northern edge of the British Isles' largest lake, Loch Neagh, made fishing more important to Heaney than to Kavanagh, they both have written about cattle trading, thatching, churning, and other ancient trades and crafts studied in Estyn Evans' *Irish Folk Ways.*

Beyond this rich shared tradition, Heaney enjoyed two early advantages over Kavanagh. First, his aptitude for learning was encouraged by his parents as he advanced through secondary school in Derry and a course of literary study at Queens University toward a profounder and more balanced view of literature than Kavanagh ever attained. Secondly, from early in his career, Heaney could benefit from the example of Kavanagh's life and work, and from that of their intermediate, John Montague.

Kavanagh offered Heaney what MacNeice gave to Mahon, proof that out of inartistic settings poetry could arise or, in Heaney's words, "a confidence in the deprivations of our condition." To the younger poet Kavanagh conveyed "an insouciance and trust in the clarities and cunnings of our perceptions."[56] In his reaction to Yeats, Kavanagh demonstrated that poetry could be written independently of "a structure and a sustaining landscape" produced from elaborate mythologizing. Yet, Heaney remained free to synthesize Kavanagh's spontaneous realism and Yeats's ordering structure. In an interview with Heaney, Seamus Deane defined the kind of synthesis Heaney hopes to achieve:

> a poetry that would be neither a matter of the day to day spontaneities alone, but a matter of making the day to day (*sic*! the myth?) become a form embedded in the day to day from which it arises.[57]

In this *Crane Bag* interview with Deane, published midway between *North* and *Field Work,* Heaney confessed his frustrations in developing a sustaining formal myth, "a kind of singular universal":

> The more one consciously tries to convey this imprint the more it seems to elude you. You see, the lift-off and push of the innocent creative moment can never be fully schematic.[58]

Heaney's first four volumes progressively evolve a "myth," what may be seen as a synthesis between Kavanagh's "day to day spontaneities" and Yeats's "schematic mythologizing." *Field Work,* however, diverges sharply from lyrical myth to a dialogue about myth-making and the poet's role.

Heaney's poetry has never been as unfreighted as Kavanagh's best verse in which merely "naming these things is the love-act and its pledge; / For we must record love's mystery without claptrap . . ." ("The Hospital," *KCP,* 280). Even in the first volume, in which the most successful poems recount "the death of a naturalist," the youthful waking from nature into self-consciousness, Heaney suggests interesting psychological themes. After an overanthologized opening poem which associates poem-making with physical activities such as gun-toting and turf-digging, the poet recollects his adolescent fear of frogs and their spawn, toward which the child was ambivalent:

> There were dragon-flies, spotted butterflies,
> But best of all was the warm thick slobber
> Of frogspawn that grew like clotted water
> In the shade of the banks.

But, his fear surfaces when the masculine and martial bullfrogs invade the breeding ground: "The great slime kings / Were gathered there for vengeance and I knew / That if I dipped my hand the spawn would clutch it" (*HP,* 5–6). "Death of A Naturalist" suggests a temporary theme—a vivid but otherwise unexceptional record of an adolescent's anxiety about metamorphosis ("The fattening dots burst . . .") and excrescence—on which no poet could afford to fixate. However, two of Heaney's enduring themes are psychologically grafted to this adolescent anxiety.

First, the child's need to define the boundary between himself and encroaching nature has its correlation in the Romanticist interest in identifying the self in the perceived experience while attempting to make a more direct contact with nature. Heaney often achieves what the phenomenologists call a "noematic reflection," a recreation of perception in which we sense the reflected eye as well as the natural object in its fundamentally inhuman essence.[59] Through a rich vocabulary of Anglo-Saxon and Gaelic cognates, he conveys precise sensations of touch and smell and temperature that represent a dense and grainy nature. In his bogland poems, particularly, he is remarkably close to Theodore Roethke's green-house poems of 1948, in which that poet rediscovered his relation to primal forms of life, and, in his fidelity to the perceived natural object, Heaney parallels Ted Hughes's more single-minded attempts to capture the unique reality of various animals.

Secondly, and more importantly, the child's concern to distinguish himself from encroaching nature evolves into mature questions about the relation of poetic perception to the actual world, of poetry to experience, and of personal expression to communal and traditional patterns of thought and action. Questions to which Heaney returns in *Field Work* concerning the poem's relation to the world are raised in the final poem of his first volume, *Death of a Naturalist*:

> Now, to pry into roots, to finger slime,
> To stare big-eyed Narcissus, into some spring
> Is beneath all adult dignity. I rhyme
> To see myself, to set the darkness echoing.
>
> ("Personal Helicon")

Heaney's next three volumes — *Door Into the Dark, Wintering Out,* and *North* (1969, 1972, and 1975) — pursue the phenomenological theme more urgently than the question of poetry. Although *Door Into the Dark* offers little evidence of poetic growth, it does deepen Heaney's concerns about our relation to the natural world. In the volume's weightiest poem, "A Lough Neagh Sequence," the threat of depersonalization becomes an overt theme. The seventh poem in the sequence, "Vision," recalls, with Freudian and animistic implications, a youthful association between eels crossing a flooded field and lice which elders had threatened would gather in his uncombed hair and drag him into the water. In a less explicit manner, many of Heaney's poems challenge the distinction, which psychologists call our ego-boundary, between ourselves and our excrescences, between our animated flesh and contiguous but alien life.

Of the volume's finest poems, "The Outlaw," "In Gallarus Oratory," "The Wife's Tale," and "Bogland," the latter summons Irish poetry from its typical bardic peregrinations to a vertical quest "into the cyclops' eye of a tarn." Anticipating the supporting evidence of P. V. Glob's *Bog People,* which Heaney read in 1969, he had represented the bog as a re-

pository where the past is rendered contemporaneous with the present—
"Butter sunk under / more than a hundred years / Was recovered salty
and white"—a modernist assumption that snaps the catena of history.
"Bogland" concludes:

> Our pioneers keep striking
> Inwards and downwards,
>
> Every layer they strip
> Seems camped on before.
> The bogholes might be Atlantic seepage.
> The wet centre is bottomless.

That *Wintering Out* (1972) extends this exploration is not at first apparent because the fallow setting and bleak tone suggest hibernation
and because a number of poems are devoted to the theme of the poet's
role through analogues such as a salmon fisher, a soul-smith, a mummer, and a thatcher. The seasonal mood pervades the volume. Like his
surrogate "Servant Boy," Heaney is "wintering out / the back-end of
a bad year," finding comfort in tactile and olfactory reminiscences ("Fod-
der") and, in the manner of Austin Clarke, regretting the loss of a more
hospitable and humane age ("The Last Mummer").

However, of the five sections into which the book divides, two seem
to reach new depths. The first section, through "Wool Trade," explores
lost traditions, the individual's relation to the land, and religious, cultural, and linguistic differences between the two Ulster heritages. Yet,
in "Anahorish," "Toome," "Broagh," "The Backward Look," "Traditions," and "A New Song," he rummages for some radical connection
between the land and the language it nurtures. The tentative resolutions of these poems—that we can achieve "a soft gradient of conso-
nant, vowel-meadow . . ." ("Anahorish") or that Irish vowels will irri-
gate consonantal English ("A New Song")—are less persuasive than his
thickly textured language, the display of gutturals and vowels that seems
as palpable as soil. Enriched by the revival of the Gaelic language and
by Clarke's experiments with assonantal patterns in Gaelic poetry, Heaney
can rival Hopkins in his ear for vowels and his etymological sense of
diction.

While this first section of *Wintering Out* is pervaded by bad weather,
the seasonal metaphor implies an eventual spring thaw. In the second

section, however, from "Linen Town," to "Veteran's Dream," "the back end of a bad year" pervades various eras in Belfast's history. Although in "A Northern Hoard" Heaney promises to find in roots and loam surrogates for suffering humanity, elsewhere in this section he cannot maintain this detachment from the zone of conflict where he is bewildered and where his lines falter and lose faith. His best poems characteristically reside, in Muldoon's phrase, at "pain's edge where we take shelter." "First Calf," from the fourth section of *Wintering Out*, epitomizes Heaney's relation to life's painful center. His attention is drawn not to the suffering cow or her new calf but to "the after-birth strung on the hedge," the mysterious margin of life, both mineral and carnal, where pain registers: "The semaphores of hurt / Swaddle and flap on a bush" (*HP*, 152).

Heaney achieves a consummate poem in this section: "The Tollund Man." Drawing on Glob's account of a recovered Iron-Age man, sacrificed to an earth goddess and mummified in a Danish bog, he compares this sacrificial death to murder in Ulster. He succeeds because his attention is drawn to details of the Tollund Man, such as his undigested meal and "the mild pods of his eyelids" which perpetuate and make contemporaneous the mysterious suspension of life's process. The deity that demanded this sacrifice is also perpetuated as some life-denying feminine force in nature:

> Bridegroom to the goddess,
>
> She tightened her torc on him
> And opened her fen,
> Those dark juices working
> Him to a saint's kept body,
>
> (*HP*, 125)

The third section of *Wintering Out* represents the woman as an unwilling adversary and, thus, introduces the fourth and most complex section of the book. The seven poems from "A Winter's Tale" through "First Calf" transcend and tend to justify the early explanatory poems. They portray woman, moved by elemental forces of moon and tide, as antithetical to the pragmatic world of man. In "Shore Woman," as in several other poems, she establishes her margin, here between the sea of violent, sexual anarchy and the land she overshadows: "And I'm walking the firm margin. White pocks / Of cockle, blanched roofs of clam and oyster / Hoard of moonlight, woven and unwoven / Off the bay." She concludes, "I have rights on this fallow avenue, / A membrane between moonlight and my shadow" (*HP,* 144–5).

The most successful poem in *Wintering Out* is "Maighdean Mara." Heaney explains the title is Irish for "mermaid," but the dedication, "For Sean Oh-Eocha," suggests some unidentified event on which the poem is based. The first and last of the three stanzas describe a drowned woman, while the second stanza recounts two seductions, the first by her husband who "charmed" her from the sea and "conjured / Patterns of home and drained / The tidesong from her voice." The second seduction by the thatcher, because it repeats the motifs of the first, breaks her spell and threatens her with land-locked recurrences: "the dead hold of bedrooms, / Dread of the night and morrow, / Her children's brush and combs." She prefers the endless rhythm of the sea's double swell, suggested by the even spacing of bacchics in the first line and of spondees in the seventh, and enacted by the two syllables of "dandled" and by the alliterative participles of the third line:

> She sleeps now, her cold breasts
> Dandled by undertow,
> Her hair lifted and laid.
> Undulant slow seawracks
> Cast about shin and thigh,
> Bangles of wort, drifting
> Liens catch, dislodge gently.
>
> This is the great first sleep
> Of homecoming, eight
> Land years between hearth and
> Bed steeped and dishevelled.
> Her magic garment al-
> most ocean-tinctured still.
>
> (*HP,* 146)

Sibilants and sonorants imitate the hiss and wash of the sea, whose movement is suggested through tempo and vowel change. The return at the conclusion of the third section of the poem's opening two lines stresses recurrence.

Although the form of the poem is elaborate, it creates the effect of a ballad or other basically oral form where artifice — rhyme and refrain — serves only to emphasize some undigested fact, whose mystery no abstraction can reduce. Heaney achieves this same oral quality in "A Winter's Tale," "Limbo," and "Bye-Child." The source of the mystery in "Maighdean Mara" may be sought in the allusion to *The Tempest* (2.2.68–69, 99) in the last two lines of the first section. The poem is about a counterspell, a ritual of immersion that breaks the conjuration of love and allows her to return to her natural, inhuman state. We wonder at, as we are threatened by, her beautiful form of nonbeing: she "doth suffer a sea-change / Into something rich and strange." The next two poems also represent the woman as governing dark domains, "a far briny zone" and "lunar distances . . . beyond love."

*North* attempts both to extend this myth and its application to the Troubles and to reestablish an ad-hoc, Kavanagh-like association with Heaney's audience. This calculated schizophrenia is reflected in a prefatory poem, the book's structure, and even the cover. The book's Part I 18 poems) and Part II (9 poems) are preceded by two dedicatory poems, one of which we have discussed. The second poem is significant, however, because it suggests the distinct modes of Parts I and II. It begins with the poet declaring self-consciously,

> They seem hundreds of years away. Breughel,
> You'll know them if I can get them true.

and concludes:

> O calendar customs! Under the broom
> Yellowing over them, compose the frieze
> With all of us there, our anonymities.
> ("The Seed Cutters," *HP,* 163)

Does the imperative suggest that the poet has yielded the composition of his art to "calendar customs," ritual and tradition? The book's cover sustains the question by giving equal space to the poet's binary modes: the front cover is a "frieze" of stylized round-bottomed Vikings, sailing under the crane-bills of their swords: anonymities in the northern ritual of murder. The back cover presents a pop-portrait of Heaney "getting them true." The book's two parts develop these two modes. In Part I a bardic persona enlarges the Ulster violence to include the state of mind called *north*, the sinister side of man, inhabited by Norsemen, *Njal*'s Ice-

landic heroes, and Jutland Celts. Current inhumanity is displaced by
ancient inhumations, the victims sacrificed to the Earth Mother, Nerthus. The invaders are Vikings or Elizabethans; the poet sings from the
crannog, or meditates on history, or the bog, that

> casket, midden,
> floe of history.
>
> Ground that will strip
> its dark side,
> nesting ground,
> outback of my mind.
>                   ("Kinship," *HP,* 196–97)

In Part II the scop yields to the Ulster poet commenting on the car-
nage in Northern Ireland, which results in some uncharacteristically awkward poems. We may excuse section II as Heaney's dues paid to his compatriots and a response to prodding from Patrick Galvin, Padraic Fiacc,
and other Belfast writers.[60] In drawing close to the violence, Heaney's
sensitive ear numbs, and he mocks the evasive clichés without renewing
them:

> We tremble near the flames but want no truck
> With the actual firing. We're on the make
>
> As ever. Long sucking the hind tit
> Cold as a witch's and as hard to swallow
> Still leaves us fork-tongued on the border bit:
>         ("Whatever You Say Say Nothing," *HP,* 213)

Part I offers pleasure as a lyric sequence that also contains some of
Heaney's finest individual poems. Bound by two "Antaeus" poems, the
sequence begins with "Belderg," where the poet engages in a neighborly chat about querns, ancient millstones recovered from the bog's
trove. The poem concludes:

> I passed through the eye of the quern,
>
> Grist to an ancient mill,
> And in my mind's eye saw
> A world-tree of balanced stones,
> Querns piled like vertebrae,
> The marrow crushed to grounds.
>                         (*HP,* 169)

Read in light of this conclusion, the opening of the subsequent poem suggests the individual bearing the crushing burden of the north's funereal ritual—

> I shouldered a kind of manhood
> stepping in the lift the coffins
> of dead relations.
>
> ("Funeral Rites," *HP*, 170)

—in a poem that anticipates the macabre beauty of the bog mummies, the subjects of later bog poems. In describing a funeral session, the poet expands the scope of "neighborly murder" to a full northern and historical dimension which section I sustains.

> Quiet as a serpent
> in its grassy boulevard
>
> the procession drags its tail
> out of the Gap of the North
> as its head already enters
> the megalithic doorway.
>
> (*HP*, 172)

Heaney's standard quatrain is particularly flexible here, yielding some dramatic emphases while seeming spare and understated. We hear the voice of the bard for whom the Icelandic hero Gunnar is a proxy as the next poem, "North," confirms.

The succeeding poem, "Viking Dublin: Trial Pieces," ostensibly maintains the same archaeological approach and northern theme in random musings on a Viking child's microscopic carvings on a bone. "These are trial pieces, / the craft's mystery / improvised on bone:" lines that would also characterize Heaney's poem, a trial incursion into Joyce's city, but on different terms from Joyce's. Alluding to *Portrait*, Heaney invokes, not the mythological Dedalus, old artificer, but the murderous Vikings, "cunning assessors":

> Come fly with me,
> come sniff the wind
> with the expertise
> of the Vikings—
> . . . . . .

> Old fathers be with us
> Old cunning assessors
> of feuds and sites
> for ambush or town.
>
> (*HP*, 178–9)

And so the carefully coordinated sequence continues. By contrast with Joyce's use of Dedalus's story, we can clarify the implications of what the jacket-blurb terms Heaney's "myth." Rather than a universal literary myth of man's creativity, Heaney constructs a hemispheric myth, inherent in the Viking foundations of Dublin, of man's homicidal nature, which is as inexplicable as nature's unconscious processes from which it is derived. Heaney associates war rites, ritual sacrifice, and sacrificial victims with the return of spring, sexuality, generation, and attachment to the mother, as they are associated in the ancient Celtic worship of Nerthus, to suggest that current Ulster killings are conditioned by preconscious forces.

The association of bog-burials—which were "northern" but not Irish—with mother-worship—a form of which preceded Christianity in Ireland—with the current atrocities in Ulster becomes too explicit to be historically accurate in certain poems, such as "Kinship":

> report us fairly,
> how we slaughter
> for the common good
>
> and shave the heads
> of the notorious,
> how the goddess swallows
> our love and terror.

Although the narrow, slean-like lines slice quickly and effectively toward this truth, efforts to extract from even a metaphorical bog a mythological and historical cause for "northern" behavior strain the authority of the speaker who must slide too quickly from *I* to *we*.

Assuming the collective point of view becomes more difficult for Heaney because his poetic voice has been nearly unvarying. In 1974 Heaney declared that in the opening poem of his first volume, he had found his voice:

Finding a voice means that you can get your own feeling into your own words and that your words have the feel of you about them; and I believe that it may not even be a metaphor, for a poetic voice is probably very intimately connected with the poet's natural voice. . . .[61]

So consistently had Heaney employed this voice—orchestrated assonance, consonantal textures, a plurality of words with Gaelic and Anglo-Saxon roots, Latinate words etymologically tuned, discrete specific detail— that he had acquired *timbre*. His *timbre,* a sound so familiar that it could border on self-parody, left little room for tone, the assumption of new voices or the adjustment of voice to audience.

My final point about the bog-poems concerns Calvin Bedient's accusation that "The Tollund Man" proves to be about Heaney's interest in the Tollund Man.[62] This charge could be made about other bog-poems as well, although finally it would be unfair. For example, consider "Strange Fruit," which begins,

> Here is the girl's head like an exhumed gourd.
> Oval-faced, prune-skinned, prune-stones for teeth.
> They unswaddled the wet fern of her hair
> And made an exhibition of its coil,
> Let the air at her leathery beauty.
> Pash of tallow, perishable treasure:
>
> (*HP,* 194)

This ironic title requires the startled reader to refocus, just as does the folksong with the same name which informs us chillingly that the strange fruit ripening under a Dixie sun is actually black humans lynched by a hysterical mob. Heaney's metaphors—gourd and prune—abet the bog in metamorphosing the girl from a human state. The metaphorically rich statement, "They unswaddled the wet fern of her hair," depicts the girl realistically as it also transforms her into artifact. *They* sounds ominously anonymous, and *exhibition* is tinged with the erotic, so the verb *let* becomes both the second action of *they* and the imperative of a complicit speaker. He too squanders her mysterious beauty as he exhibits it. As he says in the preceding poem, he is "the artful voyeur," as fascinated by his own embalming powers as by the mummified victim, who also provides a metaphor for his art.

What I am suggesting is that we are unfair to expect Heaney's vertical quest, striking inward and downward, to recover historical or mythological truths because his actual concern is the relation of his art to life. (No saffron tinges Heaney's theme: his concern is ontological and epistemological rather than aesthetic.) He can plumb himself, sounding to various levels, or establish a dialogue between private and public selves, between self and other, or between poet and community or tradition. Because his timbre could not bear the weight of further mythologizing and because his poetic subject must eventually gravitate toward his obsessional theme, implicit in his earliest poetry, Heaney shifted into a subtle dramatic mode in *Field Work,* a book that departs radically from his earlier work.

So thoroughly has Heaney revised his voice that readers attuned to the Heaney timbre could fail to identify the author of the following lines in *Field Work*:

> The way we are living,
> Timorous or bold,
> will have been our life.
> Robert Lowell,

This elegy fails for reasons to be discussed, but in its imitation of Lowell, particularly in the exaggerated Lowellian rhyme "bold / Lowell," it pays tribute beyond the capability of the younger Heaney. Such a relinquishing of timbre was forecast in Heaney's essay on William Butler Yeats, which I quoted in Chapter One, when he assessed Yeats's influence on "*a* poet approaching middle age":

> He bothers you with the suggestion that if you have managed to do one kind of poem in your own way, you should cast off that way and face into another area of your experience until you have learned a new voice to say that area properly. He encourages you to experience a transfusion of energies from poetic forms themselves, reveals how the challenge of a metre can extend the resource of the voice.[63]

This middle-aged poet follows his own prescription in *Field Work*. Whereas someone casually thumbing through *North* would discover recurrent tablets of four- and five-line stanzas, *Field Work* introduces a remarkable variety of stanzas and metres, which as he predicted gives Heaney "resources of the voice": not different dramatic speakers so much as strategies toward the reader and adjustments of tone. *Field Work* dilates the range of allusions and, within the geometry of poetic relations, attends to the relation between speaker and audience, as Heaney redefines his tradition.

Of the forty-one poems in *Field Work,* one-third are elegies or elegiac, one-third take as theme poetry or poetic tradition, and a less memorable remainder concern love and troubled Ulster. The volume also dedicates or addresses a higher incidence of poems to individuals than previous volumes, but unlike Derek Mahon, who uses dedicatees or recipients of epistolary poems as a coterie, Heaney specifies this ostensible audience to widen his range of address. Among those addressed or alluded to, the genii of the volume are Robert Lowell and William Wordsworth, masters of the elegiac and pastoral or antipastoral modes, respectively. In self-consciously relating himself to these traditional modes, Heaney moves into the immediate center of this volume questions about his own craft, about his tradition, and about his audience, as he redefines them.

For example, we know that elegies are not merely salutes to the dead. We no longer send to ask for whom the bell tolls. We mourn, above all, mortality, and writers of elegy serve the elegiac tradition so that tradition may serve them. "So may some gentle Muse / With lucky words favor my destined urn," implores Milton's elegist before he renews himself, like the sun and Christ: "he rose, and twitched his mantle blue: / Tomorrow to fresh woods and pastures new."

In Heaney's own prologue to his series of revisions of the elegiac tradition, he recollects a kind country woman who gave thirsty neighbors "A Drink of Water":

> Nights when a full moon lifted past her gable
> It fell back through her window and would lie
> Into the water set out on the table.
> Where I have dipped to drink again, to be
> Faithful to the admonishment on her cup,
> *Remember the Giver* fading off the lip.
>
> (*HFW,* 16)[64]

In readings Heaney has related the slogan to the muse.[65] Remembering the giver, Heaney re-etches the admonishment and restores it to the lip and, thereby, places the elegiac muse in an interdependency with the poet.

"A Drink of Water" comments on the elegiac mode as it introduces a series of six parochial elegies for Ulster friends or neighbors. The poems are seances. They do not visit the dead, victims of Ulster violence, but invite them into the poem as spirits of a less violent, more traditional Ireland. The dead return as badgers or seals, according to folk tales; the poet levitates the victim — "I lift you under the arms and lay you flat" — or invokes him: "Dawn-sniffing revenant, / Plodder through midnight rain, / Question me again."

Of the volume's elegies, I find most affecting "A Postcard from North Antrim," in memory of an Ulster Protestant friend Sean Armstrong. The elegy opens with an echo of Stevie Smith's "Not Waving But Drowning" which Heaney admires:

> A lone figure is waving
> From the thin line of a bridge
> Of ropes and slats, slung
> Dangerously out between
> The cliff-top and the pillar rock.
> A nineteenth-century wind.
> Dulse-pickers. Sea campions.
>
> A post card for you, Sean,
> And that's you, swinging alone,
> Antic, half-afraid,
> In your gallowglass's beard
> And swallow-tail of serge:
> *The Carrick-a-Rede Rope Bridge*
> Ghost-written on sepia.

$$(HFW, 19)$$

Because "Carrick-a-Rede" means something like "the stone in the midst of the current," this elegy may trope Yeats's depiction of the 1916 martyrs whose stony hearts "troubled the living stream." Throughout the poem Armstrong — "Prince of no man's land" — is neutrally situated: on a rope bridge "Dangerously out between / The cliff-top and the pillar rock," on a houseboat beside "those warm-planked, democratic wharves of Sausalito," or beside a boat in an Ulster lake. The poet invites this spirit to return to this lake and set up "his local, hoped for, unfound commune," to sing again a ballad about Henry Joy McCracken, another Protestant who died in the nationalist conflict, hanged in 1798 as a leader of the United Irishmen, and to lead the ecumenical communion of friends sharing cheap Irish wine and a crowded apartment floor.

The concluding stanza opens a road to the past, on which traffic moves both ways: "Fifteen years ago, come this October" — lines that remind us that the postcard recreated in the opening stanza, "ghost written on sepia," seems to be both to and from Sean Armstrong:

> Fifteen years ago, come this October,
> Crowded on your floor,
> I got my arm round Marie's shoulder
> For the first time.
> 'Oh, Sir Jasper, do not touch me!'
> You roared across at me,
> Chorus-leading, splashing out the wine.
>
> (*HFW*, 20)

In the manner of Hamlet addressing the boney Yorick — "Where be your gibes now? your gambols? your songs? your flashes of merriment, that were wont to set the table on a roar?" — Heaney recovers his friend at his liveliest moment, and most carefree. The concluding line suggests, to me at least, Alkinoos' feast in the *Odyssey* where, weeping over songs of his slain comrades, Odysseus shades his eyes and spills his wine to hide his grief. Dense with parochial allusions, the poem, nevertheless, relies on and evokes the elegiac tradition. As the poet knits himself into the poem as singer and subject — even recalling that he and Marie are the only lovers who parallel Henry Joy McCracken and Mary Ann — he raises the elegist's theme: "Remember the Giver."

The self-reflective intention of Heaney's elegies is confirmed by the more blatant, and therefore less successful, appeals to tradition in "Elegy" for Robert Lowell. Placing himself in a filial relationship with Lowell, Heaney concludes

> you found the child in me
> when you took farewells
> under the full bay tree
> by the gate in Glanmore,

> opulent and restorative
> as that lingering summertime,
> the fish-dart of your eyes
> risking, 'I'll pray for you.'
>
> (*HFW,* 32)

After appreciating the subtle fluency of roles in "Postcard . . . ," we see too obviously who controls all prayer in "Elegy."

The best gloss on Heaney's pastoral poetry may be a review in *Preoccupations,* Heaney's own collection of prose essays published in 1980. Describing the course of the pastoral, he writes,

> . . . the idealized landscape with contended figures, the garden, the harmonious estate, all the recurring features of the convention, are sanctioned by the race's nostalgia; yet they misrepresent the quotidian actualities of the world man inhabits outside Eden, and in the end beget a form of antipastoral in which sweat and pain and deprivation are acknowledged. [66]

The pastoral heart of *Field Work* is the sequence of ten Glanmore Sonnets which begin with self-conscious strategies for recovering the pastoral and devolve into antipastoral poems. This same review, which he wrote several years after moving from Belfast to Glanmore, an estate in Wicklow south of Dublin, begins in this manner:

> I have occasionally talked of the countryside where we live in Wicklow as being pastoral rather than rural, trying to impose notions of a beautiful landscape on the word, in order to keep 'rural' for the unselfconscious face of raggle-taggle farmland. [67]

In the opening sonnet he begins the self-conscious tilling of this new land, digging outward rather than downward as in the early volumes (in *Preoccupations* he compares the tilled furrow to the poetic line and derives *verse* from *versus,* the turning of the plow at the row's end). [68] The realistic detail of "mist band over furrows, a deep no sound" silently foreshadows a harvest of poems. Conventionally, Heaney closes off the octave here with the phrase, "My lea is deeply tilled." The next three lines—

> Old ploughsocks gorge the subsoil of each sense
> And I am quickened with a redolence
> Of the fundamental dark unblown rose.

—Calvin Bedient decries as a "painted abyss."[69] Employing Keats against Bedient, I would suggest that these lines function like the self-conscious straining toward the nightingale "on the viewless wings of Poesy" that precedes the real but momentary encounter with the nightingale's song. Heaney's eleventh line evokes Dylan Thomas, Shelley, Blake, Yeats, and even, in the hidden "roisin dubh," the dark rose, Mangan and earlier poets in Irish. Yet, the muse cannot be forced: "Wait then . . ." and in wise passiveness, the poet receives the seminal spirits of his poetic tradition:

> Wait then . . . Breasting the mist, in sowers' aprons
> My ghosts come striding into their spring stations.
> The dream grain whirls like freakish Easter snows.
> (*HFW,* 33)

This sestet embodies Heaney's contrast between two poetic methods, which he ascribes to Yeats and Wordsworth. In *Preoccupations* he could be describing this first Glanmore Sonnet:

> What we are presented with is a version of composition as listening, as a wise passiveness, a surrender to energies that spring within the centre of the mind, not composition as an active pursuit by the mind's circumference of something already at the centre.[70]

In the sonnets that follow, Heaney's ghost-sowers are Hopkins, Thomas, Frost, Lowell, and, especially, Wordsworth, who is drawn into the third sonnet forcefully, in almost a parody of the Wordsworthian method Heaney had described in his essays. Speaking of Dorothy and William in *Preoccupations,* he had said, "The couple listen, they surrender, the noise of water and the voice of the air minister to them," a stance he imitates in the third sonnet:

> This evening the cuckoo and the corncrake
> (So much, too much) consorted at twilight.
> It was all crepuscular and iambic.
> Out on the field a baby rabbit
> Took his bearings, and I knew the deer
> (I've seen them too from the window of the house,
> Like connoisseurs, inquisitive of air)
> Were careful under larch and May-green spruce.

I had said earlier, 'I won't relapse
From this strange loneliness I've brought us to.
Dorothy and William—' She interrupts:
'You're not going to compare us two . . . ?'
Outside a rustling and twig-combing breeze
Refreshes and relents. Is cadences.

(*HFW,* 35)

Describing this same wind as it stirs in Wordsworth's poetry Heaney writes, "This is perhaps an obvious moment, when the wind of heaven and the 'corresponding mild creative breeze' of inspiration sustain the voice and suspend the consciousness in its hovering."[71] When this wind appears in Heaney's own poem, even the reader who hasn't the advantage of knowing Heaney's self-gloss should recognize it is more than "an obvious moment." By troping Wordsworth, Heaney confesses a readiness to engineer the poem, to make "an active pursuit by the mind's circumference of something at the center," in the manner Heaney ascribed to Yeats. The meaning of the poem, therefore, is found no longer merely in Heaney's *timbre* but in the play the audience experiences between a characteristic voice and its Wordsworthian and Yeatsian traditions; in *tone,* consequently.

If we rotate Heaney's terms for Yeats's method to "an active pursuit by the mind's surface of something at its depth," we remind ourselves of Heaney's dilemma, or his honest statement of a modern dilemma: whether he actively delves to reach the poetic object or passively waits for it to rise to him, the poetic object, the visionary subject, the substance of belief withholds its epiphany.

Many critics on Heaney's own island would have him abandon the quiet experiential poem represented by the Glanmore sonnets and write of social injustice, as he does in the closing poem in *Field Work.* Heaney renders Dante's infernal encounter with Pisa's betrayer, Count Ugolino, who feeds on Archbishop Roger's skull, "Gnawing at him where the neck and head / Are grafted to the sweet fruit of the brain, / Like a famine victim at a loaf of bread" (*HFW,* 61). In response to Dante's question, "What hate / makes you so ravenous and insatiable?" Ugolino describes his imprisonment with his four young sons:

When I heard the door being nailed and hammered
Shut, far down in the nightmare tower.

I stared in my sons' faces and spoke no word.

. . . . ` . . . . . . . . . . . .

                            Then when I saw
The image of my face in their four faces
I bit on my two hands in desperation
And they, since they thought hunger drove me to it,
Rose, suddenly in agitation
Saying, "Father, it will greatly ease our pain
If you eat us instead, and you who dressed us
In this sad flesh undress us here again."
So then I calmed myself to keep them calm.
We hushed. That day and the next stole past us
And earth seemed hardened against me and them.
For four days we let the silence gather.
Then, throwing himself flat in front of me,
Gaddo said, "Why don't you help me, father?"
He died like that, and surely as you see
Me here, one by one I saw my three
Drop dead during the fifth day and the sixth day
Until I saw no more. . . .

. . . . . . . . . . . . . . .

Pisa! Pisa, your sounds are like a hiss
Sizzling in our country's grassy language.
And since the neighbour states have been remiss
In your extermination, let a huge
Dyke of islands bar the Arno's mouth, let
Capraia and Gorgona dam and deluge
You and your population. For the sins
Of Ugolino, who betrayed your forts,
Should never have been visited on his sons.
Your atrocity was Theban. They were young
And innocent: Hugh and Brigata
And the other two whose names are in my song.

                             (*HFW,* 62–64)

Although the first starvations in Long Kesh occurred nearly two years after this portion of the *Inferno* was translated, we can hardly wonder what drew Heaney to this passage. He says,

> I sensed there was something intimate, almost carnal, about those feuds and sorrows of medieval Pisa, something that could perhaps mesh with

and house the equivalent and destructive energies in, say, contemporary Belfast.[72]

Dante's function as Ugolino's intermediary with the upper world—

> Is there any story I can tell
> For you, in the world above, against him?
> If my tongue by then's not withered in my throat
> I will report the truth and clear your name.

—could be Heaney's. As in several poems of *Wintering Out* and Part II of *North,* Heaney might descend to various levels of the past and return to "the world above" with messages of social justice. Yet, Heaney has expressed his wariness of "plying the pros and cons of the Ulster situation in an editorializing kind of way. . . . That would only have ratified the sectarian categories which had us where we were."[73] Without Dante's catholic authority, Heaney's political poems in *North* seem evasive and not fully credible. In contrast, the honesty of the Glanmore sonnets we could fairly call courageous. Skeptical of recovering the object, Heaney enforces the relationship with the reader. The recognizable Heaney voice, his *timbre,* becomes only one voice in a dramatic strategy that involves the reader in field work: the poetic tilling, the passive seed-time, and the blighted harvest, with "blood on a pitch-fork, blood on chaff and hay."[74] The sequence into which the reader is drawn is underwritten by a premise, perhaps Heaney's article of faith, that is expressed in the final Glanmore Sonnet:

> I dreamt we slept in a moss in Donegal
> On turf banks under blankets, with our faces
> Exposed all night in a wetting drizzle,
> Pallid as the dripping sapling birches.
> Lorenzo and Jessica in a cold climate.
> Diarmuid and Grainne waiting to be found.
> Darkly asperged and censed, we were laid out
> Like breathing effigies on a raised ground.

The setting, a combination of dream, real geography, and literature, shifts from the more English pastoral of Wicklow to the free county of Heaney's province Ulster. It combines the Shakespearean and Irish romances, allusions to the Penshurst-like country house and to the Irish west, and finds the dream-subjects blest and dreaming. But of what do lovers in the pastoral dream? Just as Yeats's Byzantine golden bird can sing only of the world of process—"of what is past, or passing, or to come,"—so the dreamers remote in a literary setting reflect their own embowering, the actual world of convening and separating.

> And in that dream I dreamt—how like you this?—
> Our first night years ago in that hotel
> When you came with your deliberate kiss
> To raise us towards the lovely and painful
> Covenants of flesh; our separateness;
> The respite in our dewy dreaming faces.
>
> (*HFW*, 42)

The dream offers an actual moment from their past life with Wyatt's line "how like you this" which literate lovers may remember is followed by "It was no dream, I lay broad waking." The final line returns to the pastoral dreamers for whom the dream of the actual life has offered *respite,* not merely "a reprieve" but also "a looking back," in this case from the more literary and traditional toward the present.

The Glanmore Sonnets, and the recent elegies, suggest that Heaney could now revise a statement he made in 1974 that the present must be brought "into a significant relationship with the past."[75] If the past cannot be reached by the delver or emerge under the poet's cultivation, it can inspirit a poetry of experience, which involves a relationship between poet and audience. Just as the prehistoric birdsong can live only in the present singer, the ear of the listener, and the moment of the song, so the Irish tradition is renewed only within the present. The numerous critics who have admired "Song" and used its conclusion, "the music of what happens" to characterize Heaney's poetry, overlook the fact that Heaney has reset the conclusion of an ancient Fenian episode, which Austin Clarke had revised in a similar manner.[76] Heaney's Irish auditor would hear in this endorsement of spontaneous poetry a discourse with the past.

Although *Station Island* extends Heaney's dialectic in a complex manner, this volume, which arrived at my home only a week before the galley sheets for this book, is too newborn to be a suitable topic for reflection. However, because the shelf-life, and even the lap-life, of this book depends somewhat on the justness of its response to new poetry, some assessment of *Station Island* must be ventured.

The volume is divided into three parts: a gathering of twenty-five lyrics, a Dantesque pilgrimage in twelve cantos, and twenty lyrical digressions from or glosses on the Sweeney myth, Heaney's translation of which appeared in 1983 as *Sweeney Astray*.[77] The third part, which contains memorable imagery and a vague political allegory, seems less remarkable than the first two complementary parts. "The Underground" opens the volume and most of its concerns mid-stride, the youthful poet and his love racing through the Underground to Albert Hall or other sites of past pleasure. He can return to these moments, when like an enamoured god he pursued his nymph, through memory ("as Hansel . . . / Retracing the path back, lifting the buttons") or imagination, addressing the past through the transformations of mythic poetry, as a Pan, a Hansel, and an Orpheus. Finally, he is compelled to relate to her, who once led him, through his Orphic role, in which he leads her: "Bared and tense as I am, all attention / For your step following and damned if I look back."[78] The final statement of fact is also a statement of the poet's will, as he seems to accept the indirection of the underground or mythic method.

Through complex implication, the poem raises questions about not only poetic method but also the burden of the poet's personal role and how he may re-approach reality. He may re-gain reality by seeing as a child, by suffering with his compatriots, by reclaiming his geographical place, and by seeing through the eyes of nature, part one suggests. Yet, this recovery is blocked by his very success, like the rich young man who is told by Christ to sell all and give to the poor, the text which underlies *Station Island*.[79]

For example, the volume approaches the small miracle "The Railway Children" through four previous poems that comment on the poet's childhood view and on his poetic legacies for his two sons and his daughter. The poem recalls the child's startling elevated view from a railway slope through the wires and white cups of telegraph poles:

> We were small and thought we knew nothing
> Worth knowing. We thought words travelled the wires
> In the shiny pouches of raindrops,

Each one seeded full with the light
Of the sky, the gleam of the lines, and ourselves
So infinitesimally scaled

We could stream through the eye of a needle.

(HSI, 45)

Such a passage — of selves immeasurably minute and therefore scaled for infinity — the Apostles declared impossible, but Christ demurred.

Heaney attempts to recover this perspective of radical innocence in two previous poems in which he offers to Catherine a stick from the poet's sacred tree, the hazel, and to his sons a kite, an emblem of the soul. In "A Kite for Michael and Christopher," he would also give the poem, and perhaps the gift of poetry. Such is implied by the play on words such as "line," "furrow," "strumming," and "strain," which pertain more to poetry than to kites. With "A Hazel Stick for Catherine Anne," he would give also the gift of fresh vision, to himself as well as his daughter. Like the rich young man, however, Heaney is challenged to abandon his word-horde and speak as a child. The poem vacillates between an adult's language and a child's ad lib as he describes the hazel stick:

Seasoned and bendy,
it convinces the hand

that what you have you hold
to play with and pose with

and lay about with.
But then it points back to cattle

and spatter and beating
the bars of a gate —

the very stick we might cut
from your family tree.

(HSI, 42)

Other poems in this volume are energized by this tuning in and out of his timbre. We hear a resumption of the onomatopoeic nouns, as in this mason's labor: "he stands / remembering his trade, the song / of his trowel dressing a brickbat, / the tock and tap of its butt . . ." (*HSI*, 54). We see fossilized metaphors — "venerators," "untrammeled," "inanition" — stir in their Latinate beds. We experience syllables harmonized with natural sounds, but less often the squelch of bog and loam, in this volume, than a new ethereality, perhaps borrowed from Sweeney:

> . . . I closed my eyes
> to make the light motes stream behind them
> and my head went airy, my chair rode
> high and low among branches and the wind
> stirred up a rookery in the next long *Aye*.
>
> (*HSI*, 51–52)

Yet, Heaney also mimics other voices, as in the Muldoonesque "Widgeon," dedicated to Muldoon:[80]

> he found, he says, the voice box —
>
> like a flute stop
> in the broken windpipe —
>
> and blew upon it
> unexpectedly
> his own small widgeon cries.
>
> (*HSI*, 48)

As this suggests, he will speak for others — Sweeney, Catherine, Wordsworth (in "Changes"), and for the dramatis personae of "Station Island."

Heaney's vacillation between his own and others' language, between lyric and dramatic modes, and between active and contemplative responses to suffering raises ambivalence to nearly a thematic level. This division of mind polarizes his grammatical pairings which often appear Janus-like: sloe gin is "bitter and dependable"; a hampered lobster is "fortified and bewildered"; a woman's breasts are "inviolable and affronting" (actually, a divergent rather than Janus-like pairing); travelers "nourish and resist" words such as *birthplace* and *hearth*.

These apparent contradictory pairings are actually oxymora, rhetorical paradoxes which may resolve ambiguity. They can serve as poetic resolutions of questions about the poet's role, the most troublesome of which concerns Heaney's response to suffering in his native province of Ulster. Whereas the various comments on Heaney's response to the

Troubles — apologies for holding his tongue, admonitions from others to guard his individuality — still add up to ambivalence in this volume, "Away from it All" seems to comment on this ambivalence. Savoring a prolonged lobster dinner, the poet ruminates on challenging lines from the Polish poet Czeslaw Milosz:

> I was stretched between contemplation
> of a motionless point
> and the command to participate
> actively in history.

Then, as if to answer the poet's question "*Actively? What do you mean?*", the coastal landscape demonstrates "the motionless point":

> The light at the rim of the sea
> is rendered down to a fine
> graduation, somewhere between
> balance and inanition.

Finally, the poet rejects *inanition* — "an emptying out," in its radical meaning — in order to define the sort of "balance" or nonparticipation in history he may maintain:

> And I still cannot clear my head
> of lives in their element
> on the cobbled floor of that tank
> and the hampered one, out of water,
> fortified and bewildered.
>
> (*HSI*, 16–17)

Not only will he sympathize with the victim, but he will also reinterpret the oxymoron that characterizes it. The positive and negative associations of "fortified and bewildered" are recognized in Heaney's poem as actually terms of imprisonment and freedom, respectively. As indirect as this poetic statement seems to be, it nevertheless suggests that rumors of Heaney's "politicization," raised by his name on the Field Day masthead, have misrepresented the honest ambivalence of one "balancing" between sympathy for and detachment from suffering among his Ulster compatriots.

Personal questions of Heaney's disposition toward oppression in the North and his need for independence as an artist are raised in the central part of the volume, "Station Island," not lyrically here but in dialogues with and evocations of the past. In direct references to Dante, the subject of pilgrimage, sporadic use of terza rima, dialogues with the notable dead, and the placement of the individual artist against a tumultuous political background, "Station Island" summons up the spirit of Dante, particularly of the *Purgatorio*. The poem also returns to a setting —the site of the ancient pilgrimages, mentioned by Dante, to Lough Derg on the border between Donegal and Tyrone—already explored in long poems by Devlin and Kavanagh and a prose sketch by William Carleton. Only the latter two writers figure overtly in the dialogues of "Station Island."

Carleton greets the poet with "O holy Jesus Christ, does nothing change?", adapting a Tyrone voice to iambs but not to the "I am" of Heaney's characteristic diction. Kavanagh upbraids his understudy: "Sure I might have known / once I had made the pad, you'd be after me / sooner or later. Forty-two years on / And you've got no farther!" (*HSI*, 73) Neither Kavanagh's nor Heaney's best lines, this credible japing demonstrates Heaney's willingness to suspend his timbre to serve his dramatic purpose.

The dead pilgrims who waylay the poet have visited the stations of the poet's mind and uncovered his most troubling anxieties. For example, the poet first encounters Simon Sweeney, a figure from his childhood who, as a notorious Sabbath-breaker, haunted the child's dreams. The significantly named Sweeney recalls these dreams to the poet and establishes the volume's keynote with the warning: "Beware of the empty forms." Other characters needle the poet concerning his tendencies to conform, his overinvolvement with the Irish dialect, and the remoteness of his art from life. Yet, in recounting these revenants' deaths, the poem depicts the horror of political murders more starkly than in any previous Heaney poem excepting his translation of the Ugolino passage from the *Inferno*.

The strongest rebuke is delivered by Colum McCartney, a murdered cousin Heaney commemorated in a *Field Work* elegy "The Strand At Lough Beg." Just as Virgil daubs Dante's eyes with dew and plaits into his belt the reeds of humility to prepare him for Purgatory, so in his elegy Heaney asperges and adorns his murdered cousin. In "Station Island" the cousin reproaches the poet for translating his gory death into art:

"You confused evasion and artistic tact.
The protestant who shot me through the head
I accuse directly, but indirectly, you
who now atone perhaps upon this bed
for the way you whitewashed ugliness and drew
the lovely blinds of the *Purgatorio*
and saccharined my death with morning dew."

(*HSI*, 85)

Later, the poem suggests the necessity of art translating life, as a familiar kitchen mug was borrowed for a local play and thereby "dipped and glamoured from this translation."

The speaker's principal literary advisors are William Carleton and James Joyce. Joyce admonishes him to abandon poems about Irish and English dialects: "The subject people stuff is a cad's game." For both his elders, writing is natural functioning, not self-expression so much as self-maintenance. Carleton says, "We are earthworms of the earth, and all that / has gone through us is what will be our trace" (*HSI*, 66).

Joyce, however, provides the last speech in the closing canto, advising the "dolphin's way":

"Swim

out on your own and fill the element
with signatures on your own frequency,
echo soundings, searches, probes, allurements,

elver-gleams in the dark of the whole sea."

Abandoning a monumental view of literature, Heaney's advisors espouse an art that is sinuous and ephemeral. Even with echoes of "A Lough Neagh Sequence," Joyce's imperative characterizes the author of *Finnegans Wake* more than that of "Station Island." Heaney, however, has taken on the courage of Joyce, and of Yeats, in his willingness to swim out beyond the shallows. Although he has written poetry of extraordinary accomplishment, the innovativeness of *Field Work* and *Station Island* promises even further development of his talent.

Finally, in giving his closing speech to a character named Joyce, Heaney recognizes the need for narrative complexity, for the dispersal of narrative authority among various speakers, as he follows the progression Stephen Dedalus outlines in *A Portrait* as the necessary stages in the growth of all literary art: from the lyrical toward the epical and the dramatic.

## CHAPTER FOUR

# Devlin & Montague

As we dispel the shadow Yeats cast over his successors, we recognize that some of these poets have generated their own obscurity. Denis Devlin (1908–59) is known to be a difficult poet when nothing else is known of him. John Montague (b. 1929), on the other hand, presents himself so directly to readers that his complexities are often overlooked. Consequently, what are needed for an understanding of Devlin's and Montague's poetry are not accounts of their careers so much as essays, attempts to penetrate their works where they are most obscure or most subtle.

Compared with even Clarke, Kavanagh, and MacNeice, his major Irish contemporaries, Devlin has attracted few readers, and even fewer re-readers. Yet, a corps of formidable poet-critics, including Samuel Beckett, Allen Tate, Robert Penn Warren, Brian Coffey, John Montague, and Hayden Carruth have advised readers that Devlin's poetry rewards effort.[1] The fact that these defending voices arise from Paris, Boston, Washington, and Southampton, as well as Ireland, can only deepen the impression that Devlin belongs more to international modernist, than to Irish, poetry.

In fact, he spent only a third of his fifty-one years in residence in Ireland. Born in Scotland to Irish parents, he did not move to Dublin until his tenth year, and he remained only through his college years and a brief tenure as English assistant at University College, Dublin. He was appointed to the Department of External Affairs and soon assigned to the legation in Italy, from which he advanced in the hierarchy of foreign diplomacy. Although as an Irish diplomat he remained tethered occupationally to Ireland, the manifest influence of places and poets in Europe and America offers readers, who may be seeking Irishness, an excuse for ignoring Devlin, in addition to that based on his difficulty as a poet.

As I have suggested generally, to question whether or not Devlin is an Irish poet, as if there existed strict cultural dogma against which heresy can be measured, seems not only irrelevant but pernicious. To the living tradition of Irish poetry Devlin can contribute an eclectic receptivity toward literature and philosophy, an Irish-Catholic sensitivity toward the flesh, a modernized Mariolatry in which women offer access to the divine, and a poetic reticence, which soon became integral with his subject but which also may have reflected Devlin's uncertainty about a primary audience.

Although Devlin may have influenced the poetry of Montague and Kinsella, we can repatriate him to a province within the Irish poetic tradition only when the complex contents of his poetry have been fully declared. It is a propitious time for such a declaration. Devlin's editor, bibliographer, and friend, Brian Coffey, has contributed a useful collection of Devlin's verse and an excellent edition of his long masterpiece *The Heavenly Foreigner.*[2] Recently, Coffey and Mervyn Wall have written biographical sketches; Coffey and Stan Smith have given us reasonable reinterpretations of some poems, and James Mays has written a brief but exemplary study of one long poem.[3] If critics as capable as Mays and Smith would undertake a monograph study of Devlin's poetry, we might recover a flawed but deeply affective poet, one of the indispensable poets in the generation after Yeats. In this briefer space, we can recognize his essential poems, examine his rhetoric as an embodiment of his ideas, and suggest some major influences on his work.

We might begin, and end, by reflecting on Devlin's essential works. In their American selection, Tate and Warren have misled anthologizers and readers by preferring the more finished and tonally consistent poems such as "Lough Derg," "Ank'hor Vat," and "From Government Buildings." Using such finished poems as standards, a reader might be repelled by *The Heavenly Foreigner* and "The Colours of Love," "Meditation at Avila," "Old Jacobin," "Eve in My Legend," "Farewell and Good," "Royal Canal," "Little Elegy," and another dozen spiritual love poems that may also contain patches of bad rhetoric, jangling couplets, or otherwise bad rhyme or sound effects. Yet these poems, more than the anthologized standards, can affect the whole human, if we keep in mind that we are at least nine parts liquid. We value these poems not only because they open ducts and move us but because the poems themselves also are wonderfully fluid, catching multiple meanings in their urgent motion.

Difficulties in Devlin's verse are usually fluidities; where we cannot grasp meaning, we must trace it in a motion that has a definable course. Devlin employs a rhetoric that includes substitution, ambiguity, paradox, and perpetual reference to launch the reader into a circular reasoning or an otherwise continuing pursuit of meaning which, in effect, teases us out of thought.

For example, Devlin sometimes denies us an expected word in order to create play between the missing word and its surrogate. In "The Colours of Love," we read "The cliffs fell faster than tears / Reaching that pain where feeling does not matter" (*DCP*, 17). When *pain* replaces *plain,* we are reminded of the psychic nature of the Fall, but we also visualize a flat expanse of suffering. Similarly, in "Farewell and Good," the poet weighs the loneliness after the lover has departed: "What use my hermit grief to a world bitten in self" (*DCP*, 85). The suggestion in *world* and *self* of the words *apple* and *half* introduces the theme of this poem, the idea that this fall from Edenic love leads to the discovery of his distinctive self. In "The Colours of Love," because we are told that "Those beautiful women shone against the dark / With flowers upon the breast . . . ," we should be surprised by these lines: "It was as if eternity were breathing / Through the small breathing of the flowers / Shining upon its breast . . ." (*DCP*, 18). When *its* referring to "eternity" replaces the anticipated *their* referring to "those beautiful women," a successor to Shelley's Intellectual Beauty or Yeats's or Dante's Rose haunts the poem.

In addition to surprising us with substituted words, Devlin will often violate our grammatical expectations by failing to complete a compound verb or by shifting into another grammatical form at the end of a sentence. We see an example of this anacoluthon in "The Passion of Christ":

> One, Simon, in excess of passion,
> Trusted his unreflecting hands;
> What is this genius of compassion
> That comprehends, nor understands!
>
> (*DCP*, 12)

Where we might anticipate "and understands," we have a denial of clear reason that complements the skewed logic of "unreflecting hands." In another form of anacoluthon the verb in the longest line of this stanza from "Little Elegy" shifts tense and number:

> This is all I can remember
> Quarrelling, gusts of confidence
> The class climbing through faun nights
> And her I would meet
> As though I were unconscious
> In vacant, bright-columned streets
> And brings in love's tunic scattered to the four winds
> For no reason at all
> For no reason that I can tell.
>
> (*DCP*, 83)

The speaker uses the surprising unassigned verb *brings* because he is reclaiming *she* as its subject from the objective *her*, or because the speaker remembers that it is only memory that "brings in" this gathering of scattered friends. As we vacillate between possible subjects for the verb *brings* and sense both the immediacy and the remoteness of remembered love, we advance beyond reason toward the ineffable: "For no reason that I can tell."

More often we vacillate between explicit alternatives as in the opening section of "The Passion of Christ":

> From what did man fall?
> From the Archangel Michael's irritated wing?
> Man is so small,
> Without him first the universe did sing,
> So fortunate since the Christ endued his caul:
>
> (*DCP*, 8)

Three sources of ambiguity actually enrich the meaning. We are told neither with what the caul is endued, nor whether the caul is Christ's or man's. If the caul is first Christ's, then the topic is the Incarnation, and the word *endues* assumes both its rare meaning of "to put on, to dress in" when applied to Christ and a more general meaning of "to bless" when applied to man. As the Fall is compensated for, the ambiguous "so fortunate" becomes a meaningful characterization of both "the universe" and "Man."

Devlin will risk awkwardness in order to set several lines in motion with reflective meanings. However, he can also appoint the smallest words to reflect various meanings as he does in the beautiful poem "Veronica's Veil" from "The Passion of Christ":

> They tend His fierce divinity, shy saviours,
> From the calvaries of the dispossessed,
> Ragged mothers who give milk to their neighbours
> While the husband fails, and the child undressed
>
> Scrabbles at the empty plate, some holy women
> Will take their last white linen from the drawer
> And saying: "God is ours as He is human,"
> Wipe the blood from the unbearable scar.
>
> (DCP, 11)

In the woman's brief explanation, *as* means "because," "while," "in so far as," and "in the manner that," each alternative enriching the meaning.

Devlin enjoys activating the ambiguities implicit in most colloquialism. For example, in *The Heavenly Foreigner,* from his objective vision of a woman the poet creates a vision of the beloved which dissolves her actual qualities:

> How she stood, hypothetical-eyed and metaphor-breasted
> Weaving my vision out of my sight,
> Out of my sight, out of my very sight,
> Out of her sight,
> Till the sight I see with is blind with light
> Other than hers, other than mine;
>
> (DHF, 36–37)

Devlin also develops ambiguities through his syntax and punctuation. In "Royal Canal," for example, one stanza contains two "squinting" metaphors, each of which could modify the element that precedes or follows the phrase. The poem describes a dowager beseiged by time:

> The gruff mongrels in aimless exercise
> With boys shouting; and then a silence.
> All shouting waves around
> Silence like a blind egg
> Terror fills her old eyes as in girlhood
>
> She turns from the window; . . .
>
> (DCP, 42)

"As in girlhood" extends "terror fills" or modifies "she turns from the window." On the rereading, she turns because of terror, and a mere causal statement comes to characterize a life's withdrawal. The other remarkable simile deserves fuller attention. "Like a blind egg" mediates between "silence" and "terror" or perhaps between the actions that involve them. Silence enfolds and broods, to hatch some unspecified future. This anxiety makes her eyes glaucous to the present. Through the ambiguity Devlin describes both a causal sequence and a stasis which our mind must become active to apprehend.

The metaphor of the blind egg seems surreal enough to justify a brief digression from our discussion of Devlin's rhetoric to a consideration of his imagery and its relation to that of French poets. For all of its similarity to French surrealism, Devlin's imagery remains only quasi-surrealist, closer to that of the inheritors of symbolism, such as Valery or St. John Perse whom Devlin translated so capably. For contrast to Devlin's "blind egg," we might consider the following description by André Breton of a newspaper:

> But most beautiful of all is the space in between certain letters
> Where hands whiter than the midday cornucopia of stars
> Disconcert a nest of white swallows
>
> ("The Writings Recede")[4]

Beyond the idea of things hidden in overexposure, one probably cannot unravel these lines. Perhaps they fulfill Breton's own definition of surrealism: "Dictated by thought, in the absence of any control exercised by reason. . . ."[5] Even when Devlin's images startle us, they are pervious to reason and therefore conceived, somehow, rationally, as another reference to "Royal Canal" will demonstrate. One line introduces an implicit analogy for the dowager: "The druid elms, closed in their lost language." A redundancy hidden in "druid elms" acts out the idea in the participial phrase that follows. In this rare case when Devlin's images are purposefully static and self-contained, we can see with what wit and reason they are constructed. Roger Callois's advice concerning Perse's poetry can be applied to Devlin's as it could not be to the French surrealists': "Slow research and a kind of yielding to its powers can force it to give up its secrets."[6]

Rearmed with such advice, we can return to a final example of Devlin's ambiguity which appears in the complex poem "Farewell and Good."

Speaking of his indelible first love, he begins with a standard elegiac opening: "She I loved so much will not appear again / Brilliant to my eyes as once she held me. . . ." Of course she does return to him, in leaf-clones and dreams:

> At any time of the day and night, struck by a wind-flash
> In snood of leaves or in phantasms of sleep assembling her form,
> I restore my kingdom in her, the real that deepened the dreamed-on
> (*DCP,* 85)

The point of the poem, however, is that he has fallen from her as implied by the phrase discussed earlier, "a world bitten in self." The poem concludes:

> Still the complaint still no comfort to her and me split
> Like a glass, like life split by some Sistine hand,
> Our life that brimmed over like diamonds in our light.

Because the first occurrence here of *split* means merely "to divide or separate," the primary reference of "Sistine hand" probably should be to the focus of Michelangelo's Sistine mural, God's hand, which, extended and deft, separates from, as it creates, Adam. The second sense of *split,* implied in God's touch and in Michelangelo's hand, becomes realized in the final lines when splitting creates not broken glass but the beauty of faceted diamonds. Because in their split they realize their distinctive selves, this Fall is both tragic and fortunate, as the title "Farewell and Good" implies.

The rhetorical term for the repetition of a word in a different or contrary sense, as with *split,* is *antistasis,* a word that also suggests Devlin's intention. Meaning in Devlin's poetry is dynamic rather than static. He breaks stasis not only through the volleying between alternative meanings of a word but also through active paradoxes: oxymorons such as "divine dissidence" (*DHF*) or "sacred bane" ("Lough Derg") or enigmatic statements such as "they live forgotten in each others heart" ("Little Elegy"). More frequently, by omitting full stops, Devlin increases tempo and creates ambiguities, as in the example, cited earlier, of "Royal Canal":

> All shouting waves around
> Silence like a blind egg

Terror fills her old eyes as in girlhood

She turns from the window . . .

*(DCP,* 42)

Devlin will also disrupt stasis and set meaning in motion through various forms of internal reference, frequently to some antecedent in a remote line of the poem. In "Edinburgh Tale" he characterizes the woman's effect on him with numerous metaphors that suggest legends of Queen Mary or other Scottish tales. The traffic in meaning is accelerated as the metaphorical vehicles accumulate:

The tale ends for having been
No secret after all but the ungovernable, scared birds of the heart and
   the blood risen and the lute like an idiot

*(DCP,* 79)

Finally, perhaps Devlin's most characteristic "antistatic" device is the use of internal references, what Joyce calls "ipso-relative" allusions, which sometimes occur in a sequence: one term will refer to another which refers to a third, setting in motion a relay or short circuit of reasoning.

To illustrate this complex allusiveness, and other antistatic devices, we might turn to "The Colours of Love" and *The Heavenly Foreigner,* which are among Devlin's major poems. Both poems appeared in journals in the fifties — *Heavenly Foreigner* in *Poetry Ireland* (1950) and "Colours of Love" in the Roman journal *Botteghe Oscure* (1952), but they remained uncollected until after Devlin's death in 1959. In his most recent essay on Devlin, Brian Coffey suggests that Devlin's poetry reveals an acceptance of Christ as an incarnation of God's otherness, which formerly had been a barrier between humanity and God.[7] In his preface to Devlin's *Collected Poems,* Coffey suggests the place in that progression of "The Colours of Love": "There is plenty of evidence in the poems of this volume of a conflict of ravaging intensity which for many years finds expression only in a love poetry so positive that the opposing pole of the conflict hardly comes clearly into sight." He continues,

And in "The Colours of love," in verses which, although they were not written out of the tradition of courtly love (of which like so many of Gaelic poets, Denis Devlin was well aware), might well sum up the European sentence upon that extraordinary phenomenon: Better no love than love, which, through loving leads to no love: the poet seems to free himself from his conflict in its overt form, and thus, mature, turn inward to the personal life out of which issued *The Passion of Christ.* (*DCP,* xiii)

"The Colours of Love" is a difficult poem, as Coffey acknowledges in his qualifying "seems to." Although the poet assumes a greater distance from the beloved than in most poems in *Lough Derg and Other Poems* (1946), I cannot find that Devlin pronounces "sentence upon" courtly love, or that he slackens that cord between carnal and spiritual love, on which he plays.

"The Colours of Love" might even be read as a playful extension of the *dolce stil nuovo* with its emphasis on eyes and smiles, in the manner of Guido Guinizelli, and the dialectic between polar values — sunlight, daytime, father-farmer, business, and the acceptance of death, on the one hand, and starlight, night, women, Venereal pursuits, and fear of death, on the other. The polarities are recollected with more or less reference to the poet's own life.

The complexities of this poem, which often spring from the types of "antistasis" already discussed, may justify a brief paraphrase of the thirty-seven stanzas of quatrains, couplets, and five-line verses that comprise the 135 lines of "The Colours of Love."

The poem opens with a paradox: although the beauty of beloved women, which is mortal, depends on the lovers' eyes, it becomes absolute through the imagination. As the poet yields to the night-realm of Venus, he joins the priests of venery who expound Love's legends. He recalls that within their tragic foreshadowing women came to shine for him, and he fell, experiencing both transcendence and pain, reflections of eternity and death. Repenting his surrenders to love, he nevertheless relapses. Even within the rational realm, where light is "husbanded by our father," he is haunted by memory and Venus who tempts him as poet to extend love's fables. At times, intense reason can devalue life and, thereby, reduce the fear of death which is engendered by, and depends on, our love of beauty. As the poet ages and the fear of death is mollified, he imagines his own Dantean exile within an Irish setting. Bereft of love, he prays, and his prayer is answered by "a kinsman," presumably a "hunting priest" who restores his courage with this legend: "love fails but love of love stays true." The poem's dia-

lectic continues through a discussion of unity by means of formal restraint, presented in couplets, to an abandonment of absolutist devices
and an acceptance of rebirth and multiplicity, to a synthesis in ascetic
love: he "thinks on" Saint John whose attempts to transcend his own
drama through love were unrequited but who continued to love nevertheless.

The poem concludes with three autobiographical quatrains, in the
complex interpretation of which I differ from Coffey. In the "Bar du
Depart," Devlin's Parisian local and last call, he offers a parting glass
to love and poetry. This farewell is followed by the concluding antistatic
quatrains:

> Down the boulevard the lights come forth
> Like my rainflowers trembling all through Spring,
> Blue and Yellow in the Celtic North . . .
> The stone's ripple weakens, ring by ring.
>
> Better no love than love, which, through loving
> Leads to no love. The ripples come to rest . . .
> Ah me! how all that young year I was moving
> To take her dissolution to my breast!
>
> (*DCP,* 21)

The deliquescent lights, corresponding to the Irish rainflowers, are
a weaker ripple of that earlier Celtic spring. In the final stanza, apparently foreswearing love, the poet actually only accepts the stillness in
which we begin and end, but does so with a final ripple in the poem's
movement: in memory he returns to the beginning of that process, the
disturbing love of that youthful year which already had implied its own
ending. For Devlin, "the stone in the midst of all" is memory's recur-
ring incident.

As epitomes for "The Colours of Love," we might employ statements
of two poets whose influence is discernible in Devlin's poetry. Yeats's
epigram—"Man is in love and loves what vanishes, / What more is
there to say?"—finally cannot say quite enough to summarize "The Colours of Love." Shelley's lines from "Adonais"—"Heaven's light forever
shines . . . / Life, like a dome of many coloured glass, / Stains the white
radiance of eternity"—suggest a source for, and the fuller meaning of,
Devlin's title. Such static or spatial abstracts, however, ignore Devlin's

primary intention: to manifest in his poetry the dynamic, elusive, and even paradoxical relation of ideal and realized love.

This idea is reflected in the elaborate dynamics of Devlin's masterwork, *The Heavenly Foreigner.* The poem recollects an actual arch-love, perhaps a woman Devlin knew in Europe in the thirties. In the "absolute woman of a moment" he observes or imagines some essential movement, ripples of which the poem traces through encounters with other women, which are as actual as, and even conditioned by, the cathedral towns or other architectural sites associated with that love. These sites become the titles of the poem's eleven sections. As the leaves of the beech or the beach's waves refract one sun, these diverse experiences with beauty and love hint of one source, some unity. This oneness may be the essence of that woman or a projection from the poet himself, or nothingness, death, or God, but while the poet is within time, he cannot know: "Time virtual is what keeps me in Time: / Leave me in abeyance" (32–33).

In tracing the various references to Oneness, we cannot hope to isolate one reference that would identify the Heavenly Foreigner; rather, we might accept the circle, or circulation, of references as Devlin's embodiment of this elusive idea of unity. In the few cases in which Devlin refers to this principle of unity as masculine, he usually associates it with death. For example, in the "Irvine" section, after recognizing other men's attachments to diverse, particular experiences, he confesses:

> Something there was other
> Always at my elbow,
> I sang, hunted and hated one;
> He sings and hunts and hates me;
> Say heaven or hell,
> Say well or ill,
> I cannot make it different,
> Anything, or even other.
>
> (*DHF,* 35)

This contradictory statement seems to refer both to the unity of which "both thousand leaves and sea / Sang . . ." twenty lines previously as well as to an alarming tempter referred to early in the poem: "the needling of some old hair-splitter from the dark. / The thing behind your elbow" (19–20). A closer, if not clearer, association of death and the Heavenly Foreigner closes the "Irvine" section toward the end of the poem. He records the sudden brightening of life at the intrusion of some unspecified force:

> When the foreign power intervened and made all the difference
> Between the bog and the road,
> Making the present, making life
> Where the bull is silent in his shadow
> And the farmhouse in its handmaid ring of trees;
>
> There is the light small in the dark;
> There is the heart filled with oil which will burn,
> Which will be quenched.
>
> The world glows with mortal divinity;
> The red turns gray,
> The ash creeps up on the flame
> O Heavenly Foreigner! Your price is high.
>
> (*DHF,* 35–36)

That the source of this radiant intervention may be the human heart is suggested by lines that invoke Yeats's "Two Songs From A Play": "Whatever flames upon the night / Man's own resinous heart has fed," but this glow of "mortal divinity" is given value by the consuming ash, rather as Shelley's imagination is fed by "Intellectual Beauty," "that to human thought art nourishment, / Like darkness to a dying flame!" ("Hymn to Intellectual Beauty," 44–45). That God may be the source of reflected radiance is suggested in only one section, which echoes Shelley's "Mount Blanc," where Alpine heights, "Plains of desolation above the eyes, / Each inch and acre more and more dead," house the Lord whom he can serve only by "stepping down" to the human, to "the absolute woman of a moment" (*DHF,* 26–27).

One other masculine reference makes this source of value dependent on the particular woman, whom he addresses in the "Chartres" section:

> had you but come,
> Our absolute Lord had not been me, not me or you,
> But an instant preconising eternity
> Borne between our open eyes,

With no perceptible bank of land between,
Nor oblique eyesight deciding other objects were there.
                                                                                    (*DHF*, 21)

The "bank of land" and the little world of the eyes' mirroring seem
to allude to Donne's "Ecstasy" where the souls rise to negotiate between
the two lovers. In any case, Devlin's "absolute Lord" is dependent on, but distinguishable from, the woman. As the poem concludes,
however, the poet seems to differentiate the Heavenly Foreigner from
the woman:

I know there is one thing, which is You, it is the unique
Which also in part is she,
You, not seen by her,
You, not to be reduced by my eyes' famine of her.
                                                                                    (*DHF*, 37)

He seems also to distinguish the Heavenly Foreigner from Death:

Being of my being, say of my say!
We are pulled up short by death,
Our hands make the final signal on the same high-voltage wire;
Like the mob which stampedes across a racecourse and is pulled up
    at the palisade, its members turning, regarding each other, surprised
    into violent introduction;
And know themselves—with eye and skull, with skeleton.
As I know You, there, behind my back. As I know as far as I can
    think and have thought You.
                                                                                    (*DHF*, 38)

Yet, again, internal references unsettle this abstracted ideal: *You* assumes
the sinister place, "there, behind my back," and the obstructing pali-
sade recalls lines in the "Galway" section when the poet, "pulled up
short" at "the breakwater of humanity," confronts his mortality.

The final line, which seems to arrive at a conclusion, actually re-
immerses us in the paradox: "There is none so much as You, none You,
I think of." If we recall that as definitions of *none*, equal status is ac-
corded to *no one*, and *not one* and *nobody*, then we can recognize how
the poem recommences the circuit of alternative meanings and returns
us to the ripple's stone, as it must, because:

> Time virtual is what keeps me in Time:
> Leave me in abeyance.
>
> (*DHF,* 32–33)

These important lines from the poem's opening section terminate in an anacoluthon; we either have to reconstruct the subject for *leave* to be the compound "Time virtual and Time," meaning his conception of time's boundaries, the enclosing "miniscus of discontent," and his actual experience, I suppose, or accept the verb as imperative: meaning we must not try to extract him from his condition. In "abeyance," he is in a state of undetermined ownership, a state of suspension, which is, to revert to the radical meaning, a suspension of the condition of desiring, or gaping at, some unachieved prize. The prize may be eternity, "precognised" in a hypothetical moment of *The Heavenly Foreigner,* or the divine reconciliation offered in Devlin's "The Passion of Christ": "There will be something more when this is over / The Lion and the Lamb adopt His voice, / Beloved submit to lover . . ." (*DCP,* 11).

Most of Devlin's poetry, however, is set in the condition of "abeyance" rather than of submission. Until "this is over," the poet must remain suspended, over Blaise Pascal's void, perhaps, confronting which Pascal had gambled on God. However, in his motion above the void, Devlin seems within the company of the effectual angel Shelley and of St. John Perse, Valery, and Hart Crane.[8] From the void he seems to turn, at the poem's conclusion as in the Geneva Section, toward the woman whom he had called "his term," his limit in time and his possession within the limits of time. Until that term expires, the identity of the Heavenly Foreigner for whom she is a surrogate, "this other one, this similar, this One," must remain undetermined, within this poetry of fluid indeterminacy.

*&*

In 1972, John Montague praised Devlin as "the most dedicated poet of his generation" and declared him "the first poet of Irish Catholic background to take the world as his province."[9] In that year Montague had returned to Ireland from France, where he had lived for ten years. Perhaps because both poets were born outside of Ireland, were repatriated with some discomfort, and later became accommodated to other cultures, they were self-conscious about their national identity which is more like a vestment than a second skin.

Like Devlin, Montague's parents emigrated before his birth, but they provided him a remoter and harsher birthplace than did Devlin's— Brooklyn at the beginning of the Depression.[10] When he was four, his mother shipped him and his two older brothers back to County Tyrone. She placed the older sons with her parents in Fintona, to whom she returned three years later, and farmed out her youngest to in-laws in Garvaghey, seven miles away, much as Wordsworth was relegated to the day-and-night care of the Lake District. In the absence of his mother, Montague, like Wordsworth, pitched his affections on the landscape—the drumlins, glens, and moorland of Tyrone—and on his father's two sisters, who served as foster mothers. The poet explores this painful mother-son relationship in his most recent volume, *The Dead Kingdom.* (1984).[11] Perhaps sensitized by his status as an immigrant, the boy lived intensely in this turbulent "fair seedtime" and collected detailed memories which became the basis for his first full volume of poems, *Poisoned Lands* (1961), and a book of short stories, *Death of a Chieftain* (1964). He earned baccalaureate and master's degrees from University College, Dublin, and embarked on three years of literary studies in America with such teachers as Robert Penn Warren, John Crowe Ransom, and Thomas Parkinson. Marrying a French woman, a Fulbright scholar whom he met in Iowa, he worked in Dublin and then in Paris as a journalist. His marriage and its dissolution became the basis for *Tides* (1970) and *The Great Cloak* (1978), respectively. In 1972, after his marriage had disintegrated, he accepted a lectureship at University College Cork, remarried, and settled into his permanent residence. From this southern edge of Ireland, he maintained a doleful and loving perspective on his native Ulster and a current passport for his frequent departures to America or the continent.

This dual cultural perspective has imbued him with a sensitivity to his nation's tortured history which he expresses in his two most successful volumes, *The Rough Field* (1972) and *A Slow Dance* (1975), as well as in *The Dead Kingdom*. Devlin never developed, or never divulged, such a sensitivity toward Ireland. Despite the plaintive exile's note in "Lough Derg" and "The Tomb of Michael Collins," Devlin's community became more Catholic and ideal than Irish and local, whereas Montague acknowledges a tension between the universal, international, and local aspects in his poetry. Within this comparison, Devlin remains the international poet, his ideal incarnated but not localized, while Montague would situate the ideal within the local or, like Kavanagh, discover in the provincial crossroad lines of the world's network.

A fuller comparison between Kavanagh and Montague might cast more light on the younger writer's poetry than would the comparison with Devlin. Under Joyce's bracing influence, Kavanagh erased Yeats's commandment to sing the Irish peasantry by speaking for the small farmer of his province. This example eased Montague's access to the local and particular. Such a comparison could profit from an expansion on Seamus Deane's acute observation:

> Montague has brought the regionalism of Kavanagh one step further and deeper. The border between his Tyrone and Kavanagh's Monaghan has a certain appropriateness now. It encloses Montague in history as much as it releases Kavanagh from it. Montague has a religious sense of the local and the past, Kavanagh of the local and the present.[12]

In offering an international audience water from his local well, Montague has, in turn, influenced younger poets, so that a study that discriminated more carefully between stages of recent poetry would comprehend Kavanagh-Montague-Heaney, or the latter two, in a sequence of influence.

Consequently, the comparison between Devlin and Montague may seem somewhat arbitrary. Montague raised this objection himself in Henchy's, a pub which opens on a village-like square in Cork, a short walk and one hill over from his home on Grattan Hill. As he wound his disputation, his Devlin text fell open to "Love from Time to Time," where in the margin under these lines "For the first time I see you clear, / Where is the source of tears?" — and beside these lines from Devlin — "The underswell of Time whispers me away" — Montague had penciled the word *Tides* and an embryonic draft of "Down":[13]

> Seen
> as in a pallid
> lightning flash

a grieving woman
& not a goddess.

We begin
  the slow
    climb
      down.

(*MT,* 28)

Both poems express a momentary ebb in the tidal embrace of spirit, ideal, or even numen with the lover's body.

Perhaps in reaction to Irish Jansenism, which would inculcate in the Irish conscience a strong opposition between spirit and flesh, Devlin and Montague insist on an incarnate love, in which the spirit is inextricable from the flesh. They thereby contribute to a tradition of literature about spiritual love that extends from the *Symposium* to "The Blessed Damozel" or even to Crazy Jane: the lover embodies a beauty she does not fully possess, which can live in memory, and which may lead us to a source of higher truth. We sense in Devlin's poetry that his truth may find its source, ultimately, in the Christian godhead, whereas for Montague the lover may reflect powers of some pre-Christian force—the White Goddess or Mutability. Pound offers a ground for comparison of Devlin's and Montague's attitudes toward love in his translation of Cavalcanti's thirteenth-century "Canzone d'amore":

Where memory liveth
    it [love] takes its state
Formed like a diafan from light on shade
. . . . . . . . . . . . . .
Cometh from a seen form which being understood
Taketh locus and remaining in the intellect possible
Wherein hath he neither weight nor still-standing.[14]

Whereas through his techniques Devlin insinuates, as I have demonstrated, that love "hath . . . neither weight nor still-standing," Montague would emphasize that love "taketh locus" and "where memory liveth, it takes its state." Yet while Devlin remains uncertain but hopeful about the sources of love and truth, Montague is highly skeptical. Our personal sense of meaningful continuity derives from memory, he implies, as public traditions depend on the collective memory enclosed in legend, local lore, history, and place-names. Private and public memories falsify as they preserve, just as the poem itself must render process more static and the private more public and otherwise invalidate truths that depend on it. Because of its intensity, Montague's poetry about recollected love emphasizes the paradox of memory's, and poetry's, atemporal preservation.

Any illustration of this paradox with one lyric might easily exaggerate the photographic and static moment out of which memory creates a meaningful sequence. Yet, with some explanation of its place in the volume *The Great Cloak* (1978), "Tracks" might illuminate Montague's concern for memory and poetry's function. The book opens with a forewarning and summary of its "plot," which closely parallels D. H. Lawrence's "Introduction" to *Look! We Have Come Through!*[15]

> These poems should not only be read separately. A married man seeks comfort elsewhere, as his marriage breaks down. But he discovers that libertinism does not relieve his solitude. So the first section of the book ends with a slight affair which turns serious, the second with the despairing voices of a disintegrating marriage, the third with a new and growing relationship to which he pledges himself. (*MGC*, 7)

"Tracks," which first appears in *Tides,* is relocated in the "libertine" first section following an ambiguous four-line poem, "Snowfield":

> The paleness of your flesh.
>
> Long afterwards, I gaze happily
> At my warm tracks radiating
>
> Across that white expanse.
>
> (*MGC*, 11)

In the sequence of these ephemeral encounters, where "habitual sounds of loneliness / resume the mind again" ("Do Not Disturb"), the phrase "long afterwards" suggests that he views the blossoms of touched flesh not in that room but in memory "across the white expanse" of duration. Within the context of this volume, "Snowfield" also implies oblivion and the page against which memory and poem are printed.

A retrospection of a hotel-room tryst recounted in the present tense, "Tracks" establishes an ironic correspondence between a transient, erotic process and a fixed, static memory. The poem appears in four stanzas:

I

The vast bedroom
a hall of air,
our linked bodies
lying there.

II

As I turn to kiss
your long, black
hair, small breasts,
heat flares from
your fragrant skin,
your eyes widen as
deeper, more certain
and often, I enter
to search possession
of where your being
hides in flesh.

III

Behind our eyelids
a landscape opens,
a violet horizon
pilgrims labour across,
a sky of colours
that change, explode
a fantail of stars
the mental lightning
of sex illuminating
the walls of the skull;
a floating pleasure dome.

IV

*I shall miss you*
creaks the mirror
into which the scene
shortly disappears:
the vast bedroom
a hall of air, the
tracks of our bodies
fading there, while

> giggling maids push
> a trolley of fresh
> linen down the corridor.

The opening quatrain stalls process by associating memory and space
—"a hall of air" distanced by the rhyme with "there"—and by substituting a participial qualifier for an active verb. Conversely, the second
stanza reactivates the process of love-making: "as I turn . . .", "heat
flares . . . ," "your eyes widen. . . ." The rapid adverbial sequence dis-
persing meaning to direction, attitude, and frequency conveys a sense
of actual occurrence as he delves for her being hidden within the transient flesh. In this stanza and throughout the poem, the straitened, mostly
two-stress lines destabilize the normal horizontal motion of reading to
a rapid downward thrust, thus emphasizing movement, process, and
descent.

In this case, descent leads to ecstasy, transporting the lovers from
a particular hotel setting to "a landscape" within "the walls of the skull."
Naming this place "a floating pleasure dome," he alludes, through "Kubla
Khan," to its other locations in dream and poetry.

By offering another standard metaphor for art, the mirror, the final
stanza would embody both the transient and memorialized aspects of
the scene. Whereas the vast room disappears *into* the mirror, as the poem
absorbs the scene, the rhyming words *air* and *there,* repeated from the
first stanza, are now concealed within lines that enjamb: "lying there"
is replaced by "fading there while" which thrusts the process forward
to its termination, into the mirror or poem, and into the endless sequence of such trysts for which the giggling maids offer blank sheets.

Several poems further in the same section of *The Great Cloak,* the
more optimistic "Talisman," repeats the scene and many elements of
"Tracks." Whereas "Tracks" suggested the incapacity of memory and
poetry faithfully to record the process of love, "Talisman" recognizes
at the moment of lovemaking the future restorative virtues of this remembered act. Here, the reflecting surface—"the shield of the lake"—
as observed from the window returns rather than absorbs the light as
it epitomizes the shielding talismanic memory.

Montague recognizes that memory and poetic memoir, whether reflecting back on, or anticipated within, the moment, affect being in

time. Consequently, through various means he acknowledges the limits of language and the untold truth in silence and blank space.

We have observed in "Herbert Street Revisited," discussed in chapter one, the irony of the wife's plea, "Don't betray our truth": The suppositious dramatic monologues in which the wife bares her pain also remind us of the actual wife and of her silence. As Montague acknowledged in praising John Berryman's *Homage to Mistress Bradstreet,* "One cannot, after all, penetrate the secret and total meaning of another's life. . . ."[16]

Emotional intimacy, if not physical, often resides just beyond the border of Montague's direct statement, entering only indirectly, and therefore more truthfully, into the poem. Seamus Deane has commented eloquently, and cryptically, on Montague's wise discretion: "Even his love poems make of silence a supreme and chaste virtue as in 'All Legendary Obstacles', one of the most beautiful. In a Montague lyric, silence rides on the words, we hear the mild thunder of their passage and then the silence comes again like an aftertaste."[17] A later poem from *The Great Cloak,* "Working Dream," equates the ineffable with the unprinted word:

> At the end of a manuscript
> I was studying, a secret message.
> A star, a honeycomb, a seashell,
> The stately glory of a peacock's tail
> Spiralled colour across the page
> To end with a space between a lean I
> And a warm and open-armed You.
>
> An hour later, you were at the door;
> I learnt the word that space was for.
>
> (*MGC,* 51)

Beyond the charm of personifying the letters and the coyness of withholding obvious copulas between *I* and *You,* we recognize the tribute to privacy, blankness, and silence.[18]

Perhaps the strongest limitation to full poetic disclosure is each viewer's fixed perspective which can add up only to a public fiction. For example, the second section of *A Slow Dance* develops binary, mutually excluding perspectives: an abandoned Tyrone famine cottage contrasts with a Victorian Killarney estate as if Wordsworth's "Ruined Cottage"

were set beside Tennyson's castles from *The Princess* lyrics; Catholic and
Protestant neighbors in Ulster reach the limits of their shared world.
An allegory about snails prepares us for "A Song for Synge" in which
the speaker tries to assume various viewpoints on the landscape. At the
conclusion, as in Mahon's Surrey poems discussed in chapter 5, the viewer
accepts his limited perspective within the metaphor- and myth-making
mind:

> Creation bright
> each object shines & stirs like
> the dark waves the swaying
> pine crests & the mind
> turns again on its root
> back into the secret shell
> of loneliness.
>
> (*MSD*, 22)

In one of Montague's major lyrics, "Courtyard in Winter," our shared
language cannot bare the secrets of private grief, which lead to the self-
destruction of a friend who had barred the poet from her secret pain.
The poem opens with a refrain—"Snow curls in on the cold wind"—
which, repeated, absorbs the cryptic messages of successive stanzas much
as snow absorbs the "faltering flake" and gathers to a blinding glare:
"As if that / Ceaseless, glittering light was / All the truth we'd left. . . ."
The poet recalls delivering a telegram announcing a grief he could not
share to a rural family he did not know, and then leaving their farmhouse:

> The tracks of foxes,
> Wild birds as I climbed down
> Seemed to form a secret writing
> Minute and frail as life when
>
> Snow curls in on the cold wind.
>
> (*MSD*, 17)

The poet's accumulated speculation, sympathy, and intuitions—"seemed,"
"as if," "I know," "I imagine"—locate the poet midway between this
woman's grief and a not yet comprehending audience. Originally a mne-
monic in oral poetry, a refrain brings into occasional singable focus the
poet's individual story and absorbs the soloist's voice in the choral, as

the private story becomes progressively public. The idea that this process distorts as it reveals is reinforced in this poem by the collective imagery of snow:

> As if that
> Ceaseless, glittering light was
> All the truth we'd left after
>
> *Snow curls in on the cold wind.*

When the poet closes by affirming this paradoxical loss-and-gain of the private made public, the conventional rhyme—*grows, rose*—reminds us that the restoration of the unique, ephemeral life remains conditional and poetic, rather than actual.

> I still affirm
> That nothing dies, that even from
> Such bitter failure memory grows;
> The snowflake's structure, fragile
> But intricate as the rose when
>
> *Snow curls in on the cold wind.*

The refrain of "Courtyard in Winter" is only one of Montague's various devices for converting a personal poetic voice to a communal voice, or for alternating subtly between a personal and a "tribal" viewpoint. Whereas under Hopkins' influence Heaney often selects words etymologically, to be as multilayered as the bog, Montague takes equal care to pitch his diction slightly above, but consistent with, current usage and actual speech. While Kinsella and Heaney employ tactile images to probe the past, Montague raises the past to the surface of the visible world. With "At times I see it, present . . . ," he opens an earlier poem which has strong affinities with the stories of the Irishman John Mac-Gahern, to whom it is dedicated. In this poem Montague declares his intention to write as "luminously as possible":

> Not the accumulated richness
>   Of an old historical language—
> That musk-deep odour!
>   But a slow exactness

> Which recreates experience
>         By ritualizing its details—
> Pale web of curtain, width
>         Of deal table, till all
>
> Takes on a witch-bright glow
>                 (from "A Bright Day," *MCL*, 36)

More often than resonating between etymological levels, Montague's diction conveys surface details along a series of poems much as personal memory records recurrent events.

In Montague's poetry the past has no assured monumental life. It survives precariously in the present as shared recollection tossed in the blanket of communal gossip or as geographical history glinting through place-names. In an essay published in 1970, Montague points out that Irish geographical names can provide a primer class in Gaelic: "The least Irish place name can net a world with its associations."[19]

These associations are unavailable to the uninitiated or forgetful. In "The Errigal Road," Ulster "landmarks . . . celebrated in local myth" have become secrets that momentarily draw together the poet, who is visiting from Cork, and his former Protestant neighbor. An ancient cross has become "a heavy stone hidden in grass." "Whiskey Hollow" is indicated only by "a line of lunar birches," and the pair must imagine the poteen-makers "plotting against the wind . . . while the secret liquid bubbles & clears." "Foxhole Brae," which "used to be crawling with them" offers parenthetically only a glimpse of the slinking fox. In this narrow region "The mysterious saddle shape / Of Knockmany Hill" opens "perspectives beyond our Christian myth," but when they look out beyond their townland, toward Monaghan or Cork, a divisive note enters. In this troubled region of Ulster the bond between neighbors is incomplete and as tenuous as their landmarks. "Soon all our shared landscape will be effaced, / a quick stubble of pine recovering most" concludes the mirroring poem into which these shared secrets are absorbed (*MSD*, 26–27).

The poem's chronicling function becomes an implicit theme in Montague's celebrated sequence *The Rough Field*: "The whole landscape a manuscript / We had lost the skill to read, / A part of our past disinherited" (*MRF*, 35). Montague associates the poetic sequence with the social chronicle although he never clearly distinguishes between the uses of the lyric sequence and the long poem. He opened an essay on the Scots poet Hugh MacDiarmid by confessing that "sooner or later, if one continues to write poetry, the desire grows to write a long poem or sequence, something more expansive than the lyric . . . something which is co-terminous with at least one whole aspect of one's experience. . . ."[20] He complains that modern lyric poets have restricted themselves "to certain complex, asocial tones." As I suggested earlier in discussing Montague's love poetry, the lyrics often imply their own reluctance to stand as moments' monuments.

The various means by which he destabilizes individual lyrics contributes to the development of sequences. For example, although Montague's poems are embodied in a great variety of forms, the thin line has come to predominate in the later poetry. Consequently, his poetry does not invade space so much as it flows downward in time. As full stanzas become leaner in his poetry, we get not a tilled field of verses but tracks, as if through snow or wasteland, of someone moving on. Montague himself said, "When the poet is aware of space, then the poem achieves a Giacometti tension, surrounded by silence. . . ."[21] Montague's lines usually maintain both tempo, by means of some alliteration and a fairly even number of stresses, and momentum, through enjambment, lines thrusting on by ending often in verbs, participles, or adverbs, as in this passage from *The Rough Field*. Visiting his childhood home, the poet, jarred on the native Hippocrene, sets in motion the fifth stanza of Keats's "Ode to a Nightingale" as he lurches through the countryside:

> Snowdrop
> In March, primrose in April,
> Whitethorn in May, cardinal's
> Fingers of foxglove dangling
> All summer: every crevice held
> A secret sweetness. Remembering,
> I seem to smell wild honey
> On my face.
> And plunge
> Down the hillside, singing
> In a mood of fierce elation.
> My seven league boots devour

Time and space as I crash
Through the last pools of
Darkness. All around, my
Neighbours sleep, but I am
In possession of their past
(The pattern history weaves
From one small backward place)
Marching through memory magnified:
Each grassblade bends with
Translucent beads of moisture
And the bird of total meaning
Stirs upon its hidden branch.

(*MRF,* 53)

"Marching through memory magnified," this passage arrives at an uncharacteristic lyric close, which pays tribute to Kavanagh's *The Great Hunger.* Although usually Montague's sentences conclude themselves, he sometimes leaves the endings of the poems unpunctuated, most notably in "Omagh Hospital," "A New Siege," and the "Epilogue," of *The Rough Field.* Other poems simply trail off in the manner of William Carlos Williams of which Barbara Hernstein Smith writes,

> By stopping . . . the poem announces its own sufficiency, and compelling the reader to accept that sufficiency, gives a retrospective emphasis more or less to every element in it. It is as if the poet were saying, "What did you expect more? Look again, it's all there."[22]

Although this applies to Montague's conclusions as well, our first response to *The Rough Field*'s unstopped or unclimactic closures is not retrospective. Rather, carried by the momentum of the lines, we read on, treating even familiar lyrics transplanted from previous volumes as interludes in the sequence.

Of course, patterns form as the poem progresses, but, chiefly as alternations and counterpoint, they maintain the process rather than drawing it to a conclusion. On a first reading, *The Rough Field* seems to invert the quest's pattern as it represents the poet returning to his homeland in County Tyrone, Northern Ireland, attempting to recover a compensatory understanding of the embittering changes there, and then setting out again inconclusively. Yet, the volume's ten sections tend to chart separate topical returns, attempts to recover an aunt, the father, the topography, and the religious and cultural community, each of which concludes elegiacly. Within these separate circlings, the poet's voice is counterpointed by historical documents, Elizabethan journal entries, passages of bigoted hate mail, and old rhymes, the effect of which is to dissolve any sense of an authoritative causal history into separate documents defining sectarian histories.

Consequently, the contrapuntal voices help define the poet's tone ultimately as confessional elegiac. In a recent interview, Montague responded to a question on *The Rough Field* by claiming, "I do speak for a tribal consciousness in that poem."[23] For this epic ambition the poet develops a voice adaptable to narrative verse and occasional lyric, regional history, and personal disclosure. Montague's sentences are usually simple, elaboration occurring within participial phrases. His diction is spare; Gaelic cognates are reserved for geographical and agrarian terms, and regionalisms for patches of local speech seeded throughout the narrative. Frequently, so strong is the poet's sympathy for his Gaelic predecessors that the historical and personal subjects almost merge, as in this account of post-Famine suppression of the Irish language:

> An Irish
> child weeps at school
> repeating its English.
> After each mistake
>
> The master
> gouges another mark
> on the tally stick
> hung about its neck
>
> Like a bell
> on a cow, a hobble
> on a straying goat.
> To slur and stumble
>
> In shame
> the altered syllables
> of your own name;
>
> (*MRF,* 39)

*The Rough Field* opens teetering between epic and mock-epic as a woodcut representing the roasting of the prodigal's fatted calf contrasts with the laconic greeting the father gives his poet son:

> Lost in our separate work
> We meet at dusk in a narrow lane.
> I press back against a tree
> To let him pass, but he brakes
> Against our double loneliness
> With: 'So you're home again!'
>
> (*MRF,* 11)

We might assume that the triumphant seventeenth-century entrance of Lord Mountjoy into his new Ulster colony, which is related in the margin, depreciates the poet's own southwestern journey from Belfast which begins, "*Catching a bus at Victoria Station. . . .*" Yet, on retrospection the volume suggests that the poet represents the true native and the conscience of a passing culture. The lost generations are encoded in his genes:

> I assert
> a civilisation died here;
> it trembles
> underfoot where I walk these
> small, sad hills:
> it rears in my blood stream
> when I hear
> a bleat of Saxon condescension,
>
> (*MRF,* 45)

In "A New Siege" the poet becomes eponymous for the Ulster Catholic culture:

> message scrawled
> Popehead: Tague
> my own name
> hatred's synonym
>
> (*MRF,* 74)

Yet, the book reveals that the current generation is dissociated from that culture, elders besotted and youth clambering "over each other, brief as mayflies in their hunger . . . ," having abandoned the ceili for

Americanized Roselands. Speaking of *The Rough Field* in that 1979 interview, Montague said of his Ulster compatriots, "It is they who are
being taken away from what they had, and it is I who am the possessor,
and with the older people, the guardian, of what had been there."[24]

The narrator's autobiographical position in *The Rough Field* contrasts
sharply with the memoirist stance in another long poem, *Autumn Journal,* where Louis MacNeice characterized his age through the voice of
an average contemporary, as we shall see in chapter 5. Conversely, Montague develops a Rousseauesque confession in which the self is imperial,
summoning other characters to take on its shape: "what I assume you
shall assume," in the words of Whitman. Like a Tennysonian Whitman, Montague sings the elegy of himself and of the land lost with youth.

Consequently, we would mislabel *The Rough Field* to call it epic[25]
because the "episodes of a people's heroic tradition," celebrated in the
poem, depend on the poet's memory or on his music and translations
of the landscape. Even the elegiac tone is suffused with ambivalence.
The poet recognizes, for example, that the fires of memory he would
rekindle in "The Leaping Fire" have also been destructive[26] and that the
pastoral we revere in memory falsifies the past's brutal farm conditions:

> Only a sentimentalist would wish
> to see such degradation again:
> heavy tasks from spring to harvest;
> the sack-cloth pilgrimages under rain
>
> to repair the slabbery gaps of winter
> with the labourer hibernating
> in his cottage for half the year
> to greet the indignity of the Hiring Fair.
>
> (*MRF,* 82)

If we comprehend the volume as an ambivalent but elegiac confession,
we are less likely to read the climactic Section IX, "A New Siege," as
historical interpretation or vaticism than as a stylized but forthright report of one poet's impressions of changes that have altered his province,
so carefully preserved in memory. Having embodied these changes in
Section IX, the poem returns to celebrate heroic endurance and long-
suffering and to elegize "our finally lost dream of man at home / in a
rural setting!" (*MRF,* 83).

These lines and the volume's concluding quatrain restate the paradox of elegies, which Montague would assign to all poetry, as I have suggested.

> Harsh landscape that haunts me,
> well and stone, in the bleak moors of dream
> with all my circling a failure to return
> to what is already going
>
>        going
>         GONE
>          (*MRF,* 83)

Auctioned to the highest bidder, "our finally lost dream" nevertheless circles back into the poetic imagination.

One detractor has argued that in *The Rough Field* Montague's "sense of what *was* works ineffectively in his poems as a way of feeling about what is actually happening in Ireland," asserting that his "hopeless pastoral-political sentiment" is "static."[27] If we must debate the political efficacy of the poem, we can point out that in a country encumbered by ancient hatred, a discovery of what can be loved from the past, specifically, the patient endurance of his aunts and of the Cailleach in "The Wild Dog Rose," becomes analeptic. Conventionally, the elegy faces in two directions: it honors the past in order better to encounter the future. "Tomorrow to fresh woods, and pastures new" concludes the most famous English elegy.

So, *The Rough Field* has the authority only of one consciousness and the continuity of memory, a memory of personal experience augmented by a tribal legend and song. Montague succeeds in fulfilling the aspiration he stated in 1967, quoted above, "to write a long poem or sequence . . . co-terminous with at least one whole aspect of one's experience." The poem transcends the limitations of this one experience only as the reader accedes to the confessor's assumption, stated by Whitman, that "what I assume you shall assume, / For every atom belonging to me as good belongs to you."[28]

If *The Rough Field* is Montague's most celebrated book, it is not his only sequence. All of his seven volumes, especially the last five, have been carefully plotted, with *The Rough Field,* the dramatized sequence *The Great Cloak,* and *The Dead Kingdom* being nearly indivisible units.

Behind this structuring of individual volumes looms the larger architecture of the opus, a more general but definable pattern. Robin Skelton has offered extraordinary praise of the edifice of Montague's poetic career: "Steadily, slowly, with a meticulousness and integrity that astonish, he has made a body of poems that will outlast time if any poetry can."[29] Montague himself has judged it a sign of greatness when "a man's life-work can be seen as a pattern, with individual works existing not so much in themselves but as part of a total elaboration and investigation of themes. . . ."[30]

More or less directly, *Poisoned Lands* (1961) examines his Ulster childhood and tainted aspects of his region. *A Chosen Light* (1967) and *Tides* (1970) have less to do with the region than with erotic love, the woman, and a loose myth of the feminine principle in history expressed through images of the moon, the tides, and the ancient woman, the cailleach. Derived from the Irish pre-Christian worship of female deities, Montague's ideas were reinforced by Graves's sometimes fanciful compendium, *The White Goddess*.[31] As we have seen, *The Rough Field* (1972) concentrates on the region, *The Great Cloak* (1978) on love and the woman, whereas, *A Slow Dance* (1975) loosely associates the feminine principle and the land.

Because Montague's newest sequence, *The Dead Kingdom* (1984), deliberately combines the theme of the region with that of the feminine principle, in this case invested most fully in the character of the poet's mother, we will end our examination of Montague's poetry by discussing this volume. Finally quite different in effect from *The Rough Field*, *The Dead Kingdom* is at the same time more intimate and more universal than the earlier sequence concerning Ulster.

The book retains its title-page connotation of death and morbidity, which we might assume from the beginning pertains to Ulster. Ironically, Munster, the province from which the poet departs at the beginning of the book to attend his mother's funeral in Ulster, retains ancient legendary right to that morbid title. The landing-place of the first invaders, the province of female deities and supernatural hags, such as the Hag of Beare, and the corner of Ireland associated with the dead, Munster was called "the dead kingdom."[32] As the sequence traces the poet from his home in the South to the midlands of Ireland and the North, the grim connotations of the title are extended to all of Ireland.

The title also forewarns us, as in the *nekyia*,[33] the hero's descent into the underworld, that the poet will encounter the spirits in the manner of Odysseus's questioning his mother among the shades. The encounter occurs in the last two of five sections in *The Dead Kingdom,* after the poet has explored his childhood memories in Goldsmith's county, Longford. There he visited his cousin, crossed the border with its chilling associations, and reached his childhood home in Tyrone. The ulcerous fact, which the poet must mitigate, is the mother's rejection of the son, emotionally from birth and overtly when he was four, as mentioned earlier in this chapter: "All roads wind backwards to it. / An unwanted child, a primal hurt" ("Flowering Absence"). In 1933 she sent her three sons back to Ireland from Brooklyn and separated John by placing him with his paternal aunts. When she herself returned, she did not bring her youngest into the family circle:

> a mother cat,
>
> intent on safety,
> dragging her first
> batch of kittens back
> to the familiar womb-warm
> basket of home
>
> (all but the runt,
> the littlest one, whom
> she gave to be fostered
> in Garvaghey, seven miles away;
> her husband's old home).
>                    ("A Muddy Cup," *MDK,* 68)

At great risk, Montague dips into the pathos of this relationship without altogether escaping a note of self-pity.

Yet, the audacious intimacy of Montague's disclosures yields major triumphs, most notably "Northern Lights" and "The Silver Flask," a poem which recounts a rare family reunion for a Christmas Eve mass, to which the parents and grown sons drove:

>                    as father sang,
>      and the silver flask went round.
>
> Chorus after chorus of the *Adoremus*
> to shorten the road before us,

The family resume rituals and familiar song as the recurrent *or* and *us* rhymes rope them in. The presence of the father and the mother becomes the central mystery:

> my father joining warmly in,
> his broken tenor soaring, fathering,
> A legend in dim bars of Brooklyn
> (that sacramental moment of stillness
> among exiled, disgruntled men)
> now raised vehemently once again
>
> in the valleys he had sprung from,
> startling the stiff congregation
> with fierce blasts of song, while
> our mother sat silent beside him,
> sad but proud, an unaccustomed
> blush mantling her wan countenance.

Before the warmth of the family ritual, the eucharistic rite fades:

> Then driving slowly home,
> tongues crossed with the communion
> wafer, snowflakes melting in
> the car's hungry headlights,
> till we reach the warm kitchen
> and the spirits round again.
>
> (*MDK*, 72–73)

The success of *The Dead Kingdom* may depend on how each reader judges the sequence's climax, "The Locket," which offers balm for the "primal hurt." The poem's final revelation, that his mother always bore his picture in a locket, can seem only pathetic if it is not amplified beyond this individual, but hardly unique, case of maternal rejection. The amplifying apparatus in this volume is the richly evocative epigraphs to each section, a round-a-bout of related images, the echo of countless popular songs, and the italicized "universal" poems which end each section. Of the relation of these terminal poems to the volume Montague has said, "Another, less autobiographical, urge kept adding distancing poems (how many mothers have died? countries been sick?) to enlarge the framework. . . . It is not especially Irish, but invokes many archetypes; mythical and maternal."[34]

In magnifying the significance of "The Locket" beyond autobiography, the crucial poem is "The Well Dreams," the terminus toward which the water music of the first two sections flows. These sections introduce central themes: life is a constant process, fluid as water, which is governed by a female principle—"mother of destinies," "the goddess Mutabilitie," or the guardians of the well. Although a male principle—Ashurbanipal, King of Babylon—is invoked in the italicized ending to Section I, ironically this king stands behind the section's epigraph, which is from *The Book of Gilgamesh,* and which begins, "There is no permanence. Do we build a house to stand for ever. . . ?" In the fluid world we form only a "marginal civilization," leaning on devices frail as the curragh in "Upstream," which has affinities with the ship of death suggested in the opening section, or as unsteady as "swaying rope-ladders" and rustic bridges.

Ultimately, the world's ephemera are contained within the divine vision:

> only the earth and sky
> unchanging in change,
> everything else fragile
> as a wild bird's wing;
> bulldozer and butterfly,
> dogrose and snowflake
> climb the unending stair
> into God's golden eye.
> ("Process," *MDK,* 18)[35]

Analogies to "God's golden eye," other containers of the flux, emerge in several poems. For example, in one poetic reminiscence of Longford the poet and his cousin return from the stream bearing "jamjars of fresh water / . . . / in which minnows twisted / and turned in prison, or / stared out, enlarged / to gross-eyed monsters, / mouths kneading . . ." ("A Murmuring Stream," *MDK,* 19). A related container within flux appears in "Red Island" where he recalls finding "a ravenous pike; / inside its stomach, like / an embryo, an undigested perch" (*MDK,* 30). In "Lake Dwelling: Crannog," early Irish settlers, "plumping / Fat stones, logs down into the lake's stomach," build their houses on water (*MDK,* 31).

The ambiguity of the title "The Well Dreams," whether substantive or statement, suggests that either meaning is a reflection of the human mind. Venerated as a holy site, the well reflects or absorbs all that approach it. A contained fluidity and a source of life, the well also is composed of silence and emptiness which we humanize:

> There the wellhead pulses,
> little more than a tremor,
> a flickering quiver,
> spasms of silence;
> small intensities of mirth,
> the hidden laughter of earth.

In the poem's fourth stanza, the poet pays a six-line tribute to silence:

> Even a pebble disturbs
> that tremor laden miniscus,
> that implicit shivering.
> They sink toward the floor,
> the basement of quiet,
> settle into a small mosaic.
>
> (*MDK*, 40)

These lines refer the reader back to the eight-line prologue to Section II:

> I cast a pebble down, to
> set the well's walls echoing.
> As the miniscus resettles
> I see a strange face form,
> A wrinkled female face,
> Sweeny's Hag of the Mill,
> The guardian of the well,
> Source of lost knowledge.
>
> (*MDK*, 24)

From the Irish legend *Buile Suibne*,[36] Montague combines the characters of Sweeney's goading derider and a benefactor to represent the female principle as the old woman, who appears throughout the volume in various forms. Another terminal poem recognizes that we create "Deities" "from our own needs." Similarly, in this contained reflection of himself, he recognizes a "source of lost knowledge," an anima or mask of himself as the old woman.

This circuit of associations enlarges the final image of containment in "The Locket" beyond the pathos of the poet and his mother. After the mother's death, he discovers

> that, always around your neck
> you wore an oval locket
> with an old picture in it,
> of a child in Brooklyn.
>
> (*MDK*, 93)

Through a complex mirroring of the well-image in the prologue to Section II, the locket suggests a reconciliation between the feminine and masculine aspects of the self.

How specifically this psychological reconciliation would relieve the troubles of Ulster the volume cannot say, although the imbalance in the political realm in favor of male values is apparent in Section III. In this most political section of the book, the poet attributes the dissociation of Ireland to two masculine forces that may have constructed the border: the legendary Black Pig or "some burrowing Worm" ("The Black Pig"). A male god Cromm Cruaich, who supplanted the White Goddess in a portion of pre-Christian Ireland, instituted the evil practice of sacrificing rather than generating life ("The Plain of Blood").[37] Yet, the poet ascribes the Northern malevolence to "our own harsh hearts," and he charges, sarcastically, that "wise imperial policy" nurtured bitterness, "hurling the small peoples / against each other" ("The Plain of Blood," *MDK*, 47–48).

Montague differs from the other major living Irish poets in the frequency with which he confronts the political situation in the North. However, ultimately he shares with them a stereoscopic vision of their small island. The view of particular troubled lives within his community, including those of his family, enlarges in certain poems even beyond a tragic scope which sees "the punishment slowly grown / more monstrous than the crime" ("Red Branch"). From this broader view, Montague addresses "a marginal civilization," built on water or on bogland, "our land's wet matrix" ("Bog Royal"), and governed by the "goddess Mutability, / dark Lady of Process." Attempts to contain process may be necessary as they are illusory:

> Each close in his own
> world of sense & memory,
> races, nations locked
> in their dream of history,

Paradoxically, Montague's most successful poetry honors the world's passing details by representing them in their process, as he imitates the evolving motion of our transient lives:

> only love or friendship,
> an absorbing discipline
> (the healing harmony
> of music, painting, poem)
> as swaying ropeladders
> across fuming oblivion
> while the globe turns,
> and the stars turn, and
> the great circles shine,
> gold & silver,
>
> > sun & moon.
>
> > ("Process," *MDK,* 18)

## CHAPTER FIVE

# MacNeice & Mahon

Unless one ferrets out the misery west of Donegall Square, traces of which are in the harried citizens' faces, the visitor to Belfast will not find this industrial and cultural center of Northern Ireland to be a hell-hole, a tinderbox, or a running sore, as headlines would have it. In the Victorian architecture, the broad avenues that open vistas to the cradling hills, the botanical gardens and Queen's University, much of the beauty remains that greeted the youthful Louis MacNeice when he accompanied his father, who later would become an Anglican Bishop, on his trips into town from the rectory in Carrickfergus. On various occasions in the late forties, when MacNeice returned on assignment from the BBC in London to work with colleagues in Ormeau Avenue, he and Derek Mahon shared their native city. Perhaps Mahon was the child in blue shortpants, skinned knees, and sturdy brown shoes who barged out of Bruce Street into the lunchtime crowd on the Dublin Road, and the tall, fortyish, hawk-faced man with whom the boy tangled in a moment's loose scrum was Louis MacNeice guiding Bertie Rodgers and Sam Hanna Bell into the Elbow Room for a liquid lunch.

From within Belfast the paths of Mahon and MacNeice seem divergent. However, viewed in relation to the island's poets, the two Protestant Belfast poets who took all or some of their studies abroad, who became editors and writers in London, who were influenced strongly by Yeats and Auden, and who assumed an ironic stance in their poetry, seem familial. Mahon's comment that MacNeice's "example has provided a frame of reference for a number of younger poets in much the same way as Kavanagh's has done in the South"[1] amounts, in the reserved idiom of Belfast Protestants, to a filial embrace.

The essential poetry of Louis MacNeice (1907–63) would not make a thicker volume than the essential Clarke or Kavanagh, or, for that

matter, the selected Kinsella, Montague, or Heaney. Yet, MacNeice's
poetry has received more critical attention than that of any other Irish
poet after Yeats: numerous articles, three monographs, three full critical
studies by Terence Brown, William T. McKinnon, and Robyn Marshak,
a festschrift, and a full study of the poet's career in radio.[2] MacNeice
has escaped the relative obscurity of most Irish poets by merging his
light with Auden's in the thirties and by gaining access to a wider British audience through London publications and the BBC. Although it
might seem that his cup is brimming with critical verbiage and that
a new commentator can only contribute spillage or take sides on three
or four controversial points, the need remains to characterize MacNeice
as a poet.

The most disputed point involves detractors' claims that MacNeice
is merely superficial and skeptical and the counter-assertion, developed
at length by Brown and McKinnon, that MacNeice is philosophical and
profound. Then, among the few critics who believe that his last volumes break through to a new poetic level, W. H. Auden has said, "His
later poems show an advance upon his earlier, are more certain in their
craftsmanship, brilliant though that always was, and more moving."[3]
Other critics, however, have believed as Walter Allen that there

> is no obvious development in his poetry. The verses in his second vol-
> ume, *Poems,* which made his reputation, are as good as anything he ever
> wrote. What he did in the thirty years that followed was to go on writ-
> ing poems that were often as good but were scarcely different in kind.[4]

A third dispute, that over MacNeice's poetic nationality, we could hap-
pily assign to a passport office except that this poet — tourist to the British, emigrant to the Irish — frequently gets slighted in anthologies and
critical studies of Irish literature. Maurice Harmon ignores him in his
critical anthology, *Irish Poetry After Yeats*; in a 300-page study of the
Irish Renaissance, Richard Fallis accords him seventeen lines because
"MacNeice's poetry seems only sporadically Irish."[5] Curiously, among
even those anthologists who slight MacNeice there remains a recognition of MacNeice's influence on younger Ulster poets. For example, the
editor of *The Book of Irish Verse,* who misrepresents MacNeice by printing only one section of the *Autumn Journal* and one of his most bathetic
poems, confesses that MacNeice "is very much a father figure for the
poets of the province."[6] Ignoring the question of whether or not Mac-

Neice is fundamentally or primarily an Irish poet, an extraliterary question, we shall wave MacNeice into this study as an influence and argue later in this chapter, after we have addressed three other critical questions, that his poetry is deeply influenced by his Irish background.

MacNeice's Irishness, like the questions of his profundity and his development, should follow from some resolution of the fourth critical crux, concerning MacNeice's tone, before all the most characteristic feature of his poetry. Michael Longley refers to his "poetic personality which was so soon assured and recognizable."[7] On the other hand, G. S. Fraser expresses doubts about that poetic personality: "He is both in life and in poetry a man whose manner, at once sardonic and gay, suggests that he is going, perhaps, to let one in on a disquieting secret about something; one finds that he hasn't."[8] Before we can hope to resolve this difference of opinion concerning what Fraser calls MacNeice's "evasive honesty," we must listen to tone in a characteristic poem, "Sunday Morning," which appeared in the second volume *Poems* (1935):

> Down the road someone is practising scales,
> The notes like little fishes vanish with a wink of tails,
> Man's heart expands to tinker with his car
> For this is Sunday morning, Fate's great bazaar;
> Regard these means as ends, concentrate on this Now,
> And you may grow to music or drive beyond Hindhead anyhow,
> Take corners on two wheels until you go so fast
> That you can clutch a fringe or two of the windy past,
> That you can abstract this day and make it to the week of time
> A small eternity, a sonnet self-contained in rhyme.
>
> But listen, up the road, something gulps, the church spire
> Opens its eight bells out, skulls' mouths which will not tire
> To tell how there is no music or movement which secures
> Escape from the weekday time. Which deadens and endures.
>
>                                        (*MCP*, 23)

This is a social history that depends on a special personal point of view. We suppose that fish leaped in the poet's mind from the suggestion of *scales,* then connected through speed and ephemerality, reinforced by *wink,* which suggests *plink,* and the tails on musical notation. The opening lines remind us that they are poetry and that the poet, like the motorist and musician, is creating a moment's monument, "a sonnet self-contained in rhyme." The poet is located in the middle-class neighborhood he addresses: "Down the road someone . . ." and "But listen, up the road. . . ." He may be more ambivalent than his neighbors about this Sunday: the heroic diastole, "Man's heart expands," leads him only to tinker, as light as the fishes' *wink*; the apparent imperative: "Regard . . . concentrate on this Now," becomes a conditional clause, and the exalted moment *Now* is undercut by the equivocal "anyhow." By concluding equivocally and anticlimactically, the poem ironically saves what honest chance exists for the privileged moment. The sonnet's volta occurs in the eleventh line, "But listen . . ." which leads to this startling image: "the church spire / Opens its eight bells out, skulls' mouths which will not tire / to tell. . . ." What the bells tell is not what Donne's tolled. As in other MacNeice poems, bells like clocks, banisters, windscreen wipers, and ladder rungs represent the increments of time that bring tedium and boredom: "How there is not music or movement which secures / Escape from the weekday time. Which deadens and endures."9 The intensity of rhyme degenerates from *spire* to *tire* to *secures* asnd *endures,* in imitation, I assume, of the subject confronted, what Gerard Manley Hopkins called "time's tasking." MacNeice admired Hopkins whose very lines he borrows in two poems. The conclusion of "Sunday Morning" evokes Hopkins' termination of "St. Alphonsus Rodriquez" in which the poet unlaces his stressful lines to imitate the quiet endurance of the Spanish saint.10

If we begin by reassuming the basic meaning of tone—the speaker's attitude toward the subject and toward the audience—then we can arrive at a characterization of tone in "Sunday Morning." The speaker in this poem sounds like the speaker in most MacNeice poems, a poetic personality, as Michael Longley says, "assured and recognizable." We need to distinguish two audiences: first, the implied middle-class neighbor who may also have a piano or a fast car and who is told to "listen, up the road" and then the reader, rather like the neighbor, whom MacNeice elsewhere defines as, ideally, a "normal man who is an educated member of his own [the poet's] community and is basically at one with the poet in his attitude to life."11

In "Sunday Morning" no romantic vision separates the poet from his audiences. The ironic gap of lines 3 to 6 and line 10 closes as soon as the poet has delivered his forceful reminder that "weekday time" may finally prevail over Sunday escapes. As in other poems he restores to his audience a double vision, an awareness of the darkness that gives intensity to man's occasional moments of light. The poet may be, as MacNeice said in *Modern Poetry,* the "conscience" of his community, "its critical faculty, its generous instinct," but within this poem he represents himself as merely a citizen of that community—a community which is not depicted as different from the reading audience who might also "secure escape" on Sundays. If the poet believes sonneteering to be more profound than music or motoring, he is reticent to proclaim this belief. The personal, poetic activity demonstrated in the first two lines and named in the tenth line of "Sunday Morning" emerges to the surface of "Fate's great bazaar."

If we know anything about MacNeice, we probably have encountered his often-quoted curriculum vita of the exoteric poet: "I would have a poet able bodied, fond of talking, a reader of the newspapers, capable of pity and laughter, informed in economics, appreciative of women, involved in personal relationships, actively interested in politics, susceptible to physical impressions."[12]

Having characterized MacNeice's tone, we can now recognize it in most of his successful works, including the masterpiece *Autumn Journal,* MacNeice's poetic record of the last five months of 1938. Among the fifty-three pages and twenty-four cantos of this poem, we encounter lines that could be construed as confessional, private, or distinctly personal. Three cantos address a recent lover or describe her in personal and specific terms. He asks, ". . . how can I assess / The thing that makes you different?"

> I shall remember you in bed with bright
>    Eyes or in a cafe stirring coffee
> Abstractedly and on your plate the white
>    Smoking stub your lips had touched with crimson.
> <div align="right">(Canto IV: <i>MCP,</i> 108)</div>

These recurrent but particular moments are restored to the present only through memory. Yet, memory casts her as a shadowy but persistent character in this particular time, autumn 1938, and this specific place, London.

September has come, it is *hers*
  Whose vitality leaps in the autumn,
Whose nature prefers
  Trees without leaves and a fire in the fire-place;
So I give her this month and the next

.   .   .   .   .   .   .   .   .   .   .   .   .

Who has left a scent on my life and left my walls
  Dancing over and over with her shadow,
Whose hair is twined in all my waterfalls
  And all of London littered with remembered kisses.
                              (Canto IV: *MCP,* 106–07)

She does not pervade, however, twenty-one of the twenty-four progressive moments that comprise this poem. In Canto XI, through implicit phoenix images of "banked" love's rekindling, her return is projected into the future:

I see the future glinting with your presence
  Like moon on a slate roof,
And my spirits rise again. It is October,
  The year-god dying on the destined pyre
With all the colours of a scrambled sunset
  And all the funeral elegance of fire
In the grey world to lie cocooned but shaping
  His gradual return;
No one can stop the cycle;
  The grate is full of ash but fire will always burn.
Therefore, listening to the taxis
  (In which you never come) so regularly pass,
I wait content, banking on the spring and watching
  The dead leaves canter over the dowdy grass.
                              (*MCP,* 123)

Although realization of the prediction seems improbable, it is appropriate, in a journal filled with anxious concern for the future, to forecast her appearance, just as the speaker anticipates air raids, the eruption of the Third Reich, and the liberation of Barcelona.

At Canto XI we do not know that his presage of her return was false and that love would die just as so much in this elegiac record—

the year, a plumber-father, liberty in Spain, the trees on Primrose Hill. Remarkably, despite the specific "autobiographical" detail, this woman, who may be commemorated as "Nancy" in the dedication to *The Earth Compels* (1938), remains the unnamed assembly of the *Journalist*'s impressions and therefore another event in the history of this autumn as seen by one poet-observer.[13] He declares,

> Now I am free of the stars
>    And the word 'love' makes no sense, this history is almost,
> Ripe for the mind's museum—broken jars
>    That once held wine or perfume.
>
> (MCP, 140–41)

The sense of history in these lines—a dead and encased exhibit— contrasts ironically with the dynamic history of other cantos in which the present observer measures the dangerous trajectory from the past toward the future. In an astute essay on "Yeats and the Poets of the Thirties," which preceded his book *The Auden Generation*, Samuel Hynes characterizes "political poetry" between the wars in terms applicable to *The Autumn Journal*:

> Indeed the younger poets did share one crucial belief with Yeats—what we might call a faith in the momentum of history. In Yeats' later poems, and in poems of the Thirties poets, futurity exists: the rough beast slouches, the Old Gang dies. . . . You may call that pattern the collapse of capitalism and the rise of socialism, or the end of one great year and the beginning of another, but in either case there is a sense of history implied. And it seems obvious that a sense of history is necessary to political poetry, and equally obvious that *The Waste Land* does not have it; it has only a sense of the past.[14]

To define the form that this "political poetry" took in the thirties, Hynes employs a passage from Yeats's autobiographies:

> This whole passage seems to me a clear example of what Spender meant, of how the true poetry of politics must be, not submission to the political definition of man's destiny, but a willed assimilation of political experience, the public emotion, into personal life. Yeats was the first modern poet to do this, to accept contemporary history as a subject, and to respond to it as a poet.[15]

Hynes continues:

> "Easter, 1916" is a poem that achieves what Spender was trying for: it states a public emotion that has become a private one. . . .[16]

Hynes's statement would have to be inverted to describe MacNeice's poetry where private thoughts and emotions, whether concerning making sonnets or love, emerge on the public level. If we compare "Nineteen Hundred and Nineteen" or "Meditations in Time of Civil War" to *Autumn Journal,* we see that Yeats's poems move from reflections on the Black-and-Tans or the Irish Civil War to the poet's situation in the tower, to a prediction cast in the form of arcane legend: of unicorns, Jacques Molay, and Robert Artisson. MacNeice speculates as well but in terms familiar to that educated common reader. While Yeats peers down from the tower, a perspective that MacNeice depreciates in several cantos as appropriate only to dead heroes commemorated in bronze, MacNeice's narrator moves with the epochal traffic—on escalators, in cars, on trains, in taxis, and to the rhythm of the windscreen wiper or passing telephone poles. Yeats's "willed assimilation of political experience . . . into personal life" could exemplify the "egotistical sublime," whereas MacNeice's willed assimilation of personal life into the public history displays his "negative capability," as Keats defined these terms. "We cannot of course live by Keats's Negative Sensibility alone," MacNeice said in his autobiography; "all the same what I feel makes life worth living is not the clever scores but the surrenders—it may be to the life-quickening urge of an air-raid, to nonsense talked by one's friends, to a girl on top of the Empire State building. . . ."[17]

Such surrender requires discretion, "a sympathy . . . in the writer with those forces which at the moment make for progress. The important events outside him must penetrate him in the same way as Euripides was penetrated by the Peloponnesian War. . . ."[18] MacNeice's ability to chart even his personal muddle within history's currents grew from his belief in his own typicality:

> I am 33 years old and what can I have been doing that I still am in a muddle? But everyone else is too, maybe our muddles are concurrent. Maybe, if I look back, I shall find that my life is not just mine, that it mirrors the lives of the others. . . .[19]

MacNeice's collaborative relation with his contemporary audience and their shared historical situation lead him toward poetic memoir, an oxymoron only to those who insist that poetry be private or visionary. As a major form of modern autobiography, memoir can be distinguished from *confession* and *apologia* if we consider the autobiographer's relation to his audience and to history. The apologist wishes to establish his own integrity, the interrelated self that defies change in order, finally, to be free from historical flux. Through discovery of some unique, essential, and continuous quality in himself, the apologist separates himself from his contemporaries and addresses himself to some future or ideal audience. On the other hand, the writer of confession addresses his contemporary as well as future audiences with the intention of drawing them and their sense of history into his own unique view. In the manner of Rousseau he may claim to be extraordinarily sinful or distressed in order to gain the audience's sympathy and finally to seduce the reader to accept the standards and practices of his private life. The memoirist, by contrast, seeks to identify or merge his private self with some public role or historical movement. Memoir takes place when history threatens to overshadow the individual, and it saves at least the individual view of history, as F. R. Hart has argued in his revaluation of the sub-genre.[20]

As vivid examples of the memoirist's blend of highly individual perspective and a public subject, we can consider two passages from *Autumn Journal*. Canto XXII opens:

> December the nineteenth: over the black roofs
>    And the black paint-brush poplar
> The white steam rises and deploys in puffs
>    From the house-hidden railway, a northern
> Geyser erupting in a land of lava,
>    But white can be still whiter for now
> The dun air starts to jig with specks that circle
>    Like microbes under a lens; this is the first snow;
> And soon the specks are feathers blandly sidling
>    Inconsequent as the fancies of young girls
> And the air has filled like a dance-hall,
>    A waltz of white dresses and strings of pearls.
> And the papers declare the snow has come to stay,

A new upholstery on roof and garden
Refining, lining, underlining the day,
    And the sombre laurels break parole and blossom
In enormous clumps of peonies; and the cars
    Turn animal, moving slowly
In their white fur like bears,
    And the white trees fade into the hill behind them
As negroes' faces fade in a dark background
    Our London world
Grown all of a piece and peaceful like the Arctic,
    The sums all cancelled out and the flags furled.

                                    (*MCP*, 145–46)

The passage seems absolutely faithful to his window-level perspective (e.g. "puffs / From the house-hidden railways") although it is also richly metaphorical. The passage begins with a public fact, moves through impressions, and returns to the level of public fact, "this is the first snow." The passage then quickens into a swirl of new impressions before the newspaper arrives to confirm them: "And the papers declare the snow has come to stay."

The London watchers of the sky then relax into the gaiety of a cease-fire or interregnum with the appearance of "specks that circle / Like microbes under a lens." Because sky watching has become a leitmotif in *Autumn Journal,* the microbic snow reminds us of a sinister image that closes Canto VII:[21]

                        Hitler yells on the wireless,
    The night is damp and still
And I hear dull blows on wood outside my window;
    They are cutting down the trees on Primrose Hill.
The wood is white like the roast flesh of chicken,
    Each tree falling like a closing fan;
No more looking at the view from seats beneath the branches,
    Everything is going to plan;
They want the crest of this hill for anti-aircraft,
    The guns will take the view
And searchlights probe the heavens for bacilli
    With narrow wands of blue.

                                    (*MCP*, 113)

Irony arises simply as martial usage replaces peaceful meanings in "Everything is going to plan" and "the guns will take the view." The phrase "Each tree falling like a closing fan," which is a perfect miniature for the sound and motion of a falling tree, suggests the close of that style of life appropriate to a place named "Primrose Hill." More significantly, the citizens' scanning of "the heavens," the memoirist's attention to public detail, and the poet's sense of futurity, which Hynes defined, must all merge when the future may suddenly collapse from the sky.

In his provocative essay on the autobiographical sub-genre, F. R. Hart associates memoir with eras of public anxiety: "Other autobiographical modes flourish at other times: confession abounds in times of soul-searching, apology in times of confrontation. But ours is a time of survival, and memoir is the autobiography of survival."[22] Characterizing MacNeice as a memoirist in these terms may free him from certain associations. A memoirist has more responsibility to the larger movements of history than does a reporter or journalist. In this light, Fraser's term "evasive honesty" can become merely descriptive of the memoirist's intention to draft selective personal facts into the public history and to suppress personal facts that might seem merely genetic or otherwise nonhistorical.

MacNeice's preference for public over private history must have been shaped, in part, by the social theories of Auden, Spender, and Day Lewis and by the insistence of Matthew Arnold, to whom MacNeice referred often in *Modern Poetry* and elsewhere, that noble actions are the proper poetic subject. The manner in which the poet addresses an audience of peers and coevals may have been influenced by his contact with a radio audience in his roles, which he assumed in 1941, as producer and writer for the BBC. However, four years earlier, MacNeice had defined his attitude toward an audience: "A poet should always be 'collaborating' with his public, but this public, in the mass, cannot make itself heard and he has to guess at its requirements and its criticisms. But what it requires will be largely what he requires himself. . . ."[23] In that same year, 1937, the poet completed two journalistic monographs which Barbara Coulton characterizes as maintaining a "conversational tone that takes the reader into the author's confidence" and appearing "not unlike the best kind of features being done, or which were to be done in the future, for radio."[24] Such evidence indicates that the twenty-two-year career at BBC could only confirm or perhaps make routine MacNeice's memoirist stance—subjective toward the object, collaborative toward the audience—which he had acquired at an early age. If we sought earlier causes, we could even speculate that his concept of a collaborative audience was influenced by his father's loving association with his parishioners. Whatever the causes, MacNeice addresses a contemporary audience about current events as they unfold, and he is extremely sensitive to the rate of change in his society.

The quality of poetic memoir may depend on the magnitude of the public event. As if girding his loins for the coming war, MacNeice wrote in 1938: "One grows into a belief more quickly, and more solidly, in a crisis and a crisis might make these poets [Auden, Spender] better or produce other and better poets."[25] Anticipation of World War II, the siege of London, and the immediate aftermath of the War inspired some of MacNeice's strongest volumes of poetry. His collaborative attitude toward his audience must have been enforced by the sense of bunker interdependence developed among artists and intellectuals in wartime London, as characterized by the editor John Lehmann: "We *needed* one another, and for purposes larger than our own security or ambitions. This sense of cohesion was extraordinarily stimulating."[26] Beyond inspiration from such colleagues as William Empson, Benjamin Britten, V. S. Pritchett, and Dylan Thomas, MacNeice felt the gratification of providing war-related features for an audience for whom such information was a necessity as well as occasionally a comfort.

In his poetic responses to the War, MacNeice's subjugation of his private emotions and personal history to the impending public crisis creates a peculiar tension characteristic of his best poetry, such as *Autumn Journal* and "The Closing Album." We become attentive to the individual plight, which he shares with others, as he is rushed through his days in a public conveyance, in a crowded train, or among a swarm of taxis. Even the most intense personal experience of love can only suspend this traffic, as in "Meeting Point" when "Time was away and somewhere else," though more often history conveys humans beyond love, as in "Trilogy for X."

As the crisis of World War II passes, the poetic tension subsides and the quality of MacNeice's poetry abates in the fifties. To measure this decline, one needs only to compare the relatively torpid retrospective

*Autumn Sequel* (1953), with its avowal of achieved love for his wife Hedli, to the sharply poignant *Autumn Journal* (1938) with its reticence about personal loss and its anxious anticipation of the future. A glance at the titles within *Visitations* (1957) and *Solstices* (1961) reveals the extent to which during the fifties MacNeice was relying on formulae for grouping, and perhaps inventing, poems: four poems developed as "A Hand of Snapshots," "Donegal Triptych," "Jigsaws: I–IV," "Visitations: I–VII," four "Dark Age Glosses," four "Indoor Sports," four "Nature Notes," four "Sleeping Winds," as well as many companion poems and a majority of poems that rely on puns or other superficial devices for their internal development.

MacNeice recovered poetic vitality in the three years prior to his unexpected death from pneumonia in 1963. No specific public crisis galvanized his imagination, but private distress—the dissolution of his eighteen-year marriage, a love-affair that accentuated his sense of mortality "because she was young and thus too late" (*MCP*, 531), and a dark foreboding of some unspecified crisis—pitched the poems to the recognizable MacNeice note. Although the poems usually avoid a specific historical situation, they address a contemporary audience and they assimilate private emotions into a public, even political, experience. For example, in "Perspectives" a poignant sense of succeeding lives is generalized as a lecture on perspective:

> Yet sometimes for all these rules of perspective
> The weak eye zooms, the distant midget
> Expands to meet it, far up stage
> The kings go towering into the flies;
>
> And down at the end of a queue some infant
> Of the year Two Thousand straddles the world
> To match the child that was once yourself.
> The further-off people are sometimes the larger.
>
> (MCP, 519)

We accept MacNeice's conclusion more readily because, in the two stanzas that precede these, his examples—grandparents, tax-collectors, dentists, and magnates—are reassuringly familiar and contemporary and because the startling volta is rendered as a flat academic summary: "The further-off people are sometimes the larger."

Several poems of this posthumous volume *The Burning Perch* (1963) posit life as a game whose time is running out ("all our games funeral games") not merely for each mortal but implicitly for the race, as the volume's title insinuates. While on his burning perch the parakeet Budgie postures and chatters, "the human race recedes and dwindles" and "giant reptiles cackle in their graves." As in the earlier poetry MacNeice "collaborates" with his readers and generalizes his private anxieties. In "The Pale Panther," for example, the sinister fate is as common as the artifacts he shares with his contemporaries—electric fences, golf greens, airplanes, and milk bottles. In its opening lines "The sun made a late and lamented / Spring"—the poem draws out the subject of the two preceding poems, "Spring Cleaning" and "Another Cold May." To the reader led obliquely by puns, the sun's tardy arrival implies, initially, death ("late and lamented"), potential force in retraction (the late sun made a spring), and the panther's pounce ("Spring. Yellow teeth tore . . ."). Words elide in a progression of sinister expectations. The poem addresses the milkman, whose "milkrun" may associate him with the airman:

> you surely
> Know about bugs in the sun,
> Runways in rut, control
> Towers out of touch, and burns
> Whose gift is not to cure.
>
> As for you, airman, your empties
> Are broken test tubes or shards
> Of caddis, it is too soon
> To order replacements according
> To the state of play since the green
> Lies in shadow now and the tractor
> Stalled when the sun stopped play.
> (*MCP*, 526–27)

The germinating bugs suggest *rut* which evokes runways for planes. *Runways* may suggest runaways which require control towers. The burnt shell of planes or empty bomb casings approximate the form of discarded larval cases of the ephemeral caddis fly which in turn approaches the golf green through the suggested homophone *caddies* and perhaps through *replacements*.

At least two critics agree that the "third stanza about airmen, broken test tubes and shards, makes it clear that the poet is talking about both atomic and chemical warfare,"[27] although William McKinnon, author of the longest critique of this poem, cannot reconcile this reference with his assumption that the poem is about entropy. He fishes out and tosses back another interpretation which W. H. Auden had placed in the stream of oral literary criticism:

> MacNeice's old friend John Hilton told me that W. H. Auden, in a discussion of the poem with him, therefore summed up its theme as the last judgment. While I agree that judgment—not necessarily the last—is an important part of the theme, I still think the overall theme is failed renewal.[28]

Auden could have supported his interpretation by reminding us that standard references to Christ—in the panther and the sun's renewal[29]—and the two overdue arrivals, of the spring and the milkman, suggest a frustrated Second Coming whose preceding apocalyptic fire may be a nuclear explosion. The poem's dreamlike elisions discourage the sort of precise equations that McKinnon forces on the images in his essay. The poem's truth resides in the experience of anxiety it educes. As in MacNeice's society, so in the poem, two major anxieties within our Western tradition—fear of a final judgment and of the holocaust—emerge from below the surface play, occupied by dairy deliveries, golf greens, and frustration over a tardy spring, only through seemingly random associations of words. The sinister Second Coming is not proclaimed in a vatic Yeatsian tone; it lurks within the common language which MacNeice's narrator shares. Although "The Pale Panther" departs as widely from his earlier poetry as dream from journalism, characteristically in this poem, MacNeice assimilates private fears into a public anxiety, characteristic of a particular era, and retains his poetic posture as a memoirist.

Although many of the poems of *Solstices* (1961) and *The Burning Perch* (1963) register an uneasiness about the future, throughout MacNeice's poetry optimism characteristically outweighs anxiety, as it does in these mid-war lines from "Prospect": "Though the evil Past is ever present / And the happy Present is past indeed / . . . / And though to-day is arid / We know—and knowing bless— / That rooted in futurity /

There is a plant of tenderness" (*MCP*, 212–13). These lines echo the concluding sentiments of *Autumn Journal,* written three years earlier: "Sleep, the past, and wake, the future, . . . / And the equation will come out at last" (*MCP*, 153).

If we recall Hynes's distinction between political poetry—"in poems of the Thirties poets, futurity exists"—and T. S. Eliot's *The Wasteland* —"it has only a sense of the past"—then MacNeice's verse may seem securely "political." Hynes's terms remind us, however, of how rarely MacNeice concerns himself with the historical past. Among MacNeice's frequent homages to the present-becoming-past we find very few poems about historical subjects. Only in the last three volumes, in which the poet's optimism clouded somewhat, can we find even a sprinkling of historical poems, such as "Visit to Rouen," "Dark Age Glosses," and "Ravenna." Yet, the few poems we might call "historical" develop a sense of typology rather than of historical causation.

Consequently, we find MacNeice's poetry peculiarly barren of "a faith in the momentum of history" which Hynes declared was the "crucial belief" of the Thirties poets. MacNeice files his reports during a cease-fire, awaiting history's resumption in a fiery rain from heaven and a peaceful aftermath. Like Matthew Arnold, whom he refers to a dozen times in *Modern Poetry,* MacNeice writes as a voyager, "wandering between two worlds." His prose autobiography, *The Strings are False,* is framed by his own transatlantic crossings which establish the declared theme of life as a preparatory stage, or an "interregnum." Whereas his destination is imminent but vague, his place of departure remains totally obscure.

MacNeice's Irish background seems to have determined his memoirist bias. The collected poetry and the prose autobiography reveal MacNeice's memoirist mode and future tense as a reflexive turning away from his own childhood in Belfast which he recollects as a life begun in disjuncture from a meaningful past. Several factors account for MacNeice's sense of deracination which according to his autobiographical recreations began with birth rather than with departure for an English boarding school at age ten.

Because MacNeice's parents followed the Irish practice of identifying themselves with their place of origin, in the West of Ireland, rather than their present home, in Belfast, the family reminiscences created a coastal Eden in Louis's mind, an ideal place long before it materialized as the site of summer vacations. Then, the social elevation of MacNeice's father, as rector and later bishop in the Church of Ireland, set the Mac-Neices apart from even Protestant neighbors in Belfast and Carrickfergus. The social isolation was enforced by the discomfort of bringing Louis's older brother, who had Down's syndrome, into public so that recollections of childhood center on cloisters, such as the nursery, the garden, and the study. His father's heterodox support of Home Rule and his sense of justice must have made Louis, more than most Protestant youths, conscious of his minority status within Ireland. As he recalls in "Carrickfergus": "I was the rector's son, born to the anglican order, / Banned for ever from the candles of the Irish poor" (*MCP*, 69). A stern Protestant nanny made Catholic Ireland seem, by contrast, even more human and appealing, as he explains in a digression from *Zoo*:

> A harassed and dubious childhood under the hand of a well-meaning but barbarous mother's help from County Armagh led me to think of the North of Ireland as prison and the South as a land of escape.[30]

This escape would be a return to the spiritual home from which he was exiled at birth:

> Torn before birth from where my fathers dwelt,
> Schooled from the age of ten to a foreign voice,
> Yet neither western Ireland nor southern England
> Cancels this interlude; what chance misspelt
> May never now be righted by my choice.
>
> Whatever then my inherited or acquired
> Affinities, such remains my childhood's frame
> Like a belated rock in the red Antrim clay
> That cannot at this era change its pitch or name—
> And the pre-natal mountain is far away.
>                    ("Carrick revisited," *MCP*, 225)

The word *interlude,* as a term for the first decade of his life, bristles with ambiguity. MacNeice feels deeply the poignancy of his childhood and the futility of understanding or reclaiming it: "Our past we know / But not its meaning—whether it meant well" ("Carrick revisited"). In certain poems he expresses clearly the attraction and repulsion of his past: "But I cannot deny my past to which my self is wed, / The woven figure cannot undo its thread." Two dozen lines later in this same poem, "Valediction," he returns to a fabric image without acknowledging the contradiction between the images that manifest his dilemma.

> And not to have my baby-clothes my shroud
> I will acquire an attitude not yours
> And become as one of your holiday visitors,
> And however often I may come
> Farewell, my country, and in perpetuum;
>
> (*MCP*, 53)

The poet's efforts in *The Strings are False* to make meaningful history of his childhood seem unsuccessful to me, and often bathetic: "My mother was comfort and my father was somewhat alarm and my sister wore yellow shoes and a bow on her hair and my brother, who was a Mongolian imbecile, . . ."[31] By association, perhaps, Ireland's preoccupation with its own past seemed equally futile, a sort of arrested development. In his early "Eclogue from Iceland," (1936) he wrote: "My diehard countrymen like drayhorses / Drag their ruin behind them" (*MCP*, 41). Years later, with less rancor he could draw the same equation between the past, Ireland, and an irresponsible suspension of time:

> So the kiss of the past is narcotic, the ocean
> Lollingly lullingly over-insidiously
> . . . . . . . . . . .
> For the western climate is Lethe,
> The smoky taste of cooking on turf is lotus,
> There are affirmation and abnegation together
> From the broken bog with its veins of amber water,
>
> ("Western Landscape," *MCP*, 255)

MacNeice did not resolve his memories of Ireland into meaningful biography. In his poetry he set his face to the future and entertained these memories as sidesteps from history, or more precisely, as digressions from his memoir. Occasionally the poet's modes conflict: the exile's timeless Ireland and the memoirist's impending future seem incongruous, as in "The Closing Album." Of Dublin, he says, "You give me time for thought / And by a juggler's trick / You poise the toppling hour—" (*MCP*, 164). In "Cushendun," where he vacationed in Antrim, the two worlds seem irreconcilable:

> Forgetfulness: brass lamps and copper jugs
> And home-made bread and the smell of turf or flax
> And the air a glove and the water lathering easy
>     And convolvulus in the hedge.
>
> Only in the dark green room beside the fire
> With the curtains drawn against the winds and waves
> There is a little box with a well-bred voice:
>     What a place to talk of War.
>
> <div align="right">(<i>MCP</i>, 165)</div>

In Derek Mahon's assessment of MacNeice, these sidesteps from history evoke the otherworlds of Greek and Irish myth which are co-extensive with this world:

> The islands of the Blest, the Hesperides, Tir na nOg, the Land of the Ever Young—call it what you will, it crops up regularly in MacNeice's poetry and is usually associated with the West of Ireland.[32]

In the draft of the opening chapter of an autobiography that was to bear the title *Countries in the Air,* MacNeice confesses the extent to which he mythologizes the West of Ireland:

> From a very early age I began to long for something different, to construct various dream worlds which I took it were on the map.
>     The first of these dream worlds was 'The West of Ireland', a phrase which still stirs me, if not like a trumpet, like a fiddle half heard through a cattle fair. My parents came from the West or, more precisely, from Connemara, and it was obvious that both of them vastly preferred it to Ulster. The very name Connemara seemed too rich for any ordinary place. It appeared to be a country of windswept open spaces and mountains blazing with whins and seas that were never quiet, with drowned palaces beneath them, and seals and eagles and turf smoke. . . . But I was not to visit Achill or Connemara until I had left school. So for many years I lived on a nostalgia for somewhere I had never been.[33]

Acquisition of the West as his dream world seems fully deliberate:

                                    Where I was born,
        Heckled by hooters and trams, lay black to the west
        And I disowned it, played a ticklish game
        Claiming a different birthplace, a wild nest
        Further, more truly, west, on a bare height
        Where nothing need be useful and the breakers
        Came and came but never made any progress
        And children were reborn each night.
                              ("Day of Renewal," *MCP,* 309)

As he says in a late poem, "lanes of fuchsias / Bleed such hills as . . . /
. . , later shine / More than ever, with my collusion" ("Donegal Triptych," *MCP,* 446).

   Occasionally, the Edenic West represents more than a deliberate escape, as it does in a pocket of poems written toward the close of the
war and published in *Holes in the Sky* (1948). In "Last Before America"
the perspective is more distant than usual, reminding us of the viewpoint from pedestal or tower, rejected in the memoirist's poems. The
poem presents two ideal, timeless worlds, and two images of longing.
The first world is the poet's ideal, from which he is distanced or shut out:

        A spiral of green hay on the end of a rake:
        The moment is sweat and sun-prick—children and old women
        Big in a tiny field, midgets against the mountain,
        So toy-like yet so purposed you could take
        This for the Middle Ages.

        At night the accordion melts in the wind from the sea
        From the bourne of emigrant uncle and son, a defeated
        Music that yearns and abdicates; chimney-smoke and spindrift
        Mingle and part as ghosts do. The decree
        Of the sea's divorce is final.

Then the poem turns to the ostensible subject as implied by the title:
the countrymen's longing for America:

        Pennsylvania or Boston? It was another name,
        A land of a better because an impossible promise
        Which split these families; it was to be a journey

Away from death—yet the travellers died the same
As those who stayed in Ireland.

The poem ends with a curious image, presumably representing the Irish attraction to emigration:

Both myth and seismic history have been long suppressed
Which made and unmade Hy Brasil—now an image
For those who despise charts but find their dream's endorsement
In certain long low islets snouting towards the west
Like cubs that have lost their mother.

                                        (*MCP*, 226–27)

Zoologically, an indigenous animal would have been more satisfying. Cartographically, cub snouts are about right for Ireland's western coast. Historically, mothers lost their offspring to western migration. Emotionally, however, the association of dependent childhood, the lost mother, and this landscape of longing captures MacNeice's deepest feelings for the West of Ireland. Most likely the loss of the mother, to an emotional breakdown when Louis was five and to death two years later, was the crucial event that clouded his Belfast decade and assigned his Irish background to some realm aside from history and beyond loss.

&

The facts that the Belfast-born poet Derek Mahon has lived outside of Ireland during most of the last decade and that he addresses the Troubles in Ulster only rarely and indirectly have misled one *TLS* reviewer to label him "the least locally attached" of the recognized Ulster poets, such as John Hewitt, John Montague, Seamus Heaney, Michael Longley, James Simmons, and Paul Muldoon.[34] Except in Montague's *Rough Field* and Heaney's *North,* however, Ulster poets have chosen to treat the Troubles obliquely. We can also recall that writers such as Joyce, O'Casey, Beckett, and MacNeice have made living outside of Ireland seem very Irish.

Derek Mahon was conceived, according to my fallible math, during the first Nazi bombings of Belfast, or perhaps in an "all-clear," and born in November, 1941, to Protestant parents. His father, who followed his grandfather into the Belfast shipyards, became an inspector of engines.

Derek enrolled in Trinity College, Dublin, attended the Sorbonne for one year, and returned to Trinity to earn a degree in French, as well as in English and philosophy, in 1965. He sojourned in Toronto and Boston and endured a year of teaching in Belfast and two in Dublin before his hegira to London in 1970. An attempt to return to Ulster, as poet-in-residence at the New University between 1977 and 1979, left Mahon temporarily depressed and in bad health and resolved "never to live in Northern Ireland again."[35] Disaffected particularly by his repugnance for the Protestant extremist ("God, you could grow to love it, God-fearing, God- / chosen purist little puritan that"), he may appear, to the undiscerning, to be at home in the English tradition. For example, one critic, Roger Garfitt, has misplaced him with the British minimalist poets such as Empson, Fuller, and Porter, in this manner: "His very English insistence on the limitations of poetry inhibits him from proceeding to any . . . imaginative restructuring."[36] Although Mahon looks forward to the day when the question "Is so-and-so really an Irish writer?" will clear a room in seconds,[37] mislabeling leads to misinterpretation, as Garfitt illustrates, and therefore a more helpful characterization of Derek Mahon is required.

Mahon extends the tradition of those Irish exiles—Joyce and Beckett—whose writing elevates character and place, or setting, over history and ideology, particularly the Irish version of history. Goaded by a killing Irish rectitude, they reject political formulations about humanity and find man most human among the waste spaces, alone or with his own fool. Throughout Mahon's five volumes, *Night-Crossing* (1968), *Lives* (1972), and *Snow Party,* from which selections are gathered with "new poems" in *Poems 1962–1978,* and his most recent volume *The Hunt by Night* (1982), Mahon's poems are set in an actual specified place, often Belfast, or, more frequently, in some barren, primitive, or post-holocaust site.[38] Value resides not in society or the force-march of history but in survival and in the respites when one knows love or light from the hills. Through his five volumes Mahon discards social and historical values, stripping his subject to the bare forked creature.

The history Mahon discards includes the Troubles in Ulster but is larger and less defined than that ineluctable homicidal process. As Terence Brown has characterized it, "History for Mahon is no saga of land and people but a process, . . . which casts one man as coloniser, another as colonised, and man in innumerable roles."[39] The stripping of these roles down to unaccommodated humanity, Mahon's most persistent theme, was obscured among other concerns in his first volume, *Night-Crossing,* much of which was written at Trinity. The volume opens with an ironic love poem, worthy of MacNeice, which is addressed to "Girls in Their Seasons" ("matches go out in the wind"). It includes four cocksure love poems that have been dropped from *Poems 1962–1978,* the poet's personal selection, published in 1979. In the earlier volumes Mahon often loses his deftness in love poetry and either unzips emotions or tarts them up. Although *The Hunt by Night* contains a very moving missive to his wife, within the earlier four volumes only one love poem seems totally successful, "Two Songs," a recent harmonious marriage of short poems that were printed separately in *Lives.* Despite a distracting arrangement, several poems in *Night-Crossing—* "Four Walks . . . ," "An Unborn Child," "Epitaph for Robert Flaherty" —point to the remarkable archaeological poems of *Lives* (1972) and *Snow Party* (1975), in which the survivor of an unspecified holocaust locates himself:

> We are
> Holing up here
> In the difficult places —
>
> In caves,
> Terminal moraines
> And abandoned farmhouses,
>
> ("Entropy," *Lives,* 30)

or artifacts of a dead civilization disclose themselves:

> Having spent the night in a sewer of precognition, consoled by moon-glow, air-chuckle, and the retarded pathos of mackerel, we wake among shoelaces and white wood to a raw wind and the cries of gulls. Deprived of use, we are safe now from the historical nightmare . . .
>
> ("The Apotheosis of Tins," *Snow Party,* 27)

We hear also the voice of the archaeologist who fingers shards and reflects on the striae of civilizations within himself:

> So many lives,
> So many things to remember!
> I was a stone in Tibet,

A tongue of bark
At the heart of Africa
Growing darker and darker . . .

.    .    .    .    .    .    .    .    .    .

I know too much
To be anything any more —
And if in the distant

Future someone
Thinks he has once been me
As I am today,

Let him revise
His insolent ontology
Or teach himself to pray.

("Lives," *Lives,* 15–16)

All three excerpts are from poems animated by an elaborate rhetoric and florid diction which may be the most valuable artifacts of the otherwise defunct culture. Precisely when the culture collapsed remains uncertain, even vaguer in Mahon's revisions of earlier poems for *Poems 1962–1978.* In these revised poems trade-names on the junk have peeled off, the Citroen has become "the car," and topical references, to Mailer, the CIA, Cambodia, etc., have been erased in the last quarter of *Poems 1962–1978.*[40] More significantly, in the new poems, a quarter of the volume, he has chastened his diction, simplified his rhetoric, and shifted most of the irony from his tone to the formal strategies of the poems. In the "new poems" we may miss the bite of lines such as these from *Snow Party*:

Your great mistake is to disregard the satire
Bandied about among the mute phenomena.
Be strong if you must, your brusque hegemony
Means fuck-all to the somnolent sun-flower
Or the extinct volcano.

("After Nerval")

In the eighteen "new poems," Mahon's distinctive voice is nearly submerged in the stream of conventional British diction and rhetoric:

Yet even today the earth disposes
Blue bells, roses and primroses,

The dawn throat-whistle of a thrush
Deep in the dripping lilac bush,
                    ("Ford Manor," *MP*, 81)

Some reviewers find the adroit control of assonance and rhythm and
onomatopoeia, represented in the last two lines, an inadequate compensation for the biting imperatives and rich diction of the earlier poetry.
If we recognize, however, Mahon's intention to shuck off ostentatious
personality and to comment on history through his form, we can accept
the poet's own selection and revisions as canonical. I will base my obser-
vations of the earlier poetry on this volume, *Poems 1962–1978,* and then
observe how theme and tone are extended or modified in Mahon's new
volume, *The Hunt by Night* (1982).[41]
In "The Last of the Fire Kings" the escaping monarch declares,

I am
Through with history—
Who lives by the sword

Dies by the sword.
Last of the fire kings, I shall
Break with tradition and

Die by my own hand
Rather than perpetuate
The barbarous cycle.

He recognizes, however, that

. . . the fire-loving
People, rightly perhaps,
Will not countenance this,

Demanding that I inhabit,
Like them, a world of
Sirens, bin-lids
And bricked-up windows—

Not to release them
From the ancient curse
But to die their creature and be thankful.
                    (*MP*, 64–65)

The Belfast battlescape establishes grounds for arguing that Mahon's "ancient curse" is more malign than Stephen Dedalus's "nightmare," to which Mahon alludes in "The Apotheosis of Tins." Joyce is drawn into "The Snow Party," also, when from a window, a characteristic Mahon setting, the writer Basho and Japanese friends observe that

> Snow is falling on Nagoya
> And farther south
> On the tiles of Kyōto.
>
> Eastward, beyond Irago,
> It is falling
> Like leaves on the cold sea.
>
> Elsewhere they are burning
> Witches and heretics
> In the boiling squares,
>
> Thousands have died since dawn
> In the service
> Of barbarous kings;
>
> (*MP*, 63–64)

"Barbarous Kings" directs us to "The Last of the Fire Kings," the next poem in *Poems 1962–1978*. "Snow Party" also mirrors the last sections of Yeats's "Lapis Lazuli" and points in other directions: toward the slaughter of Aughrim and the Boyne, contemporary with Basho's tour to Nagoya and to northern Japan, but also away from history toward Gabriel Conroy's snow-dream in "The Dead" that life is brief compared to our endless citizenship among the dead.

Mahon is not so concerned with history's indeterminacy, one of Joyce's themes in *Finnegans Wake*, as with its determinism, which Stephen attempts to evade in *Ulysses*. In the Ithaca episode, when the typal characters Stephen the artificer and Bloom the voyager practice an ancient rite under the ageless constellations, they seem to rise out of history's causal net. Mahon terms such a liberating perspective "the theoptic view." His comments on Hugh MacDiarmid could apply to Joyce as well: "He had a lively sense of the planet earth as one stone among many, albeit the most interesting because peopled by the peculiar creatures we call people."[42] To achieve this theoptic view of man's fragility and ephemerality, Joyce would not sacrifice his alternative realistic view of the urban world (as Bloom reenters from under the dizzying heaven-tree of stars, he knocks his head against a walnut sideboard). Mahon, too, maintains a dialectic between some point beyond history and a historical urban setting, usually Belfast. Early poems, such as "De Quincey at Grasmere," "Van Gogh in the Borinage," "Teaching in Belfast," and "Canadian Pacific," a poem from the middle volumes "Afterlives," and the "new poem" "The Return" and most poems from *The Hunt by Night* provide a historical perspective to which the poet commutes. However, he often resides in a perspective we might term "phenomenological."

The term seems appropriate when Mahon attempts to reveal or ease "the metaphysical disjunction between 'subject' and 'object,' between the perceiving sensibility and everything external to it," an intention he attributes to Beckett.[43] His most effective attempts, in *Lives* and *Snow Party*, are forays along the border that barely separates the animate from the inanimate, the inert, articulate Beckett-like character from the bones, tins, and shards. "Consolations of Philosophy" concludes with Mahon's recurrent image for this border:

> . . . When the broken
> Wreath bowls are speckled with rain-water
> And the grass grows wild for want of a caretaker,
>
> Oh, then a few will remember with delight
> The dust gyrating in a shaft of light;
> The integrity of pebbles; a sheep's skull
> Grinning its patience on a wintry sill.
>
> (*MP*, 47)

Interchanges across this sill between the animate and inanimate are maintained through Mahon's sound effects, his metaphors, and even his titles. In the excerpt above he relates the quick and the dead through assonance and feminine rhyme ("integrity," "grinning," "wintry") and through the near-anagrams, "rain*water*" and "care*taker*" (in *Lives* he pairs *sugar* and *Fergus*).

Even more than by rhyming effects his phenomenological intention is served by metaphors that confuse the living and insensate. For example, in a trope on the metaphor of leaves as souls of the dead, as developed by Virgil, Milton, and then Beckett, Mahon writes,

> The prisoners of infinite choice
> Have built their house
> In a field below the wood
> And are at peace.
>
> ("Leaves," *MP*, 59)

He describes "A stadium filled with an infinite / Rustling and sighing,"
lines that are echoed in a poem on gypsies, "After Jaccottet":

> There are fires under the trees
> Low voices speak to the sleeping nations
> from the fringes of cities.
> . . . . . . . .
> perpetual murmur
> around the hidden light.
>
> (*MP*, 84)

The two poems collaborate to render gypsies and leaves referents to
each other.

A more concentrated metaphorical exchange occurs in the highly
praised "Disused Shed in Co. Wexford":

> Deep in the grounds of a burnt-out hotel,
> Among the bathtubs and the washbasins
> A thousand mushrooms crowd to a keyhole.
> This is the one star in their firmament
> Or frames a star within a star.
> What should they do there but desire?
> So many days beyond the rhododendrons
> With the world waltzing in its bowl of cloud,
> They have learnt patience and silence
> Listening to the rooks querulous in the high wood.
>
> (*MP*, 79)

Most reviewers have taken the actual subject of this poem to be dispossessed humans, "the lost people of Treblinka and Pompeii" to whom
the mushrooms are compared; however, the engaging subject, the one
Mahon is engaged with, is the tenacious marginal life of the mushroom
colony.[44]

The most interesting of such metaphorical inversions occurs between
wraiths and shift-workers in "Going Home," a poem that might appro-

priately exchange titles with the next poem after those from *Lives,* "Afterlives." "Going Home" clearly begins beyond mortality:

> Why we died
> Remains a mystery,
> One we shall never solve.

In the ninth stanza these spirits move into an indefinite metaphorical
relation to dispirited laborers from Hull:

> For ours is the afterlife
> Of the unjudgeable,
> Of the desolate and free
>
> Who come over
> Twice daily from Hull
> Disguised as shift workers
>
> And vanish for ever
> With a whisper of soles
> Under a cindery sky,

Stepping upon the material sense of *soles,* the poem continues within
a sterile and recognizable contemporary landscape:

> A sunken barge rots
> In the mud beach
> As if finally to discredit
>
> A residual poetry of
> Leavetaking and homecoming,
> Of work and sentiment;
>
> For this is the last
> Homecoming, the end
> Of the rainbow—
>
> And the pubs are shut.
> There are no
> Buses till morning.
>
> (*MP,* 61–3)

By rendering a metaphor's reference and referent interchangeable, Mahon often exposes the animistic roots of poetry.

Mahon does entertain ideas of animism. He says of the Irish novelist Brian Moore:

> An object, for Moore, is more than the sum of its atoms. It preserves within it the racial memory of its raw material, as a wardrobe might have heard of the Crucifixion.[45]

He wittily extends to the Ulster Calvinists this notion of things having memory:

> The chair squeaks in a high wind,
> Rain falls from its branches,
> The kettle yearns for the
> Mountain, the soap for the sea.
> In a tiny stone church
> On the desolate headland
> A lost tribe is singing 'Abide With Me.'
>
> ("Nostalgias," *MP,* 68)

At this point we might remind ourselves that Mahon is not a pioneer in following Husserl's first directive to return to the "things themselves." For example, this work has asserted that Mahon's fellow Irishmen, Thomas Kinsella and Seamus Heaney, employ a peculiar hinged image and a textured language, respectively, to restore the aseity of things. Mahon's method is distinguishable from theirs, however, and from that of such poets as Ted Hughes and Gary Snyder, because his wit and elaborate rhetoric remind us of the observing speaker and of "the metaphysical disjuncture between 'subject' and 'object.'" Mahon's objects usually speak only through their eloquent attorney: "Your great mistake is to disregard the satire / Bandied among the mute phenomena." Whether the speaker is unidentified or identified as an anthropologist or survivor, we are charmed by his advocacy of objects' "viewpoints," as of umbrellas in this poem:

> We know they have also shivered
> In the cold draught of despair
> And are, therefore, the more
> Ecstatic after rain—
>
> ("A Kind of People," *MP,* 29)

The "new poems" depart from earlier verse by dispensing with elo-
quence and advocacy and making the poet's relation to nature an important subject of the poem. For example, one of four "Surry Poems" begins as if it were from *Lives* or *Snow Party*:

> Ancient bathtub in the fallow field—
> midges, brown depths where once
> a drift of rainbow suds,
> rosewater and lavender.
> Now cow faces, clouds,
> starlight, nobody there.

Then imagination returns home to the poet, as it has not in the earlier poems:

> Nobody there for days and nights
> but my own curious thoughts
> out there on their own
> in a rainstorm or before dawn
> peering over the rim
> and sending nothing back to my warm room.
>
> ("Field Bath," *MP*, 85)

We become aware of the "watchful heart" that encounters the blank of
nature in this gentle troping of poems about nothingness, such as Shelley's "Mount Blanc," Stevens' "The Snow Man" and perhaps Frost's "For
Once, Then, Something."

Tracing the point of view becomes one of the pleasures of such "new
poems" as "Midsummer" where the speaker takes up his vigil only "when
the people have gone home" or "The Home Front" where the innocent
source of the poem's recollected journalistic images is revealed in the closing lines:

> Americans in the art-deco
> Milk bars! The released Jews
> Blinking in shocked sunlight . . .
> A male child in a garden
> Clutching *The Empire News*.
>
> (*MP*, 88)

The angle of vision and the source of light become the actual subjects
of the suite of twenty-five short lyrics entitled "Light Music," as we
can see in this poem about the poet's son:

> He leads me into
> a grainy twilight
> of old photographs.
>
> The sun is behind us,
> his shadow in mine.
>
> ("Rory," MP, 93)

In the "new poems" the watcher is neither the anthropologist, master of the "light meter," nor the voluble survivor. In "The Attic" Mahon
writes from the home of the poet John Montague in Cork: "Listen can
you hear me / Turning over a new leaf?" He has suppressed the imperative voice, active verbs, ornate diction, and elaborate rhetoric of the early
poems. He frequently pleads ignorance and asks only for a little room
in nature. To the trees and grasses he says, "there is no need for fear— /
I am only looking . . . ," and he makes the meager claim,

> I have a right to be here too.
> Maybe not like you—
> like the birds,
> say, or the wind blowing through.
>
> ("Dry Hill," MP, 86)

With a self-deprecating humor characteristic of these later poems, he
even contemplates metamorphosis, "into a tree / Like somebody in
Ovid / —a small tree certainly / But a tree nonetheless—" ("The Return"). This suppression of self one reviewer labels "Eastern." Certainly
relative to the earlier poems the new poems move Lao-tze's way, as the
new title of the restructured prose poem "Mayo Tao" suggests.

Many of the "new poems" seem autobiographical; we identify the
poet as the unassuming watcher at the window, his eye attracted to
landscape and light rather than to society. He is represented as isolated,
especially, from the Catholic and Protestant citizens of Ulster, "*Un beau
pays mal habite.*" He shares with the speakers of the earlier poems an
alienation from Gaelic traditions ("In the Aran Islands") as well as from

the majority of his countrymen. An earlier poem, "As It Should Be,"
which demonstrates Mahon's deft control of idiom, makes a wry, allusive comment on the poet's role. An outlaw, perhaps an IRA pariah,
is gunned down "in a blind yard / Between ten sleeping lorries / And
an electricity generator."

> Let us hear no idle talk
> of the moon in the Yellow River.
> The air blows softer since his departure

This middle line, which refers to Denis Johnston's play "The Moon in
the Yellow River," accepts implicitly Johnston's association of the luna-
tic, the bomber, and the poet; by alluding to Johnston's source in a Chinese poem Mahon's line substitutes the poet for the bomber. In both
Johnston's play and Mahon's poem, however, the poet is opposed by
homicidal methodology:

> Since his tide burial during school hours
> Our kiddies have known no bad dreams.
> Their cries echo lightly along the coast.
>
> This is as it should be.
> They will thank us for it when they grow up
> To a world with method in it.
>
> (*MP*, 46)

In "Afterlives" he considers the alternative to his exile:

> Perhaps if I'd stayed behind
> And lived it bomb by bomb
> I might have grown up at last
> And learnt what is meant by home.
>
> (*MP*, 58)

More likely, "The Return" suggests, he would have gained the harsh
tenacity of a thorn tree, grotesque but nearly tragic, like Milton's "burnt-
out angel / Raising petitionary hands."

Eschewing "the fire-loving people" of Ulster, Mahon turns to an audience of one reader, the confiding tone implies, or to that sizable lodge
of writers and friends to whom poems are dedicated. One-fourth of
the poems that appear in *Poems 1962–1978* are dedicated there or in ear-

lier editions. As in the two verse-letters—"Beyond Howth Head" and "Sea in Winter"—the dedications render the poems confidential and the addressee complicit in a poetic idea. Through translations, allusions, and references the poet recognizes, beyond the implied reader, a poetic community that stretches from Sophocles to Jaccottet. *The Hunt by Night* extends this community through poems written about or to a dozen writers and friends.

The community is international. We would be seriously misreading the English pastorals among the "new poems" if we inferred that one nation, England say, was freer of historical illusions than another. Consider "Penshurst Place," which takes as epigraph "And if these pleasures may thee move . . . ," Marlowe's opening to "The Passionate Shepherd to his Love":

> The bright drop quivering on a thorn
> In the rich silence after rain,
> Lute music from the orchard aisles,
> The paths ablaze with daffodils,
> Intrigue and venery in the air
> *A l'ombre des jeunes filles en fleurs,*
> The iron hand and the velvet glove—
> Come live with me and be my love.
>
> A pearl face, numinously bright,
> Shining in silence of the night,
> A muffled crash of smouldering logs,
> Bad dreams of courtiers and of dogs,
> The Spanish ships around Kinsale,
> The screech owl and the nightingale,
> The falcon and the turtle dove—
> Come live with me and be my love.
>
> (MP, 82)

As the historical references to Elizabethan intrigue imply, treachery resides at Penshurst as well as in Belfast. Whatever comfort the poem offers derives from the playful extension of the troping poems by Marlowe, Ralegh, Donne, and modern poets, such as Day Lewis, whose refrains the poem borrows, from the imported title of Proust's novel, from more remote allusions to Dunbar and others, and from evocation of the tradition of topographical poems that celebrate the home of Philip

Sidney, such as Waller's "At Penshurst" or Ben Jonson's "To Penshurst."
The irony of the speaker's invitation arises less from his tone than from
the conflict of traditions, literary and historical.

The tradition of literature and art offers an escape, or at least a diver-
sion, from the world of method, determined roles, and homicidal causality. In "The Sea in Winter" the speaker finds nested in the patterns
of art our various dreams of an ideal future:

> In Botticelli's strangely neglected
> Drawings for *The Divine Comedy*
> Beatrice and the rest proceed
> Through a luminous geometry—
> Diagrams of that paradise
> Each has his vision of. I trace
> The future in a colour-scheme
> Colours we scarcely dare to dream.
>
> One day, the day each one conceives—
> The day the Dying Gaul revives,
> The day the girl among the trees
> Strides through our wrecked technologies,
> The stones speak out, the rainbow ends,
> The wine goes round among the friends,
> The lost are found, the parted lovers
> Lie at peace beneath the covers.
>
> (*MP*, 114)

This passage is reinforced by other passages among the "new poems"
that celebrate a perpetual, ideal world comprised of the colors and patterns of art and the timeless features of a landscape that is recognizably
the west and north coast of Ireland. Furthermore, because this idealized
world abounds with Ovidian nymphs or Herrick's rustic maidens, offering "a glimpse of skin in the woods," Mahon's ideal might be labeled
*Tir na Mna* (the land of women), one version of the otherworld from
which the ancient Irish poet derived his authority. As I have mentioned,
Mahon has recognized in Louis MacNeice's poetry a similar version of
the Irish otherworld:

The Islands of the Blest, the Hesperides, Tir na nOg, the Land of the
Ever Young—call it what you will, it crops up regularly in MacNeice's
poetry and is usually associated with the West of Ireland.[46]

Beyond the similarity of their Edens lies a lifelong attraction, shared by Mahon and MacNeice, for the permanencies of Irish landscape. Although Mahon has composed poems specifically about the Aran Islands and Mayo, the landscape that pervades his poetry, not merely as setting but as a source of value as well, could as easily be Ulster as Connaught. The principal features of this poetic landscape are variability (created in fact by saturated land and sky), stark outlines yielding a sense of bound spaciousness, and that capricious light, which must be peculiar to Ireland. In Mahon's home-city, although the sky is "cindery" and changes have occurred "bomb by bomb," "the hills are still the same / Grey-blue above Belfast," ("Afterlives"), and major avenues lead toward the West where "the fields are bright with sunlight after rain" ("Teaching in Belfast"). The West radiates a distinctive light and color, "a dream of limestone in sea light" ("Thinking of Inishere in Cambridge"). In "The Mayo Tao" we hear that

> The nearest shop is four miles away.
> When I walk there
> through the shambles of the morning
> for tea and firelighters,
> the mountain paces me
> in a snow-lit silence.
>
> (*MP*, 72)

Mahon's poems depict this peculiarly Irish light, undependable and therefore a gift, a sign of grace; "the light / of heaven upon the mountains of Donegal," he says in one poem, or:

> The fields dark under
> a gunmetal sky, and one
> tiny farm shining
> in a patch of sunlight
> as if singled out
> for benediction.
>
> ("October," from "Light Music," *MP*, 96)

In addition to light and the stark outlines, this Belfast poet celebrates the spaciousness of rural Ulster and of the West of Ireland. "Yet distance is the vital bond / Between the window and wind" he states in "The Sea in Winter." Of this sense of spaciousness in other Irish writing Norman Jeffares has said, "This is what the Irish writer realizes Irish space can do for him or his characters; it can take them out of time, out of the past—a thing particularly to be hoped for—into a blessed sense of timelessness. . . ."[47]

Both Mahon and MacNeice find the English landscape always within earshot of machines and too humanized to escape change (cf. Mahon's "Ford Manor" and MacNeice's "Woods"). For both poets the permanencies of Western Ireland can win us, or give us respite, from the illusory concerns of society. MacNeice seems closer than Mahon to society which he represents in specific and political terms:

> All over the world people are toasting the King,
> Red lozenges of light as each one lifts his glass,
> But I will not give you any idol or idea, creed or king,
> . . . . . . . . . . . . . . . . . . . . .
> I give you the toy Liffey and the vast gulls,
> I give you fuchsia hedges and whitewashed walls.
>                 ("Train to Dublin," *MCP*, 28)

MacNeice's glances westward seem wistful beside Mahon's more developed "cold dream of a place out of time." On the other hand Mahon's returns to Belfast offer us few particulars of that city mangled by history.

MacNeice never develops an inhuman view of nature or attempts to penetrate its otherness. He offers impressions that are often magical:

> White Tintoretto clouds beneath my naked feet
> This mirror of the wet sand imputes a lasting mood
> To island truancies . . .
>                 ("The Strand," *MCP*, 226)

They are transmitted, however, through the viewpoint of a civilized observer who does

> . . . not envy the self-possession of an elm-tree
>     Nor the aplomb of a granite monolith.
> All that I would like to be is human, having a share
>     In a civilised, articulate and well-adjusted
> Community . . .
>                 (*Autumn Journal*, XII, *MCP*, 125)

This contrasts sharply with Mahon's attitudes and approach, especially as reflected in the phenomenological poems of *Lives* and *Snow Party* in which he explores imaginatively the unconscious state of rock, trees, wind, and sea.

In his recent volume *The Hunt by Night* (1982) Mahon returns to stark isolated landscapes and dusts off his urbane diction as he abandons his brief flirtation with the British landscape tradition. In one poem, "Woods," he explicitly bids farewell to the English estate Ford Manor he celebrated, although ambivalently, in the "new poems." The poem's conclusion relates this pastoral demesne to the lemon-yellow air and tamed setting of Uccello's ritualized "Hunt by Night," a fifteenth-century painting to which several poems in the volume refer:

> we travelled on
> to doubt and speculation,
> our birthright and our proper portion.
>
> Another light
> than ours convenes the mute
> attention of those woods tonight—
>
> while we, released
> from that pale paradise,
> ponder the darkness in another place.
>
> (*MHN*, 58)

The British immigrant of the "new poems" is replaced by the writer-as-exile in *The Hunt by Night*. The volume's initial exile is the poet who projects himself into de Hooch's seventeenth-century painting of a court-yard in Delft, a setting not unlike Calvinist Belfast, where "house-proud, the wives / Of artisans pursue their thrifty lives / Among scrubbed yards, modest but adequate." Separated by his poetic temperament from the "hard-nosed" Boers, the poet in this imaginary life is distanced from re-ality by the frozen lambency, the Grecian Urn stasis, of the painting. In other poems the poet represents himself as a stranger in London and North Carolina or speaks through or to other writers in exile such as Bertolt Brecht in Svendborg, Knut Hamsun, Paul Durcan, and Ovid.

Characteristically, Mahon establishes a "theoptic" view in which hu-man endeavor dwindles before the vastness of history and the heavens. The particular conditions of our exile may matter only to us; however, that they matter nevertheless is Mahon's new note. Of "A Lighthouse in Maine" he says,

> It might be anywhere —
> Hokkaido, Normandy, Maine;
> But it is in Maine.

With his deft wit he directs us to a specific lighthouse and to all such isolated places that we can't help but get to from here:

> You make a right
> Somewhere beyond Rockland,
> A left, a right,
>
> You turn a corner and
> There it is, shining
> In modest glory like
>
> The soul of Adonais.
> Out you get and
> Walk the rest of the way.
>
> (*MHN,* 44)

To the relativist generalization in "A Garage in Co. Cork" that "we might be almost anywhere," he responds, "But we are in one place and one place only. . . ." In the volume's concluding poem, "The Globe in North Carolina," the fact that the poet abides in one place, his wife in another, recalls him from his "theoptic" revery:

> . . . You lie, an ocean to the east,
> Your limbs composed, your mind at rest,
> Asleep in a sunrise which will be
> Your mid-day when it reaches me;
> And what misgivings I might have
> About the true importance of
> The merely human pale before
> The mere fact of your being there.
>
> (*MHN,* 63)

To my mind this metaphysical valediction is Mahon's most successful love poem and more engaging than the epistolary poems — "Beyond Howth Head" and "The Sea in Winter" — that conclude two previous volumes, and which are similar to this poem in length and confidential tone. Because he openly addresses his wife only toward the conclusion, we might term this poem a missive, thoughts transmitted to the recipient which the reader intercepts. The effect, nevertheless, is characteristic of Mahon: to juxtapose the enormous perspective with the "merely human" view, to address a restricted audience, and to establish — through slant rhyme, lines from popular songs, and direct colloquial address — a tone as appropriate to correspondence as to art.

The efficacy of art is questioned in four or five poems in this volume, perhaps most subtly in the title poem, "The Hunt by Night." The poem contrasts primitive depictions of the hunt — "Swift flights of bison in a cave / Where man the maker killed to live" — explicitly with Uccello's fifteenth-century pageant of hunters and horses "tamed and framed to courtly uses" in which "the ancient fears mutated / To play . . ." and implicitly with the abstraction or exhaustion of the survival impulse within the poet's culture, an explicit theme in "A Postcard from Berlin": "the fires / Of abstract rage, exhausted there, / Blaze out of control elsewhere —" (*MHN,* 49).

The stanzaic form of the title poem supports the evolution of the hunt through primitive, civilized, and decadent stages. Although Mahon disguises his pattern of rhyme in apocopated and slant rhyme and rushes us past line-endings and even stanza-endings to complete sentences, he employs a recurrent anticlimactic rhyme scheme of ABCCBA, as evident in stanza three:

> But rampant to
> The pageantry they share
> And echoes of the hunting horn
> At once preemptory and forlorn.
> The mild herbaceous air
> Is lemon-blue,

The stanza's movement from dimeter lines to the tetrameter couplets back to dimeter lines complements the movement from rhymeless lines to a concentration of rhyme, which reveals itself initially in the fourth line, to attenuated rhyme. As with cultures, the conclusion (or decadent stage) imitates the beginning (or primitive stage), but the latter phase embodies self-consciously the entire pattern not apparent in the opening. In most of the stanzas the final lines dissipate the energy anticipated or recovered in the opening lines, as the last three stanzas indicate:

The glade aglow
With pleasant mysteries,
Diuretic depots, pungent prey;
And midnight hints at break of day
Where, among sombre trees,
The slim dogs go

Wild with suspense
Leaping to left and right,
Their cries receding to a point
Masked by obscurities of paint —
As if our hunt by night,
So very tense,

So long pursued,
In what dark cave begun
And not yet done, were not the great
Adventure we suppose but some elaborate
Spectacle put on for fun
And not for food.

(*MHN*, 30–31)

A revision in the first of these stanzas indicates how far Mahon has detoured to pay tribute to W. H. Auden. As Mahon eases the bridle on his urbane diction and irony in this volume he often reminds us of Auden (consider the imperative and tone in Auden's "Alonso to Ferdinand": "Sit regal and erect / But imagine the sands where a crown / Has the status of a broken-down / Sofa or mutilated statue"). By substituting in this revision of "The Hunt by Night" "diuretic depots" for his earlier phrase "sylvan excitements,"[48] he echoes Auden's description of "a corner, some untidy spot / Where the dogs go on with their doggy life" which is where suffering is set in the Old Masters' paintings ("Musee des Beaux Arts"). In the work of Brueghel and of the other masters that Auden salutes, "the dreadful martyrdom" occurs off-center in the background. In Mahon's version of Uccello's painting, terror has departed or hidden "among sombre trees" or receded to "a point / Masked by obscurities of paint."

In *The Hunt by Night,* especially, Mahon frequently directs our attention to art's reticence or failure, not by confining us to the boardroom or parlor, in the manner of those poets who exercise "a very English insistence on the limitations of poetry," but by transporting us to landsend to hear the "North Wind: Portrush" "blasting the subler arts, / That weird, plaintive voice / Choirs now and for ever" or by challenging us, as he does the author of *Finnegans Wake,* to "cmome to a place"

> Beyond cumminity
> Where only the wind synges.
> Words faoil there
>
> Bifar infunity,
> One evenereal stare
> Twintwinkling on the si.
>
> This is the dark adge
> Where the souil swails
> With hurtfealt soang,
>
> Hearing the sonerous
> Volapuke of the waives,
> That ainchant tongue,
>
> Dialect of what thribe,
> Throb of what broken heart—
> A language beyond art
>
> That not even you,
> If you lived
> To a hundred and wan,
> Could begin to danscribe.
> ("The Joycentenary Ode," *MHN,* 47–48)

One of Mahon's writer-exiles, "Ovid in Tomis," ironically letters his praise of the blank page:

> Better to contemplate
> The blank page
> And leave it blank
>
> Than modify
> Its substance by
> So much as a pen-stroke.
>
> Woven of wood-nymphs,
> It speaks volumes
> No one will ever write.

> I incline my head
> To its candour
> And weep for our exile.
>
> > (*MHN,* 41–42)

"Our exile" recalls the wood-nymphs metamorphosed to the page as well as Ovid's origins in Rome. Even the surprising word *candour* recalls its origins, far from the current bland meaning of "frankness," in meanings such as "purity," "whiteness," and "glow."

If he does not "speak volumes" for blankness or "danscribe," Mahon would listen at the edge "Wherever that edge may be" and enlarge the scope and perspective of poetry. He hardly insists "on the limitations of poetry" as our critic charged. When asked if poetry makes nothing happen, Mahon has invoked Shelley's assertion in the *Defense* that "poetry enlarges the circumference of the imagination" which is "the great instrument of moral good."[49] Mahon might adopt as the basis for his theoptic view Shelley's belief that the emotions aroused by poetry make "self appear as what it is, an atom to a Universe."

Poetry's legislative powers, consequently, seem to Mahon no basis for arrogance. When he departs from his family and crosses London twice daily, in the guise of an editor and writer, as MacNeice did for two decades, he knows that poetry cannot free us physically from the roles in which history has cast us. He knows too that if poetry helps shape man's acceptance of mortality, it also shares mankind's fate:

> You will tell me that you have executed
> A monument more lasting than bronze;
> But even bronze is perishable.
> Your best poem, you know the one I mean,
> The very language in which the poem
> Was written, and the idea of language,
> All these things will pass away in time.
>
> > ("Heraclitus on Rivers," *MP,* 107)

## CHAPTER SIX

# Toward
# "A Broader and More Comprehensive Irish Identity"

To establish a contrast with the Irish poetic audience, the basic subject of this chapter, let me quote Charles Molesworth's "darker view" of the American poetic audience, which reveals

> a breakdown in any shared aesthetic assumptions, a realization that poetry now occurs only among isolated groups, each with its own content, its own accepted shibboleths.[1]

Relative to this social fragmentation, Irish readers could be mistaken for the kind of homogenous culture once defined by F. R. Leavis:

> To be born into a homogenous culture is to move among signals of limited variety, illustrating one predominant pervasive ethos, grammar and idiom (consider what the eighteenth century did with Homer) and to acquire discrimination as one moves.[2]

Although most Irishmen have not enjoyed such a homogenous culture probably since the early eighteenth century, nevertheless they have often proclaimed their own "unity of culture."

Before the Easter Rising and Ireland's partial disemcumbrance of England, Irish antiquarians labored with the falsifying aspirations of romantic nationalism: Gaelic would be recovered as the mother tongue, and the island would be purified racially and reenfranchised by "ourselves, alone." The name *Sinn Fein* suggested a monolithic culture which even today many Irishmen and interested non-Irish identify as "the Irish tradition." According to this prevailing concept, Ireland is racially Celtic, linguistically Gaelic, religiously Catholic, politically Anglophobic and republican, organizationally antinomian, sociologically clannish, aesthetically zoomorphic, and socially gregarious and alcoholic. In practice, of course, many nontraditional Irishmen have refused to emigrate, and the super-traditionalists must dimly recognize the contradiction in desiring both a racially pure Gaeldom and a reincorporation of one million Unionists from the North.

In five previous chapters, we have seen how Yeats's poetic successors, following his example, have resisted orthodox nationalist positions by assuming antithetical positions. They have asserted their independence even more fiercely because they continue to receive "signals of limited variety" from the tradition from which they feel dispossessed. We shall conclude this study, then, by considering the poets' relation to this tradition in face of rapid change within their society. As I have argued, the poet's relation toward his tradition entails his relation to all adherents of that tradition or, specifically, to the poetic audience. Consequently, as we return to the question of tradition, we reopen the question of *tone* and its basis in the writer's uncertain relation to his audience. Secondly, I would like to illustrate the variety of interpretations of the Irish tradition by discussing several poets not covered in chapters 2 to 5. Finally, I would close by considering the implications of this variety for the currently troubled Irish society.

Of the legacies lost to the poet, the crucial ones may be the Irish language and the rich tradition of Gaelic poetry that withered in the eighteenth century. Looking back over the millenium of Irish literature Kinsella acknowledges

> a great inheritance and, simultaneously, a great loss. The inheritance is certainly mine but only at two century's silence and through an exchange of worlds.[3]

As inheritors "of a gapped, discontinuous, polyglot tradition,"[4] the poets themselves have been recently the most active retrievers of the lost literature. As I explained in Chapter 1, they have translated major works, edited anthologies of translations, employed topics from Irish myth or history, and commented critically on the older literature. In fact, Kinsella's translation of the *Tain,* Montague's edition of *The Book of Irish Verse,* Heaney's version of *Buile Suibne,* and Sean O Tuama's and Kinsella's collection and translation from Irish poetry, *An Duanaire,* have become major legacies. Kinsella's recoveries, especially, can remind us that tradition means not "a handing down" but "a handing over." His translation of the *Tain* has altered the context in which we approach Yeats's Cuchulain, as *An Duanaire* presents the keel and hull of which

Yeats's Georgian heroes, such as Swift and Berkeley, now seem the visible rigging, so that tradition becomes the present giving to the past. In fact, the surer antiquarianism of current poets has helped free them from Yeats by so enlarging the past that they and not Yeats seem close to an authentic tradition.

The most stable continuous aspect of Irish poetry would seem to be the landscape which has provided the setting or even foreground of Irish poetry since its beginning. However, in a culture so old on an island so small, the landscape has become humanized, acquiring detailed place-names and legends. Montague's "The Road's End" offers two views of the landscape:

> a landscape
> So light in wash it must be learnt
> Day by day, in shifting detail.
> 'I like to look across,' said
> Barney Horisk, leaning on his *slean,*
> 'And think of all the people
> Who have bin.'
>
> (*MCL*, 32)

The Horisk view of the landscape, which is often presented effectively by Montague and Heaney especially, is not quite spatialized history because the human associations are legendary, a recollection of types and exploits free of historical causality or precise time-frames. On the other hand, the Horisk topography offers no escape from the "nightmare of history" or the poet's ambivalence toward the tradition. Yet the post-Yeatsian poets, especially MacNeice and Mahon, evade historical associations by emphasizing the "shifting details" in the Irish setting — the sea and sky, the variable weather, and the capricious light — which must be "learnt day by day." In these lines by Derek Mahon, for example, light becomes a form of grace:

> The fields under
> a gunmetal sky, and one
> tiny farm shining
> in a patch of sunlight
> as if singled out
> for benediction.
>
> (*MP,* 96)

By playing on and transforming the fixed associations of a familiar scene, light becomes a metaphor for the poetic imagination altering as it illuminates the tradition. Implicitly, this is a theme of Mahon's sequence "Light Music," from which the above lines are excerpted, and of much recent Irish poetry.

The poetic landscape is in as much need of imaginative recreation as other components of Irish culture. To the fluidity of the culture itself we can add a second factor to account for the Irish poet's unstable relation to his audience. The Irish audience is itself unstable and fractured synchronically as the tradition is broken diachronically. Although Ireland is not a fully pluralistic society, neither does it maintain the tribal purity portrayed on a Uris calendar or in certain Irish-American journals. Denis Donoghue summarizes the writers' uncertain situation:

> They live upon a fractured rather than an integral tradition; they do not know which voice is to be trusted. Most of them speak English, but they have a sense, just barely acknowledged, that the true voice of feeling speaks in Irish, not a dead language like Latin but a banished language, a voice in exile. English, Irish: Protestant, Catholic: Anglo-Irish, Gael: in Ireland today we do not know what to do with these fractures.[5]

To Donoghue's list of divisions we might add city-dwellers, farmers: socialists, capitalists: developers, environmentalists.

Unwilling to reduce their poetry to partisan or sectarian positions, the poets nevertheless feel political responsibility and, in some cases, moral indignation. They usually restrict themselves to indirect comment on the Troubles, but occasionally indignation flares into poetic expression, as in Kinsella's "Butcher's Dozen," a Swiftian excoriation of Judge Widgery's whitewash of thirteen murders by British soldiers on Bloody Sunday, 1972. Kinsella has also satirized the gombeen developer who has decimated the Georgian architecture of Dublin. However, the most outspoken political poet among the major Irish writers is John Montague, who argues that "politics in the widest sense — the spiritual atmosphere of a country, one's concern for its spiritual health, is one of the strongest strains in contemporary poetry."[6] When he adds, "Certainly, I think a poet should speak for his own people, out of his people's pain,"[7] he sounds more tribal than his poetic contemporaries. Yet recently Montague has advocated "the unpartitioned intellect," a unification of Irishmen through tolerance of differences and an acceptance of a diversity, if not a plurality, of beliefs.[8]

Jane Tomkins has asserted that critical questions concerning the writer's relation to an audience "do not arise until artistic activity has been cut off from the centers of political life and the art product loses its power to influence public opinion on matters of national importance."[9] Let me exempt from her arraignment of reader-response criticism my discussion of "tone in recent Irish poetry" by insisting that I am not conducting a postmortem, that I am describing an actual emphasis within the poetry on the poet's relation to his reader, and that Irish poetry may still be quoted in the premier's major policy speeches, denounced or debated in the daily paper, studied in national schools as required subjects for leaving certificates, or even, to the poets' chagrin, "held up by the chairman of the Northern Ireland Arts Council as examples of the essential health of the state."[10]

Yet, the ancient authority of the Irish poet, somewhat restored by Yeats, could vanish within a generation, so precarious is the poet's relation to his audience. The widening scope of both the poet and his audience may further diminish an Irish poetic community of those "who share interpretive strategies." We can well wonder if those who live closest to the "tradition" are among that audience the poet addresses. Richard Murphy has confessed that the highest praise he could have received for his narrative poem "The Cleggan Disaster" came from a fisherman in the story.[11] That seems unique praise, especially solicited by a poet. Montague, who believes he can speak for "a tribal consciousness," nevertheless acknowledges some separation from the people of whom he writes which he attributes to "false cultures that have come into their lives."[12] He never speaks of these Ulstermen as his readers, nor does Seamus Heaney, for whom the primary dialogue is maintained with the literate reader in "a pure pursuit of excellence — the covenant between you and the literate reader that excellence will be celebrated if it's arrived at."[13] The home-ground does not yield readers for Heaney but generations of active and nonliterary ancestors whose history raises in him doubts about the value of his craft. At an early stage of his career, he was able to address a local readership comprised of his friends among the Belfast poetry circle founded by Philip Hobsbaum in the early sixties. This group offered a model of a poetic community for Derek Mahon, who was not a regular member of the group, Michael Longley, and other Belfast poets. From such an audience Mahon evolved "a community of imagined readership" which provides a nongeographical location for many of his poems beyond the specific settings of Belfast and North Antrim.[14]

Doubtless, the Irish poets, all of whom read effectively from their own poetry, derive their sense of audience in part from frequent poetry readings sponsored by universities or arts councils within Ireland. It seems equally likely that readings in England or the United States or on the Continent must also contribute, at least an upper tier, to that imagined audience.

Consequently, at present no poet of intelligence considers Irish problems, or addresses an Irish audience, insularly, as the poets of the Palace Bar might have done. For other considerations, the Irish economy is interdependent with that of other Common Market nations. Furthermore, the Irish suspect that unless international negotiations for nuclear disarmament begin and conclude successfully, neutrality can win for Ireland only a somewhat slower extinction. BBC and RTE television, which have now penetrated pubs and other outposts of Irish culture, convey ample forewarnings of the world's "closing time," as they also make international the most spectacular aspects of other cultures. For example, I recently made the acquaintance of a Meath farmer, a "cap man" whose travels were confined within the five miles from cottage to village and who projected in a dark, turbary dialect an imaginative map of the United States which rivaled Steinberg's New Yorker-view of America for exaggerated features and foreshortened spaces. Over his head, transported by satellite from a live concert in Los Angeles to a screen in Phil Reilly's pub, Rod Stewart was humping the stage and moaning because, it seems, tonight was the night. If the sheepfarmer had borrowed the line from Joyce's *Portrait* — "Ah there must be terrible queer creatures at the latter end of the world" — that notion need no longer originate in the mind's eye of his countrymen.

Even before this internationalizing of Irish culture, however, Irish poets were reaching beyond the English channel and the Atlantic ocean for new poetic models and variations on the formal patterns bequeathed by Yeats and Austin Clarke. John Montague credits Denis Devlin with being "the first poet of Irish Catholic background to take the world as his province,"[15] and behind Devlin, Montague acknowledged, was

Joyce. From Valery and Eluard, Devlin adapted a vivid, superreal image, and from American poetry he developed "an increasing ease both in line and language."[16] Yet, Devlin's example seemed to register immediately only with Montague who became himself the most active courier of international ideas. Between 1953 and 1956 Montague took an intensive course in American poetry and culture at Yale, Indiana University, the Iowa Workshop, and the University of California at Berkeley, making the acquaintance or friendship of many of the American poets who fill the anthologies of recent decades. He also served a literary apprenticeship in Paris as a correspondent for the *Irish Times.* Kinsella, who began teaching in the U.S. in 1965, and Montague both record their discovery of William Carlos Williams as a crucial liberating experience, in Kinsella's phrase, a "leverage out of a rather clamped condition."[17] Until very recently poets from the North chose more conservative American models, such as Frost, or remained faithful to the orthodox British standards of Hardy and Edward Thomas. In the last decade, Heaney has absorbed and manifested the influence of Robert Lowell and Elizabeth Bishop, and Mahon has translated or openly imitated European poets such as Jaccottet and Cavafy.

Whereas only a half-dozen Irish poets are seriously influenced by European or American poets, many more find readers beyond the Atlantic or Irish sea. Many Irish poets are published or distributed in Britain, and at present ten poets — Kinsella, Montague, Murphy, Heaney, Longley, Mahon, Ní Chuilleanáin, Boland, Carson, and Muldoon — enjoy regular American publication. It seems unlikely that these poets would alter their styles or subjects to accommodate the wider audience, but questions concerning the universality of their own experience may trouble them and even affect their tone.

Finally, we might remind ourselves that among the factors that separate the Irish poet from his audience exists one continuous alienating condition which affected Yeats and perhaps all true poets. Because the poet develops his understanding of his past and inherited values independently of received opinion and through his own deeper processes, he will hold a radical view of tradition. He may even represent his tradition as antithetical to the orthodox view, as Yeats and Joyce did, but it will be both more personal and more fundamental than the popular conception of what is essential to the nation. I would accept Gary Snyder's assertion that "poetry is ultimately linked to any culture's fundamental world view, . . . which is the myth-base, its symbol-base, and the source of much of its values . . . ,"[18] only if we recognize the necessary and strengthening alloy of the poet's unique experience and his concern for macrocosmic issues, such as the universal courtship of nuclear disaster. As John Montague has observed,

> The real position for a poet is to be a global-regionalist. He is born into allegiances to particular areas or places and people, which he loves, sometimes against his will. But then he also happens to belong to an increasingly accessible world. . . . So the position is actually local *and* international.[19]

As a consequence of this dual address, contemporary Irish poets offer some of the intensity and discrimination of a unified culture and the variety of a more heterogeneous society, as with sincerity and insecurity they compose their audiences. The variety of the Irish poetic response could be demonstrated more convincingly in the anthologies edited by Anthony Bradley, John Montague, or Peter Fallon and Sean Golden,[20] or in an extension of this study. Such an extension would include more commentary on the poetry of Ulster, especially that of John Hewitt, whose late-flowering has surprised most of us who have admired his slender, honest canon; of Michael Longley, whose intensity and passion in *The Echo Gate* (London: Secker & Warburg, 1979) signaled the escape of a potentially major talent from straitening forms; and of James Simmons, whose raids on the f——able retain the immediacy of such rustling and who has reached an audience with his candid voice unapproached by more finely-tuned poets.[21]

As an installment on such an extended study, I can further illustrate the variety of Irish poetry by discussing new work by Richard Murphy and Paul Muldoon as well as the belated emergence of a distinctly feminine voice in the work of three young women.

Although recently Richard Murphy's bibliography has featured gaps of silence, he must be given serious attention in any book on Irish poetry. With Montague and Kinsella he appeared as a major new talent in the 1950s. In a pioneering recognition of Irish poetry since World War II, M. L. Rosenthal devoted, among studies of numerous British and American poets, four pages to Murphy's poetry. There he observed that "Richard Murphy is the least introspective or tempted toward confessional writing" of the Irish poets who had emerged in the fifties. What could only appear nearly two decades ago as "old-fashioned, rather conventional"[22] elegiac and narrative qualities in the author of *Sailing to an Island* (1963) and *The Battle of Aughrim* (1968), now seems like restraint and reticence in the author of *High Island* (1974) and *The Price of Stone* (1984), especially when we recognize that this relatively thin collection of four volumes has been squeezed out, or more likely screened, from three decades of poetry writing.

Eight years after Rosenthal, Edna Longley could recognize in *Sailing to an Island* the suppression of an autobiographical impulse:

> The archaeology, the exteriority, the deliberate "tasting of vintage terror" . . . the combination of search and research, seems indeed to result from Murphy's excessive consciousness of being an outsider, of needing to work his passage and establish credentials for naturalization.[23]

In a 1977 essay Seamus Heaney could read *Sailing to an Island* as "a parable of another journey between cultures, from the sure ground of a shared but disappearing Ascendancy world to the suspecting community of the native islanders."[24]

Now, after another decade, Murphy's poetic approach to Ireland's western islands seems like a not-so-tight-jawed substitution of Ireland/Inishboffin for England/Ireland which places the residents of the larger island at one remove from the Gaelic tradition as represented by these island fishermen. Through this strategy, Murphy implies the distance, or even inaccessibility, of any essential Irish tradition for all Irishmen. He emphasizes, however, his own alienation. For example, in this account of a drinking session, Murphy himself claims no stable footing among the island's natives:

> The bench below my knees lifts, and the floor
> Drops, and the words depart, depart, with faces
> Blurred by the smoke. An old man grips my arm,
> His shot eyes twitch, quietly dissatisfied.
> ("Sailing to an Island," *MHI*, 5)[25]

Murphy's ancient mariner also suggests Stephen Dedalus's red-eyed Irish-speaking adversary with whom all contemporary Irish writers must struggle.

In *High Island,* this subtheme of isolation from the native traditions associated with nature deepens to the phenomenological theme that a human's needs and moral disposition are irrelevant impositions on the nature we observe. Our perceptions "maroon" us, and even our insular world is fragmented:

> Fissile and stark
> The crust is flaking off,
> Seal-rock, gull-rock,
> Cove and cliff.
>
> Dark mounds of mica schist,
> A lake, mill and chapel,
> Roofless, one gable smashed,
> Lie ringed with rubble.
>
> (MHI, p. 118)

That these perceptions dissociate us from our past as well as from nature is an idea developed in other poems, as well ("Little Hunger" and "Walking On Sunday"). This realization intensifies Murphy's characteristic tone of moral neutrality, the most striking aspect of the *High Island* volume.

The irrelevancy of man's vision becomes an overt subject in "Seals at High Island" (*MHI*, 87–88). While sea and seals relate harmoniously —"Swayed by the thrust and backfall of the tide"—and responsively— "With endless malice of the sea's tongue / Clacking on shingle, they learn to bark back"—the human observer must remain spatially and emotionally detached: "I watch from cliff top, trying not to move." Yet, he cannot resist being moved: as he describes the copulation of two seals, his analogies mount toward a climactic synesthetic metaphor:

> She opens her fierce mouth like a scarlet flower
> Full of white seeds; she holds it open long
> At the sunburst in the music of their loving;

He continues anticlimactically, but as he slips into cliché, he catches himself projecting his own emotions on nature:

> And cries a little. But I must remember
> How far their feelings are from mine marooned.

He observes the languid stud being attacked and finally killed by a jealous rival. When the cows beach the bull's body and sound "An improvised requiem that ravishes / Reason, while ripping scale up like a net," the observer self-consciously but unavoidably resorts to metaphor and pathetic fallacy:

> Brings pity trembling down the rocky spine
> Of headlands, till the bitter ocean's tongue
> Swells in their cove, and smothers their sweet song.

Caught in the net of language, the poet remains marooned on High Island. Although his reintegration into nature cannot be achieved through seeing, Murphy suggests that it may arrive through a "selving," Gerard Manley Hopkins' word for the discovery and performance of a self-characterizing function. In "Coppersmith," by chanting the same word, the poet gains a mystical but momentary sense of unity: "I and the bird, the word and the tree, were one." Through six bird-poems, Murphy implies, first, that like the corncrake, the coppersmith, and the petrel, his function is to compose and recompose the same minimal statement:

> A song older than fossils,
> Ephemeral as thrift.
> It ends with a gasp.
> ("Stormpetrel," *MHI,* 113)

A second implication, that Murphy accepted his own reticence and his willingness to advance only as his corncrake—never "upward into the sun / And never where you're likely to be seen" (*MHI,* 95)—seemed borne out by a decade of poetic silence, broken only by periodical publication.

However, when *The Price of Stone* offered poetic reticence as a theme as well as a strategy, readers may well have been surprised by an heroic decubiculation of the self, obliquely confessional poetry in the form of a sonnet-sequence. In the tradition, the sequence sings of love: filial, homosexual, marital, but especially love of place. Somewhat archaic language consorts with the Renaissance function of the sonnet to commemorate the lover: "Here, too, buried in rhyme, lovers lie dead, / Engraved in words that live each time they're read" ("Friary").

In each of these fifty poems in the sequence, the speaker is a building or site, often an intimate of some period in the poet's life and sometimes a monumental correlative for the disposition of the poet or that of his Anglo-Irish forebears. To an extent, *The Price of Stone* may be seen as a literal, and therefore parodic, poetic rendering of the "big house" novel, pathologies of the Anglo-Irish Ascendancy by such writers as Kevin Casey, Aidan Higgins, and Jennifer Johnston. For example, an Ascendancy extravaganza, a "Folly," remains epicene, useless, and "Bricked up against vandals"; an anachronistic Victorian "Lead Mine Chimney" can only "go on uttering, while I may, / In granite style, with not a word to say." Other structures address the poet about his poetry. Wellington College, in Berkshire, which Murphy attended between 1943 and 1945, is made to speak candidly about poetic reticence:

> Fear makes you lock out more than you include
> By tackling my red brick with Shakespeare's form
> Of love poem, barracked here and ridiculed
> By hearty boys, drilled to my square-toed norm.
> . . . . . . . . . . . . . . . . .
> Poetry gives you unconscripted choice
> Of strategies, renaissance air to breathe.
>
> ("Wellington College")

"Lecknavarna," the flagstone of the alders beside Lough Fee, divulges the poet's conception of the sonnet as learned from a waterfall:

> Hearing that strong cadence, you learned your trade
> Concerned with song in endless falling, stayed.

Less directly, other structures declare their affinities with the sonnet, as a Traveler's "Wattle Tent" is constructed of "fourteen lithe rods, carved into wish-bones."

The "you" accused or addressed by conversant structures is usually the poet but also, because of irreversible convention, the reader. Consequently, as the stones confess or insinuate aspects of the poet's life, we share an intimate address with the poet. This approach to tone works with remarkable subtlety throughout the sequence as the referents for the second- and first-person pronouns converge or separate. For example, a "Georgian Tenement" appeals to youthful protestors who would block its demolition:

> Young lovers of old structures, you who squat
> To keep my form intact, when guards arrive
> With riot gear and water gun, we cannot
> Under such tonnage of cracked slate survive.

By such appeals a poet has drawn his audience to his tradition, which elsewhere is portrayed as anachronistic or reactionary.

As the sequence advances, it subtly revises Murphy's tradition. Evolving from isolated Anglo-Irish obelisks through cryptic witnesses of youthful intimacies, the volume ends with derelict dwellings accounting for themselves. The theme of poetry plays lightly across the desecrated dead or outcasts from life, itinerant or illegitimate, with whom the poet sympathizes. A comparison of the sequence's concluding sonnets with the conclusion of the penultimate version of *The Price of Stone* reveals much of Murphy's intention. Earlier, the volume's final line, offered lightly and ironically by a skating rink—"Old scores ironed out, tomorrow a clean sheet"—could be understood as a sign of personal poetic renewal. In this revised ending, two final sonnets about birth also foretell renewal, but one in which the poet is midwife, perhaps the ministering angel in line eleven of "The Beehive Cell." This poem celebrates the heroic feminine role in that sea-going tradition whose masculine side Murphy portrayed in *Sailing to an Island.*

> There's no comfort inside me, only a small
> Hart's-tongue sprouting square, with pyramidal headroom
> For one man alone kneeling down: a smell
> Of peregrine mutes and eremitical boredom.
>
> Once, in my thirteen hundred years on this barren
> Island, have I felt a woman giving birth,
> On her own in my spinal cerebellic souterrain,
> To a living child, as she knelt on earth.
>
> She crawled under my lintel that purgatorial night
> Her menfolk marooned her out of their coracle
> To pick dillisk and sloke. What hand brought a light
> With angelica root for the pain of her miracle?
>
> Three days she throve in me, suckling the child,
> Doing all she had to do, the sea going wild.

Replacing his vocal structures in the final sonnet, the poet comforts a mother and invites "to share our loneliness" a newborn "natural son," who has just left life's most complete abode. Through enlarged poetic sympathies in this volume, Murphy expresses the ephemerality and value of our abiding places.

Among the variety of voices in Irish poetry over the years, a feminine viewpoint has often been expressed. That this woman's voice must depend on the ventriloquism and negative capability of men—Jonathan Swift or Brian Merriman or William Butler Yeats or John Montague—seems a limitation to the actual variety of poetic expression in Ireland. From the generation of Clarke and Kavanagh and of Kinsella and Montague, which fostered fiction writers such as Mary Lavin, Edna O'Brien, and Jennifer Johnston, no serious poet emerged who was a woman, unless we name Maire Mhac an tSaoi, who published only one volume and that in Irish.

Yet at present, three younger women poets can invite serious attention. In their mid-thirties or early forties, they have not produced poetry as consistently as the best of their contemporaries, Mahon and Muldoon, but in addition to the poet's requisite second career, reviewing or teaching, they have maintained a third career of motherhood which may account for their inconsistency or late-flowering and which may ultimately enrich their poetry and that of Ireland.

Eavan Boland has focused much of her recent poetry on motherhood and the domestic woman. As if recalling Kavanagh's injunctions to write out of one's parish and to make one's epics out of local rows, she looks with wonder, wit, and anger at home and home-body:

> She jockeys him to her hip,
> pockets the nappy liner,
> collars rain on her nape
> and moves away
>
> but my mind stays fixed:
> If I could only decline her—
> lost noun,
> out of context—
>
> stray figure of speech
> from this rainy street
> again to her roots
> she might teach
>
> me a new language,
> to be a sybil

able to sing the past
in pure syllables,

limning hymns sung
to belly wheat or a woman,
able to speak at last
my mother tongue.

Declension of "The Muse Mother"[26] would lead Boland to a hymn of
wonder, the Kavanagh mode, or toward the less-limited "mother-tongue,"
presumably an articulation of the subconscious responses to maternity.

Although the poetry of Medbh McGuckian often shares a domestic
and sexual subject with Boland's, in its metaphorical complexity it contrasts sharply with the honest clarity of Boland's *Nightfeed* or her *In
her own Image*. Metaphors shoal in McGuckian's two volumes — *The Flower
Master* (1982) and *Venus and the Rain* (1984) — darting off at right angles
to any anticipated directions. We see this in the movement of the quatrain from *The Flower Master* on the ephemerality of Mayflies:

The mayflies' opera is their only moon, only
Those that fall on water reproduce, content
With scattering in fog or storm, such ivory
As elephants hold lofty, like champagne.
("Champagne")

Whereas certain effects recur in her verse almost like formulae — the
abstract and concrete nouns incongruously linked by a preposition; an
incongruous appositive or a metaphor that shifts into another mode
or level of thought; the Leonard–Cohenish title ("Something Like A
Wind") — these effects seem part of a rich vocabulary which she probably employs intuitively, so dizzying can be the twists in meaning. These
twists become tortuous, and interpretation torturous, in certain poems
of *Venus and the Rain*. Without abandoning the reader's essential pleasure of making startling and semiconscious connections in poetry, we
can wait to learn her vocabulary of poetic effects and savor, in the mean-
time, the poems in which we sense coherence. The best of these are
infused with sensual language and often a rich eroticism, even when
the subject is flowers or domestic interiors or, as in "The Mast Year,"
the hummock-making of the beech:

It makes an awkward neighbour, as the birch
Does, that lashes out in gales, and fosters
Intimacy with toadstools, till they sleep
In the benevolence of each other's smells,
Never occupying many sites for long:
The thin red roots of alder vein
The crumbled bank, the otter's ruptured door.

Eiléan Ní Chuilleanáin blends some of McGuckians' brilliancy of images with a degree of Boland's clarity. To the rapid tempo and fish-dart of McGuckian's metaphors, however, we can contrast Ní Chuilleanáin's tempo, often slowed to the pulsations of gestation. By transferring action to participles and otherwise suppressing active verbs, by rearranging chronology, and by focusing on timeless aspects of landscape adjunct to any action in the poem, she slows motion to a frieze, as in her fine long poem, "Site of Ambush":[27]

The clouds grew grey, the road grey as iron,
The hills dark, the trees deep,
The fields faded; like white mushrooms
Sheep remote under the wind.
The stream ticked and throbbed
Nearer; a boy carried a can to the well
Nearer on the dark road.
The driver saw the child's back,
Nearer; the birds shoaled off the branches in fright.

So self-effacing are the points of view in some of Ní Chuilleanáin's poems that we cannot initially recognize the source of the lucid images or assign the voice, which become mysteries in the poem. To the extent that the discreet point of view, the static imagery and light-weirs, the pace of habitual inactivity are nurtured in the following poem, rather than treated as a source of silent terror as in Mahon's "A Disused Shed . . . ," to that extent this might be identified as a woman's creation:

'A l'usage de M. et Mme van Gramberen'
—the convent phrase (nothing is to be mine,
Everything ours) marks the small round enclosure,
Its table and bench. Distinguished
From the other old people, from the nuns' gravel

They sat in the windmill's afternoon shadow, half
Hidden by a moving carthorse's huge blond rump
And quarrelled over their sins for Saturday:
*Examination of Conscience before Confession*

Prepared and calm in case one thought
Struck them both, an attentive pose
Eluding me now, at ten in the morning, alone
With a clean college pantry: piled rings
Of glass rising, smooth as a weir.

The moment sways
Tall and soft as a poplar
Pointing into a lifetime of sky.

("The Rose Geranium")[28]

This sacramental view of the passive moment, received meditatively rather than ministered, suggests one innovative dimension these women poets offer to Irish poetry.

Innovation is not one of the principles of the Irish poetic trade as espoused by Yeats. Through emulation of Yeats's integrity, his successors have been true to their own experience and thereby created various interpretations of the Irish tradition. Excepting recent volumes by Kinsella, however, they have produced no works we could honestly label avant garde, until the appearance of *Quoof* in 1983 which confirmed Paul Muldoon's remarkably innovative talent.

Even from the publication of the precocious *New Weather* when Muldoon was twenty-one, the three successive volumes—*Mules* (1977), *Why Brownlee Left* (1980), and *Quoof*—have demonstrated the growth of his poetic powers. On the other hand, each volume, comprised of brief, often enigmatic, lyrics, yields its own complex, unifying theme, rendering the whole volume greater than the sum of its parts. Individual poems are often enthymemes with a suppressed premise or a neglected narrative stage. As if referring to his own early poem "Vampire," Muldoon told one interviewer,

I've become very interested in structures that can be fixed like mirrors at angles to each other—it relates to narrative form—so that new images can emerge from the setting up of the poems in relation to each other.[29]

*Mules* "concerns mixed marriages—between delicacy and bestiality, Grace and Will, humble and heavenly, jackass and mare. . . ."[30] The poet himself describes an idea that arose from his own background: "I was trying to explore these lives that couldn't quite reproduce themselves . . . lives caught between heaven and earth."[31] In *Mules,* mystery resides within hybrid characters such as Ribera's bearded woman and her husband, a merman, and girl-women courted by the uninitiated poet.

The twenty-seven lyrics and long mock-heroic voyage poem that comprise *Why Brownlee Left* seem Waterford-clear poem by poem. The enigmas develop as the poems reflect each other, directing us to somewhere outside the poem, to a place whose mystery is enhanced incrementally. The reader is introduced to this place-out-of-time almost off-handedly, as in the "Geography Lesson" in which the ripening of bananas is described: "Their sighing from the depths of a ship / Or from under the counter in Lightbody's shop, / How all that greenness turned to gold / Through unremembering darkness, an unsteady hold" (*MWBL,* 10).[32] The final line characterizes also the mysterious place of the poet's conception, the subject of the preceding poem, "October 1950."

> Whatever it is, it goes back to this night,
> To a chance remark
> In a room at the top of the stairs;
> To an open field, as like as not,
> Under the little stars.
> Whatever it is, it leaves me in the dark.
>
> (*MWBL,* 9)

This place, within reach only of the imagination, or just beyond, also hoards Roanoke Island's lost colonists in "Promises, Promises":

> We are some eighty souls
> On whom Raleigh will hoist his sails.
> He will return, years afterward
> To wonder where and why
> We might have altogether disappeared,
> Only to glimpse us here and there
> As one fair strand in her braid,
> The blue in an Indian girl's dead eye.
>
> (*MWBL,* 24)

The place out of time may simply be what imagination makes of distant places or lost possibilities, or as in "Immrama" the destination of a cancelled journey, when the man who would become his father "disappeared / And took passage, almost, for Argentina. / . . . That's him on the verandah, drinking rum / With a man who might be a Nazi, / His children asleep under their mosquito-nets" (*MWBL,* 23). The long version of the voyage of Melduin, "Immram," written in Byron-esque stanzas and Los-Angelic idiom, sends a Raymond Chandler hero to discover this truant father, who may appear as a Howard-Hughes recluse in a hidden Park Hotel suite:

> We were spirited to the nineteenth floor
> Where Caulfield located a secret door.
> We climbed two perilous flights of steps
> To the exclusive penthouse suite.
> A moment later I was ushered
> Into a chamber sealed with black drapes.
>
> (*MWBL,* 47)

The volume's title and the title poem, the sonnet "Why Brownlee Left," assure us that we are not reading off the page when we infer this place-out-of-time. The book intends to evoke this space incrementally. In the final rhyming couplet, "foot to / Foot" translates the word *enjambment* and leaves us mid-stride to a future.

> Why Brownlee left, and where he went,
> Is a mystery even now.
> For if a man should have been content
> It was him; two acres of barley,
> One of potatoes, four bullocks,
> A milker, a slated farmhouse.
> He was last seen going out to plough
> On a March morning, bright and early.
>
> By noon Brownlee was famous;
> They had found all abandoned, with
> The last rig unbroken, his pair of black
> Horses, like man and wife,
> Shifting their weight from foot to
> Foot, and gazing into the future.
>
> (*MWBL,* 22)

Muldoon has defended his attraction to the notion of alternative lives against the charge of escapism:

> One of the ways in which we are most ourselves is that we imagine ourselves to be going somewhere else. It's important to most societies to have the notion of something out there to which we belong, that our home is somewhere else . . . there's another dimension, something around us and beyond us, which is our inheritance.[33]

Muldoon embodies this other dimension in a dozen poems of *Why Brownlee Left* where he suggests the concept, discussed in chapter 2 of this book and indelible to the Irish imagination, of another world co-extensive with our world of process, but timeless. A dying ex-Bishop invites us to cross the curtain, the *faed fiad,* into this space which he has discovered in a snowy yard:

> His favourite grand-daughter
> Would look out, one morning in January,
> To find him in his armchair, in the yard.
>
> It had snowed all night. There was a drift
> As far as his chin, like an alb.
> 'Come in, my child. Come in, and bolt
> The door behind you, for there's an awful draught.'
> (*MWBL,* 14)

We might read the subsequent poem, "The Boundary Commission," only as a political poem if it did not follow "The Bishop." It extends and makes visible, however, the idea of a curtain between ontological states:

> *You remember that village where the border ran*
> *Down the middle of the street,*
> *With the butcher and baker in different states?*
> Today he remarked how a shower of rain
>
> Had stopped so cleanly across Golightly's lane
> It might have been a wall of glass
> That had toppled over. He stood there, for ages,
> To wonder which side, if any, he should be on.
> (*MWBL,* 15)

Similar on its surface to *Why Brownlee Left, Quoof* contains twenty-seven lyrics and a long mock-heroic alternative to the immram, perhaps a mock invasion-poem. In language that may be droll or coy but always carefully and delicately structured, *Quoof* draws to its surface the theme of violence, evaded in much Irish poetry and submerged in the earlier Muldoon volumes. Although to this moment *Quoof* has attracted only enthusiastic reviews, we might not be surprised if it were characterized as "a combination of dissimilar images, or discovery of occult resemblances in things apparently unlike . . . [in which] the most heterogeneous ideas are yoked by violence together; nature and art are ransacked for illustrations, comparisons, and allusions."³⁴ Samuel Johnson's comment on the Metaphysicals reminds us not only of Muldoon's interest in these poets³⁵ and of the fallibility of critical judgment, but it also suggests that the greatest of critics has recognized in metaphor-making some inherent violence. The relationship between violence and poetry may be essential to *Quoof.*

The opening poem "Gathering Mushrooms," which is the longest of the lyrics before the long concluding narrative, seems to construct a parable of a localized violence, the Troubles of Northern Ireland, as a mushroom-induced hallucination evokes the H-block and Belfast ghettos:

> Beyond this concrete wall is a wall of concrete
> and barbed wire. Your only hope
> is to come back. If sing you must, let your song
> tell of treading your own dung,
> let straw and dung give a spring to your step.
> If we never live to see the day we leap
> into our true domain,
> lie down with us now and wrap
> yourself in the soiled grey blanket of Irish rain
> that will, one day, bleach itself white.
> Lie down with us and wait.
>
> (*Quoof,* 9)

This admonition is spoken by a kind of Pegasus, the poet himself transformed in a vision he has cultivated. As the poet shadows his father, parallels are suggested between the father, active mushroom-grower and heroic sacker of Troy, on the one hand, and the son, passive mushroom-eater and singer of violence, on the other.

The subsequent poems develop the themes of hallucinogenics, the child's imagination, and the entrance to another state ("Trance"), hands that maintain the past, and the past shaped by the accidents of language and imagery, before arriving at the title poem "Quoof" which concerns nonce language leading the speaker into an uncharted future.

The nineteen poems that link "Quoof" to the long narrative "The More a Man Has, The More a Man Wants" often tell brief stories, as incomplete as narratives heard on a bus, and sometimes develop hidden implications of colloquialisms. In an article that places *Quoof* in the forefront of what the reviewer calls "The New Narrative," John Kerrigan has characterized the genre of *Quoof*: "Reflexive, aleatory, and cornucopian, the New Narrative deploys its fragmented and ramifying fictions to image the unpredictability of life, and its continuous shadowing of What Might Be."[36] The poems are replete with shape-changers: women become trees; unicorns become East-Village innocents; butterflies from an earlier volume become destroying angels. Within one poem, "The Salmon of Knowledge," a master-metamorphoser transforms from semen-like lymph to informant of Finn MacCool, to icon of Christ, to culinary delight—changes inherent in the legends of salmon.

A human shape-changer is the protagonist of Muldoon's long narrative, comprised of forty-nine sections, whose fourteen-liners play all of the changes on the sonnet-form. Gallogly—a.k.a. Golightly, Ingoldsby, English, a gallowglass, the Green Knight, and Sweeney—shares the central role with a Sioux or Apache who is his dope-dealer, contact man, assassin, or, if we track the pronoun-references from the second to third stanzas, a version of himself. Gallogly's actions are set in contemporary Belfast, the orchards of Armagh (near Muldoon's childhood home), and (transported by Picasso, Hopper, and drugs) New York and Boston —in other words, the theatre of the Troubles or stages of a universal condition of violence. So confident is the narrative, so confidential the transitions, as if we are all in on the jokes (it's our choice to be or not), so clear the imagery and fragmented scenes, and so rapid the cinemagraphic tempo that we experience delight and anxiety before enlightenment. As one reviewer has wisely stated, "We have been given the whole texture of a political world and an implicit judgment of it.

We have been denied a simple answer, but we have been granted an understanding."[37]

In addition to the seamy texture of life in Northern Ireland, this poem, particularly, insinuates a relation between violence and metaphorical language. We might correct one of the few misconceptions in John Kerrigan's review—"Muldoon . . . seems drawn to violence for its immediate grotesqueness and what he can make of it verbally"[38]—by counterarguing that Muldoon draws out violence and grotesqueness inherent in contemporary verbiage. In the *Poetry Book Society Bulletin,* Muldoon disclosed of this poem which concerns the use, or abuse, of the English language in Ireland: "I hoped to purge myself of the very public vocabulary it employs, the keenings of the hourly news bulletins."[39] Consider, for example, this report on Gallogly's U.D.R. victim:

> You could, if you like, put your fist
> in the exit wound
> in his chest.
> He slumps
> in the spume of his own arterial blood
> like an overturned paraffin lamp.
>
> (*Quoof,* 49)

The obscenity of "*exit* wound," "*arterial* blood," and the concluding simile could be the envy of ABC's Geraldo Rivera, reporting Garry Gilmore's execution, CBS's Dan Rather in his chest-high verbal dribbling, or their BBC and RTE equivalents because they convey information that has only voyeuristic value.

Yet Gallogley's Portean exploits imply a deeper connection between this shape-changer and our language. First, we notice that the volume aligns itself with the literature of shamanism. The Faber jacket-notes relay the poet's assertion that this narrative has parallels to the trickster cycle from the Winnebago Indians. The epigraph extends the source to a shamanistic legend of the Netselik Eskimos in which a female shaman transmogrifies snow into a dog and herself into a man. The poem makes its first transition in setting by traveling three miles "as the crow flies," insinuating Ted Hughes's trickster borrowed from Indian legends. In stanza 21, a legend from Ovid's *Metamorphosis* concerning a punishment for ungenerosity interrupts as it parallels a parody of Heaney's

Sweeney[40] in which Gallogly laps from a barnyard heel-print milk brought by a Muirghil-like maiden.

Because Gallogly seems less master than victim of these changes, and because other characters also metamorphose (e.g., Alice who is sometimes Lewis Carroll's mushroom-nibbling heroine and sometimes Gertrude Stein's brownie-baking associate), we might identify the trickster with the narrator-poet rather than any character. Whether for Aristophanes' Dionysius in *Frogs* or Shakespeare's mercurial Autolychus or Marlowe's devil, we can seek the prototype for all tricksters in "the divine trickster of Greek mythology, Hermes."[41] Inventor of the lyre and god of messengers, Hermes becomes associated with poetry not as a benign bringer of light and order, like Apollo, but as the ur-trickster and morally neutral conveyer of truth, which necessarily includes the dark and disorder. As one mythologist has written: "His function . . . is to add disorder to order and so make a whole, to render possible within the fixed bounds of what is permitted, an experience of what is not permitted."[42] As Hermetic poetry, Muldoon's *Quoof* may violently yoke together comparisons, but it more often trips off a chain reaction of nominatives, a series of re-namings that necessarily include the dark side of the creature named. If a comparison between love and a cultivated garden seemed truthful for the Apollonian Renaissance poet, then Muldoon's bizarre horticultural comparison, between a bomb-blast victim's dismembered foot and "a severely pruned-back shrub" seems an equally truthful description of this Hermetic poet's dark world. Furthermore, the hermetic shape-changer seems intent on showing us that the benign face of the world is a disguise, so that in Muldoon's poetry our habitual and comfortable disposition toward the domestic and everyday is continually violated.

In fact, this poetic shape-changing and re-naming depend on the reader's familiarity with the stable form and standard names that Muldoon's poems transform. For example, the last short lyric of the volume before "The More a Man Has . . . ," entitled "Aisling," should bring to mind the political vision poems of Aogán Ó Rathaille and Eoghan Rua Ó Súilleabháin in which a beautiful, disguised personification of Ireland mourns her captivity and appeals for ransom.[43] For example, Ó Rathaille's "An Aisling" associates promise of a bounteous harvest with the beautiful vision, and O Súilleabháin, as Austin Clarke after him, offers as possible identifications for this messenger a series of names of legendary women. Coming latest in this subgenre, Muldoon's "Aisling" requires reflexiveness of the reader:

> I was making my way home late one night
> this summer, when I staggered
> into a snow drift.
>
> Her eyes spoke of a sloe-year,
> her mouth a year of haws.

> (*Quoof,* 39)

From this surprising unseasonal image, the reader interprets the encounter as drug-induced before adjusting the interpretation to a figure: the woman's eyes and smile, like a drift of blackthorn and hawthorn blossoms, forecast bounteous fruit. Identified only by the conventional series of anonyms (which includes the unconventional "Anorexia"), the girl yields the speaker "a lemon stain on my flannel sheet." The image repels the reader by confounding the appetites, a frequent nasty practice of Muldoon's, so that in place of fruits we have the symptoms of a venereal disorder, which drives the speaker to the ironic thanksgiving, "It's all much of a muchness," and to the hospital for a urine test. By metonym rather than overt metaphor the poem draws in a hunger-striker, recovering in a Belfast hospital ward:

> In Belfast's Royal Victoria Hospital
> a kidney machine
> supports the latest hunger-striker
> to have called off his fast, a saline
> drip into his bag of brine.
>
> A lick and a promise. Cuckoo spittle.
> I hand my sample to Doctor Maw.
> She gives me back a confident *All Clear.*

The Royal Victoria actually employs a Dr. Maw, but the physician's gender has been altered to align her with the visionary woman and to evoke the voracious female principle—Nerthus, the sea-goddess, Cathleen Ni Hoolihan—in the work of Heaney, Montague, and earlier Irish poets. Echoing the tannoy's All Clear, the last line declares that the speaker and the hunger-striker have survived another "close call" from this vision of great promise.

The squeamish reader of Muldoon's poetry must trade the pleasure of noble sentiments for the pleasure of truth: for example, that the Irish aisling wears many disguises and pseudonyms and that she can swallow up the unwitting, or allow them a narrow escape. Muldoon's best reader, however, will prefer the Protean experiences of his poems, often unpleasant, to the tired shibboleths and false truths they replace. The readers who wrestle with these experiences in *Quoof* and derive a truth confirm, to various degrees, Muldoon's version of the Irish tradition, which complements rather than supplants the various versions of Kinsella, Montague, Heaney, and Mahon. However, the method of *Quoof* suggests a new way of addressing the issue of violence in the Irish tradition: by unmasking it and disclosing its various universal aliases rather than by giving it a purely Irish or regional character. As Muldoon adds a distinctive new tone to Irish poetry, he also confirms the strength of this variable tradition. Of the poets studied in this book, the tanist seems to have appeared and the succession to have been assured.

The drafters of a recent celebrated report calling for a New Ireland would "allow full participation by all traditions in the affairs of the island. This would require," they emphasize, "a general and more explicit acknowledgement of a broader and more comprehensive Irish identity."[44] We can argue that the "traditions" referred to in this report as constituents of the broader identity, which is based on sect, region, and national origin, and defined by political spokespeople, can be supplemented, or even supplanted, by the traditions of individual writers and their audiences — the traditions of Yeats, Joyce, Kinsella, Montague, Heaney, Mahon, and so on. These poetic versions of the Irish tradition comprehend a wider vision of the universe and include in "the more comprehensive Irish identity" Joyce's sense of humanity's universal plight . . . and flight "between a micro- and a macrocosm ineluctably constructed upon the incertitude of the void."[45]

# Notes

## Chapter One

1. Peter Costello, *The Heart Grown Brutal: The Irish Revolution in Literature from 1891–1939* (Dublin: Gill & Macmillan; Totowa, New Jersey: Rowman and Littlefield, 1978), 246.

2. Louis Gillet, "The Living Joyce," in *Portraits of the Artist in Exile: Recollections of James Joyce by Europeans,* ed. Willard Potts (Seattle: University of Washington Press, 1979), 185.

3. Ibid., 186.

4. Deirdre Bair, *Samuel Beckett: A Biography* (New York: Harcourt Brace Jovanovich, 1978), 305.

5. Richard Ellmann, *James Joyce,* rev. ed. (Oxford: Oxford University Press, 1982), 738.

6. Bair, *Samuel Beckett,* 308–13.

7. Mervyn Wall, "Denis Devlin Remembered," *Advent VI,* Denis Devlin Special Issue (Southampton: Advent Books, 1976), 20.

8. Louis MacNeice, *Collected Poems,* ed. E. R. Dodds (London: Faber & Faber, 1966); cited parenthetically as *MCP* with page numbers.

9. F. S. L. Lyons, *Ireland Since the Famine,* rev. ed. (London: Fontana, 1973), 589.

10. Augustine Martin, "Literature and Society, 1938–1951," in *Ireland in the War Years and After, 1939–1951,* ed. Kevin B. Nowland and T. Desmond Williams, (Dublin: Gill & Macmillan, 1969), 169.

11. Sean O'Faolain, "Ireland After Yeats," *The Bell* 17, no. 11 (Summer 1953): 46.

12. Anthony Cronin, *Dead as Doornails* (Dublin: Dolmen Press, 1976), 76.

13. Cyril Connolly, "Comment," *Horizon* 5, no. 25 (January 1942): 9.

14. John Ryan, *Remembering How We Stood: Bohemian Dublin at the Mid-Century* (Dublin: Gill & Macmillan, 1975), 66; Maurice Harmon, "Notes Toward A Biography," *Irish University Review,* Austin Clarke Special Issue, 4, no. 1 (Spring 1974): 22.

15. Lyons, *Ireland Since the Famine,* 554–56.

16. *Irish Times,* 31 June 1941; "The War Years," *The Honest Ulsterman* 64 (September 1979–January 1980): 13.

17. Seamus Heaney, *Preoccupations: Selected Prose 1968–1978* (London: Faber & Faber; New York: Farrar, Straus & Giroux, 1980), 22; *Honest Ulsterman* 64: 28–37.

18. Ryan, *Remembering How We Stood,* 9.

19. Connolly, "Comment," 6.

20. *Irish Times,* 15 March 1941.

21. *Irish Times,* 15 March 1941. The esteemed Cuala Press, omitted from the *Irish Times*'s list, actually exhibited at this fair, according to Liam Miller. Interview at Wynn's Hotel, Dublin, June 1983.

22. R. M. Smyllie, "Preface" to *Poems from Ireland,* ed. Donagh MacDonagh (Dublin: The Irish Times, 1944), v.

23. O'Faolain, "Ireland After Yeats," 47.

24. Michael Adams, *Censorship: The Irish Experience* (Tuscaloosa: University of Alabama Press, 1968), 250. Although blemished by near-silence on the special case of *Ulysses* and by insensitivity to literary value, this book gives the only thorough account of modern Irish censorship.

25. Costello, *Heart Grown Brutal,* 269.

26. Clarke wrote against censorship in "Books Beyond Reach," *Irish Times,* 18 September 1943, and "Banned Books," *New Statesman* 65, no. 1159 (23 May 1953): 606 ff.

27. For example, see Geoffrey Taylor's "The Poetry of John Hewitt," *The Bell* 3, no. 3 (December, 1941): 229–231.

28. Dermot Foley, "Monotonously Rings the Little Bell," *Irish University Review,* Sean O'Faolain Special Issue, 6, no. 1 (October 1940): 5.

29. Martin, "Literature and Society," 172.

30. O'Faolain, "This is Your Magazine," *The Bell* 1 (October 1940): 5.

31. *The Bell* 5, no. 5 (February 1943): 399.

32. *The Bell* 5, no. 6 (March 1943): 423.

33. Geoffrey Taylor, "Sense and Nonsense in Poetry," *The Bell* 7, no. 2 (November 1943): 423.

34. "The Belfry," *The Bell* 1, no. 5 (February 1941): 88.

35. "Diary," *Envoy* 2, no. 7 (June 1950): 85.

36. Frank O'Connor, "The Future of Irish Literature," *Horizon* 5, no. 25 (January 1942): 59.

37. Sean O'Faolain, *The Irish: A Character Study* (New York: Devin Adair, 1956), 166–67.

38. Kavanagh never bothered to call on Yeats; Denis Devlin's request to

meet with Yeats was refused because "so many young poets sought to see him, that he had to refuse them all." MacNeice records his only encounter with Yeats in September 1931, in the comic-ironic mode in which so much of Yeats's later life is recast. MacNeice recalls that, in the company of E. R. Dodds, at tea with Yeats, who had just retired from a croquet match with his daughter, the poet's conversation hovered around the topic of the spirits whom Yeats confessed he had never seen although "he had often *smelt* them." *Lace Curtain* 4 (Summer 1971): 82; Louis MacNeice, *The Strings are False* (London: Faber & Faber, 1965), 147–48.

39. Austin Clarke, *A Penny in the Clouds* (London: Routledge and Kegan Paul, 1968), 201.

40. Edward O'Shea, *Yeats as Editor* (Dublin: Dolmen Press, 1975), 58.

41. Yeats, ed., *The Oxford Book of Modern Verse, 1892–1935* (Oxford: Oxford University Press, 1936), xv.

42. Francis Stuart in *The Yeats We Knew,* Thos. Davis Lectures, ed. Francis McManus (Cork: Mercier Press, 1965), 27.

43. Frank O'Connor, "Reminiscences of Yeats," *Leinster, Munster, and Connaught* (London: R. Hale, 1950), 237–43, reprinted in *W. B. Yeats: Interviews and Recollections,* ed. E. H. Mikhail, 2 vols. (London: Macmillan, 1977), 2: 335.

44. Mary M. Colum, "Memories of Yeats," in *W. B. Yeats,* ed. Mikhail, 2: 243.

45. Richard J. Loftus, *Nationalism in Modern Anglo-Irish Literature* (Madison: University of Wisconsin Press, 1964), 282.

46. O'Connor, "Future of Irish Literature," 57.

47. W. B. Yeats, *The Poems,* new edition, ed. Richard J. Finneran (New York: Macmillan, 1983); cited parenthetically as *YP* with page numbers.

48. John Montague, "Under Ben Bulben," *Shenandoah,* Yeats and Ireland Issue, 16, no. 4 (Summer 1965): 23.

49. James Randall, "An Interview with Seamus Heaney," *Ploughshares* 5, no. 3 (1979): 17.

50. F. S. L. Lyons, *Ireland Since the Famine*; William Irwin Thompson, *The Imagination of an Insurrection* (New York: Harper & Row, 1967).

51. Comment by Desmond Ryan in W. R. Rodgers, ed., *Irish Literary Portraits* (New York: Taplinger, 1973), 210.

52. Heaney, *Preoccupations,* 101.

53. James Kilroy, *The Playboy Riots* (Dublin: Dolmen Press, 1971), 19.

54. Ibid., 32.

55. F. S. L. Lyons, *Culture and Anarchy in Ireland, 1890–1939,* Ford Lectures 1978 (Oxford: Oxford University Press, 1979), 82.

56. "The Playboy of the West," *Sinn Fein* 9 (Feburary 1907), 2. Quoted in Kilroy, *Playboy Riots,* 91.

57. Kilroy, *Playboy Riots,* 24.

58. George Moore, *Vale,* vol. 3 of *Hail and Farewell* (London: William Heinemann, 1947), 147.

59. Seamus Deane, "The Literary Myths of the Revival: A Case for their Abandonment," in *Myth and Reality in Irish Literature,* ed. Joseph Ronsley (Waterloo, Ontario: Wilfred Laurier University Press, 1977), 322.

60. W. B. Yeats, *Autobiography,* Anchor edition (Garden City, N.Y.: Doubleday, 1958), 137.

61. In "The History of Ireland," Davis wrote, "If we attempt to govern ourselves without statesmanship — to be a nation without knowledge of the country's history . . . we will fail. . . ." *Essays,* Centenary edition (Dundalk: Dundalgan Press, 1914; repr. New York: Lemma, 1974), 381–82.

62. Ibid., 376.

63. Robert Langbaum, *The Poetry of Experience* (New York: W. W. Norton, 1963), 10.

64. Thomas R. Whitaker, *Swan and Shadow: Yeats's Dialogue with History* (Chapel Hill: University of North Carolina Press, 1964), 8.

65. Ibid., 217.

66. Quoted in Whitaker, *Swan and Shadow,* 6.

67. Incorporated in *The Autobiography,* 132.

68. Ibid., 184.

69. Just as in the nineties the randy and reckless Gaelic poet Red Hanrahan contrasts with the absentee landlady Victoria so in the thirties Crazy Jane represents a foil to one of the Free State's new landlords, the Bishop. The character of Crazy Jane represents only one aspect of a complex truth, "learned in bodily lowliness," which she espouses: "Fair and foul are near of kin, / And fair needs foul. . . ." The individual apprehends a personal truth when he recognizes the shadowy cailleach within himself; the nation might lose the mad illusion of racial purity if it could embrace the degraded Cathleen Ni Houlihan or sluttish Hag of Beare or her truth of the interdependency of soul and hole. (Some of these assumptions are developed by Barbara J. Hall in *Yeats's Sean Van Voght: A Study of Crazy Jane,* Master's Thesis, Wake Forest University, 1980; see also Loftus (*Nationalism in Anglo-Irish Literature,* 261) who suggests that Crazy Jane may have been derived from Austin Clarke's "Young Woman of Beare.")

Futhermore, Ribh, in "Supernatural Songs," counterbalances both Patrick's masculine Trinity and his occidental and puritanical doctrine of love with a pre-Western trinity that includes a feminine goddess and whose perfect conjugation is a model for man's efforts to become complete through coition. Ribh's paradoxical assertion that "Hatred of soul may bring the soul to God" echoes Blake's idea that good and evil, love and hatred, which appear as antinomies within cloven thought, are ultimately one reality.

70. Yeats, *Essays and Introductions* (New York: Macmillan, 1961), 397.

71. In a 1910 article in the *Manchester Guardian,* Yeats wrote: "Irish national politics dated from the Young Ireland Movement, when Thomas Davis and his friends had created by journalism a national ideal which was to take the place of national institutions. The images they had created of the ideal peasant and charming colleen had spread . . . abstract virtues had taken the place of realities. . . . By this time an industrial class had arisen, the first the country had ever seen, and having neither leisure nor a traditional culture its leaders were banded together only by a political hatred and suspicion. . . ." Quoted in Donald T. Torchiana, *W. B. Yeats and Georgian Ireland* (Evanston: Northwestern University Press, 1966), 30.

72. Yeats, *Essays and Introductions,* 401–403.

73. Yeats, *Uncollected Prose,* ed. John P. Frayne and Colton Johnson, 2 vols. (New York: Columbia University Press, 1976), 2: 56.

74. Yeats, *Explorations* (New York: Macmillan, 1962), 347, n. 1.

75. *The Senate Speeches of W. B. Yeats,* ed. Donald R. Pearce (Bloomington: Indiana University Press, 1960), 159–60.

76. Among Conor Cruise O'Brien's several versions of this argument, see especially "Passion and Cunning," in *In Excited Reverie: A Centenary Tribute to William Butler Yeats 1865–1939,* ed. A. Norman Jeffares and K. G. Cross (New York: Macmillan, 1965), 207–78. In addition to shorter responses, O'Brien elicited two full-length rebuttals—Elizabeth Cullingford's *Yeats, Ireland and Fascism* (New York: New York University Press, 1981) and Grattan Freyer's *W. B. Yeats and the Anti-Democratic Tradition* (New York: Barnes and Noble, 1981).

Yeats's aestheticist maxim—"Art is art because it is not nature" (*Autobiography,* 187)—raises questions about the distinctiveness of art and life that we are foolish to ignore in such arguments. Ezra Pound's confusion about Mussolini's area of mastery—"Take him as anything save the artist and you will get muddled with contradictions" (*Jefferson and/or Mussolini* [1935; rpt. New York: Liveright, 1970], 34)—seems an inversion of O'Brien's. Curiously enough, O'Brien, in his most extended arraignment of Yeats as fascist, also recognizes the distinction between the poetic impulse and the political (but irresolutely and on his last pages) and between the possible priority of Yeats the poet over Yeats the politician (but in a footnote which is inexplicably enclosed in parentheses):

(There is a sense of course in which the poet, actually engaged in writing his poetry, is the true Yeats, but that is another matter.) "Passion and Cunning," 258.

77. *The Variorum Edition of the Poems of W. B. Yeats,* ed. Peter Ault and Russel K. Alspach (New York: Macmillan, 1968), 835.

78. Ibid., 833.

79. Yeats, *Explorations,* 442.

80. Heaney, *Preoccupations,* 110.

81. Samuel Hynes, "Yeats and the Poets of the Thirties," in *Modern Irish Literature,* ed. Raymond J. Porter and James D. Brophy (New York: Iona College Press, 1972), 5.

82. Stephen Spender, "The Influence of Yeats on Later English Poets," *Tri-Quarterly* 4 (1965): 86.

83. After *all, old* is the most frequently employed word in Yeats's poetry, according to the frequency list in *A Concordance to the Poems of W. B. Yeats,* ed. Stephen Maxwell Parrish, programmed by James A. Painter (Ithaca: Cornell University Press, 1963).

84. Derek Mahon, Interview, 14 June 1979, New Haven, Connecticut.

85. W. R. Rodgers, ed., *Irish Literary Portraits,* 19.

86. T. S. Eliot, *On Poetry and Poets,* Noonday ed. (New York: Farrar, Straus and Cudahy, 1961), 296.

87. Davis, *Essays,* xix.

88. Yeats, *Essays and Introductions,* 251.

89. Heaney, *Preoccupations,* 110.

90. Daniel Corkery, *Synge and Anglo-Irish Literature* (Cork: Cork University Press, 1931), 19.

91. Frank O'Connor, "Yeats's Phantasmagoria" in *W. B. Yeats,* ed. Mikhail, 2: 266–67.

92. Thomas Flanagan, "Yeats, Joyce, and the Matter of Ireland," *Critical Inquiry* 2, no. 1 (Autumn, 1975): 45.

93. Yeats, *Autobiography,* 132.

94. Ibid., 48.

95. Ibid., 115.

96. James Joyce, *The Critical Writings,* ed. Ellsworth Mason and Richard Ellmann, Compass Edition (New York: Viking Press, 1964), 71.

97. *Letters of James Joyce,* ed. Stuart Gilbert and Richard Ellmann, 3 vols. (New York: Viking Press, 1957–66), 1: 62–63. Cited in Dominic Manganiello, *Joyce's Politics* (London: Routledge and Kegan Paul, 1980), 232.

98. Ibid.

99. James Joyce, *A Portrait of the Artist As a Young Man* (New York: Viking Press, 1964), 187; hereafter cited parenthetically as *JP* with page numbers.

100. Seamus Heaney, *Station Island,* (London: Faber & Faber, 1984; New York: Farrar, Straus & Giroux, 1985), 93; hereafter cited parenthetically as *HSI* with page numbers.

101. Ellmann, *James Joyce,* 728.

102. For examples, see Ellmann, 504, 527ff, 588, 703.

103. Joyce, *Stephen Hero,* ed. John J. Slocum and Herbert Cahoon, new ed. (New York: New Directions, 1963), 86.

104. Flanagan, "Yeats, Joyce," 59.

105. Bernard Benstock, *James Joyce: The Undiscover'd Country* (Dublin: Gill & Macmillan; New York: Barnes & Noble, 1977), 35.

106. For example, see Don Gifford, *Notes for Joyce* (New York: E. P. Dutton, 1967), 186–87.

107. Ellmann, *James Joyce,* 505.

108. Patrick Kavanagh, *Collected Pruse* (London: Martin Brian and O'Keeffe, 1973), 282.

109. Lecture to English 282, Wake Forest University, 8 January 1980, at Kelly's Hotel, Dublin.

110. Seamus Deane, "The Literary Myths of the Revival," 323.

111. Kavanagh, *Collected Pruse,* 260.

112. Hugh Kenner, *Joyce's Voices* (London: Faber & Faber, 1978), 83.

113. A. Walton Litz, "Ithaca," in *James Joyce's Ulysses: Critical Essays,* ed. Clive Hart and David Hayman (Berkeley: University of California Press, 1974), 396.

114. Joyce, *Stephen Hero,* 211.

115. Ellmann, *Ulysses on the Liffey* (New York: Oxford, 1972), 167.

116. Litz, "Ithaca," 400.

117. James Joyce, *Ulysses* (New York: Modern Library, 1961), 703.

118. Robert Stawall Ball, *The Story of the Heavens,* new and rev. ed. (London: Cassell and Company, 1897).

119. Joyce, *Ulysses,* 698.

120. Ibid., 701.

121. Joyce, *Letters,* 1:160.

122. Ellmann, *Ulysses on the Liffey,* 141–42.

123. Kenner, *Joyce's Voices,* 47–48.

124. Ibid., 49.

125. Joyce, *Ulysses,* 34.

126. Terence Brown, *Ireland: A Social and Cultural History, 1922–79* (London: Fontana, 1981), 226.

127. Spender, "Influence of Yeats," 82.

128. Yeats, "Nationality and Literature," in *Uncollected Prose,* ed. John P. Frayne, 2 vols. (New York: Columbia University Press, 1970), 1:269.

129. Joyce, *Portrait,* 213–14.

130. F. S. L. Lyons, *Ireland Since the Famine,* 684.

131. O'Faolain, "This is Your Magazine," 5.

132. Brown, *Ireland,* 236.

133. In "The Head," consider this description of an Orphean head, river-bound like "The Lady of Shallot," and singing its last song to "the Woman":

> So it was the wind
> That used the tattered wizen of the throat
> As well as the sockets of the eyes, the earholes
> And the pit behind the nose for hollow music,
> Not overlooking the jewels of the mouth
> That still smiled
> For yet no wound was felt.
>
>                     *Poems* (Dublin: Dolmen Press, 1974), 47.

The imagination that gives tautness to the second, third, and fourth lines lulls off in the fifth line's "overlooking," as Fallon ignores the awkward ambiguity of subjects for the participle and forgets that the reader is all eyes only because the wind is all sound. That same slackness pervades the poem's ending where the poet has not conceived the woman-muse, the theme of the head-song, beyond a cardboard stereotype.

134. Fallon, *Poems,* 39.

135. Sean O'Faolain, "Signing Off," *The Bell* 12, no. 1 (April 1946), 1.

136. Valentin Iremonger, "Poets and Their Publishers," *The Bell* 14, no. 1 (April 1947), 79.

137. Quoted in Brown, *Ireland,* 233.

138. Liam Miller, *Dolmen XXV: An Illustrated Bibliography of the Dolmen Press 1951–1976* (Dublin: Dolmen Press, 1976), 13.

139. Robin Skelton, "Twentieth-Century Irish Literature and the Private Press Tradition: Dun Emer, Cuala, and Dolmen Presses 1902–1963," in *Irish Renaissance: A Gathering of Essays, Memoirs, and Letters for the Massachusetts Review,* ed. Robin Skelton and David R. Clarke (Amherst: University of Massachusetts Review, 1965), 165.

140. E. Estyn Evans, *The Personality of Ireland: Habitat, Heritage and History,* enlarged and rev. ed. (Belfast: Blackstaff Press, 1981), 86.

141. Brown, *Ireland,* 258.

142. Evans, *Personality of Ireland,* xi.

143. Liam Miller believes the Black Church Reading preceded another early reading at the Lantern Theatre (interview at Wynn's Hotel, 24 June 1983); Peter Fallon, "Introductions," *The First Ten Years: Dublin Arts Festival Poetry,* ed. Peter Fallon and Dennis O'Driscoll (Dublin: Dublin Arts Festival, 1979), 7.

144. Blake Morrison, *Seamus Heaney,* Contemporary Writers' Series (London: Methuen, 1982), 11 and 56.

145. F. S. L. Lyons, "T. W. M.," in *Ireland Under the Union: Varieties of Ten-*

*sion, Essays in Honor of T. W. Moody,* ed. F. S. L. Lyons and R. A. J. Hawkins (Oxford: Clarendon Press, 1980), 1.

146. Ibid., 23.

147. E. Estyn Evans, *Irish Folk Ways* (London: Routledge and Kegan Paul, 1957); idem, *Irish Heritage: The Landscape, The People and Their Work* (Dundalk: Dundalgan Press, 1942); Henry Glassie, *Passing the Time in Ballymenone* (Philadelphia: University of Pennsylvania Press, 1982).

148. Based on figures in Brown, *Ireland,* 268.

149. Survey, Market Research Bureau of Ireland, published in the *Irish Times,* 27 June 1983.

150. Sean MacReamoinn, "Introduction," *The Pleasures of Gaelic Poetry,* ed. Sean MacReamoinn (London: Allen Lane-Penguin Books, 1982), 13.

151. Thomas Kinsella, "Another Country . . . ," *Pleasures of Gaelic Poetry,* 178.

152. Paul Muldoon, *Quoof* (London: Faber & Faber; Winston-Salem: Wake Forest University Press, 1983), 13.

153. Kinsella, "A Selected Life" and "Vertical Man," *Peppercanister Poems 1972–1978* (Dublin: Dolmen Press; Winston-Salem: Wake Forest University Press, 1979); Montague, "O'Riada's Farewell," *A Slow Dance* (Dublin: Dolmen Press; Winston-Salem: Wake Forest University Press, 1975); Heaney, "In Memoriam Sean O'Riada," *Field Work* (London: Faber & Faber; New York: Farrar, Straus & Giroux, 1979).

154. MRBI Survey, *Irish Times.*

155. Evans, *Personality of Ireland,* xi.

156. Ibid., xii.

157. Ibid., 24.

158. Liam dePaor, *Divided Ulster,* 2nd ed. (London: Penguin, 1972), 2.

159. F. S. L. Lyons, *Culture and Anarchy in Ireland*; Evans, *Personality of Ireland.*

160. Terence Brown, *Northern Voices: Poets from Ulster* (Dublin: Gill & Macmillan; Totowa, New Jersey: Rowman and Littlefield, 1975), 1; Ormsby, *Poets from the North of Ireland* (Belfast: Blackstaff, 1979).

161. Blake Morrison and Andrew Motion, "Introduction," *The Penguin Book of Contemporary British Poetry,* ed. Morrison and Motion (Harmondsworth, Middlesex: Penguin, 1982), 13.

162. Ibid., 16.

163. Seamus Heaney, *An Open Letter* (Derry: Field Day Publications, 1983).

164. For example, see Gregory Schirmer's review of *Quoof* in the *Christian Science Monitor,* 13 January 1984.

165. "The Belfast Group: A Symposium," *Honest Ulsterman* 53 (November/December 1976): 53–63.

166. Interview with Paul Muldoon and Ciaran Carson, Belfast, May 1983.

167. "The Belfast Group," 53, 57.

168. John Haffenden, *Viewpoints: Poets in Conversation* (London: Faber & Faber, 1981), 74.

169. Ibid., 74–75.

170. Tom Paulin, *A New Look at the Language Question*; Seamus Heaney, *An Open Letter*; Seamus Deane, *Civilians and Barbarians* (all Derry: Field Day Publications, 1983); idem, *Heroic Styles: The Tradition of the Idea*; Richard Kearney, *Myth and Motherland*; Declan Kiberd, *Anglo-Irish Attitudes* (all Derry: Field Day Publications, 1984). For information and ideas about Field Day, I am indebted to Mitch Harris.

171. Seamus Deane, "The Writer of the Troubles," *Threshold* 25 (Summer 1974): 17.

172. Thomas Kinsella, *Peppercanister Poems*, 66–67; hereafter cited parenthetically as *KPC* with page numbers.

173. Christopher Clausen, *The Place of Poetry: Two Centuries of an Art in Crisis* (Lexington: University of Kentucky Press, 1981), 92.

174. Kinsella's use of *The Book of Invasions* is explained in part by Maurice Harmon in *The Poetry of Thomas Kinsella* (Dublin: Wolfhound, 1974) and in detail by Carolyn Rosenburg, in her unpublished dissertation, *Let Our Gaze Blaze: The Recent Poetry of Thomas Kinsella* (Ph.D. Diss., Kent State University, 1980). The latter work promises to be our most reliable guide to the poetry of Kinsella.

175. Daniel O'Hara, "An Interview with Thomas Kinsella," *Contemporary Poetry: A Journal of Criticism* 4, no. 1 (1981): 6–7.

176. Charles Altieri, "Sensibility, Rhetoric, and Will: Some Tensions in Contemporary Poetry," *Contemporary Literature* 23, no. 4 (Fall 1982): 469.

177. Hugh Kenner, "Thomas Kinsella: An Anecdote and Some Reflections," *Genre* 12, no. 4 (Winter 1979): 597. You may also wish to consult my "A Response to Hugh Kenner: Kinsella's Magnanimity and Mean Reading," *Genre* 13, no. 4 (Winter 1980): 531–537.

178. You may recall Cleanth Brooks' widely accepted definition of poetic *tone*: "The tone of a poem indicates the speaker's attitude toward his subject and toward his audience, and sometimes toward himself. The word is, strictly speaking, a metaphor drawn from the tone of voice in speech or song" (*Understanding Poetry*, 4th edition [New York: Holt, Rinehart & Winston, 1960], 112). When we attempt to translate Brooks's statement of what tone does to a definition of what tone is, we begin anticipating the quarrel of I. A. Richards and John Crowe Ransom. For Richards, successful use of tone depends primarily on "the perfect recognition of the writer's relation to the reader in view of what is being said and their joint feelings about it" (*Practical Criticism* [New York: Harcourt Brace, 1954], 207). As he goes on to characterize

successful tone as a form of good manners, we recognize that Richards is treating the poem as a missive between friends, forgetting that we encounter the poet only through his poetic speaker within the act of reading and that the speaker's manner may vary according to the poetic truth with which he engages the reader.

In contradicting Richards, who associates *tone* with manners, audience, and even style, Ransom prefers to gather all of these relationships under the phrase "dramatic situation":

> Dramatic situation is evidently a kind of structural principle. But it is one which in part contends against and mitigates the structural principle we call the 'argument', 'idea', or 'thesis' of the poem. . . . If the latter is the structural principle proper, Dramatic Situation must be regarded as an anti-structural principle. (*The New Criticism* [Norfolk, Conn: New Directions, 1941], 62)

By characterizing the dramatic situation as "anti-structural," Ransom would preclude the possibility of poets developing a structure that emphasizes tone or, in other words, of poets developing strategies for presenting "the object with the context." Ransom's definition exposes contemporary poetry to misreadings of the other extreme. Reacting to formalist criticism that interprets a poem in terms of a transmissive speaker, autonomous images, and clear theme, certain reader-response critics approach the poem as a purely dramatic reading in which the text and reader play leading roles and in which meaning and character become irrelevant to the moment of the poem.

In a *Sewanee Review* essay we find Denis Donoghue, in paraphrasing Stanley Fish, caught at this phenomenological extreme: "We should not ask what the words mean, as though they contain secrets, but what they are doing, as though they embody actions." Donoghue would also forewarn us from rendering the text as an impression of a completed character. Although he attributes this fallacy—"Given the words, find the speaker"—to critics of fiction, he does not preclude application of his warning to any genre that depends on a narrator or speaker:

> . . . it is just as reductive to translate words into an impression of their speaker as it is to translate them into a sequence of ideas, thoughts, or feelings. In the first case we go through the notions of character-building, and we regard the work as concluded when the character seems to be built, in the second we think of the sentences as delivering more and more of an otherwise secret meaning, the disclosure of which will end the book. (Donoghue, "The Sovereign Ghost," *Sewanee Review* 84, no. 1 [Winter 1976], 118)

179. Stanley Plumly, "Rhetoric and Emotion," *American Poetry Review* 7,

no. 1 (Jan/Feb 1978): 21. Although Plumly's characterization of tone is different from mine, his article presents the only full discussion of *tone* that I have encountered.

180. David Kalstone, *Five Temperaments* (New York: Oxford, 1977), 10–11.

181. Even in Browning's crucial transitional poetry, such as "My Last Duchess," the stanzaic form, in this case couplets, is a major clue to the poet's strategy.

182. *Princeton Encyclopedia of Poetry and Poetics,* ed. Alex Preminger *et al.,* enlarged ed. (Princeton: Princeton University Press, 1974), 856.

183. Georges Poulet, "Phenomenology of Reading," *New Literary History* 1, no. 1 (Fall 1969): 67.

184. Muldoon, *Quoof,* 19.

185. Derek Mahon, *Poems 1962–1978* (London: Oxford, 1979); cited parenthetically as *MP* with page numbers.

186. Wolfgang Iser, *The Act of Reading: A Theory of Aesthetic Response* (Baltimore: Johns Hopkins University Press, 1978), 10.

187. John Hollander, *Vision and Resonance* (New York: Oxford, 1975), 24.

188. Seamus Heaney, *Poems 1965–1975* (London: Faber & Faber; New York: Farrar, Straus & Giroux, 1980); cited parenthetically as *HP* with page numbers.

189. Helen Vendler, "The Music of What Happens," *New Yorker* 57 (28 September 1981): 151.

190. John Montague, *The Great Cloak* (Dublin: Dolmen Press; Winston-Salem: Wake Forest University Press, 1978); cited parenthetically as *MGC* with page numbers.

191. Stanley Fish, "Interpreting the Variorum," in *Reader-Response Criticism,* ed. Jane P. Tompkins (Baltimore: Johns Hopkins University Press, 1980), 174.

## Chapter Two

1. Brown, *Ireland,* 16.

2. Austin Clarke, *Twice Round the Black Church* (London: Routledge and Kegan Paul, 1962), 26–27; hereafter cited parenthetically as *CBC* with page numbers.

3. Austin Clarke, *Poetry in Modern Ireland,* Cultural Relations Series (Cork: Mercier, 1962), 30.

4. Stephen MacKenna quoted in Gregory Schirmer's "'A Mad Discordancy': Austin Clarke's Early Narrative Poems," *Eire-Ireland* 16, no. 2 (Summer 1981): 16.

5. For information on Clarke's chronology I have relied on Maurice Harmon, "Notes Towards a Biography."

6. Donald Davie, "Austin Clarke and Padraic Fallon," *Poetry Nation* 3 (1974): 91; rept. in *Two Decades of Irish Writing,* ed. Douglas Dunn (Cheadle: Carcanet, 1975), 38.

7. Davie, "The Guest Word," *New York Times Book Review,* 23 May 1976, 55.

8. Michel Leiris, *Manhood,* trans. Richard Howard (New York: Grossman, 1963), 141.

9. According to a conversation overheard on a Dorset Street bus in 1975, the number of laps around the Black Church requisite for an appointment with Satan has inflated to nine, perhaps indicating the growth of skepticism, ecumenicalism, or athletic prowess in Dublin.

10. Austin Clarke, *Collected Poems* (Dublin: Dolmen Press, 1974), 3; hereafter cited within parentheses as *CCP* with page number.

11. Augustine Martin, "The Rediscovery of Austin Clarke," *Studies* 14, no. 216 (Winter 1965): 416; quoted in Davie, "Clarke and Fallon," 91.

12. Clarke's note to *Later Poems* (1961), reprinted in *Collected Poems,* 545.

13. See James Carney's recapitulation of Clarke's public controversy in the *Irish Times* with Osborn Bergin concerning the Irish poem "Feuch Fein . . ." in *Studies in Irish Literature and History* (Dublin: Institute for Advanced Studies, 1955), 243ff.

14. Clarke, "Gaelic Ireland Rediscovered: The Early Period," *Irish Poets in English,* ed. Sean Lucy (Cork: Mercier Press, 1973), 30–43. On several occasions Clarke reworked the Buile Suibne legend but probably with reference to the translation by J. G. O'Keefe (London: Irish Texts Society, 1913). See also Craig Tapping, *Austin Clarke: A Study of his Writing* (Totowa, N.J.: Barnes & Noble, 1981), ch. 1 and 2, for an assessment of Clarke's Irish scholarship.

15. Robert Welch, "Austin Clarke and Gaelic Poetic Tradition," *Irish University Review* 4, no. 1 (Spring 1974): 41.

16. John Montague, "Global Regionalism," An Interview with Adrian Frazier, *The Literary Review* 22, no. 22 (Winter 1979): 161.

17. William John Roscelli, "The Private Pilgrimage of Austin Clarke," *The Celtic Cross: Studies in Irish Culture and History,* ed. Ray B. Browne, W. J. Roscelli, and Richard Loftus (W. Lafayette, Ind: Purdue University Press, 1964), 59.

18. Martin, "Rediscovery of Clarke," 422.

19. Tapping, *Austin Clarke,* 172.

20. Adrian Frazier, "'The Cod-Bewildered Schoolboy': Austin Clarke's Later Poetry," *Eire-Ireland* 14, no. 2 (Summer 1979): 64.

21. Austin Clarke, *Penny in the Clouds,* 43.

22. Austin Clarke, *Collected Plays* (Dublin: Dolmen, 1963), 166.

23. Ibid., 183. Lines of such beauty demonstrate that Clarke never abandoned poetry but merely redirected it into poetic dramas. Therefore, as the best explanation of Clarke's seventeen-year silence, I prefer Clarke's own in the *Later Poems*: "The lapse of years between two of the small collections here was due to the fact that I found intense pleasure in the writing of verse plays" (*CCP*, 545).

24. Frazier, "Cod-Bewildered Schoolboy," 64.

25. Martin Dodsworth, "'Jingle-go-Jangle': Feeling and Expression in Austin Clarke's Later Poetry," *Irish University Review* 4, no. 1 (Spring 1974): 120.

26. Davie, "Clarke and Fallon," 84.

27. Denis Donoghue, "Fire in the Great Vein, *The New Review* 1, no. 5 (August 1974): 70.

28. Davie, "Clarke and Fallon," 94.

29. Austin Clarke, "Review of *Aithdioghluim Dana: A Miscellany of Irish Bardic Poetry, Historical and Religious* . . . ," *Dublin Magazine* 16, no. 1 (January/March 1941): 62–63.

30. Vernon Young, "Poetry Chronicle," *Hudson Review* 29, no. 4 (January 1977): 623.

31. Denis Donoghue, "One More Brevity," in *A Tribute to Austin Clarke on his Seventieth Birthday*, ed. John Montague and Liam Miller (Dublin: Dolmen, 1966), 21.

32. James Carney, *Studies in Irish Literature and History* (Dublin: Institute for Advanced Studies, 1955), 229.

33. Consider the photographs of Clarke on the covers of the *Irish University Review*, Clarke Issue, 4, no. 4 (Spring 1974). In his autobiography Clarke said, "I am used to being mistaken for a priest and so I am no longer embarrassed by the respect paid to my cloth. As a provincial youth . . . I believed that a poet must wear a wide-brimmed black hat and grave suit" (*CBC*, 32). For Kinsella on Irish tradition, see Kinsella, "The Divided Mind," in *Irish Poets in English*, 216–17.

34. For early examination of Kinsella's poetry, see Maurice Harmon's essays in *Emory University Quarterly* (Spring 1966) and *Eire-Ireland* (Summer 1973) and M. L. Rosenthal's *The New Poets* (Oxford and New York: Oxford University Press, 1967).

35. Calvin Bedient, *Eight Contemporary Poets* (Oxford: Oxford University Press, 1974), 119.

36. *Lebor Gabála Érenn: The Book of the Taking of Ireland*, ed. and trans. by R. A. Stewart Macalister, 4 secs. (Dublin: Irish Texts Society, 1938–1941), 3: 211.

37. Maurice Harmon, *Poetry of Kinsella*; Carolyn Rosenberg, *Let Our Gaze Blaze*; see ch. 1, n. 179.

38. C. G. Jung, *Two Essays in Analytical Psychology*, trans. R. F. C. Hull, vol. 7 of *Collected Works*, ed. Sir Herbert Read *et al.* (New York: Pantheon Books; Princeton: Princeton University Press, 1953–79), 171–72.

39. *Lebor Gabála Érenn*, sec. 1, p. 165.

40. Rosenberg, *Let Our Gaze Blaze*, 445–449.

41. Thomas Kinsella, *Poems 1956–1973* (Winston-Salem: Wake Forest University Press, 1979; Dublin: Dolmen Press, 1980); cited parenthetically as *KP* with page numbers.

42. O'Hara, "Interview with Thomas Kinsella"; Haffenden, *Viewpoints*, 111; conversation at Kinsella residence, Philadelphia, November 26, 1982.

43. O'Hara, "Interview with Kinsella," 3–4.

44. As printed in *Poems & Translations* (New York: Atheneum, 1961), 26.

45. I am thinking of parallels between *Alastor* and "Downstream" and between the conclusion of "Mirror in February" and *Prometheus Unbound*, 3.4.193–94. Interesting parallels exist between Kinsella's poems and Clarke's imaginative forays, such as "Loss of Strength" and "The Flock at Dawn" and Clarke's "Forget me-Not," although Kinsella may be the influence in one of these parallels. Consider also Auden's "From the narrow window of my fourth floor room / I smoke into the night, and watch reflections," from *Look, Stranger* and "Baggot Street" and "Nightwalker."

46. For Kinsella's chronology I have relied on Rosenberg's dissertation, cited above, and on my own conversations with the poet.

47. "Does Kinsella Lead the Poets?" *The Sunday Independent*, 14 October 1962.

48. Calvin Bedient, "Review of *Notes from the Land of the Dead and Other Poems*," *New York Times Book Review*, 16 June 1974.

49. Haffenden, *Viewpoints*, 101.

50. "Poetry Since Yeats: An Exchange of Views—Stephen Spender, Patrick Kavanagh, Thomas Kinsella, W. D. Snodgrass," in *Tri-Quarterly* 4 (1965): 105.

51. Ibid., 108.

52. O'Hara, "Interview with Kinsella," 6, 9.

53. Haffenden, *Viewpoints*, 106.

54. O'Hara, "Interview with Kinsella," 7.

55. Kinsella has said, "I myself derive increased understanding from the brilliant teaching and work of many friends. I believe I might have festered and gone sterile if we hadn't managed to come back to Dublin." Haffenden, *Viewpoints*, 105, 112.

56. Ibid., 104.

57. O'Hara, "Interview with Kinsella," 15.

58. Haffenden, *Viewpoints*, 102.

59. Pierre Teilhard de Chardin, "My Fundamental Vision," *Toward the Future*, trans. Rene Hague (London: Collins, 1975), 181, 190.

60. C. G. Jung, *Psychology and Religion: East and West,* trans. Hull, vol. 11 of *Collected Works,* 236.

61. C. G. Jung, *Mysterium Coniunctionis,* trans. Hull, vol. 14 of *Collected Works,* 503–4.

62. Harmon, *Poetry of Kinsella,* 67.

63. C. G. Jung, *Psychological Types,* trans. H. G. Baynes, rev. R. F. C. Hull, vol. 6 of *Collected Works,* 207.

64. Rosenberg, *Let Our Gaze Blaze,* 286; Jung, *The Development of Personality,* trans. Hull, vol. 17 of *Collected Works,* 198.

65. Jung, *Aion,* trans. Hull, vol. 9, pt. 2 of *Collected Works,* 20.

66. Ibid., 16.

67. Jung, *Development of Personality,* 200.

68. Ibid., 201.

69. Mircea Eliade, *Images and Symbols: Studies in Religious Symbolism,* trans. Philip Mairet (New York: Sheed & Ward, 1969), 50, 78.

70. *New Larousse Encyclopedia of Mythology,* intr. Robert Graves, trans. Richard Aldington and Delano Ames (New York: Hamlyn, 1968), 152, 165.

71. Jung, *Psychology and Alchemy,* trans. Hull, vol. 12 of *Collected Works,* 52, n.2.

72. Rosenberg, *Let Our Gaze Blaze,* 269.

73. *New Larousse Encyclopedia of Mythology,* new ed., trans. R. Aldington and Delano Ames (New York: Hamlyn, 1968), 15.

74. Rosenberg, *Let Our Gaze Blaze,* 292–93.

75. Jung, *Two Essays in Analytical Psychology,* 175, 172.

76. Haffenden, *Viewpoints,* 112.

77. Charles Molesworth, *The Fierce Embrace: A Study of Contemporary American Poetry* (Columbia: University of Missouri Press, 1979), 25.

78. *New Larousse Mythology,* 128.

79. "Poetry Since Yeats," 108.

80. This lyric has some parallels to the Irish mythological tale, "The Wooing of Étain," in which Étain metamorphoses into pool, worm, and then a purple fly which when it falls into a woman's cup and makes her pregnant is reborn as Étain.

81. Seamus Deane, "Unhappy and at Home: Interview with Seamus Heaney," *Crane Bag* 1, no. 1 (Spring 1977): 64.

## Chapter Three

1. Patrick Kavanagh, *Collected Poems* (London: Martin Brian & O'Keefe, 1972; 1964); *The Complete Poems of Patrick Kavanagh,* ed. Peter Kavanagh (New

York: The Peter Kavanagh Hand Press, 1972). I will refer parenthetically to *The Complete Poems* as *KCP* with page number.

2. Samuel Taylor Coleridge, *Biographia Literaria,* ed. James Engell and W. Jackson Bate, vol. 7 of *The Collected Works,* ed. Kathleen Coburn (Princeton: Princeton University Press, 1983), pt. 1, 80.

3. Basil Payne, "The Poetry of Patrick Kavanagh," *Studies* 49 (1960): 291.

4. Patrick Kavanagh, *Collected Prose,* 235.

5. Ibid., 149.

6. Heaney has jumped claim on this phrase by applying it to Kavanagh himself: "There is a feeling of prospector's luck—which may be deliberately achieved, but I don't think so—about many of his best effects." *Preoccupations,* 118.

7. Kavanagh, *Collected Prose,* 228.

8. Ibid., 20.

9. *Ploughman and Other Poems* (London: Macmillan, 1936); *The Green Fool* (London: Michael Joseph, 1938); *The Great Hunger* (Dublin: Cuala, 1942); *Tarry Flynn* (London: Pilot Press, 1948).

10. Kavanagh, *The Green Fool,* 63.

11. Ibid., 246.

12. Patrick Kavanagh, *November Haggard: Uncollected Prose and Verse,* ed. Peter Kavanagh (New York: The Peter Kavanagh Hand Press, 1971), 33.

13. Kavanagh, *Complete Poems,* 2, 10.

14. Alan Warner, *Clay is the Word: Patrick Kavanagh 1904–1967* (Dublin: Dolmen, 1973), 48.

15. Kavanagh, *Complete Poems,* "The Intangible," 1. See also "Ascetic," 5; "A Star," 6; and "To a Child," 7.

16. Padraic Colum, *The Poet's Circuits,* Centenary Edition (Dublin: Dolmen Press, 1981; Oxford, 1960), 14.

17. John Montague, "A Primal Gaeltacht," *Irish Times,* 30 July 1970.

18. I am assured by the poet Peter Fallon who has, in a fine poem, himself memorialized "cowshit and horseshit and sheepshit" that Kavanagh's fancy has raised the caloric count of the dung. (See Fallon's *Winter Work* [Gallery Press, 1982].)

19. Kavanagh, *Collected Prose,* 278.

20. Ibid., 282.

21. I can remember my understanding of this poem being enlarged by Coilin Owens in a conversation in the Spring of 1982.

22. Heaney, *Preoccupations,* 118.

23. John Jordan, "Mr Kavanagh's Progress," *Studies* 49 (1960): 297.

24. Terence Brown, "After the Revival: The Problem of Adequacy and Genre," *Genre* 12, no. 4 (Winter 1979): 579, 587.

25. "The HU Business Section," *The Honest Ulsterman* 60 (July/October 1978): 77.

26. Ibid., 75.

27. "Jude the Obscure" extols "Lough Derg" as "the first long poem to come out of Ireland and one of the few great long poems of the century" ("The HU Business Section," 61). Alan Warner appreciates it as "a poem of real power and originality" (*Clay is the Word*, 62).

28. Warner, *Clay is the Word*, 62.

29. *The Bell* 8, no. 4 (July 1944): 199.

30. "Public Opinion," *The Bell* 7, no. 3 (December 1943): 255–57.

31. Kavanagh, *November Haggard*, 18. In an interview in Winston-Salem (30 September 1984), John Montague stressed the importance, to younger poets in 1947, of this essay which seemed to depose Yeats's heir-apparent, F. R. Higgins.

32. Kavanagh, *Collected Pruse*, 13.

33. Recorded in Peter Kavanagh's *Sacred Keeper: A Biography of Patrick Kavanagh* (The Curragh: Goldsmith Press, 1979), 266.

34. John Nemo, *Patrick Kavanagh* (Boston: Twayne, 1979), 85.

35. Patrick Kavanagh, *A Soul for Sale* (London: Macmillan, 1947).

36. Ryan, *Remembering How We Stood*, 97.

37. Kavanagh, "Diary," *Envoy* 2, no. 7 (June 1950): 90.

38. Robert F. Garratt, "Patrick Kavanagh and the Killing of the Irish Revival," *Colby Library Quarterly* 17, no. 3 (September 1981): 176.

39. Kavanagh, *Collected Pruse*, 255.

40. Anthony Cronin, *Dead as Doornails* (Dublin: Dolmen Press, 1976), 84.

41. See Kavanagh, *November Haggard*, 68, 89, and *Collected Pruse*, 15, 16, and 157.

42. Ryan, *Remembering How We Stood*, 158.

43. See Kavanagh, *Collected Pruse*, 238, 260, 285, and *Sacred Keeper*, 159–60.

44. Garratt, "Patrick Kavanagh," 175.

45. Kavanagh, *Collected Pruse*, 282.

46. Ibid., 21.

47. Kavanagh, *November Haggard*, 87.

48. Alan Warner says only that "the energy of happiness" is in the poem (*Clay is the Word*, 92). Darcy O'Brien follows a full quotation of the poem with "Poetry has become all" (*Patrick Kavanagh*, Irish Writers Series [Lewisburg, Penn.: Bucknell University Press; London: Associated University Presses,

1975], 60). More helpfully, John Nemo sees the poem as a comment on three stages of Kavanagh's career (*Patrick Kavanagh,* 125).

49. Kavanagh, *November Haggard,* 65.

50. Kavanagh, *Collected Pruse,* 22.

51. Kavanagh, *November Haggard,* 92.

52. For the most pathetic of the self-parodies see the middle stanza on page 313 of *The Complete Poems* and the late poem "Shancoduff" which merely itemizes articles of the landscape before saying, "So does a poem bring a world alive in my mind" (*CP,* 346–47).

53. Seamus Deane, "Unhappy and at Home," 66.

54. Feature stories on Heaney have appeared in the *New York Times Magazine* (Francis X. Clines, "Poet of the Bogs," 13 March 1983); *New Yorker* (Helen Vendler, "The Music of what Happens," 18 September 1981, 146–52, 155–57, and Anthony Bailey, "A Reporter at Large: A Walk along the Boyne," 2 June 1980, 92, 95–122), and *Newsweek* (Peter Prescott, "Bard of the Irish Soul," 2 February 1981, 67–69).

55. Blake Morrison says that *North* sold 6,000 copies in England during its first month of publication. *Seamus Heaney,* Contemporary Writers Series (London: Methuen, 1982), 56.

56. Deane, "Unhappy and at Home," 66.

57. Ibid.

58. Ibid., 67.

59. For example, see M. Merleau-Ponty, *Phenomenology of Perception,* trans. Colin Smith (London: Routledge & Kegan Paul, 1962), x.

60. For example, see Padraic Fiacc, "Fiacc Answers Back," *Honest Ulsterman* 50 (Winter 1975): 134.

61. Heaney, *Preoccupations,* 43.

62. Calvin Bedient, "The Music of What Happens," *Parnassus* 8 (Fall/Winter 1979): 111.

63. Heaney, *Preoccupations,* p. 110.

64. Seamus Heaney, *Field Work* (New York: Farrar, Straus & Giroux, 1979), 16; cited parenthetically as *HFW* with page numbers.

65. Reading at Kelly's Hotel, Dublin, 10 January 1980.

66. Heaney, *Preoccupations,* 176.

67. Ibid., 173.

68. Ibid., 65.

69. Bedient, "The Music of What Happens," 120.

70. Heaney, *Preoccupations,* 63.

71. Ibid., 66.

72. Heaney, Preface, *Ugolino* (Dublin: Andrew Carpenter, 1979), n.p.

73. James Randall, "An Interview with Seamus Heaney," *Ploughshares* 5, no. 3 (1979): 16–17.

74. Of course, "Field Work" has anthropological implications, as well as agricultural.

75. Heaney, *Preoccupations,* 60.

76. See James Stephens, *Irish Fairy Tales* (New York: Collier, 1962), 48–49; reprinted in *The Book of Irish Verse,* ed. John Montague (New York: Macmillan, 1974), 80. In "The Hippophagi," Clarke asks, ". . . Could self have learned / In woody, ferny glen to choose / With Fionn the music of what happens, / Found in some Clapham an honest sect / Of intellect?" *Collected Poems,* 235.

77. *Sweeney Astray* (Derry: Field Day; New York: Farrar, Straus & Giroux, 1983).

78. *Station Island,* 13; cited parenthetically as *HSI* with page numbers.

79. Christ's encounter with the rich young man is recorded in Matt. 19: 24, Mark 10:23, and Luke 18:23. When the Apostles declare impossible the passage of a rich man to heaven or the threading of a camel through a needle's eye, Christ responds that things impossible for men are possible for God. Heaney refers to this episode also at the conclusion of part one (*HSI,* 58) and in part three (*HSI,* 119).

80. In reviewing *Station Island* for the *London Review of Books* (Nov. 1–14, 1984), Muldoon chose "Widgeon" "above all . . . small masterpieces" in the volume to quote in full.

## Chapter Four

1. Beckett praised Devlin's verse briefly in 1934 and 1970, articles which appear in *Lace Curtain* 3 (Summer 1970): 41–44 and vol. 4 of that same journal (Summer 1971): 58–63. Tate and Warren's comments and preferences appear in their edition of Devlin's *Selected Poems* (New York: Holt, Rinehart, and Winston, 1963). See also Carruth's review of this volume in *Poetry* 103 (December 1963): 191–92; Montague's essay, "The Impact of International Modern Poetry on Irish Writing," in *Irish Poets in English*; and Coffey's essay in the *University Review* 2, no. 11 (1960): 3–18. I refer to Coffey's other articles in other notes. Even Devlin's distinguished detractor Randall Jarrell exhibits enough confusion to lighten our own load of perplexity. See Randall Jarrell's *Poetry and the Age* (New York: Vintage, 1955), 203–05.

2. Denis Devlin, *Collected Poems* (Dublin: Dolmen, 1964) and *The Heavenly Foreigner* (Dublin: Dolmen, 1967), both edited and introduced by Brian Coffey; hereafter cited parenthetically as *DCP* and *DHF,* with page numbers.

3. These biographical and critical studies appear in *Advent VI*, Denis Devlin special issue. Stan Smith has published a second article on Devlin in *The Irish University Review* 8, no. 1 (Spring 1978): 51–67.

4. Translated by Michael Benedikt and included in his anthology *The Poetry of Surrealism* (Boston: Little, Brown, 1974), 129.

5. Ibid., xiii.

6. Roger Callois, "The Art of St. John Perse," trans. H. M. Chevalier, appended to Perse's *Exile and Other Poems,* trans. Denis Devlin (New York: Pantheon Books, 1949), 149.

7. Brian Coffey, "Denis Devlin: Poet of Distance" in *Place, Personality, and the Irish Writer,* ed. Andrew Carpenter, Irish Literary Series, 1 (Gerrards Cross: Colin Smythe, 1977), 137–57, 152–5.

8. Several critics suggest Pascal as an intellectual ancestor. The influence of Perse and Valery, whom Devlin translated, has been recognized although it has never been carefully traced. Montague mentions the resemblance between Crane's dense style and Devlin's in his article in the Lucy edition cited above. In suggesting the probability of Shelley's influence on Devlin, I would refer readers especially to Shelley's essays "On Life" and "On Love" and to his poem "Epipsychidion."

9. John Montague, "Impact of International Modern Poetry on Irish Writing," 150, 148–49.

10. For precise dates and for confirmation concerning biographical information, I am indebted to Mark Waelder who has developed a chronology of Montague's life to be published with his edition of Montague's *Selected Prose.* This carefully selected typescript of the prose brought me to some essays I had not otherwise found.

11. John Montague, *The Dead Kingdom* (Dublin: Dolmen; Winston-Salem: Wake Forest University Press; Oxford: Oxford University Press; 1984); hereafter cited parenthetically as *MDK,* with page numbers. Montague's other volumes of poetry are cited in a similar manner: *Poisoned Lands and Other Poems* (London: MacGibbon & Kee, 1963; Philadelphia: Dufour, 1963), *Poisoned Lands,* new edition (Dublin: Dolmen; Oxford: Oxford University Press, 1977) as *MPL; A Chosen Light* (London: MacGibbon & Kee, 1967; Chicago: Swallow, 1969) as *MCL; Tides* (Dublin: Dolmen, 1970; Chicago: Swallow, 1971) as *MT; The Rough Field,* 4th ed. (Dublin: Dolmen Press; Winston-Salem: Wake Forest University Press, 1984) as *MRF; A Slow Dance* (Dublin: Dolmen, 1975; Winston-Salem: Wake Forest University Press, 1976) as *MSD; The Great Cloak* as *MGC,* as already noted. *Selected Poems* was also published in 1982 (Toronto: Exile Editions; Winston-Salem: Wake Forest University Press; Dublin: Dolmen; London: Oxford University Press). A volume of short stories, *Death*

*of a Chieftain and Other Stories,* was published in 1964 (London: McGibbon & Kee) and reissued in 1978 (Dublin: Poolbeg Press).

12. Seamus Deane, "Irish Poetry and Irish Nationalism," in *Two Decades of Irish Writing,* 16.

13. My recollection of the wording of Montague's annotation of Devlin's *Collected Poems* was confirmed and, on one point, corrected by Thomas Dillon Redshaw who wrote to me from Cork on 19 June 1984.

14. Ezra Pound, *The Cantos* (New York: New Directions, 1970), 177.

15. D. H. Lawrence, *Look! We Have Come Through: A Cycle of Love Poems* (Austin: The University of Texas Humanities Research Center, 1971), 15.

16. John Montague, "American Pegasus," *Studies* 48 (Summer 1959): 185.

17. Deane, "Irish Poetry and Irish Nationalism," 15.

18. Montague's poem could be reagrded as a trope on Celtic art where branching and zoomorphic interlacing "served to fill up all available gaps, for Celts had a horror of empty spaces," according to Peter Harbison, *Guide to the National Monuments,* rev. ed. (Dublin: Gill & Macmillan, 1975), 17.

19. Montague, "A Primal Gaeltacht."

20. Montague, "The Seamless Garment and the Muse," *Agenda* 5, no. 4 (Autumn/Winter 1967–68): 27.

21. Montague, "A Note on Rhythm," *Agenda* 10 (Autumn/Winter, 1972–73): 41.

22. Barbara Hernstein Smith, *Poetic Closure: A Study of How Poems End* (Chicago: University of Chicago Press, 1968), 258.

23. Adrian Frazier, "Global Regionalism: Interview with John Montague," *The Literary Review* 22, no. 2 (Winter 1979): 164.

24. Ibid., 165.

25. Deane speaks of "the epic attempt" in *The Rough Field (Two Decades of Irish Writing,* 15).

26. The woodcut introducing this section depicts Elizabethan soldiers torching a tenant's cottage.

27. Douglas Dunn, "The Speckled Hill, the Plover's Shore: Northern Irish Poetry Today," *Encounter* 41, no. 6 (December 1973): 75, 71.

28. Whitman, *The Complete Poems,* ed. Francis Murphy (Harmondsworth: Penguin, 1975), 63.

29. Robin Skelton, "Comment," *The Malahat Review* 62 (July 1982): 7.

30. Montague, "American Pegasus," 189.

31. Robert Graves, *The White Goddess* (1948; amended and enlarged, New York: Farrar, Straus & Giroux, 1966).

32. Alwyn Rees and Brinley Rees, *Celtic Heritage* (London: Thames & Hudson, 1961), 134–35.

33. Jung, *Psychology and Alchemy*, 52, n. 2.

34. Letter to Paul Mariani (12 July 1982), quoted in draft of essay for the *DLB: British Poets Since World War II*, ed. Vincent B. Sherry, p. 27 of draft.

35. For a similar image of containment see Yeats's *Collected Poems*, 264.

36. *Buile Suibne*, trans. J. G. O'Keefe, Irish Text Society Translations, vol. 12 (London: Irish Text Society, 1913).

37. See also Graves, *The White Goddess*, 130.

## Chapter Five

1. Derek Mahon, ed., *The Sphere Book of Modern Irish Poetry* (London: Sphere, 1972), 14.

2. John Press, *Louis MacNeice*, Writers and Their Work Series (London: Longmans, Green, and Co., 1965); D. B. Moore, *The Poetry of Louis MacNeice*, (Leicester: University of Leicester Press, 1972); Elton Edward Smith, *Louis MacNeice* (New York: Twayne, 1970); Terence Brown, *Louis MacNeice: Skeptical Vision* (Dublin: Gill & Macmillan, 1975); William McKinnon, *Apollo's Blended Dream* (London: Oxford University Press, 1971); Robyn Marsack, *The Cave of Making: The Poetry of Louis MacNeice* (Oxford: Clarendon, 1982); Terence Brown and Alec Reid, eds., *Time Was Away* (Dublin: Dolmen Press, 1974); Barbara Coulton, *Louis MacNeice in the BBC* (London: Faber & Faber, 1980).

3. "Louis MacNeice: A Memorial Address," in *Time Was Away*, 8.

4. Walter Allen, "Introduction," to MacNeice, *Modern Poetry*, 2nd ed. (1938; Oxford: Oxford University Press, 1968), xi.

5. Richard Fallis, *The Irish Renaissance* (Syracuse: Syracuse University Press, 1977), 239.

6. John Montague, *The Book of Irish Verse* (New York: Macmillan, 1976), 239.

7. Michael Longley, "The Neolithic Night: A Note on the Irishness of Louis MacNeice," in *Two Decades of Irish Writing*, 98.

8. G. S. Fraser, "Evasive Honesty: The Poetry of Louis MacNeice," in *Vision and Rhetoric: Studies in Modern Poetry* (New York: Barnes and Noble, 1960), 180.

9. In an essay published in 1949 MacNeice explained his departure from autobiography in the concluding lines of "Sunday Morning": "In this example, however (where I was thinking of the Birmingham suburbs), I have rationalized or twisted my original association which would have suggested rather 'escape from the Sunday time,' i.e., from that stony, joyless, anti-time of the church (my upbringing was puritanical) which had seemed to preclude

music and movement and the growth of anything but stalactites and stalag-
mites." MacNeice, "Experience with Images," *Orpheus: A Symposium of the
Arts,* 2 vols. (London: John Lehmann, 1949), 2:128.

10. ". . . while there went / Those years and years by of world without
event / That in Majorca Alfonso watched the door." See *The Poems of Gerard
Manley Hopkins,* 4th ed., ed. W. H. Gardner and N. H. MacKenzie (London:
Oxford University Press, 1970), 106.

11. MacNeice, *Modern Poetry,* 34.

12. Ibid., 198.

13. Barbara Coulton identifies the departed lover in *Autumn Journal* as
"Nancy," to whom MacNeice "gave" September and October of 1938 (Canto
IV), rather than Mary, MacNeice's first wife who left him in May of 1935
(*MacNeice in the BBC,* 32) and whom Samuel Hynes takes to be a subject of
the poem. Perhaps it is this mistake that leads Hynes to push the romantic
passages further into MacNeice's past and misjudge "a good deal of *Autumn
Journal*" as "retrospective autobiography." See Hynes' otherwise excellent dis-
cussion of *Autumn Journal* in *The Auden Generation: Literature and Politics in
England in the 1930s* (New York: Viking Press, 1977), 367–73.

14. Samuel Hynes, "Yeats and the Poets of the Thirties," in *Modern Irish
Literature: Essays in Honor of William York Tindall,* ed. Raymond J. Porter and
James D. Brophy (New York: Iona College Press, 1972), 10.

15. Ibid., 5.

16. Ibid., 6.

17. MacNeice, *The Strings are False* (London: Faber & Faber, 1965), 220.

18. MacNeice, *Modern Poetry,* 204.

19. MacNeice, *The Strings are False,* 35.

20. F. R. Hart, "History Talking to Itself: Public Personality in Recent
Memoir," *New Literary History* 11, no. 1 (Autumn 1979): 193–210.

21. The analogy between bombs and bacilli may have pervaded thirties
literature, but the similarity between Isherwood's account of a bombing in
China and MacNeice's, written at the same time continents apart, seems re-
markable: "The searchlights criss-crossed, plotting points. . . . It was as if a
microscope had brought dramatically into focus the bacilli of a fatal disease."
W. H. Auden and Christopher Isherwood, *Journey to a War* (London: Faber
& Faber, 1939), 71. Isherwood's passage is quoted on page 343 of Hynes's
*The Auden Generation.*

22. Hart, "History Talking to Itself," 195.

23. MacNeice, *Modern Poetry,* 196.

24. Coulton, *MacNeice in the BBC,* 29.

25. MacNeice, *Modern Poetry,* 204. Hynes argues throughout his *Auden*

*Generation* that anticipation of World War II is a major motif in British poetry from early in the thirties.

26. Coulton, *MacNeice in the BBC*, 53–54.

27. Smith, *MacNeice*, 193; *see also* William T. McKinnon, "MacNeice's 'Pale Panther'": An Exercise in Dream Logic," *Essays in Criticism* 23, no. 4 (October 1973): 388–98.

28. McKinnon, "MacNeice's 'Pale Panther'," 393.

29. See also medieval bestiaries (e.g., *A Medieval Bestiary* trans. T. J. Elliott [Boston: Godine, 1971], n.p.) where, because the panther was believed, after his kill, to sleep for three days and rise again to hunt, he was associated with Christ. See "Lycidas" for a standard Renaissance association of sun/son and rebirth.

30. MacNeice, *Zoo* (London: Michael Joseph, 1938), 79.

31. MacNeice, *The Strings are False*, 37.

32. Brown and Reid, *Time Was Away*, 121.

33. MacNeice, *The Strings are False*, 216–17.

34. Blake Morrison, "An Expropriated Mycologist," *Times Literary Supplement*, 15 February 1980.

35. Interview in New Haven, 14 June 1979.

36. Roger Garfitt, "Stability, Exile, and Cunning," *TLS*, 15 February 1980.

37. Brown and Reid, *Time Was Away*, 113.

38. The first four volumes were published by Oxford University Press in London and New York. *The Hunt by Night* was published by Oxford in Great Britain and Wake Forest University Press in the U.S.A.

39. Brown, *Northern Voices*, 198.

40. Hereafter I shall refer to these eighteen poems as "new poems," within quotations marks, to distinguish them from the more recent poems in *The Hunt by Night*.

41. Cited parenthetically as *MP* or *MHN*, with page numbers.

42. Mahon, "Lament for the Maker," review of MacDiarmid's *Complete Poems* in *The New Statesman* 96 (1 December 1978): 744–45.

43. Mahon, "The Existential Lyric," review of Beckett's *Collected Poems* in *The New Statesman* 93 (25 March 1977): 402–03.

44. For example, see Brian Donnelly, "From Nineveh to the Harbour Bar," *Ploughshares* 6, no. 1 (1980): 131–37.

45. Mahon, "Magic Casements," review of *The Great Victorian Collection*, *The New Statesman* 90 (17 October 1975): 479.

46. Brown and Reid, *Time Was Away*, 121.

47. Norman Jeffares, "Place, Space, and Personality and the Irish Writer," in *Place, Personality and the Irish Writer*, 22.

48. Mahon, *Courtyards in Delft* (Dublin: Gallery Books, 1981), 22.

49. Interview in New Haven, 14 June 1979. Both quotations are from "A Defense of Poetry," *The Complete Works of Percy Bysshe Shelley,* ed. Roger Ingpen and Walter E. Peck (New York: Scribner's, 1930), 7: 118, 136.


## Chapter Six

1. Molesworth, *The Fierce Embrace,* 198.

2. F. R. Leavis, *How to Teach Reading: A Primer for Ezra Pound* (1932; repr. Folcroft, Penn: Folcroft Press, 1969), 3.

3. Thomas Kinsella, "The Divided Mind," in *Irish Poets in English,* 209.

4. Ibid., 217.

5. Donoghue, "Being Irish Together," *Sewanee Review* 84, no. 1 (Winter 1976): 130.

6. Adrian Frazier, "Global Regionalism: Interview with John Montague," *The Literary Review* 22, no. 2 (Winter 1979): 163.

7. Ibid.

8. Talk delivered at joint American and Canadian conference of the Committee for Irish Studies, University of Vermont, April 2, 1982.

9. Jane P. Tompkins, "The Reader in History: The Changing Shape in Literary Response," in *Reader-Response Criticism,* 213.

10. Witnessed by Tom Paulin, in Haffenden, *Viewpoints,* 173.

11. Haffenden, *Viewpoints,* 147.

12. Frazier, "Global Regionalism," 164–65.

13. Haffenden, *Viewpoints,* 63.

14. Willie Kelly, "Each Poem for Me is a New Beginning: Interview with Derek Mahon," *Cork Review* 2, no. 3 (June 1981): 10–12.

15. Montague, "Impact of Modern Poetry on Irish Writing," 148–49.

16. Ibid.

17. O'Hara, "Interview with Kinsella," 6.

18. Gary Snyder, *The Real Work: Interviews and Talk 1964–1979,* ed. William Scott McLean (New York: New Directions, 1980), 290.

19. Frazier, "Global Regionalism," 174.

20. Anthony Bradley, ed., *Contemporary Irish Poetry, An Anthology* (Berkeley: University of California Press, 1980); John Montague, ed., *The Book of Irish Verse;* Peter Fallon and Sean Golden, eds., *Soft Day: A Miscellany of Contemporary Irish Writing* (Notre Dame, Ind.: University of Notre Dame Press; Dublin: Wolfhound Press, 1981); soon see also Paul Muldoon, ed., *The Faber Book of Contemporary Verse* (London: Faber & Faber, forthcoming).

21. Hewitt's publications include *Collected Poems* (1968), *Out of My Time:*

*Poems 1967–1974* (1974), *Time Enough: Poems New and Revised* (1976), *The Rain Dance* (1978), *Kites in Spring: A Belfast Boyhood* (1980), *Loose Ends* (1983), all published by Blackstaff Press in Belfast. Michael Longley's major works are *No Continuing City* (London: Macmillan 1969), *An Exploded View* (London: Victor Gollancz, 1973), *Man Living on A Wall* (London: Victor Gollancz, 1976), *The Echo Gate* (London: Secker & Warburg, 1979), *Selected Poems 1963–1980* (Winston-Salem: Wake Forest University Press, 1980). Among James Simmons works, see especially *Engergy to Burn* (London: Bodley Head, 1971) and *West Strand Visions* (1974), *Judy Garland and the Cold War* (1976), *The Selected James Simmons,* ed. Edna Longley (1978), and *Constantly Singing* (1980), all from Blackstaff Press in Belfast.

22. M. L. Rosenthal, *The New Poets: American and British Poetry Since World War II* (Oxford: Oxford University Press, 1967), 306.

23. Edna Longley, "Searching the Darkness: Richard Murphy, Thomas Kinsella, John Montague and James Simmons," in *Two Decades of Irish Writing,* 130–31.

24. Seamus Heaney, "The Poetry of Richard Murphy," *Irish University Review,* Richard Murphy Special Issue, 7, no. 1 (Spring 1977): 19.

25. Murphy, *High Island: New and Selected Poems* (New York: Harper & Row, 1974); cited parenthetically as *MHI* with page numbers.

26. Eavan Boland, *Nightfeed* (Dublin: Arlan House; Boston: Marion Boyars, 1982), 28–29; Boland's other volumes are *Introducing Eavan Boland: Poems* (Princeton, NJ: Ontario Review Press, 1981); *In Her Own Image* (Dublin: Arlan House, 1980); *The War Horse* (London: Victor Gollancz, 1975); *New Territory* (Dublin: Figiss, 1967).

27. Eiléan Ni Chuilleanáin, *Site of Ambush* (Dublin: Gallery Books, 1975); Ni Chuilleanáin's other volumes are *Acts and Monuments* (Dublin: Gallery Books, 1972); *The Second Voyage* (Winston-Salem: Wake Forest University Press; Dublin: Gallery, 1977); *The Rose Geranium* (Dublin: Gallery, 1981).

28. Ni Chuilleanáin, *Rose Geranium,* 30.

29. Haffenden, *Viewpoints,* 136.

30. Editorial copy, *Mules,* Wake Forest edition.

31. Haffenden, *Viewpoints,* 131.

32. Paul Muldoon, *Why Brownlee Left* (London: Faber & Faber; Winston-Salem: Wake Forest University Press, 1980); cited parenthetically as *MWBL,* with page numbers.

33. Haffenden, *Viewpoints,* 141.

34. Samuel Johnson, *Lives of the English Poets,* ed. George Birbeck Hill, 3 vols. (Oxford: Clarendon Press, 1903), 1:20.

35. Haffenden, *Viewpoints,* 133.

36. John Kerrigan, "The New Narrative," *London Review of Books,* 16–29 February 1984, 22–23.

37. Adrian Frazier, "Juniper, Otherwise Known: Poems by Paulin and Muldoon," *Eire-Ireland* 19, no. 1 (Spring 1984): 133.

38. Kerrigan, "The New Narrative," 23.

39. "Paul Muldoon Writes . . . ," *The Poetry Book Society Bulletin* 118 (Autumn 1983): 1.

40. Heaney, *Sweeney Astray,* 72.

41. Karl Kerényi, "The Trickster in Relation to Greek Mythology," in Paul Radin, *The Trickster: A Study in American Indian Mythology* (London: Routledge and Kegan Paul, 1956), 176. See also the notes and discussion by Paul Radin and the commentary by C. G. Jung in the same volume. The Kerenyi commentary and the entire volume can illustrate other parallels between Gallogly and the Trickster. See also Michael Grant and John Hazel, *Gods and Mortals in Classical Mythology* (Springfield, Mass: G & C Merriam Co., 1973) who remind us that Hermes was father of Hermaphroditus and Priapus, suggesting correspondences to the transexuality of *Quoof.*

42. Kerényi, 185.

43. See Kinsella, *An Duanaire 1600–1900.*

44. *New Ireland Forum Report* (Dublin: The Stationery Office, 2 May 1984), 32.

45. *Ulysses,* 697.

# Works Cited

Adams, Michael, *Censorship: The Irish Experience*. Tuscaloosa: University of Alabama Press, 1968.

Altieri, Charles. "Sensibility, Rhetoric, and Will: Some Tensions in Contemporary Poetry." *Contemporary Literature* 23, no. 4 (Fall 1982): 451–79.

Auden, W. H. and Christopher Isherwood. *Journey to a War.* London: Faber & Faber, 1939.

Auden, W. H. "Louis MacNeice: A Memorial Address." In *Time Was Away,* ed. Terence Brown and Alec Reid. Dublin: Dolmen Press, 1974.

————. *Selected Poetry.* Modern Library edition. New York: Random House, 1959.

Bailey, Anthony. "A Reporter at Large: A Walk along the Boyne." *New Yorker,* 2 June 1980, 92, 95–122.

Bair, Deirdre. *Samuel Beckett: A Biography.* New York: Harcourt, Brace, Jovanovich, 1978.

Ball, Robert Stawall. *The Story of the Heavens.* rev. ed. London: Cassell and Company, 1897.

Beckett, Samuel. "Recent Irish Poetry." *Lace Curtain* 4 (Summer 1971; reprinted from *The Bookman,* 1934): 58–63.

Bedient, Calvin. *Eight Contemporary Poets.* Oxford: Oxford University Press, 1974.

————. "The Music of What Happens." *Parnassus* 8 (Fall/Winter 1979): 109–22.

————. "Review of *Notes from the Land of the Dead and Other Poems.*" *New York Times Book Review,* 16 June 1974, 7.

"The Belfast Group: A Symposium." *The Honest Ulsterman* 53 (November/December 1976): 53–63.

Benedikt, Michael, ed. *The Poetry of Surrealism.* Boston: Little, Brown, 1974.

Boland, Eavan. *In Her Own Image.* Dublin: Arlan House, 1980.

―――. *Introducing Eavan Boland: Poems.* Princeton, N.J.: Ontario Review Press, 1981.

―――. *New Territory.* Dublin: Figgis, 1967.

―――. *Nightfeed.* Dublin: Arlan House; Boston: Marion Boyars, 1982.

―――. *The War Horse.* London: Victor Gollancz, 1975.

Bradley, Anthony, ed. *Contemporary Irish Poetry, An Anthology.* Berkeley: University of California Press, 1980.

Brooks, Cleanth and Robert Penn Warren. *Understanding Poetry.* 4th ed. New York: Holt, Rinehart & Winston, 1960.

Brown, Terence. "After the Revival: The Problem of Adequacy and Genre." *Genre* 12, no. 4 (Winter 1979):565–89.

―――. *Ireland: A Social and Cultural History 1922–1979.* London: Fontana Books, 1981.

―――. *Louis MacNeice: Skeptical Vision.* Dublin: Gill & Macmillan, 1975.

―――. *Northern Voices: Poets from Ulster.* Dublin: Gill & Macmillan; Totowa, New Jersey: Rowman and Littlefield, 1975.

Brown, Terence and Alec Reid, eds. *Time Was Away.* Dublin: Dolmen Press, 1974.

*Buile Suibne.* Trans. and ed. J. G. O'Keefe. Irish Text Society Translations, vol. 12. London: Irish Texts Society, 1913.

Callois, Roger. "The Art of St John Perse." Trans. H. M. Chevalier. In *Exile and Other Poems,* by St. John Perse; trans. Denis Devlin, 147–53. Bollinger Series XV. New York: Pantheon Books, 1949.

Carney, James. *Studies in Irish Literature and History.* Dublin: Institute for Advanced Studies, 1955.

Carson, Ciarán. *The New Estate.* Belfast: Blackstaff Press; Winston-Salem: Wake Forest University Press, 1976.

Chardin, Pierre Teilhard de. *Toward the Future.* Trans. Rene Hague. London: Collins, 1975.

Clarke, Austin. "Banned Books." *New Statesman and Nation* 45, no. 1159 (23 May 1953):606.

―――. "Books Beyond Reach." *Irish Times,* 18 September 1943, 2.

―――. *Collected Plays.* Dublin: Dolmen Press, 1963.

————. *Collected Poems.* Dublin: Dolmen Press; New York: Oxford University Press, 1974.

————. "Gaelic Ireland Rediscovered: The Early Period." In *Irish Poets in English,* ed. Sean Lucy, 30–43. Cork: Mercier Press, 1973.

————. *A Penny in the Clouds.* London: Routledge & Kegan Paul, 1968.

————. *Poetry in Modern Ireland.* Cultural Relations Series. Cork: Mercier, 1962.

————. "Review of *Aithdioghluim Dana: A Miscellany of Irish Bardic Poetry, Historical and Religious . . .*" *Dublin Magazine* 16, no. 1 (January/March 1941): 62–63.

————. *Selected Poems.* Ed. Thomas Kinsella. Dublin: Dolmen Press; Winston-Salem: Wake Forest University Press, 1976.

————. *Twice Round the Black Church.* London: Routledge & Kegan Paul, 1962.

Clausen, Christopher. *The Place of Poetry: Two Centuries of an Art in Crisis.* Lexington: University of Kentucky Press, 1981.

Clines, Francis X. "Poet of the Bogs." *The New York Times Magazine,* 13 March 1983, 42–43, 78–79, 104.

Coffey, Brian. "Denis Devlin: Poet of Distance." In *Place, Personality, and the Irish Writer,* ed. Andrew Carpenter, 137–57. Irish Literary Series, 1. Gerrards Cross: Colin Smythe, 1977.

Coleridge, Samuel Taylor. *The Collected Works.* Ed. Kathleen Coburn and B. Winer. 17 vols. London: Routledge & Kegan Paul; Princeton: Princeton University Press, 1969– .

Colton, Barbara. *Louis MacNeice in the BBC.* London: Faber & Faber, 1980.

Colum, Mary. "Memories of Yeats." In *W. B. Yeats: Interviews and Recollections,* ed. E. H. Mikhail. 2 vols., 2: 241–46. London: Macmillan; New York: Barnes & Noble, 1977.

Colum, Padraic. *The Poet's Circuits.* Centenary ed. Dublin: Dolmen Press, 1981.

Connolly, Cyril. "Comment." *Horizon* 5, no. 25 (January 1942): 3–11.

Corkery, Daniel. *Synge and Anglo-Irish Literature.* Cork: Cork University Press, 1931.

Costello, Peter. *The Heart Grown Brutal: The Irish Revolution in Literature from 1891–1939.* Dublin: Gill & Macmillan; Totowa, New Jersey: Rowman and Littlefield, 1978.

Cronin, Anthony. *Dead as Doornails.* Dublin: Dolmen Press, 1976.

Cullingford, Elizabeth. *Yeats, Ireland and Fascism.* New York: New York University Press, 1981.

Davie, Donald. "Austin Clarke and Padraic Fallon." *Poetry Nation* 3 (1974): 80–101.

———. "The Guest Word." *New York Times Book Review,* 23 May 1976, 55, 30.

Davis, Thomas. *Essays.* Centenary ed. Dundalk: Dundalgan Press, 1914.

Deane, Seamus. *Civilians and Barbarians.* Derry: Field Day Publications, 1983.

———. *Heroic Styles: The Tradition of an Idea.* Field Day Publications, 1984.

———. "Irish Poetry and Irish Nationalism." In *Two Decades of Irish Writing,* ed. Douglas Dunn, 4–22. Cheadle, Cheshire: Carcanet Press: 1975.

———. "The Literary Myths of the Revival: A Case for their Abandonment." In *Myth and Reality in Irish Literature,* ed. Joseph Ronsley, 317–29. Waterloo, Ontario: Wilfred Laurier University Press, 1977.

———. "Unhappy and at Home: Interview with Seamus Heaney." *The Crane Bag* 1, no. 1 (Spring 1977): 61–67.

———. "The Writer of the Troubles." *Threshold* 25 (Summer 1974): 13–17.

dePaor, Liam. *Divided Ulster.* 2nd ed. London: Penguin, 1972.

Devlin, Denis. *Collected Poems.* Ed. Brian Coffey. Dublin: Dolmen Press, 1964.

———. *The Heavenly Foreigner.* Ed. Brian Coffey. Dublin: Dolmen Press, 1967.

———. *Selected Poems.* Ed. Allen Tate and Robert Penn Warren. New York: Holt, Rinehart & Winston, 1963.

Dodsworth, Martin. "'Jingle-go-Jangle': Feeling and Expression in Austin Clarke's Later Poetry." *Irish University Review* 4, no. 1 (Spring 1974): 117–27.

Donnelly, Brian. "From Nineveh to the Harbour Bar." *Ploughshares* 6, no. 1 (1980): 131–37.

Donoghue, Denis. "Being Irish Together." *The Sewanee Review* 84, no. 1 (Winter 1976): 129–33.

————. "Fire in the Great Vein." *The New Review* 1, no. 5 (August 1974): 69–72.

————. "One More Brevity." In *A Tribute to Austin Clarke on his Seventieth Birthday*, ed. John Montague and Liam Miller, 20–22. Dublin: Dolmen Press, 1966.

————. "The Sovereign Ghost." *Sewanee Review* 84, no. 1 (Winter 1976): 98–118.

Dunn, Douglas. "The Speckled Hill, the Plover's Shore: Northern Irish Poetry Today." *Encounter* 41, no. 6 (December 1973): 70–76.

————, ed. *Two Decades of Irish Writing.* Cheadle, Cheshire: Carcanet Press, 1975.

Eliade, Mircea. *Images and Symbols: Studies in Religious Symbolism.* Trans. Philip Mairet. New York: Sheed & Ward, 1969.

Elliot, T. S. *On Poetry and Poets.* Noonday ed. New York: Farrar, Straus, and Cudahy, 1961.

Ellmann, Richard. *James Joyce.* rev. ed. Oxford: Oxford University Press, 1982.

————. *Ulysses on the Liffey.* New York: Oxford University Press, 1972.

Evans, E. Estyn. *Irish Folk Ways.* London: Routledge & Kegan Paul, 1957.

————. *Irish Heritage: The Landscape, the People and their Work.* Dundalk: Dundalgan Press, 1942.

————. *The Personality of Ireland: Habitat, Heritage and History.* rev. ed. Belfast: Blackstaff Press, 1981.

Fallis, Richard. *The Irish Renaissance.* Syracuse: Syracuse University Press, 1977.

Fallon, Padraic. *Poems.* Dublin: Dolmen Press, 1974.

Fallon, Peter. *Winter Work.* Dublin: Gallery Press, 1982.

Fallon, Peter and Dennis O'Driscoll, eds. *The First Ten Years: Dublin Arts Festival Poetry.* Dublin: Dublin Arts Festival, 1979.

Fallon, Peter and Sean Golden, eds. *Soft Day: A Miscellany of Contemporary Irish Writing.* Notre Dame: University of Notre Dame Press; Dublin: Wolfhound Press, 1981.

Fiacc, Padraic. "Fiacc Answers Back." *The Honest Ulsterman* 50 (Winter 1975), 133–36.

Fish, Stanley. "Interpreting the Variorum." In *Reader-Response Criticism,* ed. Jane P. Tompkins, 164–84. Baltimore: Johns Hopkins University Press, 1980.

Flanagan, Thomas. "Yeats, Joyce, and the Matter of Ireland." *Critical Inquiry* 2, no. 1 (Autumn 1975):43–67.

Foley, Dermot. "Monotonously Rings the Little Bell." *Irish University Review,* Sean O'Faolain Special Issue, 6, no. 1 (October 1940):54–62.

Fraser, G. S. *Vision and Rhetoric: Studies in Modern Poetry.* New York: Barnes and Noble, 1960.

Frazier, Adrian. "'The Cod: Bewildered Schoolboy': Austin Clarke's Later Poetry." *Eire-Ireland* 14, no. 2 (Summer 1979):52–67.

———. "Global Regionalism: Interview with John Montague." *The Literary Review* 22, no. 2 (Winter 1979):153–74.

———. "Juniper, Otherwise Known: Poems by Paulin and Muldoon." *Eire-Ireland* 19, no. 1 (Spring 1984):123–33.

Freyer, Grattan. *W. B. Yeats and the Anti-Democratic Tradition.* New York: Barnes and Noble, 1981.

Garfitt, Roger. "Stability, Exile, and Cunning." *Times Literary Supplement,* 15 February 1980, 169.

Garratt, Robert F. "Patrick Kavanagh and the Killing of the Irish Revival." *Colby Library Quarterly* 17, no. 3 (September 1981):170–83.

Gifford, Don. *Notes for Joyce.* New York: E. P. Dutton, 1967.

Gillet, Louis. "The Living Joyce," In *Portraits of the Artist in Exile: Recollections of James Joyce by Europeans,* ed. Willard Potts, 170–204. Seattle: University of Washington Press, 1979.

Glassie, Henry. *Passing the Time in Ballymenone.* Philadelphia: University of Pennsylvania Press, 1982.

Grant, Michael and John Hazel. *Gods and Mortals in Classical Mythology.* London: Routledge & Kegan Paul, 1956.

Graves, Robert. *The White Goddess.* Amended and enlarged. New York: Farrar, Straus & Giroux, 1966.

Greacen, Roy. "When Peace Breaks Out in Dublin." *The Bell* 5, no. 5 (February 1943):397–99.

Haffenden, John. *Viewpoints: Poets in Conversation.* London: Faber & Faber, 1981.

Hall, Barbara J. "Yeats's Sean Van Voght: A Study of Crazy Jane." Master's Thesis, Wake Forest University, 1980.

Halpern, Susan. *Austin Clarke: His Life and Works.* Dublin: Dolmen Press, 1974.

Harbison, Peter. *Guide to the National Monuments.* Rev. ed. Dublin: Gill & Macmillan, 1975.

Harmon, Maurice, ed. *Irish Poetry after Yeats.* Dublin: Wolfhound Press; Boston: Little, Brown, 1979.

––––––. "Notes Toward a Biography." *Irish University Review,* Austin Clarke Special Issue, 4, no. 1 (Spring 1974): 13–25.

––––––. *The Poetry of Thomas Kinsella.* Dublin: Wolfhound Press, 1974.

Hart, Francis Russell. "History Talking to Itself: Public Personality in Recent Memoir." *New Literary History* 11, no. 1 (Autumn 1979): 193–210.

Heaney, Seamus. *Death of a Naturalist.* London: Faber & Faber; New York: Oxford University Press, 1966.

––––––. *Door Into the Dark.* London: Faber & Faber; New York: Oxford University Press, 1969.

––––––. *Field Work.* London: Faber & Faber; New York: Farrar, Straus & Giroux, 1979.

––––––. *North.* London: Faber & Faber; New York: Oxford University Press, 1976.

––––––. *An Open Letter.* Derry: Field Day Publications, 1983.

––––––. *Poems 1965–1975* London: Faber & Faber; New York: Farrar, Straus & Giroux, 1980.

––––––. "The Poetry of Richard Murphy." *Irish University Review,* Richard Murphy Special Issue, 7, no. 1 (Spring 1977): 18–30.

––––––. *Preoccupations: Selected Prose 1968–1978.* London: Faber & Faber; New York: Farrar, Straus & Giroux, 1980.

––––––. *Station Island and Other Poems.* London: Faber & Faber, 1984; New York: Farrar, Straus & Giroux, 1985.

––––––. *Sweeney Astray: A Version from the Irish.* Derry: Field Day Publications; New York: Farrar, Straus & Giroux, 1983.

––––––. *Ugolino.* Dublin: Andrew Carpenter, 1979.

––––––. *Wintering Out.* London: Faber & Faber; New York: Oxford University Press, 1972.

Hewitt, John. *Collected Poems.* Belfast: Blackstaff Press, 1968.

––––––. *Kites in Spring: A Belfast Boyhood.* Belfast: Blackstaff Press, 1980.

––––––. *Loose Ends.* Belfast: Blackstaff Press, 1983.

————. *Out of My Time: Poems 1967–1974.* Belfast: Blackstaff Press, 1974.

————. *The Rain Dance.* Belfast: Blackstaff Press, 1978.

————. *Time Enough: Poems New and Revised.* Belfast: Blackstaff Press, 1976.

Hollander, John. *Vision and Resonance.* New York: Oxford University Press, 1975.

Hopkins, Gerard Manley. *The Poems of Gerard Manley Hopkins.* Ed. W. H. Gardner and N. H. MacKenzie. 4th ed. London: Oxford University Press, 1970.

Hynes, Samuel. *The Auden Generation: Literature and Politics in England in the 1930s.* New York: Viking Press, 1977.

————. "Yeats and the Poets of the Thirties." In *Modern Irish Literature,* ed. Raymond J. Porter and James D. Brophy, 1–22. New York: Iona College Press, 1972.

Iremonger, Valentin. "Poets and Their Publishers." *The Bell* 14, no. 1 (April 1947): 79.

————. "Public Opinion." *The Bell* 7, no. 3 (December 1943): 255–57.

Iser, Wolfgang. *The Act of Reading: A Theory of Aesthetic Response.* Baltimore: Johns Hopkins University Press, 1978.

Jarrell, Randall. *Poetry and the Age.* New York: Vintage, 1955.

Jeffares, A. Norman. "Place, Space, and Personality and the Irish Writer." In *Place, Personality and the Irish Writer,* ed. Andrew Carpenter, 11–40. Gerrards Cross, Buckinghamshire: Colin Smythe; New York: Barnes & Noble, 1977.

Johnson, Samuel. *Lives of the English Poets.* Ed. George Birbeck Hill. 3 vols. Oxford: Clarendon Press, 1903.

Johnston, Dillon. "Devlin's Poetry: Love in Abeyance." *Concerning Poetry* 14, no. 2 (Fall 1981): 27–43.

————. "The Enabling Ritual: Irish Poetry in the Seventies." *Shenandoah* 25, no. 4 (Summer 1974): 1–24.

————. "A Response to Hugh Kenner: Kinsella's Magnanimity and Mean Reading." *Genre* 13, no. 4 (Winter 1980): 531–37.

————. "Unaccommodated Mahon: An Ulster Poet." *The Hollins Critic* 17, no. 5 (December 1980): 1–16.

Jordan, John. "Mr. Kavanagh's Progress." *Studies* 49 (1960): 295–304.

Joyce, James. *The Critical Writings.* Ed. Ellsworth Mason and Richard Ellmann. Compass ed. New York: Viking Press, 1964.

——. *Finnegans Wake.* New York: Viking Press, 1959.

——. *Letters of James Joyce.* Ed. Stuart Gilbert and Richard Ellmann. 3 vols. New York: Viking Press, 1957–66.

——. *A Portrait of the Artist as a Young Man.* New York: Viking Press, 1964.

——. *Stephen Hero.* Ed. John J. Slocum and Herbert Cahoon. New ed. New York: New Directions, 1963.

——. *Ulysses.* New York: Modern Library, 1961.

Jude the Obscure [pseud.]. "The HU Business Section." *The Honest Ulsterman* 60 (July/October 1978):60–80.

Jung, C. G. *Collected Works.* Bollinger Series XX. Ed. Herbert Read *et al.* 20 vols. New York: Pantheon Books; Princeton: Princeton University Press, 1953–79.

——. *The Portable Jung.* Ed. Joseph Campbell; trans. R. F. C. Hull. New York: Viking Press, 1971.

Kalstone, David. *Five Temperaments.* New York: Oxford University Press, 1977.

Kavanagh, Patrick. *Collected Poems.* London: Martin Brian & O'Keefe, 1972.

——. *Collected Pruse.* London: Martin Brian & O'Keefe, 1973.

——. *Come Dance With Kitty Stobling and Other Poems.* London: Macmillan, 1960.

——. *The Complete Poems of Patrick Kavanagh.* Ed. Peter Kavanagh. New York: The Peter Kavanagh Hand Press, 1972.

——. "Diary." *Envoy* 2, no. 7 (June 1950):83–91.

——. *The Great Hunger.* Dublin: Cuala Press, 1942.

——. *The Green Fool.* London: Michael Joseph, 1938.

——. *November Haggard: Uncollected Prose and Verse.* Ed. Peter Kavanagh. New York: The Peter Kavanagh Hand Press, 1971.

——. *Ploughman and Other Poems.* London: Macmillan, 1936.

——. *A Soul for Sale.* London: Macmillan, 1947.

——. *Tarry Flynn.* London: Pilot Press, 1948.

Kavanagh, Peter. *Sacred Keeper: A Biography of Patrick Kavanagh.* The Curragh: Goldsmith Press, 1979.

Kearney, Richard. *Myth and Motherland.* Derry: Field Day Publications, 1984.

Kelly, Willie. "Each Poem for Me is a New Beginning: Interview with Derek Mahon." *Cork Review* 2, no. 3 (June 1981): 10–12.

Kenner, Hugh. *Joyce's Voices*. London: Faber & Faber, 1978.

—————. "Thomas Kinsella: An Anecdote and Some Reflections." *Genre* 12, no. 4 (Winter 1979): 591–99.

Kerényi, Karl. "The Trickster in Relation to Greek Mythology." Postscript to *The Trickster: A Study in American Indian Mythology*, by Paul Radin. London: Routledge & Kegan Paul, 1956.

Kerrigan, John. "The New Narrative." *London Review of Books*, 16–29 February 1984, 22–23.

Kiberd, Declan. *Anglo-Irish Attitudes*. Derry: Field Day Publications, 1984.

Kilroy, James. *The Playboy Riots*. Dublin: Dolmen Press, 1971.

Kinsella, Thomas. "Another Country . . ." In *The Pleasures of Gaelic Poetry*, ed. Sean MacReamoinn, 175–88. London: Allen Lane-Penguin Books, 1982.

—————. "The Divided Mind." In *Irish Poets in English*, ed. Sean Lucy, 208–18. Cork: Mercier Press, 1973.

—————, trans. *An Duanaire 1600 – 1900: Poems of the Dispossessed*. Selected by Sean O Tuama. Dublin: Dolmen Press; Philadelphia: University of Pennsylvania Press, 1981.

—————. *New Poems*. Dublin: Dolmen Press, 1973.

—————. *Nightwalker and Other Poems*. Dublin: Dolmen Press, 1968.

—————. *Notes from the Land of the Dead and Other Poems*. New York: Knopf, 1973.

—————. *Peppercanister Poems 1972–1978*. Dublin: Dolmen; Winston-Salem: Wake Forest University Press, 1979.

—————. *Poems and Translations*. New York: Atheneum, 1961.

—————. *Poems 1956–1973*. Winston-Salem: Wake Forest University Press, 1979; Dublin: Dolmen Press, 1980.

—————, trans. *The Tain*. Dublin: Dolmen Press, 1969; Oxford: Oxford University Press, 1970.

Langbaum, Robert. *The Poetry of Experience*. New York: W. W. Norton, 1963.

Lawrence, D. H. *Look! We Have Come Through: A Cycle of Love Poems*. Austin: The University of Texas Humanities Research Center, 1971.

Leavis, F. R. *How to Teach Reading: A Primer for Ezra Pound*. Cambridge: The Minority Press, 1932; rpt. Folcroft, Penn.: Folcroft Press, 1969.

*Lebor Gabála Érenn: The Book of the Taking of Ireland.* Ed. and trans. R. A. Stewart Macalister. 4 secs. Dublin: Irish Texts Society, 1938–1941.

Leiris, Michel. *Manhood.* Trans. Richard Howard. New York: Grossman, 1963.

Litz, A. Walton. "Ithaca." In *James Joyce's Ulysses: Critical Essays,* ed. Clive Hart and David Hayman, 385–405. Berkeley: University of California Press, 1974.

Loftus, Richard J. *Nationalism in Modern Anglo-Irish Literature.* Madison: University of Wisconsin Press, 1964.

Longley, Edna. "Searching the Darkness: Richard Murphy, Thomas Kinsella, John Montague and James Simmons." In *Two Decades of Irish Writing: A Critical Survey,* ed. Douglas Dunn, 118–53. Cheadle, Cheshire: Carcanet Press, 1975.

Longley, Michael. *The Echo Gate.* London: Secker & Warburg, 1979.

———. *An Exploded View.* London: Victor Gollancz, 1973.

———. *Man Lying on a Wall.* London: Victor Gollancz, 1976.

———. "The Neolithic Night: A Note on the Irishness of Louis MacNeice." In *Two Decades of Irish Writing,* ed. Douglas Dunn, 98–104. Cheadle, Cheshire: Carcanet Press, 1975.

———. *No Continuing City.* London: Macmillan, 1969.

———. *Selected Poems 1963–1980.* Winston-Salem: Wake Forest University Press, 1980.

Lucy, Sean, ed. *Irish Poetry in English.* The Thomas Davis Lectures. Cork: Mercier, 1973.

Lyons, F. S. L. *Culture and Anarchy in Ireland 1890–1939.* Ford Lectures 1978. London: Oxford University Press, 1979.

———. *Ireland Since the Famine.* rev. ed. London: Fontana, 1973.

Lyons, F. S. L. and R. A. J. Hawkins, eds. *Ireland Under the Union: Varieties of Tension, Essays in Honor of T. W. Moody.* Oxford: Clarendon Press, 1980.

MacNeice, Louis. *Collected Poems.* Ed. E. R. Dodds. London: Faber & Faber, 1966.

———. "Experience with Images." In *Orpheus: A Symposium of the Arts.* 2 vols., 2. London: John Lehmann, 1949.

————. *Modern Poetry.* 2nd ed. London: Oxford University Press, 1968.

————. *The Poetry of W. B. Yeats.* London and New York: Oxford University Press, 1941.

————. *The Strings are False.* London: Faber & Faber, 1965.

————. *Zoo.* London: Michael Joseph, 1938.

MacReamoinn, Sean, ed. *The Pleasures of Gaelic Poetry.* London: Allen Lane-Penguin Books, 1982.

Mahon, Derek. *Courtyards in Delft.* Dublin: Gallery Books, 1981.

————. "The Existential Lyric." *The New Statesman* 93 (25 March 1977):402–03.

————. *The Hunt by Night.* Oxford: Oxford University Press; Winston-Salem: Wake Forest University Press, 1982.

————. "Lament for the Maker." *The New Statesman* 96 (1 December 1978):744–45.

————. *Lives.* Oxford and New York: Oxford University Press, 1972.

————. "Magic Casements." *The New Statesman* 90 (17 October 1975): 479.

————. *Night Crossing.* Oxford and New York: Oxford University Press, 1968.

————. *Poems 1962–1978.* London: Oxford University Press, 1979.

————. *Snow Party.* Oxford and New York: Oxford University Press, 1975.

————, ed. *The Sphere Book of Modern Irish Poetry.* London: Sphere, 1972.

Manganiello, Dominic. *Joyce's Politics.* London: Routledge & Kegan Paul, 1980.

Marsack, Robyn. *The Cave of Making: The Poetry of Louis MacNeice.* Oxford: Clarendon Press, 1982.

Martin, Augustine. "Literature and Society, 1938–1951." In *Ireland in the War Years and After, 1939–1951,* ed. Kevin B. Nowlan and T. Desmond Williams, 167–84. Dublin: Gill & Macmillan, 1975.

————. "The Rediscovery of Austin Clarke." *Studies* 14, no. 216 (Winter 1965):408–34.

Mays, James. "A Poem by Denis Devlin with Some Questions and Conclusions." In *Advent VI,* Denis Devlin Special Issue, 9–14. Southampton: Advent Books, 1976.

McGuckian, Medbh. *The Flower Master.* Oxford: Oxford University Press, 1982.

————. *Venus and the Rain.* Oxford and New York: Oxford University Press, 1984.

McKinnon, William. *Apollo's Blended Dream.* London: Oxford University Press, 1971.

————. "MacNeice's 'Pale Panther': An Exercise in Dream Logic." *Essays in Criticism* 23, no. 4 (October 1973): 388–98.

*A Medieval Bestiary.* Trans. T. J. Elliott. Boston: Godine, 1971.

Merleau-Ponty, Maurice. *Phenomenology of Perception.* Trans. Colin Smith. London: Routledge & Kegan Paul, 1962.

Mikhail, E. H., ed., *W. B. Yeats: Interviews and Recollections.* 2 vols. London: Macmillan, 1977.

Miller, Liam. *Dolmen XXV: An Illustrated Bibliography of the Dolmen Press 1951–1976.* Dublin: Dolmen Press, 1976.

Molesworth, Charles. *The Fierce Embrace: A Study of Contemporary American Poetry.* Columbia: University of Missouri Press, 1979.

Montague, John. "American Pegasus." *Studies* 48 (Summer 1959): 183–91.

————, ed. *The Book of Irish Verse.* New York: Macmillan, 1976. First published as *The Faber Book of Irish Verse.* London: Faber & Faber, 1974.

————. *A Chosen Light.* London: MacGibbon & Kee, 1967; Chicago: Swallow, 1969.

————. *The Dead Kingdom.* Dublin: Dolmen; Winston-Salem: Wake Forest University Press; London: Oxford University Press, 1984.

————. *Death of a Chieftain and Other Stories.* London: McGibbon & Kee, 1964; Dublin: Poolbeg Press, 1978.

————. "Global Regionalism: An Interview With Adrian Frazier." *The Literary Review* 22, no. 2 (Winter 1979): 153–74.

————. *The Great Cloak.* Dublin: Dolmen Press; Winston-Salem: Wake Forest University Press, 1978.

————. "The Impact of International Modern Poetry on Irish Writing." In *Irish Poets in English,* ed. Sean Lucy, 144–58. Cork: Mercier, 1972.

————. "A Note on Rhythm." *Agenda* 10 (Autumn/Winter, 1972–73): 41.

————. *Poisoned Lands and Other Poems.* London: MacGibbon & Kee; Philadelphia: Dufour, 1963.

————. *Poisoned Lands.* new ed. Dublin: Dolmen Press; Oxford: Oxford University Press, 1977.

————. "A Primal Gaeltacht." *The Irish Times,* 30 July 1970, 7.

————. *The Rough Field.* new ed. Dublin: Dolmen Press; Winston-Salem: Wake Forest University Press, 1984. First published by Dolmen Press, 1972.

————. *Selected Poems.* Toronto: Exile Editions; Winston-Salem: Wake Forest University Press; Dublin: Dolmen Press; London: Oxford University Press, 1982.

————. "The Seamless Garment and the Muse." *Agenda* 5, no. 4 (Autumn/Winter, 1967–68): 27–34.

————. *A Slow Dance.* Dublin: Dolmen Press; Winston-Salem: Wake Forest University Press, 1975.

————. *Tides.* Dublin: Dolmen Press, 1970; Chicago: Swallow, 1971.

————. "Under Ben Bulben." *Shenandoah,* Yeats and Ireland Issue, 16, no. 4 (Summer 1965): 21–24.

Moore, D. B. *The Poetry of Louis MacNeice.* Leicester: University of Leicester Press, 1972.

Moore, George. *Hail and Farewell.* 3 vols. London: William Heinemann, 1947.

Morrison, Blake and Andrew Motion, eds. *The Penguin Book of Contemporary British Poetry.* Hammondsworth, Middlesex: Penguin, 1982.

Morrison, Blake. "An Expropriated Mycologist." *Times Literary Supplement* 15 February 1980, 168.

————. *Seamus Heaney.* Contemporary Writers Series. London: Methuen, 1982.

Muldoon, Paul. *Mules.* London: Faber & Faber; Winston-Salem: Wake Forest University Press, 1977.

————. *New Weather.* London: Faber & Faber, 1973.

————. "Paul Muldoon Writes . . . ," *The Poetry Book Society Bulletin* 118 (Autumn 1983): 1.

————. *Quoof.* London: Faber & Faber; Winston-Salem: Wake Forest University Press, 1983.

————. *Why Brownlee Left.* London: Faber & Faber; Winston-Salem: Wake Forest University Press, 1980.

Murphy, Richard. *High Island: New and Selected Poems.* New York: Harper & Row, 1974.

————. *The Price of Stone.* London and Boston: Faber & Faber, forthcoming.

Nemo, John. *Patrick Kavanagh*. Boston: Twayne, 1979.

*New Larousse Encyclopedia of Mythology*. intr. Robert Graves; trans. Richard Aldington and Delano Ames. New York: Hamlyn, 1968.

*New Ireland Forum Report*. Dublin: The Stationery Office, 2 May 1984.

Ní Chuilleanáin, Eiléan. *Acts and Monuments*. Dublin: Gallery Books, 1972.

————. *The Rose Geranium*. Dublin: Gallery Press, 1981.

————. *The Second Voyage*. Winston-Salem: Wake Forest University Press; Dublin: Gallery Press, 1977.

————. *Site of Ambush*. Dublin: Gallery Press, 1975.

O'Brien, Conor Cruise. "Passion and Cunning." In *Excited Reverie: A Centenary Tribute to William Butler Yeats 1865–1939*, ed. A. Norman Jeffares and K. G. Cross, 207–78. New York: Macmillan, 1965.

O'Brien, Darcy. *Patrick Kavanagh*. Irish Writers Series. Lewisburg, Penn.: Bucknell University Press; London: Associated University Presses, 1975.

O'Connor, Frank. "The Belfry." *The Bell* 1, no. 5 (February 1941): 86–88.

————. "Does Kinsella Lead the Poets?" *The Sunday Independent,* 14 October 1962.

————. *Leinster, Munster, and Connaught*. London: R. Hale, 1950.

————. "The Future of Irish Literature." *Horizon* 5, no. 25 (January 1942): 55–63.

O'Faolain, Sean. "Ireland after Yeats." *The Bell* 17, no. 11 (Summer 1953): 37–48.

————. *The Irish: A Character Study*. New York: Devin Adair, 1956.

————. "Signing Off." *The Bell* 12, no. 1 (April 1946): 1–4.

O'Hara, Daniel. "An Interview with Thomas Kinsella." *Contemporary Poetry: A Journal of Criticism* 4, no. 1 (1981): 1–18.

Ormsby, Frank, ed. *Poets from the North of Ireland*. Belfast: Blackstaff Press, 1979.

O'Shea, Edward. *Yeats as Editor*. Dublin: Dolmen Press, 1975.

Parrish, Stephen Maxwell, ed. *A Concordance to the Poems of W. B. Yeats*. Programmer James A. Painter. Ithaca: Cornell University Press, 1963.

Paulin, Tom. *A New Look at the Language Question*. Derry: Field Day Publications, 1983.

Payne, Basil. "The Poetry of Patrick Kavanagh." *Studies* 49 (1960): 279–94.

Plumly, Stanley. "Rhetoric and Emotion." *American Poetry Review* 7, no. 1 (Jan/Feb 1978): 21–32.

"Poetry Since Yeats: An Exchange of Views—Stephen Spender, Patrick Kavanagh, Thomas Kinsella, W. D. Snodgrass." *Tri-Quarterly* 4 (1965): 100–11.

Poulet, Georges. "Phenomenology of Reading." *New Literary History* 1, no. 1 (Fall 1969): 53–68.

Pound, Ezra. *The Cantos.* New York: New Directions, 1970.

———. *Jefferson and/or Mussolini.* 1935; rpt. New York: Liveright, 1970.

Preminger, Alex *et al,* eds. *Princeton Encyclopedia of Poetry and Poetics.* enl. ed. Princeton: Princeton University Press, 1974.

Prescott, Peter. "Bard of the Irish Soul." *Newsweek,* 2 February 1981, 67–69.

Press, John. *Louis MacNeice.* Writers and their Work Series. London: Longmans, Green, and Co., 1965.

Radin, Paul. *The Trickster: A Study in American Indian Mythology.* London: Routledge & Kegan Paul, 1956.

Randall, James. "An Interview with Seamus Heaney." *Ploughshares* 5, no. 3 (1979): 7–22.

Ransom, John Crowe. *The New Criticism.* Norfolk, Conn: New Directions, 1941.

Rees, Alwyn and Brinley Rees. *Celtic Heritage.* London: Thames & Hudson, 1961.

Richards, I. A. *Practical Criticism.* New York: Harcourt Brace, 1930.

Rodgers, W. R., ed. *Irish Literary Portraits.* New York: Taplinger, 1973.

Roscelli, William John. "The Private Pilgrimage of Austin Clarke." In *The Celtic Cross: Studies in Irish Culture and History,* ed. Ray B. Brown, W. J. Roscelli, and Richard Loftus. West Lafayette, Ind.: Purdue University Press Studies, 1964.

Rosenberg, Carolyn. "Let Our Gaze Blaze: The Recent Poetry of Thomas Kinsella." Ph.D. diss., Kent State University, 1980.

Rosenthal, M. L. *The New Poets: American and British Poetry Since World War II.* Oxford and New York: Oxford University Press, 1967.

Ryan, John. *Remembering How We Stood: Bohemian Dublin At the Mid-Century.* Dublin: Gill & Macmillan, 1975.

Schirmer, Gregory. "'A Mad Discordancy': Austin Clarke's Early Narrative Poems." *Eire-Ireland* 16, no. 2 (Summer 1981): 16–28.

————. *The Poetry of Austin Clarke.* Notre Dame: University of Notre Dame Press; Dublin: Dolmen Press, 1983.

Shelley, Percy Bysshe. *The Complete Works of Percy Bysshe Shelley.* Ed. Roger Ingpen and Walter E. Peck. 10 vols. New York: Scribner's, 1930.

Simmons, James. *Constantly Singing.* Belfast: Blackstaff Press, 1980.

————. *Energy to Burn.* London: Bodley Head, 1971.

————. *Judy Garland and the Cold War.* Belfast: Blackstaff Press, 1976.

————. *The Selected James Simmons.* Ed. Edna Longley. Belfast: Blackstaff Press, 1978.

————. *West Strand Visions.* Belfast: Blackstaff Press, 1974.

Skelton, Robin. "Comment." *The Malahat Review* 62 (July 1982): 5–7.

————. "Twentieth-Century Irish Literature and the Private Press Tradition; Dun Emer, Cuala, and Dolmen Presses 1902–1963." In *Irish Renaissance: A Gathering of Essays, Memoirs, and Letters for the Massachusetts Review,* ed. Robin Skelton and David R. Clarke, 158–67. Amherst: University of Massachusetts Review, 1965.

Smith, Barbara Hernstein. *Poetic Closure: A Study of How Poems End.* Chicago: University of Chicago Press, 1968.

Smith, Elton Edward. *Louis MacNeice.* New York: Twayne, 1970.

Smith, Stan. "Frightened Antinomies: Love and Death in the Poetry of Denis Devlin." In *Advent VI,* Denis Devlin Special Issue, 24–31. Southampton: Advent Books, 1976.

————. "Precarious Guest: The Poetry of Denis Devlin." *Irish University Review* 8, no. 1 (Spring 1978): 51–67.

Smyllie, R. M. "Preface." *Poems from Ireland.* Ed. Donagh MacDonagh. Dublin: The Irish Times, 1944.

Snyder, Gary. *The Real Work: Interviews and Talk 1964–1979.* Ed. William Scott McLean. New York: New Directions, 1980.

Spender, Stephen. "The Influence of Yeats on Later English Poets." *Tri-Quarterly* 4 (1965): 82–89.

Stephens, James. *Irish Fairy Tales.* New York: Collier, 1962.

Stevens, Wallace. *The Palm at the End of the Mind: Selected Poems and A Play.* Ed. Holly Stevens. New York: Vintage, 1972.

Stuart, Francis. Untitled Recollection. In *The Yeats We Knew,* ed. Francis McManus, 25–40. Cork: Mercier, 1965.

Survey. Market Research Bureau of Ireland. *The Irish Times,* 27 June 1983, 6.

Tapping, Craig. *Austin Clarke: A Study of his Writing.* Dublin: Dolmen Press; Totowa, N.J.: Barnes & Noble, 1981.

Taylor, Geoffrey. "The Poetry of John Hewitt." *The Bell* 3, no. 3 (December 1941): 229–31.

———. "Sense and Nonsense in Poetry." *The Bell* 1, no. 5 (February 1941): 86–88.

Thompson, William Irwin. *The Imagination of an Insurrection.* New York: Harper & Row, 1967.

Tompkins, Jane P. "The Reader in History: The Changing Shape in Literary Response." In *Reader-Response Criticism: From Formalism to Post-Structuralism,* ed. Jane P. Tompkins, 201–32. Baltimore: Johns Hopkins University Press, 1980.

Torchiana, Donald T. *W. B. Yeats and Georgian Ireland.* Evanston: Northwestern University Press, 1966.

Vendler, Helen. "The Music of What Happens." *New Yorker* 57 (28 September 1981): 146–52, 155–57.

"The War Years." *The Honest Ulsterman* 64 (September 1979–January 1980): 11–62.

Warner, Alan. *Clay is the Word: Patrick Kavanagh 1904–1967.* Dublin: Dolmen Press, 1973.

Welch, Robert. "Austin Clarke and Gaelic Poetic Tradition." *Irish University Review,* Austin Clarke Special Issue, 4, no. 1 (Spring 1974): 41–51.

Whitaker, Thomas R. *Swan and Shadow: Yeats's Dialogue with History.* Chapel Hill: University of North Carolina Press, 1964.

Whitman, Walt. *The Complete Poems.* Ed. Francis Murphy. Harmondsworth: Penguin, 1975.

Yeats, W. B. *The Autobiography.* Anchor ed. Garden City, N.Y.: Doubleday, 1958.

———. *Explorations.* New York: Macmillan, 1962.

———. *Essays and Introductions.* New York: Macmillan, 1961.

———, ed. *The Oxford Book of Irish Verse, 1892–1935.* London: Oxford University Press, 1936.

———. *The Poems.* new ed. Ed. Richard Finneran. New York: Macmillan, 1983.

————. *The Senate Speeches of W. B. Yeats.* Ed. Donald R. Pearce. Bloomington: Indiana University Press, 1960.

————. *Uncollected Prose.* Ed. John P. Frayne and Colton Johnson. 2 vols. New York: Columbia University Press, 1976.

————. *The Variorum Edition of the Poems of W. B. Yeats.* Ed. Peter Ault and Russell K. Alspach. New York: Macmillan, 1968.

Young, Vernon. "Poetry Chronicle." *Hudson Review* 29, no. 4 (January 1977):615–34.

# Index